BRITISH ECONOMIC DEVELOPMENT IN
SOUTH EAST ASIA, 1880–1939

CONTENTS OF THE EDITION

BRITISH ECONOMIC DEVELOPMENT IN SOUTH EAST ASIA, 1880–1939

Volume 3
The Building Blocks of Development: Governance, Transport and
Communications, and Human and Financial Capital

Edited by
David Sunderland

Routledge
Taylor & Francis Group

LONDON AND NEW YORK

First published 2014 by Pickering & Chatto (Publishers) Limited

2 Park Square, Milton Park, Abingdon, Oxon, OX14 4RN
605 Third Avenue, New York, NY 10017

Routledge is an imprint of the Taylor & Francis Group, an informa business

First issued in paperback 2020

BRITISH LIBRARY CATALOGUING IN PUBLICATION DATA

British economic development in South East Asia, 1880–1939.
1. Great Britain – Commerce – Southeast Asia – History – 19th century – Sources.
2. Great Britain – Commerce – Southeast Asia – History – 20th century – Sources.
3. Southeast Asia – Commerce – Great Britain – History – 19th century – Sources.
4. Southeast Asia – Commerce – Great Britain – History – 20th century – Sources.
5. Economic development – Southeast Asia – History – 19th century – Sources.
6. Economic development – Southeast Asia – History – 20th century – Sources.
7. Agriculture – Economic aspects – Southeast Asia – History – 19th century –
Sources. 8. Agriculture – Economic aspects – Southeast Asia – History – 20th
century – Sources. 9. Great Britain – Colonies – Asia – Economic policy – Sources.
I. Sunderland, David, 1958– editor of compilation.
330.9'5904-dc23

ISBN-13: 978-1-84893-488-7 (set)
ISBN-13: 978-1-138-75070-8 (hbk)
ISBN-13: 978-0-367-74002-3 (pbk)

Typeset by Pickering & Chatto (Publishers) Limited

CONTENTS

GOVERNANCE

Modes of Government

As discussed in the General Introduction, administrative methods varied from country to country. The Straits Settlements was a Crown colony and administered by a Governor, an Executive Council and a Legislative Council. The Executive Council comprised senior officials and local notables and had to be consulted by the Governor on all important matters, and, if its advice was not followed, this fact had to be reported to the Secretary of State for the Colonies. The Legislative Council, meanwhile, had five European members, three Chinese, one Indian, one Malay and one Eurasian. Apart from the two Europeans appointed by the British members of the two Chambers of Commerce, all were nominated by the Governor. Elections were unfeasible given that the majority of the Chinese and Indian populations were migrants and there was a fear that democracy would result a Council dominated by the Chinese, thought to be more politically mature than the other races, and by members of the Malayan aristocracy. The Council, again, had to be consulted on all issues, though the Governor had the casting vote on all the decisions made.[1]

In the FMS prior to the creation of the Federation, the States were administered by State Councils, which comprised the local Sultan, who assumed the role of President, the British Resident and later other British officials, Malay Chiefs and representatives of the British, Chinese and Indian communities. The Resident and other officials were appointed by the Governor of the Straits Settlements and provided the Sultan and State Council with 'advice' that had to be followed unless it involved cultural or religious matters. After 1896 and federation, a new government structure was introduced. Overall control was placed in the hands of the Governor of the Straits Settlements, who became High Commissioner and appointed a Resident General to supervise the administration of the States. The Resident General, in turn, was assisted by a staff of Federal Officers, each of whom concentrated on an aspect of governance, such as agriculture, mining etc. State decisions were thus increasingly made by the Resident General and Federal Officers and the influence of Residents and State Councils diminished.[2]

In both the Straits and the FMS, day-to-day administration was undertaken by civil servants; 242 in 1919, 270 in 1929 and 213 in 1935. The majority were British; in 1904 Chinese, Indians and Eurasians were specifically prohibited from joining the civil service and there were relatively few Malays, most of whom occupied lowly positions. Recruitment was via the Colonial Office. Candidates for posts across the Empire chose the territories in which they wished to serve and then sat an examination; those who attained the highest scores were sent to their first choice, the others to their second or third preferences and all could be dismissed after six months if found to be 'unsuitable'. Those arriving in Malaya had invariably attained relatively low marks in the exam; among Far Eastern candidates Ceylon was the favoured posting, followed by Hong Kong. They thus tended to be relatively inefficient and from the less prestigious public schools and Oxbridge colleges, though surprisingly few were dismissed during their probationary period. Most spent their entire careers in Malaya. To minimize transfers, which were thought to disturb the *esprit de corps* and the service's proficiency in the Malayan language, officers were paid high salaries and enjoyed an enviable standard of living; every household had a minimum of three servants and all stations offered cricket, football, golf, tennis and polo facilities, plus an active social life. From the First World War, they were permitted and indeed encouraged to bring out their wives and younger children, who were believed to have a civilizing influence, and single men often formed 'relationships' and had children with local Malay or Indian women. Given their social backgrounds and long service, they were highly suspicious of European planters and businessmen, who usually came from a lower social class, extremely sympathetic to the local Malayan community, whose values they believed were similar to their own, and were relatively honest, though many had financial interests in local tin and rubber companies.[3]

Elsewhere in South East Asia, an array of administrative systems was adopted. As discussed in the General Introduction, Burma until 1937 was a province of India, and Sarawak was governed by the Brooke family, who operated two parallel systems of administration. Indigenous chiefs were appointed to apply traditional law and levy taxes and District Officers and Regional Residents were recruited from the UK to introduce Western systems of justice and land ownership and to monitor the actions of the chiefs. Brunei from 1906 was under the control of a Resident, who took all executive decisions, rubber stamped by a State Council, and appointed State and District Officers and Penghulus (headmen). British North Borneo, meanwhile, was administered by a Governor, appointed by the Court of Directors of the British North Borneo Company, who was advised by a Legislative Council comprising nine official and five unofficial members. On the ground, administration was in the hands of Residents, each of whom was in charge of one of four residencies, each divided into nineteen districts supervised by Magistrates-in-Charge and later by District Officers and their deputies.

'Native affairs' were conducted by Governor appointed chiefs and village headmen chosen by District Officers with the approval of the relevant Resident.[4]

Public Expenditure

In comparison with the rest of South East Asia, per capita public expenditure in Malaya was relatively high. Per capita spending in 1910 was US$13 in the FMS (US$28 in 1938), US$6 in the Straits (US$17 in 1938) and US$5 (US$10 1938) in the UFMS, as compared to US$1 in French Indo-China (US$2 1938), US$2 in the Dutch East Indies (US$4 1938) and US$3 in Siam (US$4 1938). All the Malayan territories generally ran large budgetary surpluses, partly due the Colonial Office requirement that the Currency Board hold huge balances in the UK and the Straits' decision to place a proportion of opium revenue in an Opium Revenue Replacement Fund, which in 1937 held $59m. The finances of the FMS, however, temporarily tipped into deficit in the early 1930s and declining revenues from opium sales and the absence of export duties caused Singapore to suffer large and continuous deficits after 1925.[5]

From the 1880s to the early 1930s, government funds were largely spent on infrastructure, which in the FMS absorbed 40 per cent of revenues in the early 1920s, half of which financed the building of railways and the remainder the construction of roads and public buildings. Thereafter, slow economic growth and less need for new infrastructure caused capital spending to fall in 1935 to less than 10 per cent in the FMS and 13 per cent in the Straits. The vast proportion of the remaining revenues was expended on administration, which in the early 1930s consumed 34 per cent of the FMS budget and between 28 per cent and 37 per cent of that of the Straits, and, in the case of the FMS, in the servicing of its $65m (1938) public debt, largely comprising loans raised in London, which devoured 30 per cent of its income. Comparatively little was spent on health and education, in the early 1930s respectively 15 and 5 per cent in the FMS and 8 per cent and 4 per cent in the Straits. The State expected mines and plantations to provide basic health care, few Indian and Chinese migrants brought their families to the country, there was little demand for education from Malays and there was a fear that Western schooling would disrupt traditional Malay society.[6]

Public expenditure in British North Borneo in 1938 stood at $2,087m, almost half of which was spent on administration, 7 per cent on railways and a further 11 per cent on other capital expenditure. Burma expended US$3m in 1938, up from US$2m in 1910. From the late nineteenth century to 1937, when it attained financial autonomy, between 32 and 57 per cent of its annual revenues were sent to the Indian government, a subvention that represented 3.6 to 8.4 per cent of its Net National Product (1901/2–1931/2) and was much criticized for depriving the country of much needed funds. Of its other income, almost 40 per cent was spent on defence and law and order (39.6 per cent in 1901/4 and 38.9 per cent in 1937/9), from 10.1 per cent (1937/9) to 23.6 per cent (1901/4) on civil public works, between 15.5 per cent (1937/9) and 22.1 per cent (1901/4) on administration, and from 14 per cent (1937/9) and 18.4 per cent (1901/4) on irrigation, health and education.[7]

Note: Information on governance can also be found in the following sources/themes:

Topic	Source	Volume/Theme
Contribution of forestry to Malayan government expenditure/revenues	*Annual Report on Forest Administration in Malaya including Brunei, 1939*	Volume 1/Agriculture

Notes

1. R. Winstedt, 'Southeastern Asia and the Philippines', *Annals of the American Academy of Political and Social Science*, 226 (1943), pp. 97–111, on pp. 98–9.
2. R. Mahadevan, 'Pattern of Enterprise of Immigrant Entrepreneurs: A Study of Chettiars in Malaya, 1880–1930', *Economic and Political Weekly*, 13:4/5 (1978), pp. 329–58, on p. **99 [check]**; J. S. Galbraith, 'The "Turbulent Frontier" as a Factor in British Expansion', *Comparative Studies in Society and History*, 2:2 (1960), pp. 150–68, on p. 162; A. Noh, 'Small Steps, Big Outcome: A Historical Institutional Analysis of Malaysia's Political Economy', *Asia Research Centre, Murdoch University, Working Paper*, 164 (2010), pp. 1–34, on p. 19.
3. R. Heussler, *British Rule in Malaya: The Malayan Civil Service and Its Predecessors, 1867–1942* (Westport, CT: Greenwood Press, 1981); Y. K. Wah, 'The Grooming of an Elite: Malay Administrators in the Federated Malay States, 1903–1941', *Journal of Southeast Asian Studies*, 11:2 (1980), pp. 287–319; J. de Vere Allen, 'Malayan Civil Service, 1874–1941: Colonial Bureaucracy/Malayan Elite', *Comparative Studies in Society and History*, 12:2 (1970), pp. 149–78, on pp. 158–61, 165, 167, 170; A. L. Stoler, 'Rethinking Colonial Categories: European Communities and the Boundaries of Rule', *Comparative Studies in Society and History*, 31:1 (1989), pp. 134–61, on p. 144.
4. B. A. Darusssalam Hussainmiya, 'Manufacturing Consensus: The Role of the State Council in Brunei', *Journal of Southeast Asian Studies*, 31:2 (2000), pp. 321–51; A. Kaur, 'The Babbling Brookes: Economic Change in Sarawak 1841–1941', *Modern Asian Studies*, 29:1 (1995), pp. 65–109, on pp. 70–2; A. Kaur, '"Hantu" and Highway: Transport in Sabah 1881–1963', *Modern Asian Studies*, 28:1 (1994), pp. 1–49, on pp. 7, 12; G. M. Kahin, 'The State of North Borneo 1881–1946', *Far Eastern Quarterly*, 7:1 (1947), pp. 2–53, on pp. 47–8. See also A. V. M. Horton, '"I Have Taken Steps to Ensure that the Utmost Economy is Exercised": Government Finance in Brunei, 1906–1932', *Journal of the Malaysian Branch of the Royal Asiatic Society*, 67:2 (1994), pp. 47–92. Sarawak was divided into three administrative divisions to which were added two more in respectively 1885 and 1912. All decisions taken by the British North Borneo Governor had to be approved by the Court of Directors. The country's four residencies were later consolidated into just two – the East Coast Residency, with headquarters in Sandakan, and the West Coast Residency controlled from Jesselton.

5. A. Booth, 'Night Watchman, Extractive, or Developmental States? Some Evidence from Late Colonial South-East Asia', *Economic History Review*, 60:2 (2007), pp. 541–66, on pp. 249–51, 255; Winstedt, 'Southeastern Asia', p. 109; I. Sugimoto, 'Comparing Colonial and Post-colonial Government Finance Behaviour in Singapore: Revenue-raising, Expenditure Allocation and Budget Management', available online at http://keizai.soka. ac.jp/assets/pdf/dp/2010_06.pdf [accessed 13 December 2013], p. 23. Government revenues are discussed in the General Introduction in Volume 1.
6. Booth, 'Night Watchman', pp. 245, 247, 252, 255; Winstedt, 'Southeastern Asia', p. 109.
7. Kahin, 'The State', p. 52; M. Nissanke, 'International and Institutional Traps in Sub-Saharan Africa under Globalisation: A Comparative Perspective', *Centre for Economic Institutions Working Paper Series*, 8 (2011), pp. 1–20, on p. 12; Booth, 'Night Watchman', p. 258; N. Nishizawa, 'Economic Development of Burma', *Institute of Peace Studies, Hiroshima University, Japan, Research Report*, 16 (1991), pp. 1–155, on p. 118.

ANON., *REPORT ON THE WORKING OF THE MUNICIPALITIES OF BRITISH BURMA FOR THE YEAR 1882–83* (1883)

Anon., *Report on the Working of the Municipalities of British Burma for the Year 1882–83* (Rangoon: Government Press, 1883).

On acquiring Burma, the British government established municipal self-government in Rangoon, Moulmein, Akyab, Prome, Bassein, Toungoo and Henzada. Each town was administered by a committee composed of appointed and, from 1882, elected European, Burmese and Indian notables, who determined local expenditure. The following extract from the municipalities' 1882–3 annual report demonstrates how revenues were raised and spent during one twelve month period.

Anon., *Report on the Working of the Municipalities of British Burma for the Year 1882–83* (1883), extract

[...]

3. *Financial results.* – The following table shows the financial position of the several Municipalities at the beginning and end of the year under review as compared with the corresponding figures of the previous year: –

Town	Opening balance.		Incomes		Expenditure		Closing balance.	
	1881 – 82.	1882 – 83.	1881 – 82.	1882 – 83.	1881 – 82.	1882 – 83.	1881 – 82.	1882 – 83.
	Rs.	Rs.	Rs.	Rs.	Rs.	Rs.	Rs.	Rs.
Rangoon	9,02,296	2,68,466	17,90,683	10,91,803	24,24,513	13,43,338	2,68,466	16,931
Moulmein	8,689	33,805	1,58,998	1,33,058	1,33,882	1,52,927	33,805	13,936
Akyab	34,165	17,404	1,66,029	1,24,036	1,82,790	1,14,891	17,404	26,549
Prome	28,194	34,398	1,14,996	1,22,833	1,08,792	1,02,887	34,398	54,344
Bassein	33,923	41,811	1,28,593	1,28,788	1,20,705	1,37,292	41,811	33,307
Toungoo	9,845	7,735	74,818	78,295	76,928	84,489	7,735	1,541
Henzada	98,071	49,488	50,400	77,294	98,983	1,05,864	49,488	20,918
Total	11,15,183	4,53,107	24,84,517	17,56,107	31,46,593	20,41,688	4,53,107	1,67,526 /

There was thus an increase in the incomes of Prome, Bassein, Toungoo, and Henzada, and a decrease in those of Rangoon, Moulmein, and Akyab. In the case of Rangoon and Akyab the decreases is merely apparent as the receipts of the previous year were largely swelled by loans. A special contribution of Rs.1,50,000, made from provincial revenues to defray part of the cost of important sanitary works at Prome, does not appear in the accounts. There was a decrease in expenditure at Rangoon, Akyab, and Prome, and an increase at Moulmein, Bassein, Toungoo, and Henzada. The large decrease at Rangoon is chiefly due to the fact that the greater part of the cost of the new waterworks was expended in 1881 – 82. The closing balance was abnormally small at Rangoon and Toungoo, and loss than the opening balance at each of the other towns, except Akyab and Prome. At the end of the year Rangoon was indebted to the amount of Rs.11,69,446 and Akyab to the amount of Rs.46,900.

4. *Details of receipts.* – The receipts under the several heads during the past two years were as follows: –

	1881 – 82. Rs.	1882 – 83. Rs.
Taxes on houses and lands	3,54,747	3,71,595
Licenses on trades	3,33,035	3,81,586
Taxes on vehicles	42,026	46,198
Tolls on ferries	24,606	31,995
Conservancy-tax	81,947	79,443
Lighting-rate	53,131	59,094
Water-rate	18,677	12,976
Total income from taxation	9,08,169	9,82,887
Fines	43,108	23,677
Miscellaneous	13,80,912	4,50,199
Grants from provincial and local funds	1,52,328	2,99,344
Total income	24,84,517	17,56,107

The incidence of taxation per head of population was Rs.3-2-4 as compared with Rs. 2-14-7 in the previous year. The incidence varied from Rs.4-8-4 in Rangoon to Rs. 1-7-1 in Akyab. For the most part the items of receipts call for little comment. There was no change in the rate of taxation during the year, and the increase under that head is due to the fact that capitation-tax[1] for two years was credited to the funds of the Henzada Municipality during the period under review. The decrease under the head "Fines" is not altogether satisfactory. From the reports it appears that this is to be ascribed not to a better observance of municipal regulations but to laxity of supervision. It must be remembered that the Municipal authorities, and not the police, are primarily responsible for the enforcement of byelaws, and that it is the aim of the Administration to relieve the police as much as possible of the duty of suppressing petty nuisances. The very large increase of Rs. 1,47,000 under the head "Grants" is due to the allotment of provincial and local funds for the purpose of enabling the Municipalities to undertake the management of medical and educational institutions. The decrease under the head "Miscellaneous" is accounted for by the fact that no loans were raised during the year, while the figures for the previous year included loans to the amount of nearly 10 lakhs of rupees. In this item are included rents of lands, markets, &c., which cannot be accurately distinguished under the new system of account. /

5. *Expenditure.* – The expenditure of the year amounted to Rs. 20,41,688 as compared with Rs. 31,46,593 in 1881 – 82, there being thus a decrease of Rs. 11,04,905, or 35·1 per cent. The introduction of revised forms of statements renders an exact comparison of the several items in the two years impossible. The following table shows approximately the expenditure on the several major heads and the percentage of each on the total outlay: –

Head of expenditure.	1881 – 82.		1882 – 83.	
	Amount.	Percentage of total expenditure.	Amount.	Percentage of total expenditure.
	Rs.		Rs.	
Collection of taxes and head office establishment	1,44,085	4·6	1,14,049	5·6
Conservancy, cleaning, and drainage	3,20,177	10·2	2,94,633	14·4
Water-supply	11,25,873	35·8	6,41,690	31·4
Police	1,51,421	4·8	1,267	·1
Lighting	47,711	1·5	50,435	2·5
Road making and watering	2,19,553	6·9	2,27,124	11·1
Hospitals and vaccination	66,835	2·1	1,17,234	5·7
Education	38,075	1·2	1,33,956	6·6

6. *Sanitary works.* – Although some interest seems to have been taken by the Rangoon Committee in the subject of sanitary improvement, little progress was made during the year. The day and night conservancy arrangements were carried out, as in former years, at a slightly increased cost. The drainage scheme, of which mention was made in last year's report, is in abeyance pending the completion of the waterworks. Towards the close of the year a Health Officer was appointed in Rangoon, and the conservancy work and other arrangements for sanitation were placed under his supervision. This arrangement is said to have produced a marked improvement in the cleanliness of the town. The extracts from the Health Officer's report show how much remains to be done in respect of sanitation in Rangoon, and the Chief Commissioner can state from his own observation that, as compared with towns in India, Rangoon is very backward in this matter. The Chief Commissioner trusts that the elected Committee will justify the confidence reposed in them by taking energetic action in these matters. The question of burialgrounds is specially commended to the notice of the Committee. The report from Moulmein contains scanty mention of the subject of sanitary work. From the tables it is gathered that Rs. 21,213 were spent on conservancy as compared with Rs. 16,897 in the previous year, and that there was no expenditure on drainage. The Executive Engineer states that the works of the year consisted merely of "petty repairs to roads and the construction of a few culverts and drains." At Akyab Rs. 12,586 were spent on road-cleaning and Rs.4,449 on the construction of masonry drains. The failure of the Committees of these two important towns to make any attempt at sanitary improvements is very disappointing. It remains to be seen whether the new elected Committees will show a more enlightened interest in the welfare of the inhabitants. The Prome Committee has taken much interest in sanitary works. The extensive drainage and embankment scheme which will, it is hoped, radically change the sanitary condition of Prome, was carried on with energy during the year.

The expenditure was almost entirely defrayed from the provincial contribution before mentioned. From their own funds the Prome Committee / expended Rs.14,586 on road-cleaning and Rs.6,509 on night-conservancy.[2] The number of latrines has been increased and, to quote the words of the President, war has been made against unpleasant spots and strong efforts to reduce them to a minimum. At Bassein Rs. 7,651, at Toungoo Rs. 9,953, and at Henzada the large sum of Rs. 63,050 were spent on the construction of masonry drains. The expenditure of conservancy in these three towns amounted to Rs. 18,799. At Toungoo a beginning has been made towards the introduction of a system of night-conservancy.

7. *Water-supply.* – The precise progress made with the Rangoon waterworks during the year cannot readily be gathered from the somewhat technical details extracted by the President from the Engineer's report. A sum of Rs. 6,24,100 was spent, and the completion of the work may be expected before the conclusion of the current year. A draft of an enactment framed for the purpose of giving the Municipal Committee control over the Royal Lakes from which the water will be drawn, and for conferring on them the powers necessary to carry out the proposed arrangements for supplying water, is now under the consideration of the Supreme Government. At Bassein preparations are being made for supplying the town with water at an estimated cost of Rs. 2,60,000. During the year Rs.17,526 were expended, as the Commissioner expresses it, on getting up the scheme. A scheme has also been matured for supplying Prome with river water at a cost of Rs. 2,40,000. No municipal funds were expended on this object but preparations were made for starting the work, and the Committee are now engaged in negotiating a loan of Rs. 2,50,000 to provide funds. At none of the other municipal towns was any extensive work undertaken for the improvement of the water-supply.

8. *Lighting.* – The arrangements for lighting the several towns were unaltered during the year, and the trifling fluctuations in the expenditure incurred under this head are due for the most part to variations in the price of oil or to a small increase or decrease in the number of lamps. The Rangoon Committee have not yet been able to carry out their intention of introducing the electric light into their streets, and Akyab still continues in darkness.

9. *Road-making, &c.* – The expenditure under the head "Road-making" shows a small increase of Rs. 7,571. In Rangoon Rs. 1,22,238 were spent, and it is reported that some important roads were remetalled. Just complaints of the state of many roads in the town are however still frequent. While giving due attention to the large and important sanitary measures on which they are engaged, the Committee should not overlook the care of their roads, on the good condition of which the safety and comfort of the townspeople so largely depend. It is to

be hoped that they will find means to surmount the difficulty which is experiences in obtaining sufficient supplies of road metal. In the other towns a sum of
Rs. 1,04,886 was spent on making, repairing, and watering roads as compared
with Rs. 1,05,129 in 1881 – 82. It must not be forgotten that, under the revised
arrangements, roads not hitherto maintained by municipalities were placed
under the charge of the Committees and provincial funds were allotted for the
support of these additional burdens.

10. *Hospitals, &c.* – The control of all hospitals within municipal limits and the
conduct of the arrangements for vaccination having been made over to the /
Committees, the expenditure under this head was nearly doubled in the year
under review. But the increased expenditure was more than counterbalanced by
the contributions made to the municipalities from provincial funds in considerations of the additional burdens imposed upon them. The Rangoon Committee
spent Rs.68,533 in maintenance of hospitals and Rs. 2,733 on vaccination. The
report shows that the Committee take a commendable interest in these matters.
The institution of a vaccine depôt under the supervision of the Health Officer
at Rangoon, and maintained partly by municipal and partly by provincial funds,
can scarcely fail to prove beneficial both to the town and to the province at
large. At the other towns the hospital charges were duly paid; but there is little
in the reports to show that the Committees displayed any active interest in the
management of these institutions. It is observed that the amount expended on
vaccination in the six Municipalities other than Rangoon was Rs.3,896. At the
time of the adjustment of the financial relations between provincial and municipal funds the annual expenditure on this object in these towns was estimated
at Rs. 5,920. In the case of Prome only did the actual expenditure on vaccination exceed the estimate. Up to the close of the year under review none of the
Municipal Committees had finally declared in favour of the extension of the
Vaccination Act. Since the close of the year the Act has been extended to Akyab.

11. *Education.* – The expenditure on education shows a very large increase, the
figures for the two years being Rs. 38,075 and Rs. 1,33,956 respectively. The management of all town schools, with the exception of certain special institutions in
Rangoon, Moulmein, and Akyab, was vested in the Committees, and the cost
of the maintenance of these schools and of grants-in-aid and scholarships was
charged to municipal funds to which at the same time contributions were made by
Government somewhat in excess of the amounts by which it was calculated that
the educational expenditure would be increased under the new arrangements.

12. The following table shows the actual expenditure on hospitals and vaccination and education respectively, and the amount under each head on which the
financial arrangements mentioned in the two preceding paragraphs were based: –

	Hospitals, &c.		Education.	
	Actual.	Estimate.	Actual.	Estimate.
	Rs.	Rs.	Rs.	Rs.
Rangoon	71,266	88,500	51,964	72,000
Moulmein	15,401	21,400	23,453	33,800
Akyab	11,058	16,200	14,027	20,400
Prome	3,615	6,200	9,731	13,900
Bassein	5,703	8,050	16,251	22,600
Toungoo	7,616	8,500	10,792	21,500
Henzada	2,576	5,000	7,738	12,400
Total	1,17,235	1,53,850	1,33,956	1,96,600

It must be remembered also that school fees formed in each case an additional municipal asset. From these figures it appears that in no case did the medical and educational expenditure equal the amount which it was hoped that the Committees would spend upon these objects when the large provincial contributions / were made over to them in April 1882. Taking these charges together, it will be seen that the expenditure of the Municipalities on hospitals and education fell short by nearly Rs. 1,00,000 of the sums which were allotted to them from provincial revenues for expenditure on these objects. It could perhaps scarcely be expected that the Committees would be able to expend the whole of these allotments during the first year of the operation of the new system. But in future years the Chief Commissioner will expect that the average expenditure will not fall short of the estimate on which the amount of the provincial contribution is calculated, and that funds allotted for medical and educational charges will not be diverted to other objects.

13. *Town Committees.* – In conclusion brief mention may be made of the working of the quasi-Municipal Committees which were established in the following towns: –

Town.	Population.	Town.	Population.
Kyaukpyu	2,620	Yandoon	12,673
Sandoway	1,617	Ma-ubin	1,178
Pegu	5,891	Pantanaw	6,174
Shwedaung	12,373	Donabyoo	5,800
Paungdè	6,727	Thayetmyo	16,097
Thônzè	1,936	Allanmyo	5,825
Gyobingauk	837	Kawkareik	2,135
Ngathainggyaung	2,289	Thatôn	6,388
Lemyethna	5,355	Shwegyin	7,519
Myanaung	5,416	Kyaikto	1,932
Zalun	4,637	Tavoy	13,372
Kyangin	7,565	Mergui	8,633

These Committees were constituted by the appointment, on the nomination of Commissioners, of the leading official and non-official residents of the several towns. Subject to the control of the Deputy Commissioner and the Commissioner, the powers and responsibilities of these bodies are in many ways similar to those of the duly constituted Committees. But at present they have no power of imposing taxes or making byelaws. In nearly every case the Committees exercised the privilege of electing their own Presidents by choosing the District, Subdivisional, or Township officer. For the most part the Committees have shown an interest in the discharge of their duties. In some case they have been tempted to overstep the limits of their powers and to deal with matters which fall within the province of the District Officers. They have also exercised, somewhat too freely perhaps, the power which has been conferred upon them of increasing the number the number and raising the pay of municipal employés. But, as far as can yet be judged, the experiment has been attended with fair success. When the new Municipal Act becomes law, it will no doubt be possible to place these Committees on a legal basis and to define more accurately the precise limits of their powers and responsibilities. Many of these towns are small and at a distance from headquarters, and the Chief Commissioner thinks that it may be necessary, for a time at least, to give the Deputy Commissioners direct control over the proceedings of the Committees. If this is done, the Chief Commissioner / would see that the power was used judiciously and sparingly and that no undue interference was allowed to spoil the growth of these young institutions. Mr. Crosthwaite has seen the growth of municipal institutions in India and the great improvement in the condition of towns and cities due to them. He believes that similar effects will follow their establishment in Burma; and if he advocates the necessity of given them their liberty gradually, it is solely because he thinks a guiding hand at the outset will help them on their way.

By order,
E. S. SYMES,
Offg. Secretary. /

Form No. I. – Statement showing the income of the several municipalities in British Burma during the year 1882 – 83.

1	2	3	4	5	6 Number of members of committee							
Name of district	Serial number of municipality.	Name of municipality.	Act under which constituted	Population within municipal limits.	a Ex-officio.	b Nominated.	c Elected.	d Total.	e Officials.	f Non-officials.	g Europeans.	h Natives.
Akyab	1	Akyab		33,989	5	10	...	15	7	8	9	6
Rangoon	2	Rangoon		134,176	6	1	15	22	4	18	9	13
Prome	3	Prome		28,813	4	9	...	13	7	6	5	8
		Total Pegu		162,989	10	10	15	35	11	24	14	21
Bassein	4	Bassein	Act VII of 1874.	28,147	4	12	...	16	4	12	6	10
Henzada	5	Henzada		16,924	3	7	...	10	3	7	3	7
		Total Irrawaddy		45,071	7	19	...	26	7	19	9	17
Moulmein	6	Moulmein		53,107	4	...	15	19	4	15	8	11
Toungoo	7	Toungoo		17,199	6	8	...	14	6	8	7	7
		Total Tenasserim		70,306	10	8	15	33	10	23	15	18
		Grand Total, British Burma		312,355	32	47	30	109	35	74	47	62

1	2	3	4	8 Octror – (concluded).			9 Assessed Taxes. Conservancy case.						
District.	Serial No.	Name of municipality.	Act VII of 1874. Act under which constituted	g. Class VII – Cloth	h. Class VIII – Metals	Total	Arrear Collection for the previous year. Rs.	A.	P.	Collection for the current year. Rs.	A.	P.	Penalties
Akyab	1	Akyab		...	...	...	...	...	...	...	...	...	...
Rangoon	2	Rangoon		...	...	...	7,505	7	6	72,137	12	3	...
Prome	3	Prome		...	...	...	...	...	...	...	...	...	...
		Total Pegu		...	...	...	7,305	7	6	72,137	12	3	...
Bassien	4	Bassein	Act VII of 1874.	...	...	...	...	...	...	...	...	...	...
Henzada	5	Henzada		...	...	...	...	...	...	...	...	...	...
		Total Irrawaddy		...	...	...	...	...	...	...	...	...	...
Moulmein	6	Moulmein		...	...	...	...	...	...	...	...	...	...
Toungoo	7	Toungoo		...	...	...	...	...	...	...	...	...	...
		Total Tenasserim		...	...	...	...	...	...	...	...	...	...
		Grand Total British Burma		...	...	...	7,305	7	6	72,137	12	3	...

7									8					
By balance in hand at the close of last year.									Octroi					
									a	b	c	d	e	f
Deposits			Actual municipal balance.			Total.			Class I – Articles of food or drink for men or animals	Class II – Animals for slaughter.	Class III – Fuel, lighting, and washing	Class IV – Building materials.	Class V. – Drugs, gums, and spices.	Class VI. – Tobacco
Rs.	a.	p.	Rs.	a.	p.	Rs.	A.	p.						
...			17,403	9	3	17,403	9	3	...	...	...	...	...	...
62,625	8	3	2,05,840	11	2	2,68,466	3	5	...	...	...	...	...	...
...			34,397	15	0	34,397	15	0	...	...	...	...	...	...
62,625	8	3	2,40,238	10	2	3,02,864	2	5	...	...	...	...	...	...
395	10	7	41,415	2	10	41,810	13	5	...	...	...	...	...	...
...			49,487	11	4	49,487	11	4	...	...	...	...	...	...
395	10	7	91,298	8	9	91,694	3	4	...	...	...	...	...	...
...			33,805	5	8	33,805	5	8	...	...	...	...	...	...
100	0	0	7,635	4	6	7,735	4	6	...	...	...	...	...	...
100	0	0	41,440	10	2	41,540	10	2	...	...	...	...	...	...
63,121	2	10	3,89,985	11	9	4,53,106	14	7	...	...	...	...	...	... /

9

ASSESSED TAXES.

Conservancy case.			License on trades.							Other taxes in detail.			
Total			Arrear collection for the previous year.	Collection for the current year			Penalties.	Total					
Rs.	A.	P.		Rs.	A.	P.		Rs.	A.	P.			
...	...	...	...	16,202	12	0	...	16,202	12	0	... ...	...	...
79,443	3	9	...	2,58,950	4	0		2,58,950	4	0	... ...	...	...
...	...	...	...	19,488	2	0		19,488	2	0	... ...	...	...
79,443	3	9	...	2,78,438	6	0		2,78,438	6	0	... ...	...	...
...	...	...	...	26,323	0	0		26,323	0	0	... ...	...	...
...	...	...	...	11,659	2	0		11,659	2	0	... ...	...	...
...	...	...	...	37,982	2	0		37,982	2	0	... ...	...	...
...	...	...	...	41,508	0	0		41,508	0	0	... ...	...	...
...	...	...	...	7,455	0	0		7,455	0	0	... ...	...	...
...	...	...	...	48,963	0	0		48,963	0	0	... ...	...	...
79,443	3	9		3,81,586	4	0		3,81,586	4	0	... ...	...	... /

1	2	3	4	10			11			12	13		
District.	Serial number of municipality	Name of municipality.	Act under which constituted.	Tax on houses and land.			Tax on vehicles.			Tax on animals.	Tolls, &c.		
				Rs.	a.	p.	Rs.	a.	p.	Rs.	Rs.	a.	p.
Akyab	1	Akyab		27,457	0	0	1,847	12	0		3,700	0	0
Rangoon	2	Rangoon		1,63,332	8	9	23,597	5	0		16,287	8	0
Prome	3	Prome		35,754	10	10	1,936	0	0		510	0	0
		Total Pegu		1,99,087	3	7	25,533	5	0		16,797	8	0
Bassein	4	Bassein	Act VII of 1874.	42,170	1	9	1,136	0	0		7,010	0	0
Henzada	5	Henzada		33,431	8	0	6,352	0	0		470	0	0
		Total Irrawaddy		75,601	9	9	7,488	0	0		7,480	0	0
Moulmein	6	Moulmein		50,949	15	9	9,606	8	0		1,506	4	0
Toungoo	7	Toungoo		18,499	8	7	1,722	0	0		2,511	0	0
		Total Tenasserim		69,449	8	4	11,328	8	0		4,017	4	0
		GRAND TOTAL BRITISH BURMA		3,71,595	5	8	46,197	9	0		31,994	12	0

1	2	3	4	16											
District	Serial number of municipality.	Name of municipality.	Act under which constituted.	Miscellaneous receipts – (Concluded.).											
				Municipal fines.			Payments for municipal services rendered to individuals.			Grants-in-aid from provincial or local funds.			Sundries (rent of municipal lands, receipts from public gardens, &c)		
				Rs.	A.	P.	Rs.	A.	P.	Rs.	A.	P.	Rs.	A.	P.
Akyab	1	Akyab		1,035	8	0	...	...	...	44,093	8	5	7,966	1	3
Rangoon	2	Rangoon		6,489	1	0	267	4	7	2,17,000	0	0	1,25,138	5	0
Prome	3	Prome		362	4	0	...	...	...	5,000	0	0	3,472	9	4
		Total Pegu		6,851	5	0	267	4	7	2,22,000	0	0	1,28,610	14	4
Bassein	4	Bassein	Act VII of 1974.	240	11	0	...	...	...	6,250	0	0	8,050	5	4
Henzada	5	Henzada		1,327	12	9	...	...	...	...	...	...	2,464	5	6
		Total Irrawaddy		1,568	7	9	...	...	...	6,250	0	0	10,514	10	10
Moulmein	6	Moulmein		1,510	9	0	...	...	...	11,000	0	0	5,611	15	3
Toungoo	7	Toungoo		928	5	0	...	...	...	16,000	0	0	2,137	4	11
		Total Tenasserim		2,438	14	0	...	...	...	27,000	0	0	7,749	4	2
		GRAND TOTAL BRITISH BURMA		11,894	2	9	267	4	7	2,99,343	8	5	1,54,840	14	7

14						15			16										
Other taxes in detail.						Total income from taxation.			Miscellaneous receipts.										
Lighting rate.			Water-rate.			Capitation-tax			Realizations under special Acts.			Proceeds of land, &c.	Income from markets (rents, fees, sale of refuse, &c.).			Conservancy and road-cleaning (fees, sale proceeds of night-soil, street refuse, &c.).			
Rs.	a.	p.	Rs.	a.	p.	Rs.	Rs.	a.	p.	Rs.	a.	p.	Rs.	Rs.	a.	p.	Rs.	a.	p.
...	...	...	...	...	...	...	49,207	8	0	1,499	2	0	...	19,200	10	0	68	0	0
51,974	9	11	12,975	10	2	...	6,06,561	1	7	5,177	2	0	...	1,00,935	5	9	708	5	11
...	...	...	...	...	...	...	57,688	12	10	2,053	9	3	...	51,764	14	9	1,971	12	11
51,974	9	11	12,975	10	2	...	6,64,249	14	5	7,230	11	3	...	1,52,700	4	6	2,680	2	10
...	...	...	...	...	...	...	76,639	1	9	482	9	6	...	36,408	3	1	...	...	...
...	...	...	...	...	...	...	51,912	10	0	11	0	0	...	21,010	14	6	...	...	...
...	...	...	...	...	...	...	1,28,551	11	9	493	9	6	...	57,419	1	7	...	...	...
7,119	2	3	...	...	...	...	1,10,689	14	0	1,896	10	9	...	...	...	...	224	0	0
...	...	...	...	...	...	...	30,187	8	7	662	6	9	...	27,881	13	0	275	0	0
7,119	2	3	...	...	...	...	1,40,877	6	7	2,559	1	6	...	27,881	13	0	499	0	0
59,093	12	2	12,975	10	2	...	9,82,886	8	9	11,782	8	3	...	2,57,201	13	1	3,247	2	10 /

16			17							18			19			20			21			22
Misc receipts			Debt.							Total income of year, excluding balance.			Total, including balance.			Incidence of taxation column 15 per head of population.			Incidence of income shown in column 18 per head of population.			Remarks.
Total.			Loans.	Deposits, contractors' salaries unpaid, &c.			Advances.															
ws.	A.	P.	Rs.	Rs.	A.	P.	Rs.	A.	P.	Rs.	A.	P.	Rs.	A.	P.	Rs.			Rs.			
73,862	13	8	...	...	...	...	966	0	0	1,24,036	5	8	1,41,439	14	11	1	7	1	3	10	4	
4,55,715	8	3	...	25,915	9	2	3,610	6	9	10,91,802	9	9	13,60,268	13	2	4	8	4	8	2	2	
64,625	2	3	...	519	0	0	...	...	...	1,22,832	15	1	1,57,230	14	1	2	0	0	4	4	3	
5,20,340	10	6	...	26,434	9	2	3,610	6	9	12,14,635	8	10	15,17,499	11	3	4	1	2	7	7	3	
51,431	12	11	...	395	10	7	321	5	6	1,28,787	14	9	1,70,598	12	2	2	11	7	4	9	2	
24,814	0	9	...	567	12	1	...	...	...	77,294	6	10	1,26,782	2	2	3	1	1	4	9	1	
76,245	13	8	...	963	6	8	321	5	6	2,06,082	5	7	2,97,380	14	4	2	13	8	4	9	2	
20,243	3	0	...	1,925	0	0	200	0	0	1,33,058	1	0	1,66,863	6	8	2	1	4	2	8	1	
47,884	13	8	...	221	15	10	...	...	...	78,294	6	1	86,029	10	7	1	12	0	4	8	10	
68,128	0	8	...	2,146	15	10	200	0	0	2,11,352	7	1	2,52,893	1	3	2	0	1	3	0	1	
7,38,577	6	6	...	29,544	15	8	5,097	12	3	17,56,106	11	2	22,09,213	9	9	3	2	4	5	9	11	/

Form No. II. – Statement showing the expenditure of the municipalities in British Burma during the year 1882 – 83.

1	2	3	4			5			6 GENERAL ESTABLISHMENT.					
	Serial No.	Name of municipality.	Balance from previous year.			Income during the year.			Office establishment, inspection, Honorary Magistrate's establishment, &c.			Collection of municipal taxes including octroi, establishment, purchase of account-books, paper, &c.		
District.			Rs.	A.	P.	Rs.	A.	P.	Rs.	A.	P.	Rs.	A.	P.
Akyab	1	Akyab	17,403	9	3	1,24,036	5	8	3,714	1	0	1,644	2	0
Rangoon	2	Rangoon	2,68,466	3	5	0,91,802	9	9	36,823	0	8	21,340	8	0
Prome	3	Prome	34,397	15	0	1,22,832	15	1	2,657	15	6	8,986	2	3
		Total Pegu	3,02,864	2	5	12,14,635	8	10	39,481	0	2	30,326	10	3
Bassein	4	Bassein	41,810	13	5	1,28,787	14	9	9,817	7	11	3,427	15	7
Henzada	5	Henzada	49,487	11	4	77,294	6	10	1,727	6	1	1,448	5	1
		Total Irrawaddy	91,298	8	9	2,06,082	5	7	11,544	14	0	4,876	4	8
Moulmein	6	Moulmein	33,805	5	8	1,33,058	1	0	10,636	12	10	6,118	9	8
Toungoo	7	Toungoo	7,735	4	6	78,294	6	1	3,898	3	10	1,808	1	10
		Total Tenasserim	41,540	10	2	2,11,352	7	1	14,535	0	8	7,926	11	6
		GRAND TOTAL BRITISH BURMA	4,53,106	14	7	17,56,106	11	2	69,274	15	10	44,773	12	5

1	2	3	8 PUBLIC HEALTH – *concluded*											
	Serial No.	Name of municipality.	(e) Vaccination (establishment)			(f) Water-works (establishment and repairs).			(g) Road-watering (establishment, purchase of water-carts, repairs, &c.).			(h) Road-cleaning (establishment, purchase and repair of dust-bins &c.).		
District.			Rs.	A.	P.	Rs.	A.	P.	Rs.	A.	P.	Rs.	A.	P.
Akyab	1	Akyab	483	5	3	65	0	0	93	11	0	12,586	6	0
Rangoon	2	Rangoon	2,732	13	4	6,24,099	12	1	22,651	7	1	55,502	10	0
Prome	3	Prome	660	0	0	...	...	...	154	0	9	14,586	0	11
		Total Pegu	3,392	13	4	6,24,099	12	1	22,805	7	10	70,088	10	11
Bassein	4	Bassein	503	4	6	17,525	9	10	1,693	13	0	8,501	6	6
Henzada	5	Henzada	300	0	0	...	...	...	...	...	...	...	...	...
		Total Irrawaddy	803	4	6	17,525	9	10	1,693	13	0	8,501	6	6
Moulmein	6	Moulmein	1,350	0	0	...	...	...	91	8	0	14,674	9	1
Toungoo	7	Toungoo	599	8	0	...	...	...	295	3	0	6,433	9	3
		Total Tenasserim	1,949	8	0	...	...	...	386	11	0	21,108	2	4
		GRAND TOTAL BRITISH BURMA	6,628	15	1	6,41,690	5	11	24,979	10	10	1,12,284	9	9

7			8			
PUBLIC SAFETY.			PUBLIC HEALTH.			
			(a)	(b)	(c)	(d)
Fire (establishment, purchase of fire-engine, buckets, repairs, &c.).	Lighting (establishment, purchase of lamps, oil, repairs, &c.).	Police (establishment, purchase of clothing, lantern, &c.).	Registration of births and deaths.	Buildings and other works (erection of slaughter-house, Latrines, &c.).	Repairs (to market, dispensary, &c.).	Maintenance of medical institutions (dispensary establishment purchase of medicines, &c.).
Rs. A. P.	Rs. A. P.	Rs. A. P.	Rs. A. P.	Rs. A. P.	Rs. A. P.	Rs. A. P.
... ...	... ...	1,267 4 0	592 12 9	13,071 5 3	641 10 0	10,575 0 8
13,242 14 6	31,961 13 7	... ...	1,834 7 9	143 6 0	2,483 4 5	68,533 3 8
... ...	1,223 0 0	... ...	625 9 7	5,559 4 4	5,151 10 1	2,955 0 4
13,242 14 6	33,184 13 7	... ...	2,460 1 4	5,702 10 4	7,634 14 6	71,488 4 0
... ...	2,389 5 0	... ...	827 15 0	2,266 7 11	5,405 9 9	5,200 2 9
... ...	1,125 0 0	... ...	592 12 7	2,559 12 5	6,492 4 3	2,276 2 0
... ...	3,514 5 0	... ...	1,420 11 7	4,826 4 4	11,897 14 0	7,476 4 9
3,530 9 11	10,291 4 10	... ...	839 12 9	1,675 0 0	470 4 6	14,050 8 11
... ...	3,444 11 7	... ...	676 13 9	4,877 2 1	3,779 15 1	7,016 2 6
3,530 9 11	13,736 0 5	... ...	1,516 10 6	6,552 2 1	4,250 3 7	21,066 11 5
16,773 8 5	50,435 3 0	1,267 4 0	5,990 4 2	30,152 6 0	24,424 10 1	1,10,606 4 10 /

8						9
PUBLIC HEALTH – *concluded*						PUBLIC INSTRUCTION.
(i)			(j)		(k)	
Conservancy.						
Establishment, repairs, purchase of carts, dry-earth, land for burying nightsoil, &c.	Refunds, &c, of fines or over-assessments.	Remission of cess.	Drainage works (establishment, repairs).	Other measures. Markets and slaughter-houses (establishment, contingencies).	Public garden (establishment, purchase of seeds, repair of well, purchase of bullocks, &c).	Contributions to schools.
Rs. A. P.	Rs. A. P.	Rs. A. P.	Rs. A. P.	Rs. A. P.	Rs. A. P.	Rs. A. P.
... ...	... ...	... ...	4,449 9 0	2,209 0 10	... ...	14,026 13 5
50,788 7 10	... ...	... ...	27,304 3 5	23,254 9 9	8,854 8 4	51,964 7 5
6,508 8 0	... ...	... ...	... ...	1,439 2 6	7,179 13 9	9,731 6 2
57,296 15 10	... ...	... ...	27,304 3 5	24,693 12 3	16,034 6 1	61,695 13 7
2,536 11 6	179 15 0	... ...	7,651 7 10	4,197 13 7	1,257 3 6	16,251 1 1
2,498 9 5	112 8 0	... ...	63,424 9 6	4,480 14 2	... ...	7,737 12 4
5,035 4 11	292 7 0	... ...	71,076 1 4	8,678 11 9	1,257 3 6	23,988 13 5
6,538 8 5	... ...	... ...	... ...	1,627 6 6	2,337 4 0	23,452 13 6
196 8 3	... ...	... ...	10,159 5 0	1,842 6 0	821 12 6	10,791 10 2
6,735 0 8	... ...	... ...	10,159 5 0	3,469 12 6	3,159 0 6	34,244 7 8
69,067 5 5	292 7 0		1,12,989 2 9	39,051 5 4	20,450 10 1	1,33,956 0 1 /

1 District.	2 Serial No.	3 Name of municipality.	10 Public convenience.											
			Public works.											
			Establishment			Construction and maintenance of roads.			Other (new) works.			Other repairs.		
			Rs.	A.	P.	Rs.	A.	P.	Rs.	A.	P.	Rs.	A.	P.
Akyab	1	Akyab	4,362	9	3	20,698	6	0	840	12	0	753	0	0
Rangoon	2	Rangoon	37,740	5	11	99,587	5	0	75	0	0	1,777	7	5
Prome	3	Prome	5,923	7	10	24,129	10	2	1,760	0	0	830	8	8
		Total Pegu	43,663	13	9	1,23,716	15	2	1,835	0	0	2,608	0	1
Bassein	4	Bassein	9,371	6	2	737	4	9	9,431	12	5	16,210	6	8
Henzada	5	Henzada	364	4	5	9,747	2	3	...	...	...	291	5	4
		Total Irrawaddy	9,735	10	7	10,484	7	0	9,431	12	5	16,501	12	0
Moulmein	6	Moulmein	7,584	6	11	29,099	2	1	115	4	0	6,336	8	10
Toungoo	7	Toungoo	1,830	0	0	18,145	12	5	2,555	0	9	886	5	7
		Total Tenasserim	9,414	6	11	47,244	14	6	2,670	4	9	7,222	14	5
		GRAND TOTAL BRITISH BURMA	67,176	8	6	2,02,144	10	8	14,777	13	2	27,085	10	6

1 District.	2 Serial No.	3 Name of municipality.	12 Debt – cncld.			13 Miscellaneous.			14 Total expenditure.			15 Balance at close of year.					
			Advances (on account of departmental works, &c.									Deposits.			Actual municipal balance.		
			Rs.	A.	P.	Rs.	A.	P.	Rs.	A.	P.	Rs.	A.	P.	Rs.	A.	P.
Akyab	1	Akyab	...	...	...	3,536	9	0	1,14,890	10	8	...	...	...	26,549	4	3
Rangoon	2	Rangoon	3,373	7	2	1,03,138	14	1	13,43,337	12	6	16,402	7	8	528	9	0
Prome	3	Prome	...	...	...	2,806	3	5	1,02,886	10	3	...	...	...	54,344	3	10
		Total Pegu	3,373	7	2	1,05,945	1	6	14,46,224	6	9	16,402	7	8	54,872	12	10
Bassein	4	Bassein	216	15	0	1,747	4	0	1,37,291	13	10	213	4	8	33,093	9	8
Henzada	5	Henzada	...	...	...	...	...	...	1,05,864	4	10	...	...	...	20,917	13	4
		Total Irrawaddy	216	15	0	1,747	4	0	2,43,156	2	8	213	4	8	54,011	7	0

10 Public convenience.						11 Contributions to local or provincial funds.			12 Debt.												
Survey of land.			Other charges (printing, rewards, &c).						Loans (instalments paid during the year).			On account of last year.			On account of current year.			Deposits (salaries attached, contractors, &c.).		
Rs.	A.	P.	Rs.	A.	P.	Rs.	A.	P.	Rs.	A.	P.	Rs.	A.	P.	Rs.	A.	P.	Rs.	A.	P.
...	...	...	609	7	9	1,283	5	6	13,400	0	0	...	...	...	3,986	8	0	...	...	...
...	...	...	911	3	5	...	...	...	32,571	7	0	...	...	...	4,244	9	0	16,402	7	8
...	...	...	19	2	0	...	...	...	...	...	...	...	...	...	...	...	...	...	...	...
...	...	...	930	5	5	...	...	...	32,571	7	0	...	...	...	4,244	9	0	16,402	7	8
8,483	14	11	1,246	3	0	...	...	...	...	...	...	...	...	...	...	...	...	213	4	8
...	...	...	140	11	0	...	...	...	...	...	...	...	...	...	...	...	...	544	14	0
8,483	14	11	1,386	14	0	...	...	...	...	...	...	...	...	...	...	...	...	758	2	8
...	...	...	1,260	14	0	...	...	...	...	...	...	...	...	...	...	...	...	1,900	0	0
...	...	...	...			...	...	...	...	...	...	...	...	...	...	...	...	281	11	10
...	...	...	1,260	14	0	...	...	...	...	...	...	...	...	...	...	...	...	2,181	11	10
8,483	14	11	4,187	9	2	1,283	5	6	45,971	7	0	...	...	...	8,231	1	0	19,342	6	2 /

15 Balance at close of year. Total.				Remarks.	Akyab.		
Rs.	A.	P.	Memorandum of liabilities and claims		Rs.	A.	P.
			Liabilities –				
			Balance of loans		46,900	0	0
26,549	4	3	Deposits to be adjusted		...	...	...
			Claims –		46,900	0	0
			Sinking fund		...	...	...
16,931	0	8	Advances recoverable		...	...	...
54,344	3	10	Net amount of debt		46,900	0	0

Memorandum of liabilities and claims.   Rangoon.   Prome.

			Liabilities –		Rs.	A.	P.	
71,275	4	6	Balance of loans		11,49,081	15	3	...
			Deposits to be adjusted		72,138	9	9	...
					12,21,220	9	0	...
			Claims –	Rs. A. P.	...	...	...	...
			Sinking fund	50,000 0 0	51,774	8	3	...
33,306	14	4	Advances recoverable	1,774 8 3	...	...	...	...
20,917	13	4	Net amount of debt		11,69,446	0	9	...

Memorandum of liabilities and claims.   Bassein.   Henzada.

			Liabilities –				
54,224	11	8	Balance of loans				
			Deposits to be adjusted		213	4	8
					213	4	8

1	2	3	12			13			14			15					
District.	Serial No.	Name of municipality.	Debt – cncld. Advances (on account of departmental works, &c.			Miscellaneous.			Total expenditure.			Balance at close of year.					
												Deposits.			Actual municipal balance.		
			Rs.	A.	P.	Rs.	A.	P.	Rs.	A.	P.	Rs.	A.	P.	Rs.	A.	P.
Moulmein	6	Moulmein	...	...	...	8,946	8	10	1,52,927	13	7	...	...	...	13,935	9	1
Toungoo	7	Toungoo	780	0	0	3,368	15	8	84,488	15	1	...	...	...	1,540	11	6
		Total Tenasserim	780	0	0	12,315	8	6	2,37,416	12	8	...	...	...	15,476	4	7
		GRAND TOTAL BRITISH BURMA	4,370	6	2	1,23,544	7	0	20,41,688	0	9	16,615	12	4	1,51,009	12	8

15							
Balance at close of year.			Remarks.				
Total.							
Rs.	A.	P.	Memorandum of liabilities and claims			Rs.	A.	P.

Rs.	A.	P.	Memorandum of liabilities and claims					Rs.	A.	P.
			*Claims –							
			Advance recoverable					216	15	0
13,935	9	1	Net amount of debt					430	3	8
1,540	11	6								
			Memorandum of liabilities and claims.	Moulmein.				Toungoo.		
			Liabilities –							
			Balance of loans	...	...	...		...	...	...
			Deposits to be adjusted	...	...	...		...	...	...
15,476	4	7	*Claims –							
			Advance recoverable	...	...	...		...	...	...
1,67,525	9	0	Net amount of debt	...	...	...		...	...	.../

TRANSPORT AND COMMUNICATIONS

Transport and communication in the region comprised railways, discussed in the General Introduction, roads, rivers, ocean shipping, airlines and the telegraph.

Roads

Roads were given low priority by governments. The fragility and small carrying capacity of vehicles and the poor quality of routes made road transport less economically viable than railways for both the short and long distance carriage of goods. Administrations also lacked the funds necessary for their construction and maintenance and regarded them as unwanted competition to rail transport, which would damage government receipts and make it even more difficult to ensure that these gigantic enterprises broke even, and were fearful of the possible social and political consequences of an extended road system. It was a common belief that motor transport by increasing mobility would disrupt fragile social structures and lead to the spread of crime and dissent.

Relatively few thoroughfares were therefore constructed until the turn of the century when views of road transport underwent a revolution. Commercial communities and administrations gradually became more aware of the economic advantages of motor transportation. European companies experienced the benefits of road construction in other parts of the Empire and, facing greater economic turbulence, wished to avoid the high freight rates charged by monopolistic railway companies. They thus placed increasing pressure on administrations to increase spending on roads. Colonial governments were similarly more attune to the economic and revenue possibilities of motor transport and its advantages over rail. Roads were cheaper to build than railroads, could easily be abandoned if they failed to prove their commercial worth, removed the need for costly transhipment of goods and, with improvements in construction, were less subject to closure due to natural disasters. They also possessed other benefits. For officials, they were easily acquired physical evidence of achievement that could boost their social status and self-confidence and help to advance their careers. For administrations, they minimized the risk of fire in towns, and in the countryside, facilitated settlement, the spread of 'civilizing' education and, as with railways, the control and administration of indigenous peoples.[1]

Road transport was most developed in Malaya. In 1911, the FMS possessed 3,439 miles of road and the Straits Settlements 800 miles, of which 100 miles were in Singapore. The Malayan North–South highway was completed in 1922, the following year the Johore causeway linked Singapore to the Malay States, and, by 1938, the country had over 6,000 miles of roadway – 100.1 km per thousand squ. kms. The roads connected towns, replaced river transport and ran from plantations and mines to rail terminals and were built by paid and convict labour. Initially consisting of sand and compacted earth, they were increasingly constructed with broken granite and cinders, known as road metal or gravel, and, when heavier and faster moving traffic caused corrugations in the gravel, of asphalt, which was also cheaper, easier to lay and had a longer lifespan.[2]

Burmese roads were far more basic. Internally, there were all-weather highways from Rangoon to Prome and to Mandalay, from Toungoo to Loilem and from Meiktila through the Shan state. Tracks connected the country with India, though because of cheap sea transport through the Bay of Biscay and their dangerous nature these were rarely used, and with Siam, the main routes being across the Dawna range and through the Three Pagodas Pass. Communication with China was initially via paths, and, from 1938, the Burma Road. Built by the Chinese after the start of the Sino-Japanese War to move to China military supplies landed at Rangoon, the 717-mile highway started in Mandalay, ran through Lashio to Wantung on the Chinese border and thence onto Chungking.[3]

The Sarawak and British North Borneo road systems were even more basic. In Sarawak, the Brooke family initially regarded roads as an unnecessary expenditure; the dense tropical forest was difficult to penetrate and most mines/plantations were located near to rivers. Highways were thus only found in the major towns and in concessions, where companies such as the Borneo Co. and Sarawak Oilfields Ltd built roads to the nearest river. This policy changed in the early 1930s; roads were required to facilitate the implementation of the International Rubber Regulation Agreement and it was believed that they would attract Chinese farmers to the country and aid administration, helping to calm the unrest that was occurring in Dayak communities. Alas, by 1940 only one forty-mile road had been constructed – from Kuching to Seria.[4]

In British North Borneo, bridle paths initially took precedence over roads. From 1902, each District Officer had to construct and maintain bridleways in his district. The paths ran north to south, were between 2 and 2.5-metres wide, had gradients of between 1 in 12 and 1 in 15 and were built and maintained by forced labour and later by gangs of waged workers.[5] By 1929, 640 miles of path had been constructed at a cost of $300 to $500 per mile, maintenance amounting to $80 per mile per annum. Linking the main towns and connecting agricultural areas with the railway, they were largely used by District Officers. Locals preferred to travel along their own tracks, partly because bullocks were either forbidden from traversing the bridleways or owners forced to pay a hefty fee and there was a belief that the paths disturbed the spirits that supposedly inhabited the landscape. Roads began to be built only in the early 1920s. From 1920 to 1926, three thoroughfares were constructed from Jesselton to Tuaran (20 miles), from the Melalap terminus of the railway to Keningau (21 miles) and from Sandakan to Labuk. A new Governor, J. L. Humphries, then instigated a £25,000 road construction programme, and, by 1939, the country possessed 138 miles of metalled and 98 miles of earth highways. [6]

The vehicles that travelled along these new roads initially comprised bullock carts, two-wheeled vehicles pulled by a pair of beasts and used to transport both goods and people; gharries, light horse-drawn carriages owned by the wealthy; bicycles, cheap and easy to repair and store; and, in urban areas and for short-distance travel, the rickshaw and the trishaw. Rickshaws, two wheeled carts pulled by a man, first appeared in Singapore in 1880 and rapidly spread to other towns and cities. By 1921, the sector employed 22,985 in the Straits Settlements, 9,000 of whom worked in Singapore, 6,247 in the FMS and 844 in the UFMS, and was controlled by Chinese entrepreneurs, who recruited their own countrymen and kept costs to a minimum through the payment of low wages. The trishaw, a bicycle attached to a sidecar, at first proved unpopular and only became commonplace in the 1920s when its advantages over the rickshaw were recognized. More manoeuvrable and faster than its primitive counterpart, it was also able to carry heavier loads and regarded as a less inhumane form of transport.[7]

Cars were first driven in Singapore in 1896. However, initially they were relatively scarce. The compacted earth and sand roads were often impassable during the rainy season, forced cars and lorries to travel in third gear, causing boilers to overheat, and, owing to the weight of vehicles, developed ruts, mounds of earth that destroyed sumps and had to be constantly lowered. Cars, meanwhile, were expensive; possessed poor quality engines that were noisy and prone to overheating, often necessitating journeys to take place at night; their non-removable wooden-spoked wheels made long trips uncomfortable; and the rubber skins that covered these wheels often perished in the hot sun or were punctured by stones.[8]

Vehicle numbers rose in the early decades of the century. Again, Malaya led the way; in 1938 there were just thirty-eight private and hire cars in the whole of British North Borneo. From 1910 to 1915, the number of registered vehicles in the country rose by 400 per cent and in the following fifteen years by 1,000 per cent to reach in 1930 165,000, as compared to the Dutch East Indies' mere 85,000. The growth in numbers was partly related to the prosperity of the rubber and tin sectors; there being a direct correlation between the prices of the two commodities and sales of automobiles. Other factors were the increasing use of asphalt in the construction of roads and the appearance of American vehicles, such as Fords and Dodges. These were cheaper than European models and possessed technical advantages. Not only were they more durable, but spare parts were widely available, cutting repair and maintenance costs. More importantly, they had a high road clearance, reducing damage caused by ruts, were equipped with Firestone pneumatic tyres that ensured a smoother ride and were lighter and could thus travel on and did not destroy unsurfaced roads, minimizing highway maintenance costs. By 1913, imports of American automobiles into Malaya had reached $1.281m, and, by 1921, had climbed to $2.869m, largely due to the virtual disappearance of foreign competition during the First World War.[9]

The cars were purchased by Chinese entrepreneurs and Europeans working in the country. At first they were imported into Malaya and distributed by British, and, to a lesser extent, Chinese general merchants, who additionally provided maintenance and repair services. By 1928, sixteen firms operated in the sector, though the majority of sales were made by just three companies: the Australian-owned Wearne Bros (1906), an agent for Rolls-Royce, Napier, Standard, Renault and, from 1910, Ford; the Cycle & Carriage Co. (1926), which acted for six English and four American manufacturers; and Borneo Motors Ltd (1925), a subsidiary of the Borneo Co. and General Motors' and Chrysler's Malayan agent. As sales increased, it became more economical for manufacturers to part-assemble a small proportion of cars within the country and to invest in showroom and service facilities and expand into distribution. Ford vehicles began to be assembled by Wearne Bros from 1924, and, in 1926, the American company opened its own assembly plant in Singapore. An attempt by General Motors to establish a plant in Katong the following year was scuppered by the government, which rejected the application – publicly because the factory would spoil Katong, then a seaside suburb, but privately because it feared that the company's high salaries would increase general wages. Ford and General Motors also opened their own agencies, though sales were low largely because they continued to sell vehicles through merchants.[10]

The commercial vehicles purchased were used to transport passengers and freight. By 1937, there were 2,917 commercial vehicles in the FMS. Some were owned by mines and plantations, but the vast majority by small-scale Chinese entrepreneurs, 80 per cent of whom had just one lorry which they used in their own businesses, transporting raw materials to their workshops and finished goods to customers, and hired out, along with their own services, to others. Although their transportation of produce to and from railheads initially increased the amount of freight carried by railways, hauliers gradually captured an ever increasing share of the haulage market, able to offer a prompt door-to-door service and carry mixed consignments. In response, railways slashed freight rates, closed uncompetitive lines such as the Kuala Selangor and Kuala Pilah branches, established their own road haulage businesses and received government help. To protect the interests of the FMS railway, the government prohibited long distance haulage on that part of the north–south trunk road that ran alongside the railroad, limited the operations of hauliers to a specified distance from their bases and refused to renew licences to long-distance freighters who competed with the railroad between Kuala Lumpur and Singapore and other major towns. A similar restrictive policy was adopted towards Chinese taxi owners and operators of mosquitos (converted motor cars with six to nine seats) and buses, who threatened the prosperity of European competitors. Operators were required to organize themselves into limited companies, each of which was given a fixed trading area/route, the most lucrative generally being awarded to Europeans. By 1939, the number of bus companies in the FMS had been reduced to just eighty-two, though 70 per cent were Chinese-owned, and the taxi sector was dominated by the General Transport Co., a subsidiary of Wearne Bros., which operated 'yellow top' taxis in Singapore, Malacca, Penang, Kuala Lumpur, Ipoh and Rangoon.[11]

Rivers

River transportation had a number of drawbacks. Many of the countries in the region lacked easily navigable waterways and, elsewhere, tributaries were generally circuitous, increasing the distances travelled, and broken by waterfalls and rapids. Goods thus often had to be transhipped and carried for some distance by porters in wagons, increasing costs and further slowing journey times. Moreover, canoes and sampans often capsized with the loss or deterioration of their cargoes and steamers were unable to operate in shallow rivers. Nonetheless, this form of transport was of great importance before the construction of railways and roads, and, in British North Borneo and Burma, remained significant until the end of the period. In British North Borneo, most export goods and particularly timber were transported to the coast along the Kinabatangan River, navigable for steam launches as far as the mouth of the Lokan tributary, and for smaller boats, as far as Tangkulang, and along the Segama, Sugut, Paitan and Labuk rivers. The Burmese Irrawaddy Delta was crossed by a network of waterways, most of which were navigable by canoe in the dry season and, with the arrival of the monsoon, by steam launches. In 1896/7, they carried twice as much freight as the country's railways and, in 1940/1, an equal amount. The most important river was the Irrawaddy, which linked Rangoon with Upper Burma and was plied by the Irrawaddy Flotilla Co. Founded in 1865 with the help of the Indian government and Rs 60,000 capital, the firm established services from Rangoon to Mandalay/Bhamo, from Rangoon to Bassein/Henzada and from Prome to Thayetmyo. By 1940, it possessed over 600 steamers, including express boats and vessels specially designed to carry oil, and carried 8m passengers and 1.2m tons of cargo pa.[12]

Ocean Transport

The total tonnage of merchant ships arriving at and departing from the Straits Settlements increased from 14.5m tons in 1900 to 42.99m tons on 1928, roughly half of which in 1919 were British, 22 per cent Japanese and 12 per cent Dutch. The twenty-three companies transporting goods to the West and Japan in 1897 represented a host of nations. Of the many British companies, the most important were the Ocean Steamship Co. (1866), which worked in close partnership with the shipping agency W. Mansfield & Co., Ben Line Steamers (1847), the Eastern & Australian Mail Steamship Co. (1873), Ellerman & Bucknall Steamship Co., the British India Steam Navigation Co. (1856) and the Peninsular and Oriental Steam Navigation Co., the latter two businesses merging in 1914. Of the other countries operating services, Holland was represented by Stoomvaart Maatschappij Nederland (1870) and Koninklijke Rotterdamsche Lloyd (1878), which in 1908 formed an alliance with Koninklijke Paketvaart-Maatschappij under the name NV Nederlandsche Scheepvaart Unie; Scandinavia by the Danish East Asiatic Co. (1897) and the Norwegian Wilh. Wilhelmsen; France by Messageries Maritimes (1851); Japan by Nippon Yusen Kaisha (1870); and Italy by Österreichischer Lloyd (1836), renamed Austrian Lloyd in 1919. The German presence comprised the Hamburg–America Line, the German Australian Steamship Co., and Norddeutscher Lloyd (1857). The latter company from 1885 was subsidised by a government contract to provide postal services between Germany and the Far East, in 1895 took over the Ocean Steamship Co., and, after the purchase of steamers from the East Indian Ocean Steamship Co. and Scottish Oriental Steamship Co. in 1907, became the second largest steamship company in the world.[13]

The first shipping cartel (also known as a conference) was established in 1885, but collapsed two years later. After a further failed attempt, in 1897 the shipping companies plying the route to Europe formed the Straits Homeward Conference. The cartel set a common freight rate, and, to prevent competition from other lines, gave shippers that used its services a 10 per cent rebate, paid at the end of the contract period and forfeited if goods had been transported on non-conference ships. Moreover, it presented the three largest trading companies (Boustead & Co., Gilfillan Wood & Co. and Behn Meyer & Co.) with an additional initially secret 10 per cent rebate, again on condition that they only used its services, later adding a further four companies to this elite club (Patterson Simons & Co., the Borneo Co., Huttenbach Bros and Brinkmann & Co.). In 1897, freight rates were raised twice and again in 1898, and, in 1905, the cartel was extended to routes to the East coast of the United States with the establishment of the New York Freights Conference.[14]

Needless to say, the formation of the cartel generated much controversy. Conference members argued that they provided a superior service to tramp steamers – more stable rates and favourable rebates, and, more importantly, regular sailings. Independently owned ships often failed to sail during periods of poor trade or particular seasons when no return cargo was available and it was claimed that the tendering process and the need for cargoes to accumulate until the chartering of a steamer became cost effective led to delays in shipments. Critics responded that the cartel set unnecessarily high freight charges, which inhibited the economic growth of Malaya, and that the secret rebate gave its recipients an unfair advantage over their competitors. British complainants, meanwhile, protested that the presence in the cartel of foreign companies acted against the interests of the UK's shipping industry and encouraged the development of the direct trade between extra-Malayan South East Asian countries and the West, which was destroying Singapore's *entrepôt* business.[15]

Attempts by shipping companies and shippers to break the conference ended in failure. Soon after its formation, the German Kingsin line began to carry freight to Hamburg in competition with the cartel's vessels. The conference attempted to persuade the company to become a member, and, when this was unsuccessful, Norddeutscher Lloyd took over the line. A further challenge by H. J. Harrison was resolved in a similar manner, the firm being purchased by the Shire line, another conference member. Shipper defiance was similarly ineffective. Threats by four trading companies to charter tramp steamers were neutralized by simply admitting them to the elite club that received the secret rebate.

Change only came in 1911. The British government's 1907 Royal Commission on Shipping Rings condemned the cartel's secret rebate, and, on the receipt of a petition demanding action signed by 700 European, Chinese and Indian businessmen, the Straits government passed the 1910 Freight and Steamship Ordinance. The Act not only defined conference vessels as common carriers, making it illegal for them to refuse to accept cargo for shipment, but forced them to pay an additional customs duty of 20 per cent on all freight transported. Appalled, the cartel demanded negotiations and, after several days of intense activity, the government agreed to repeal the ordinance in return for the abolition of the secret rebate, though it allowed the cartel to compensate the rebate's recipients through the payment of lump sums.[16]

Shipping within South East Asia and to East Asia was initially dominated by the Chinese, who, based in Singapore and Penang, transported goods between Malayan ports and to/from Rangoon, Bangkok, Saigon, the Dutch East Indies, French Indo-China and the southern Chinese ports. The companies involved in the sector generally plied a small number of routes, were owned by families and later by shareholders, and purchased their steamships from the secondary market, Riley Hargreaves & Co., Chinese owned shipyards in Singapore or the

Hong Kong Whampoa Dockyards. Significant firms included the Koe Guan Co. (1870s–1907), operated by the Khaw family of Penang and later taken over by the Eastern Shipping Co. (1907–22); the Ho Hong Steamship Co. (1914–32), managed by Lim Peng Siang; the Heap Eng Moh Steamship Co. (1912–30), part of Oei Tiong Ham's business empire; and the Wee Brothers Steamship Co. (1893–1929). By far the largest operator was Ban Hin & Co (1874–*c*. 1900), established by Tiong Po, who also had interests in tin mining, revenue farming, rice milling, insurance and plantation agriculture. The firm opened branches in Penang, Hong Kong, Amoy and Swatow and had twelve steamers that carried tin from Perak and Phuket, rice from Saigon and coolies and a variety of goods from China.[17]

The sector began to decline from the turn of the century due to discriminatory legislation and greater British and Dutch competition. By 1935, Chinese companies had lost all the routes to the Dutch East Indies, southern China and the southern Siamese states, plus the routes to Rangoon, Bangkok, Penang, Port Swettenham and Malacca. The most damaging legislation was the prerequisite that the senior staff of steamships should possess English qualifications, which forced Chinese companies to employ expensive and difficult to recruit European captains and officers, and the 1910 Merchant Shipping Ordinance that required the owners of all locally registered steamships to be British subjects and thus barred China-born businessmen from ownership. European competition came from Koninklijke Paketvaart-Maatschappij (KPM) and the Straits Steamship Co., and, on the South China route, from British lines such as the Ocean Steamship Co., the China Navigation Co., the Indo-China Steam Navigation Co. and the China Mutual Steam Navigation Co.[18]

KPM was founded in 1888 by the shipping lines Stoomvaart Maatschappij Nederland and Rotterdamsche Lloyd, in order to move goods to Java, where they would be transported to Holland by its two co-founders. Beginning with twenty-nine steamers, the company by 1920 had ninety-two vessels and 300 ports of call, including many in Malaya, French Indo-China, Burma and Siam, and, by 1939, 146 ships, 400 ports of call and nine international routes. The Straits Steamship Co. was established in 1890 by T. C. Bogaardt, the Dutch owner of the shipping agency W. Mansfield & Co., and a number of European businessmen and Chinese merchants, such as Tan Jiak Kim, Tan Keong Saik and Lee Cheng Yan. Raising $10m nominal capital and with a government subsidy for local and regional mail services, it purchased five vessels and began to carry tin, coffee, pepper, rice, rubber and tobacco between Singapore and Malaya's west coast ports. From 1914, when the Ocean Steamship Co. took a substantial shareholding, raising European ownership to 60 per cent, it grew rapidly, operating in 1939 fifty-one vessels with a combined tonnage of 38,860 tons. Its relationship with the Ocean Steamship Co. allowed it to issue through bills of lading, extremely attractive to traders who shipped local goods to Singapore or

Penang for transhipment to Europe or the United States, and it took over three local Chinese shipping lines, including the Eastern Shipping Co. and acquired a large shareholding in the Ho Hong Steamship Co.[19]

Airlines and the Telegraph

Two other important forms of communication were air travel and the telegraph. Aviation was relatively undeveloped. Its high costs and small carrying capacities made it unsuitable for the transport of passengers and cargo, apart from mail, and, by the end of the period, although the region was connected to the major European cities the service provided was limited. International flights were provided by Imperial Airways Ltd, which was founded in 1924 through the merger of four existing firms, and, in 1939, was itself amalgamated with British Airways Ltd (1935), a European carrier, to form the State owned British Overseas Airways Corporation (BOAC). The company initially concentrated on the development of European routes and only extended its reach to South East Asia in the early 1930s. A London to Rangoon service was launched in September 1933, a London to Singapore route in December of that year, which through an arrangement with QANTAS was extended to Brisbane in 1935, and, in March 1936, a branch service from Penang to Hong Kong was inaugurated. As for internal flights, in Burma there was an air service between Rangoon and Chungking and flying boats landed at Rangoon and Akyab. In Malaya, KLM flew goods and passengers to the Dutch East Indies, a plethora of seaplanes used bases at Langkawi Island (Kedah), Lumut (Perak), Muar (Johore), Glugor (Penang) and Kallang and, from 1937, Wearne Air Services, a subsidiary of Wearne Bros, operated flights from Singapore to Kuala Lumpur and Penang, and, later, to Alor Star (Kedah), Taiping, Ipoh (Perak) and Kota Bahru (Kelantan). Malayan Airways, founded in 1937 by Imperial Airways, the Straits Steamship Co. and the Ocean Steamship Co., lay dormant until after the Second World War, its directors fearful that it would fail to compete with Wearne Air Services.[20]

The international telegraph network was heavily subsidised by the Imperial government, which recognized that the ability to transmit information in minutes as opposed to the months it usually took to ship a message to the other side of the world would permit better control and defence of the Empire and promote the expansion of trade. The laying of ocean cable linking South East Asia to the major European cities was undertaken by companies owned by John Pender. Having connected India to the UK, Pender formed the British-Indian Extension Telegraph Co., which in 1870 laid cables from Madras to Penang, from Penang to Singapore and from Singapore to Darwin, Australia via Java. The following year a further company, the China Submarine Telegraph Co., linked Singapore to Saigon and Saigon to Hong Kong, and, in 1877, the Eastern

Extension, Australasia & China Telegraph Co. connected Penang to Rangoon and used landlines to link Rangoon to Madras. Duplicate cables were then laid from Singapore to Darwin (1879), Penang to Singapore via Malacca (1879), Singapore to Hong Kong via Tonkin (1884) and Labuan, North Borneo (1894), between Ceylon, Penang, Singapore and Hong Kong (1914) and from Singapore to Batavia (1922).[21]

Note: Information on transport and communications can also be found in the following sources/themes:

Topic	Source	Volume/Theme
Burmese canals	F. Noel-Paton, *Burma Rice* (paragraphs 41–54)	Volume 1/Agriculture
FMS roads and railways	R. G. Watson, *The Land Laws and Land Administration of the Federated Malay States*	Volume 1/Agriculture
Transport re. mines	G. E. Greig, *Mining in Malaya*	Volume 2/Mining
Volume of shipping entering and leaving FMS ports	C. S. Alexander, *British Malaya: Malayan Statistics*	Volume 3/Trade

Notes

1. D. Sunderland, *Communications in Africa, 1880–1939*, 5 vols (London: Pickering & Chatto 2012), vol. 1, pp. x–xlii.
2. Ibid., p. xlv; S. Yacob, 'Anglo-American Cooperation in the Malayan Automobile Market before the Pacific War', *Jebat: Malaysian Journal of History, Politics & Strategic Studies*, 38:2 (2011), pp. 61–82, on p. 65; T. R. Leinbach, 'Transportation and the Development of Malaya', *Annals of the Association of American Geographers*, 65:2 (1975), pp. 270–82, on p. 272; R. Winstedt, 'Southeastern Asia and the Philippines', *Annals of the American Academy of Political and Social Science*, 226 (1943), pp. 97–111, on p. 108; A. Booth, 'The Transition in Open Dualistic Economies in Southeast Asia: Another Look at the Evidence', *XIV International Economic History Congress*, (2006), pp. 1–39, on p. 28; A. Kaur, *Bridge and Barrier: Transport and Communications in Colonial Malaya, 1870–1957* (Singapore: Oxford University Press, 1985).
3. V. Thompson, 'Communications in Burma', *Far Eastern Survey*, 11:2 (1942), pp. 29–31. By 1911, only 1,939 miles of road had been constructed in Burma (N. Nishizawa, 'Economic Development of Burma', *Institute of Peace Studies, Hiroshima University, Japan, Research Report*, 16 (1991), pp. 1–155, on p. 120).
4. A. Kaur, 'The Babbling Brookes: Economic Change in Sarawak 1841–1941', *Modern Asian Studies*, 29:1 (1995), pp. 65–109, on p. 103.
5. Each male in the district was required to construct and care for 22 metres of bridleway, and, in return, obtained food, drink and tobacco (A. Kaur, '"Hantu" and Highway: Transport in Sabah 1881–1963', *Modern Asian Studies*, 28:1 (1994), pp. 1–49, on p. 32).
6. Ibid.
7. Anon., *The Land Transport of Singapore: From Early Times to the Present* (Singapore: Educational Publications Bureau, 1984), pp. 61–4; J. Warren, 'The Singapore Rickshaw Pullers: The Social Organization of a Coolie Occupation, 1880–1940', *Journal of South-*

east Asian Studies, 16:1 (1985), pp. 1–15; W. T. Yuen, 'Chinese Capitalism in Colonial Malaya, 1900–1941' (DPhil. dissertation, University of Hong Kong, 2010), pp. 1–450, on pp. 294–5.

8. Sunderland, *Communications in Africa*, vol. 1, p. xliii.

9. Ibid., vol. 1, p. xliv; Yacob, 'Anglo-American', pp. 4–7; Kaur, '"Hantu and Highway", p. 39. The value of UK imports in 1913 and 1921 was $0.907m and $1.47m respectively. A small number of Italian and French cars were also imported (Yacob, 'Anglo-American', p. 7).

10. Yacob, 'Anglo-American', pp. 6, 9, 16, 20–1; G. Jones and J. Wale, 'Merchants as Business Groups: British Trading Companies in Asia before 1945', *Business History Review*, 72:3 (1998), pp. 367–408, on p. 378; C. Fyfe, *Wheels in Malaya: The Wearne Brothers and their Company* (Claremont, W. Australia: Lane Press, 2002). General Motors eventually established the plant in the Dutch East Indies at Batavia (Yacob, 'Anglo-American', p. 2).

11. Yuen, 'Chinese Capitalism', pp. 294–9; Sunderland, *Communications in Africa*, vol. 1, p. xlvi; Leinbach, 'Transportation', p. 277; Fyfe, *Wheels in Malaya*.

12. Sunderland, *Communications in Africa*, vol. 5, pp. 183–4; Kaur, '"Hantu" and Highway', p. 4; Nishizawa, 'Economic Development', pp. 22–4; Kaur, *Bridge and Barrier*, p. 347.

13. Yuen, 'Chinese Capitalism', pp. 402–3; K. A. Snow, 'Russian Commercial Shipping and Singapore, 1905–1916', *Journal of Southeast Asian Studies*, 29:1 (1998), pp. 44–63; G. A. Hardwick, 'A Century of Service: The Eastern and Australian Steam Ship Company Limited', *Journal of the Royal Australian Historical Society*, 66:2 (1880), pp. 119–32; G. Jones, *Merchants to Multinationals: British Trading Companies in the Nineteenth and Twentieth Centuries* (Oxford: Oxford University Press, 2000), p. 70; S. Yacob, 'Trans-Generational Renewal as Managerial Succession: The Behn Meyer Story (1840–2000)', *Business History*, 19:4 (2012), pp. 1–20, on p. 6.

14. C. H. Ding, 'The Early Shipping Conference System of Singapore, 1897–1911', *Journal of Southeast Asian History*, 10:1 (1969), pp. 50–68, on pp. 56–7; Yuen, 'Chinese Capitalism', pp. 403–4; Jones, *Merchants to Multinationals*, p. 74; W. G. Huff, *The Economic Growth of Singapore: Trade and Development in the Twentieth Century* (Cambridge: Cambridge University Press, 1994), p. 129. The 1893 conference failed in 1895 (Ding, 'The Early Shipping', p. 56).

15. W. L. Ken, 'Singapore: Its Growth as an Entrepot Port, 1819–1941', *Journal of Southeast Asian Studies*, 9:1 (1978), pp. 50–84, on p. 68; Ding, 'The Early Shipping', p. 58.

16. Ding, 'The Early Shipping', pp. 58–63.

17. Yuen, 'Chinese Capitalism', pp. 374–5, 432; W. Y. Tuan, 'Uncovering the Myths of Two 19th-Century Hokkien Business Personalities in the Straits Settlements', *Chinese Southern Diaspora Studies*, 5 (2011–12), pp. 146–56, on p. 150; D. W. L. W. Leng, 'Regional Links: Yangon, Penang, and Singapore', *Journal of the Malaysian Branch of the Royal Asiatic Society*, 82:297 (2009), pp. 67–79.

18. Yuen, 'Chinese Capitalism', pp. 401–2, 430–1.

19. W. Makepeace, G. E. Brooke, and R. Braddell, *One Hundred Years of Singapore, Volume 2* (Singapore: Oxford University Press, 1991, pp. 201–2; W. Bailey and K. Bhaopichitr, 'How Important Was Silver? Some Evidence on Exchange Rate Fluctuations and Stock Returns in Colonial-Era Asia', *Journal of Business*, 77:1 (2004), pp. 137–73, on p. 147; Yuen, 'Chinese Capitalism', pp. 374, 376, 400, 402–3; W. G. Huff, 'Entitlements, Destitution, and Emigration in the 1930s Singapore Great Depression', *Economic History Review*, 54:2 (2001), pp. 290–323, on p. 302; K. G. Tregonning, *Home Port Singapore:*

A History of Straits Steamship Company Limited, 1890–1965 (Singapore: Oxford University Press, 1967).

20. Sunderland, *Communications in Africa*, vol. 1, p. x; vol. 5, p. 309; Thompson, 'Communications'; B. G. Wee (ed.), *Government-Linked Companies and Other Organisations in Singapore* (Singapore: Nanyang Technological University, 2004), pp. 1–37; Fyfe, *Wheels in Malaya*; Anon., 'Malaya and its Communications', *Bulletin of International News*, 18:26 (1941), pp. 2003–7, on p. 2007.

21. Sunderland, *Communications in Africa*, vol. 1, p. xlvi; Anon., 'History of the Atlantic Cable & Undersea Communications from the First Submarine Cable of 1850 to the Worldwide Fiber Optic Network', available online at http://atlantic-cable.com/Cable-Cos/CandW/EExt/index.htm [accessed 4 December 2013].

WRAY JR, *NOTES ON PERAK WITH A SKETCH OF ITS VEGETABLE, ANIMAL AND MINERAL PRODUCTS* (1886)

L. Wray Jr, *Notes on Perak with a Sketch of its Vegetable, Animal and Mineral Products* (London: W. Clowes & Sons, 1886), pp. 29–30.

The following extract provides a very brief review of the transport and communication infrastructure of Perak in 1886. The Taiping railway was followed in 1898 by a further line constructed between Enggor and Teluk Anson.

L. Wray Jr, *Notes on Perak with a Sketch of its Vegetable, Animal and Mineral Products* (1886), extract

RAILWAY.

In 1881, a trial cutting was made between Port Weld (then known as Sapetang) and Thaipeng, the chief town of Laroot, a distance of eight miles. The jungle was felled, and the line commenced the following year. Owing to the unstable character of the ground, which consists of sea and fresh-water swamps, with a little solid ground at the Upper or Thaipeng end, vast quantities of earth have had to be taken down from Thaipeng to make the embankment, and the line has proved much more difficult and costly than was at first anticipated. The line, which is of metre gauge, was opened for traffic on the 1st of June, 1885, and the Port is now within half-an-hour's journey / of the principal town of the State. It will remain to be seen whether rice and other provisions can be profitably carried by rail to, say, the tin-mining districts of Kinta, and the tin brought down to the coast, at a cheaper rate than is now paid. In those districts where there is no river transport, this might be possible, but in those more favourably situated it seems doubtful. This, of course, only applies to the financial side of the question; but what would be considered a failure, if the line belonged to a private company, might be a success as a State undertaking, for many places which would not pay under present conditions, could, with cheap transport, be profitably worked for tin, and the increased yield of metal might produce directly and indirectly sufficient revenue to more than justify the outlay for the construction of a line.

POST AND TELEGRAPHS

The following return of the covers which passed through the Post Offices in Perak during the last four years will show what rapid strides the country is making.

1881	17,327
1882	65,035
1883	102,963
1884	160,328

Money Orders were issued from the Perak offices to the amount of $35,000 in 1884, payable in India, Ceylon, and the Straits. Post Office Orders are not yet issued in Perak for payment in England.

Until the year 1884, the only telegraph lines in existence in the State were those running between Matang, Thaipeng and Kuala Kangsa, a total distance of twenty-six miles. These lines, which met at a place called Simpang, were in a most defective state as regards insulation and resistance, and from their peculiar arrangement were most difficult to work.

In August of 1884, a new line was opened to Krian, following the main road. This line has iron tubular posts, and white double invert insulators and No. 6 galvanised iron wire. The Matang and Kuala Kangsar branches have also been divided so as to form two separate lines. A line has been laid to Port / Weld from Thaipeng, following the railway, and the line to Krian has been extended to Kuala Prai in Province Wellesley and thence to Penang by cable, so that Perak is now in direct communication with the Eastern Extension Submarine System.

Another extension of 45 miles will be finished before the end of 1885, from Kuala Kangsar to Kinta; and further sections – Tapa to Lower Perak, 24 miles, and Kinta to Ulu Bernam, 100 miles – will be completed next year.

Twenty-one thousand, seven hundred and eighty messages were sent over the Perak lines in 1884.

ROADS

Roads. – A great deal of road construction and river clearing has been done in the last ten years. Excellent metalled carriage roads connect Teluk Kertang, Matang, Taipeng, Kamunting, and Kuala Kangsar, while from this last centre 50 miles of bridle road has just been completed towards the northern limit of the State; about 50 miles out of 150 miles contracted for, to join Kuala Kangsar with the eastern boundary at Ulu Berman, is finished, and the remainder will be constructed next year, as well as a branch of 24 miles from Tapa to Teluk Anson. These roads are all graded to nothing steeper than 1 in 20, and will be converted into cart roads as the traffic justifies the increased expenditure.

An unmetalled cart road runs from Simpang on the Matang-Thaipeng road across the railway to Krian and the western boundary of the State at Parit Buntar; the Krian District also contains many miles of similar roads.
Other short sections of cart and bridle roads have been constructed in many parts of the State.

ANON., *FIFTY YEARS OF RAILWAYS IN MALAYA, 1885–1935* (1935)

Anon., *Fifty Years of Railways in Malaya, 1885–1935* (Kuala Lumpur: Federated Malay States. Railways Department, 1935), pp. 3, 5, 7, 27–9, 31, 33–5, 37–8, 40, 42, 45, 47, 49, 51–3, 77, 79, 81, 83, 85, 87–9, 95.

The following extract provides detailed information on the construction of each line and FMS Railway's various wharves, its locomotives and financial performance. No further lines were constructed until 1965 when a six mile-long branch was added to the network, spanning Jurong and Bukit Timah.

Anon., *Fifty Years of Railways in Malaya, 1885–1935* (1935), extract

INTRODUCTION

THE first railway in Malaya, that from Port Weld to Taiping, was opened for traffic in June 1885. The present year, therefore, marks the fiftieth anniversary of railways in this country. The development of the railway system in Malaya from the year 1885 onwards is dealt with in the chapters which follow. In this introduction it is intended only to give a brief description of the railway system as it exists to-day.

The main line of the F. M. S. Railways serves the western portion of the Peninsula and runs from Singapore to Prai (for Penang) with an extension to the Siamese border at a point 580 miles from Singapore where junction is made with the Royal State Railways of Siam. The Johore State Railway, which forms an integral part of the main line, is 121 ¼ miles in length and is leased by the Federated Malay States Railways from the State of Johore. From Gemas, 137 miles north of Singapore, a line, known as the East Coast Line, runs northwards for a distance of 327 miles to Tumpat on the coast of Kelantan. From this line there is also a connection with the Royal State Railways of Siam at Sungei Golok. A branch line connects with the chief port of the Federation, Port Swettenham, managed by the railway, whilst other branches serve the railway ports of Malacca, Port Dickson, Teluk Anson and Port Weld*. [...]

The total route mileage of the system is 1,067 with a total track mileage of 1,321, all of metre gauge. The railway has been constructed to a high standard and, except on a short section of 25 miles known as the "Taiping Pass Section", has a maximum gradient of 1 in 100. The main line and Port Swettenham Branch are laid with rails of 80 lbs. per yard, the remaining sections being laid with rails of 60 lbs. per yard. Sleepers of local hard-wood are used, the rails being fastened by dog spikes.[1] The average life of a local hard-wood sleeper is about 14 years. The more important lines are ballasted[2] with limestone of a maximum size of 2 ¼", sand ballast being used for lines having less traffic.

There are 213 permanent stations and 76 halts. The Railways own 178 locomotives and rail motors, 397 passenger coaches, 5,170 goods vehicles, 11 steam vessels and 80 lighters.[3] The locomotives and rolling stock are diversified in character and capacity and meet all requirements of passenger and freight services. Single loads up to 35 tons can be handled.

The headquarters of the system are at Kuala Lumpur, the capital of the Federated Malay States. The Central Workshops are at Sentul, three miles north of Kuala Lumpur. The Headquarters organization of the Railways is shown on the chart on page 6 [not included]. For operating and commercial purposes the railways are divided into two divisions, Kuala Lumpur and lines north and west thereof forming one division known as the "Western Division", whilst lines south and east of Kuala Lumpur form the "Midland Division" with headquarters at Kuala Lumpur and Gemas respectively.

The staff of the Railways, which in the year 1929 totalled 25,000, has been more than halved in consequence of the cessation of new construction, reorganization and reduction in traffic. The distribution, by nationalities, of the present staff is as follows: –

Europeans	106
Eurasians	135
Malays	1,570
Indians and Ceylonese	8,941
Chinese	868
Others	23
Total	11,643

It has been the policy of the Railway Department to house as far as possible the whole of its staff and the Railways at present own over 10,000 staff quarters.

An up-to-date and adequate organization has been provided for the recruiting and training of youths for all locally appointed grades in the Railway Service.

For the higher Subordinate Technical posts, youths having general education of Matriculation Standard are selected for a four-year course of training about two years of which is spent in the Government Technical School, Kuala Lumpur. /

For meeting the Railways' needs for artizans of all kinds, a large number of apprentices are constantly under training. These youths, most of whom are English-speaking, receive a five-year course of training in the Central Workshops supplemented by evening classes in machine drawing, workshop mechanics and similar subjects.

Apprentices for training as Guards, Signalmen, and Station and Yard staff, undergo a three-year course of training, the time being divided between courses of instruction in a Transportation Training School situated in the Head Office Building and in gaining experience at stations.

The Railways now employ no European Drivers; locally recruited youths of sound physique are given a five-year course of training in the Running Sheds, on the engine footplate on line and also in the Transportation Training School.

At all large railway centres, Railway Institutes have been provided for the benefit of the staff. These Institutes usually have ample playing fields with tennis and badminton courts, and the larger Institutes are equipped with billiard tables and spacious club buildings.

The average number of trains run daily is 250. Of these the most important are the Day and Night Expresses between Penang and Singapore. These Express trains are equipped with Restaurant and Buffet Car accommodation and the night trains have single and double berth Sleepers. The trains run to the following times:

DAILY.

Penang	dep.	8.30	a.m.	8.00	p.m.
Kuala Lumpur	arr.	6.05	p.m.	6.30	a.m.
Kuala Lumpur	dep.	10.00	p.m.	9.00	a.m.
Singapore	arr.	6.44	a.m.	5.58	p.m.
Singapore	dep.	8.40	a.m.	10.00	p.m.
Kuala Lumpur	arr.	5.49	p.m.	7.20	a.m.
Kuala Lumpur	dep.	8.30	p.m.	8.30	a.m.
Penang	arr.	6.45	a.m.	6.10	p.m.

The Railways maintain a service of ferry steamers between Prai on the mainland and the island of Penang.

In conjunction with the Royal State Railways of Siam an Express train service is provided between Penang and Bangkok twice a week in each direction. The train is equipped with Restaurant Cars and coaches adaptable for day and night use. A through Day and Night Coach is provided from Kuala Lumpur connecting with the Bangkok train. The journey between Penang and Bangkok, a distance of 713 miles, occupies 27 hours.

On the East Coast line an Express train with sleeping accommodation is run once per week in each direction. This train is provided with a Buffet and an Observation Coach.

An excellent goods train service is provided throughout the system, the more important centres being connected by fast night goods trains which, in most cases, provide for delivery the following morning. Collection and Delivery Lorry Services are provided at all the more important centres, the total number of such services being 110.

Throughout the greater part of the Peninsula, the F.M.S. Railway system is subject to intense competition from road vehicles and from coastal shipping. On page 7 will be found a statement of the receipts and profits of the system since its inception, from which it will be noticed that between 1929 and 1933 railway receipts declined by no less than 61%. This decline in receipts was due to the severe trade depression, the fall in the price of the country's chief products, tin and rubber, and also the intense competition with other forms of transport. Since 1929 the railways annual expenditure has been reduced by 40%, whilst special efforts have been made to increase railway revenue, so that at the time of writing the Railways are able to meet working expenses and make a substantial allowance for depreciation, but no interest on capital has been paid since the year 1929. Special rates are quoted for competitive traffic and a large proportion of the tonnage handled is now carried at such special reduced rates. These rates have been quoted in many different forms such as flat rates from a factory to all stations on the line; rates decreasing with increases in the tonnage, rates varying with the selling price of the commodity transported and contract rates over a period of time.

Considerable areas of godown[4] accommodation are available and favourable terms for sites and for sidings are granted by the Railways to traders who erect accommodation alongside the line.

The Railways have been relieved of the responsibility of avoiding preference in the quotation of rates, so enabling the system to compete on more equal terms with other forms of transport. /

STATEMENT OF GROSS EARNINGS 1894 – 1934

and

NET CASH SURPLUS/DEFICIENCY 1885 – 1934.

Year	Passenger Train Traffic		Goods Train Traffic		Miscellaneous Receipts	Total Gross Earnings	Net Cash Surplus
	No. of Passengers	Receipts $ c	Tonnage	Receipts $ c	$ c	$ c	$ c
1885 to 1893							1,659,162 73
1894						909,721 14	459,258 01
1895						1,237,714 46	590,711 14
1896						1,228,294 46	560,719 36
1897						1,220,378 12	519,285 31
1898						1,304,049 43	481,703 02
1899						1,605,767 60	748,423 27
1900						2,087,921 67	1,035,368 83
1901						2,340,821 45	1,079,117 90
1902						2,874,263 94	1,338,293 32
1903	4,173,242	1,915,020 95	460,348	1,391,430 77	379,382 42	3,685,834 14	1,881,685 11
1904	4,797,609	2,011,609 61	499,874	1,518,247 35	75,172 29	3,605,029 25	1,474,911 07
1905	5,514,449	2,179,463 82	514,226	1,645,892 39	115,242 48	3,940,598 69	1,663,048 15
1906	6,171,596	2,565,969 78	589,580	1,921,855 53	76,274 68	4,564,099 99	1,572,337 51
1907	6,772,340	2,879,190 54	616,287	2,136,033 58	185,686 99	5,200,911 11	1,553,617 74
1908	6,391,840	2,611,307 61	596,385	2,058,812 24	396,033 30	5,066,153 15	1,609,130 60
1909	7,262,830	2,594,862 99	624,850	2,105,848 78	487,398 59	5,188,110 36	1,488,343 34
1910	9,034,529	3,180,846 81	653,663	2,273,519 65	414,140 22	5,868,506 68	2,247,073 79
1911	10,347,896	3,932,878 92	780,780	2,685,989 31	439,820 80	7,058,689 03	3,281,274 91
1912	11,589,273	4,839,311 36	988,416	3,191,924 23	389,781 28	8,421,016 87	2,666,345 23
1913	13,143,659	5,514,531 90	1,172,794	3,718,554 25	315,287 85	9,548,374 00	2,707,696 23

Year	Passenger Train Traffic		Goods Train Traffic		Miscellaneous Receipts	Total Gross Earnings	Net Cash Surplus
	No. of Passengers	Receipts $ c	Tonnage	Receipts $ c	$ c	$ c	$ c
1914	11,974,745	5,045,850 92	1,140,253	3,685,096 21	342,812 62	9,073,759 75	2,029,187 22
1915	11,899,028	4,890,247 83	1,100,381	3,692,046 49	468,948 85	9,051,243 17	2,636,397 93
1916	14,741,066	6,542,731 99	1,267,031	4,145,449 74	928,514 77	11,616,696 50	4,027,228 54
1917	12,037,941	7,614,177 37	1,293,404	4,654,302 14	921,348 37	13,189,827 88	4,168,322 06
1918	9,356,880	6,957,872 67	1,449,973	5,229,520 77	919,119 23	13,106,512 67	3,399,358 19
1919	10,176,029	8,164,014 19	1,578,757	5,702,279 12	1,091,175 22	14,957,468 53	3,310,446 62
1920	13,401,532	9,899,363 20	1,683,562	6,122,562 71	1,294,607 78	17,316,533 69	563,185 49
1921	10,551,115	7,765,904 40	1,542,218	7,103,575 70	1,328,945 93	16,198,426 03	501,552 08
1922	8,439,333	6,212,533 36	1,669,399	6,401,153 34	1,202,637 32	13,816,324 02	2,004,005 07
1923	10,656,384	6,686,229 50	1,845,827	6,657,767 56	1,331,108 86	14,675,105 92	1,710,348 85
1924	10,814,586	6,603,910 89	1,862,866	8,005,717 88	1,600,573 13	16,210,201 90	3,278,427 81
1925	12,552,621	7,678,808 03	2,031,352	9,141,341 69	1,923,202 51	18,743,352 23	4,770,316 13
1926	14,555,190	9,833,336 98	2,259,005	9,428,593 08	2,378,615 23	21,640,545 29	6,427,444 78
1927	14,171,105	10,124,026 33	2,463,185	10,188,463 19	2,743,025 21	23,055,514 73	3,606,011 96
1928	13,475,070	9,192,275 97	2,508,476	10,363,147 84	2,792,135 73	22,347,559 54	2,591,708 60
1929	14,087,281	9,381,145 42	2,618,234	11,223,488 53	2,726,984 48	23,331,618 43	7,371,321 85
1930	11,773,129	7,977,885 02	2,159,536	8,790,022 08	2,504,996 26	19,272,903 36	4,183,104 80
1931	7,229,106	4,983,085 69	1,375,454	5,854,954 82	2,074,538 51	12,912,579 02	*319,083 78
1932	5,309,799	3,685,749 88	944,133	4,037,964 59	1,760,144 39	9,483,858 86	*1,496,996 06
1933	4,514,883	3,121,302 29	890,632	3,988,231 18	1,927,242 84	9,036,776 31	*2,039,909 57
1934	5,498,159	3,958,677 37	1,187,041	5,256,108 69	2,069,361 38	11,284,147 44	1,574,757 48
						Net Surplus	84,914,642 62

Contribution from net surplus to Railway Renewals Fund 1927 to 1934 inclusive –
$17,514,077.21.
* Deficiency. /

CONSTRUCTION

FIFTY years ago, on 1st June, 1885, the line from Port Weld to Taiping was opened. This line, 8 ¼ miles long, was the first railway to be constructed in the Malay Peninsula. The Perak Government, at the time, had no Engineers with experience of Railway construction, so it commissioned the Ceylon Government to carry out the work, and on completion the line was taken over and operated by the Perak Government. This line which now carries only one goods train a day in each direction was then of considerable importance linking up the mining centre of Larut with Port Weld, which in addition to being a port of call for local steamers, was the centre of supply of the mangrove firewood then extensively used by the mines.

The Taiping terminus of the Port Weld line occupied the present site of the King Edward VII School Padang and the Railway Headquarters offices were near the Rest House and are now the Sanitary Board and certain other Government Department offices. Taiping station was later moved to its present site.

In 1888 extensions to Kamunting and Kuala Kangsar were contemplated. In his Annual Report for 1888, the Resident Engineer and Traffic Manager writes: –

"The necessity for railway extension to Kamunting is now more evident than it was when I sent in my last Annual Report. The traffic on the cart road has considerably increased, and cattle disease has enhanced the rates for cart hire, it now being cheaper to send a load of rice from Port Weld to Taiping (8 miles) than from Taiping to Kamunting (3 ½ miles). The freight for 50 bags of Bengal rice from Port Weld to Taiping is $3.50 including loading and unloading / charges, while from Taiping to Kamunting it varies from $3.50 to $3.75, the carts being loaded by the railway.

Such heavy transport charges must militate against the opening up and working of mines in the Kamunting District and beyond.

A line to Kuala Kangsar might not prove immediately remunerative, but it would not be an expensive line to construct, there being no heavy work except at 'The Pass.'

One of the advantages immediately following would be the reduction on carriage of goods to about one half of the present rates, and Kuala Kangsar would be brought within 1 ½ hours of Taiping."

Construction of the line to Kamunting was commenced on September 30th, 1889, and the line was opened by the Resident on 6th May, 1890.

In June 1891, work commenced on a further extension northwards from Kamunting to Blanda Mabok, since renamed Ulu Sapetang on representations made by the Dutch Consul. This section was opened for traffic on 1st July, 1892.

It is interesting to note from the Annual Report of the Resident Engineer for Railways that the opening of this section was delayed through the failure of the sleeper supply. Railway construction has been similarly handicapped on many occasions.

Meanwhile during 1891 contracts were let for the construction of the Kinta Valley Railway from Ipoh to Tapah Road, a distance of 34 miles, and from Tapah Road to Teluk Anson; surveys were also made for extensions from Ulu Sapetang to Selama and from Taiping to Kuala Kangsar.

In 1893 the contract for the construction of the line from Ipoh to Tapah Road was cancelled, and in his report for 1893 the Resident Engineer for Railways states: –

"I think I may safely say that experience has shown that in Perak it is not advisable to let the Railways by contract.

My experience of Railway work, at the Cape, in Ceylon and here, is conclusive that, with an efficient staff, a Government can construct its own Railways more economically and expeditiously, and ensure better work, than if a contractor is employed." /

It may be mentioned here that from this date all Railway construction undertaken by the F.M.S. Railways has been carried out departmentally, or at piece work rates under the supervision of Railway Engineers.

During 1893 the line from Teluk Anson to Tapah Road was opened for traffic, also a portion of the Kinta Valley Railway from Ipoh to Batu Gajah which was extended to Kota Bharu in 1894; during the latter year a section of this line from Tapah to Talam was also opened to traffic.

In the Annual Report for 1894, the Resident Engineer for Railways writes under the heading "Occurrences": –

"On the evening of the 17th September a passenger train from Tapah Road to Teluk Anson came into collision with a wild elephant, at about three and a half miles from Teluk Anson. The engine and tender were derailed and the line was blocked till 22nd September. No one was injured and the passengers walked into Teluk Anson, but the driver was thrown off his engine into the jungle by the side of the line."

The head and tusks of the elephant are now in Taiping Museum together with photographs of the occurrence which is also commemorated on the spot by a monument...

During 1895 the East Section of the Kinta Valley line was completed, thus linking up Ipoh with the Port of Teluk Anson. It is worthy of note that nowhere in the annual reports is mention made of any projected railway from Ipoh to Lumut. The construction of the Kinta Valley line suggests that Teluk Anson was designed to be the Port for Kinta, and in the words of the Resident Engineer "The opening for through traffic was accompanied by an immediate rise in the monthly receipts."

In the same year construction was commenced on an extension northwards of the Kinta Valley Line from Ipoh to Tanjong Rambutan and Chemor. The extension was opened in 1896, and further extensions northwards were completed to Sungei Siput in 1897, and to Enggor in 1898.

In 1896 surveys were completed from Prai to Bagan Serai and from Ulu Sapetang to Bukit Merah, the projected line from Ulu Sapetang to Selama having been abandoned in favour of a / more circuitous route via Pondok Tanjong, Bukit Merah and Bagan Serai.

During 1897 the difficult task of finding a route over the Pass between Taiping and Padang Rengas was seriously undertaken. Two routes were surveyed each involving the construction of 3 tunnels. In the Annual Report for 1897 it is stated: "An immense amount of work has been done on the survey through the Pass in order to select the best possible route, a large extent of the ground has been contoured, and cross sections have been taken 50 feet apart on the centre line for a distance of 5 ½ miles."

The Pass Section was commenced in 1898 and completed in 1903, and for some time this was the only gap in the line between Kuala Lumpur and Prai, through passengers had to undertake the journey between Padang Rengas and Taiping by gharry.

Work on the Perak River Bridge at Enggor was commenced during 1897 but was suspended at the end of the year owing to the high floods which occurred in December as a result of which the rail level was raised by 6 feet. This was fortunate, as had it not been so raised the floods of December 1926, which rose several feet higher than that of 1897, would no doubt have caused considerable damage to or completely destroyed the bridge. Construction was resumed early in 1898 and the bridge completed in 1900.

1898 was a year of intensive railway construction. In addition to the Taiping – Kuala Kangsar section, work was in hand between Prai and Ulu Sapetang and also to the south between Tapah Road and Tanjong Malim, and in 1899 work on the section Enggor to Kuala Kangsar was commenced.

In 1899 the first section in Province / Wellesley was opened from Prai to Bukit Mertajam, this was extended to Nibong Tebal in 1900 and in 1902 joined up with the system in Perak. In connection with the Railway in Province Wellesley, Sir Frank Swettenham wrote in 'British Malaya': –

"The Malay States made, and paid for, the Province Wellesley Railway, and no benefit so great has ever been conferred on Pinang in the history of the Settlement, but the people of this place were slow to appreciate the fact and have never been demonstrative in thanks to the Malay States. . . . ."

Through communication by rail between the Perak/Selangor boundary at Tanjong Malim and Prai was established in 1903.

SELANGOR.

The first Railway in Selangor was opened in 1886 and extended from Kuala Lumpur to Bukit Kuda near Klang. Later the old Connaught Bridge over the Klang River was built and the Railway extended to Klang in 1890 from where sidings extended to the river bank and suitable wharves were constructed to accommodate local steamers. These wharves were situated near the Klang end of Belfield Bridge.

The first Kuala Lumpur Station was a temporary structure with an attap[5] roof sited near the present Customs Godown in the Goods Yard. In 1892 a permanent station was built on the present site which in turn was replaced by the present station commenced in 1909 and completed some years later.

In 1889 construction was commenced on the Ulu Selangor Line from Kuala Lumpur to Rawang and thence to Kuala Kubu. This line was opened to Rawang in 1892, to Serendah in 1893 and to Kuala Kubu (now Kuala Kubu Lama) in 1894...

The projected railway from Kuala Lumpur to Ulu Pahang was never built, neither was the line from Klang to Kuala Sungei. Dua, better known as "Deep Water Point"; this was unfortunate as it is now well known that Deep Water Point would have made a better port than Port Swettenham.

During 1892 the line from Kuala Lumpur to Pudoh was commenced and completed in 1893. This was the start on the line which eventually linked Kuala Lumpur with Singapore. This line started at Kuala Lumpur Station, ran through the present goods yard, crossed the Klang River and thence by way of Foch Avenue to Sultan Street and Pudu. It will be seen that the line wandered through the town of Kuala Lumpur and the inconvenience of the level crossings at Rodger Street, High Street, Petaling Street and Sultan Street led to the ultimate deviation of the main line in 1912 via Port Swettenham Junction and Salak South Junction to Sungei Besi.

The survey over Ginting Peras into Pahang was continued during 1892 and a line / was projected from Kuala Lumpur via Sungei Besi, Cheras and Ulu Langat crossing Ginting Peras at an elevation of 1,500 feet. Descending into Jelebu the route ran through the concession of the Jelebu Mining Company to the River Triang and thence to Temerloh, a total distance of 87 miles from Kuala Lumpur.

In 1893 the extension southwards from Pudu to Sungei Besi was commenced. The objective then was Pahang via Ginting Peras with the terminus at Temerloh. As is well known this project was abandoned and the line extended southwards with Singapore as the objective.

During the year a decision was made to extend the Klang Line to Kuala Klang, now known as Port Swettenham. In this connection the Resident Engineer writes in his Annual Report: –

"The accommodation available for shipping and the depth of the water obtainable at this point had formerly been reported upon unfavourably, but after roughly sounding[6] the proposed harbour I reported upon it as a suitable site for the construction of wharves, and with abundance of water and swinging room for vessels lying in the harbour. The question was eventually, at the Resident's request, referred by H. E. the Governor to Capt. Field, R.N., (H.M.'s Surveying Vessel Egeria), who carefully inspected the proposed harbour and reported most favourably upon it, and the whole scheme has now been sent to the Right Hon'ble the Secretary of State for the Colonies for approval."

During 1895 the line from Pudu to Sungei Besi was opened and the extension southwards to Kajang was in hand. The extension from Klang to Kuala Klang was also commenced. No new lines were opened in 1896, but the construction was in hand of the line from Klang to Kuala Klang and of the wharves at Kuala Klang. The Resident Engineer remarks in his Annual Report that contrary to expectation there was scarcely any sickness among the workmen. During the year the Resident Engineers of the Selangor and Perak Railways met to discuss working arrangements when the two systems joined up at the Selangor/ Perak boundary.

1897 saw the completion of the extensions from Sungei Besi to Kajang and from Klang to Kuala Klang although the latter line was not opened to traffic until 1899 pending the completion of the wharves. The year was notable from the fact that a scheme of Railway extension was laid down by Sir Frank Swettenham with the approval of the Secretary of State. This scheme contemplated through connection by rail from Prai to Seremban.

During 1898 and 1899 the extension from Kuala Kubu to Tanjong Malim was in hand and opened for traffic in 1900.

1901 saw the amalgamation of the Perak and Selangor State Railways under the style of "The Federated Malay States Railways" and administered by Mr. C. E. Spooner, C.M.G., as General Manager and Chief Engineer.

NEGRI SEMBILAN.

The first railway in the State now known as the Negri Sembilan was opened in 1891 and ran from Port Dickson to Seremban, a distance of 24 3/4 miles. It was constructed and owned by a private company known as The Sungei Ujong Railway Co., which operated independently of the Government for many years, and was subsequently taken over by the F.M.S. Railways system in the year 1908. No further railways were constructed in Negri Sembilan until the F.M.S. Railways were extended from Bangi to Seremban in 1903 although during 1890 and 1891 surveys were made for an extension of the Sungei Ujong Railway from Seremban to Semantan / (Pahang). This project was abandoned chiefly owing to the difficult route through the mountains.

FEDERATED MALAY STATES RAILWAYS.

It will be seen that the origin of the present system consisted of four lines linking the chief towns with the coast; thus Taiping was linked with Port Weld, Ipoh with Teluk Anson, Kuala Lumpur with Klang and Seremban with Port Dickson.

Construction continued gradually extending North and South until in 1903 there was a through line from Prai to Seremban. A further extension Southwards from Seremban to the Johore frontier, including a branch line from Tampin to Malacca, was commenced in 1903 and opened to Malacca in 1905 and to Gemas in 1906.

During 1904 an agreement was completed with the Johore State Government for the construction of a line from the Negri Sembilan/Johore frontier to Johore Bahru opposite Singapore Island and construction was commenced in the same year. This line ran through jungle for practically the whole length and great difficulty was experienced owing to lack of communications and transport facilities over 100 of the 120 miles the line was to cover. Except in the vicinity of Johore Bahru itself roads did not exist and except for the Muar River at Buloh Kasap, no navigable river was crossed.

On the 1st July, 1909, the line through Johore was opened and through communication was thereby established from Penang in the north to Johore Bahru; from there a ferry conveyed passengers across the Johore Straits to Woodlands where they joined the Singapore – Kranji Railway for Singapore. In 1910 a goods wagon ferry was opened between Johore Bahru and Woodlands thus avoiding transshipment of goods.

The Singapore – Kranji Railway constructed by the Colonial Government in 1903 was purchased by the F.M.S. Railways in 1913.

The construction of the Causeway across the Johore Straits to carry two tracks of railway and a 26 foot roadway was commenced towards the end of 1919. The Causeway was opened for goods trains on the 17th September, 1923, and for passenger trains on 1st October, 1923, the ceremonial opening being performed by H. E. the Governor and High Commissioner, Sir Laurence Guillemard, K.C.B., K.C.M.G., on 28th June, 1924. The length of the Causeway is 3,465 feet and the average depth of water in which it is laid is 47 feet at low / tide with a maximum depth, also at low tide, of 77 feet. It is constructed entirely of granite block, over 1 ½ million cubic yards being used. A lock 510 feet long, 32 feet wide and 10 feet deep at low tide has been constructed through the Causeway at the Johore end for small local craft. A rolling lift bridge,[7] the only one of its type in this part of the world, carries the railway and roadway across the lock. The bridge is 57 feet wide and the weight of the moving part is 570 tons. It is operated electrically, as also are the lock gates.

THE EAST COAST RAILWAY.

The East Coast Railway leaves the main line at Gemas and runs in a northerly direction / via Kuala Lipis to Tumpat in Kelantan, a distance of 327 3/4 miles. Reference has previously been made to the projected lines from Kuala Lumpur and from Seremban into Pahang, both had the same objective, i.e. Temerloh or Kuala Semantan. The objective of the East Coast Railway was also originally Temerloh and it was then known as the Gemas – Kuala Semantan Railway. It may be wondered why Temerloh, a Kampong on the Pahang River, should have been made the objective. Temerloh is almost on a direct line between Kuala Lumpur or Seremban and / Kuantan on the East Coast and in the early days of the railway the engineers and administrators had in view an ultimate extension to Kuantan.

When construction had been in hand some time it was decided to run the line through Pahang and Kelantan to Tumpat and the original survey to Kuala Semantan was deviated at Mengkarak and now crosses the Semantan River at

Mentakab 7 miles from the *Kuala*. Construction from Gemas end was commenced late in 1907 and the first section from Gemas to Bahau including a branch to Kuala Pilah was opened in April, 1910. Further extensions were opened from time to time until in 1913 Tembeling 117 miles from Gemas was reached. Meanwhile in 1912 construction commenced at Tumpat working south and a section from Tumpat to Tanah Merah, a distance of 32 miles was opened in 1914, and in the following year a small branch was opened from Tanah Merah to Riverside on the Kelantan River.

During the Great War construction slowed down considerably on the south section and was suspended in Kelantan. In 1917 the line from Tembeling to Kuala Lipis was opened to traffic, thus linking up the Administrative Capital of Pahang with the Railway system.

Construction in Kelantan recommenced during 1918, work being at first concentrated on a branch from Pasir Mas to Sungei Golok on the Kelantan/Siam frontier to join up with the Siamese Railways. This branch, 11 ½ miles long, was opened on the 1st September, 1920, thus giving Kelantan rail communication with the rest of the Peninsula via the Siamese Railways to Padang Besar.

During 1920 work commenced on the bridge over the Kelantan River near Tanah Merah. This is the longest bridge in the Peninsula and consists of 5 spans of 250 feet each and 5 spans of 150 feet each. Work on this bridge and on construction generally, was slowed down during the slump period of 1921/22. The Kelantan Bridge was completed in November, 1923, and opened for traffic in 1924. The official opening was performed by H. E. Sir Laurence Guillemard, and the bridge was named "The Guillemard Bridge".[8] The line from Tanah Merah to Krai was also opened in 1924. Meanwhile, construction was proceeding from the south and the line to Merapoh, the boundary between Pahang and Kelantan, was opened in 1927 and in the same year a further section from Krai to Manek Urai. The line from Manek Urai to Merapoh is very heavy and owing to difficulties in transport, progress was necessarily slow. The highest known flood which occurred in December, 1926, caused a great deal of damage to the construction works and rendered necessary a considerable deviation in the original line between Kuala Lumpar and Kuala Pergau necessitating heavier tunnelling and additional expenditure. There are 9 tunnels on the East Coast Railway of which 8 are in Kelantan, they vary in length from 309 to 2,340 feet, the total length being 7,704 feet. The East Coast Railway was completed on the 5th September, 1931, the ceremonial opening being performed jointly by H. E. Sir Cecil Clementi[9] and H. H. the Sultan of Kelantan.

THE KEDAH RAILWAY.

The Kedah line branches off from the main trunk line at Bukit Mertajam 7 miles south of Prai, and runs through Province Wellesley, Kedah and Perlis to the Siamese boundary at Padang Besar where it joins up / with the Siamese Railway System. The length of the line is 99 miles.

Construction of the line was commenced in 1912 which was opened to Alor Star, the capital of Kedah, in 1915 and to Padang Besar in 1918.

TRONOH BRANCH.

This branch runs from Ipoh to Tronoh, a distance of 15 miles, with stations at Menglembu, Lahat Town, Papan, Pusing and Siputeh. It taps a very populous mining area. Construction of this line started in April, 1907, and it was opened to traffic in October, 1908.

BATANG BERJUNTAI BRANCH.

The branch starts at Kuang on the main line 15 miles north of Kuala Lumpur and runs to Batang Berjuntai, a distance of 14 miles, with stations at Pengkalan Kundang, Batu Arang and Bukit Badong. Construction was commenced in November, 1913, and completed to Batu Arang in July, 1915. Work beyond Batu Arang was suspended for a while but subsequently re-started and the line to Batang Berjuntai opened to traffic in February, 1918.

This branch connects with the Malayan Collieries at Batu Arang.

KUALA SELANGOR BRANCH.

This branch ran from Connaught Bridge Junction on the west of the Klang River to Klang North and thence via Vallambrosa and Jeram to Kuala Selangor, a distance of 32 miles. Construction started in 1911 and the line was opened to Assam Jawa in 1913 and to Kuala Selangor in 1914. Owing to the earnings of this branch not covering working expenses on account of road competition, the line was closed down in 1931 and was dismantled in 1934.

AMPANG AND SULTAN STREET BRANCHES.

The branch from Sultan Street, Kuala Lumpur, to Salak South Junction 4 ½ miles long-was originally the main line from Kuala Lumpur to Sultan Street, Pudu and Sungei Besi. After the deviation of the main line via Port Swettenham Junction and Salak South, the portion of the old main line from Kuala Lumpur to Sultan Street was removed and the remaining line from Sultan Street to Salak South Junction became a branch line.

The Ampang line branches off from the Sultan Street branch and runs to Ampang Village, a distance of 4 ½ miles from the junction.

BATU CAVES BRANCH.

The Batu Caves Branch 5 ¼ miles long was opened in 1905. It serves the Central Workshops and the Railway township at Sentul and important quarries and other works at Batu Caves. During *Thaipusam* (Hindu Festival) it is extensively used by pilgrims and sightseers to Batu Caves.

PENANG HILL RAILWAY.

The first Penang Hill Railway built by private enterprise was a failure. The present railway was constructed by the F.M.S. Railways; it was commenced in 1920 and opened in 1923. From 1st January, 1924, it was handed over to the Colonial Government which now owns and operates it. The Penang Hill Railway is a Cable Railway, the motive power being electricity; its total length is 1 ¼ mile, the steepest gradient being 1 in 1.95. Near the top there is a tunnel 258 feet long on a gradient of 1 in 2.04. The upper station is 2,400 feet above sea level.

NAVAL BASE RAILWAY.

The Naval Base Railway which provides railway connection to H.M. Naval Base, Singapore, commences at Kranji and proceeds to the Naval Base, a distance of about 5 miles. It was constructed by the F.M.S. Railways for the Admiralty.

CHANGI RAILWAY.

A railway about 4 miles in length of 4' 8 ½" gauge was constructed by the F.M.S. Railways for the War Department near Changi in connection with the Singapore Defences.

SURVEYS OF PROJECTED LINES.

Numerous reconnaissance and preliminary surveys of projected lines have been / made in various parts of the country. As has already been stated, in the early nineties, surveys were made from Kuala Lumpur and Seremban over the range of mountains into Pahang. Recently in 1931 further surveys were made for a projected East to West Railway from Kuala Lumpur to Kuantan, Pahang, and it was ascertained that the route via Ginting Peras was the most suitable though steep grades, sharp curves and much tunnelling would be necessary. A survey was made for a rack railway from Merapoh on the East Coast Line near the Pahang/Kelantan boundary to Gunong Tahan rising to about 7,000 feet above sea level.

Surveys were also made from Kampar and Batu Gajah in Perak to Kuala Lipis in Pahang via the Cameron Highlands. Of the other surveys, the principal one was for another projected East Coast Line from Johore to Kelantan keeping near the Coast and traversing Pahang and Trengganu.

DEVIATIONS.

During the history of the railway several deviations of the existing line were carried out for various reasons. The principal ones were as follows: –

Serdang Deviation between Sungei Besi and Kajang to avoid excessive curvature and improve the alignment carried out in 1907.

Main Line Deviation from Kuala Lumpur to Salak South Junction to avoid the route through the town between Kuala Lumpur and Sultan Street completed in 1912.

In 1915 the first Kuala Kubu Deviation was constructed to avoid the silting of the Selangor River. The silting however continued so rapidly that it was soon necessary to make a second deviation; this starts at Kuala. Kubu Road and ends at Rasa and avoids Kuala Kubu altogether. It was opened in 1924.

Kamunting Deviation. This deviation, about 3 miles in length, is between Taiping and Ulu Sapetang and was constructed in 1929 largely at the expense of a Tin Dredging Company.

The Singapore Deviation is the most important one constructed by the F.M.S. Railways. In 1920, it was proposed to double the line from Woodlands to Tank Road and build a new terminal station and hotel at the foot of Fort Canning. Work was actually commenced on the doubling of the line but was stopped during the 1921 slump. Later the scheme was abandoned and a decision made to deviate the line from a point between Bukit Panjang and Bukit Timah to Tanjong Pagar with a terminal station at the latter place and / intermediate stations at Bukit Timah, Tanglin and Alexandra Road. This deviation, 8 ½ miles in length, avoids the old route through Singapore and skirts the western boundary of the town. It was opened to traffic in May, 1932.

DOUBLING OF LINE.

The line was doubled between Prai and Bukit Mertajam in 1917 in order to cope with the increased traffic to Kedah and Siam consequent on the opening of through traffic with Bangkok. In 1924 and 1925 the line was doubled between Kuala Lumpur and Batu Junction and Kuala Lumpur and Sungei Besi for suburban traffic.

[...]

WHARVES.

The F.M.S. Railways have built, own and operate the wharves at the various ports of the Peninsula (except Singapore), served by the Railway.

Port Weld. – The first wharves to be constructed were at Port Weld. These consisted of a timber structure near the station for local steamers and smaller jetties for firewood traffic. In 1929 the main wharf was rebuilt in reinforced concrete.

Teluk Anson. – The first wharves at Teluk Anson were built in 1893 alongside the river at Teluk Anson Town. The new wharves lower down the river were opened in 1909. These consist of two pontoon wharves for local steamers.

Klang. – When the line was opened to Bukit Kuda in 1886, temporary wharves were constructed there on the bank of the Klang River. In 1890 when Klang Station was opened, new wharves were built on the adjacent river bank; there were three of these, one timber and two pontoon wharves.[10] Owing, however, to the swift current, it was found very difficult to maintain the pontoon wharves, which were abandoned and replaced by timber structures.

Port Swettenham. – On the opening of the line from Klang to Port Swettenham in 1900, the first permanent wharves were built. In that year, three wharves and a passenger jetty were completed. The wharves, each with about 100 feet of frontage, were for use by local steamers. They were founded on cast iron cylinders 6 feet diameter, sunk to a depth of 70 feet below mud level. The superstructure is of steel and the deck of timber. The passenger jetty is a screw pile structure with a timber deck and timber and corrugated iron cover. It is situated near the station and is / intended for the use of passengers to and from ocean-going steamers anchored in the roads. In 1910 a pontoon wharf was opened for tongkang traffic and another wharf also for the use of tongkangs was constructed of hardwood timber in 1912. The main wharf for ocean-going steamers was completed in 1914. It is constructed of steel screw piles[11] sunk to a depth of about 40 feet below mud level. The superstructure is of steel and the original timber deck has recently been replaced by reinforced concrete. The wharf is 1,010 feet long and 50 feet wide, it has rail access and powerful electric cranes for working cargo.

Port Dickson. – In 1892 the Sungei Ujong Railway Co., constructed a steel screw pile wharf at Port Dickson. This was taken over with the Sungei Ujong Railway in 1908 and operated by the F.M.S. Railways until 1926 when it was reconstructed.

Tumpat. – In 1912, a timber jetty was constructed at Tumpat mainly for the discharge of railway material for the construction of the line from Tumpat southwards. It has, however, been kept going for general cargo. Owing to the shallow water inside the bar at Tumpat, the depth of water at the Wharf is only about 2'6" at low tide. Steamers anchor outside the bar and cargo is brought to and from the wharf in special shallow draught lighters.

Kota Bharu & Palekbang. – The Kelantan River separates the town of Kota Bharu, the Capital of the State of Kelantan, from the railway at Palekbang. A ferry service is maintained between the two and for this purpose pontoon jetties were constructed in 1914 at Palekbang and at Kota Bharu. In addition a small timber wharf for goods traffic was provided at Palekbang.

Prai. – In 1899, when the line was opened to Prai, a passenger pontoon jetty was constructed on the river bank opposite the station for use of the railway passenger ferries between Penang and Prai. Two timber jetties for general merchandise / were also built. In 1914 the Railway Department took over from the Prye Dock Co., a screw pile wharf which accommodated small ocean-going steamers and was chiefly used for coal traffic. In 1916, this wharf was demolished to make room for the present wharves which were commenced in 1916, and completed in 1923. The wharves consist of a main wharf for ocean-going steamers 1,100 feet long by 142 feet wide, constructed entirely of reinforced concrete and founded on concrete cylinders sunk to a hard foundation about 40 feet below mud level. The landward side of this wharf was dredged to form a basin for lighters. In addition there is another 1,000 feet of wharf frontage of solid block construction. As is well known the rapid silting at the mouth of Prai River has prevented full use being made of these wharves.

Penang. – The railway jetty at Penang was constructed in 1901 for the use of the ferry steamers. At the landward end it is carried on brick piers for a distance of 114 feet from the quay wall. This portion being 45 feet wide originally accommodated the station master's, and booking offices now situated in the main building at the corner of China Street Ghaut and Weld Quay. The jetty then narrows to 16 feet for a length of 400 feet with a Tee head 96 feet by 30 feet at the seaward end. This portion is on screw piles with a timber deck and corrugated iron roof. /

LOCOMOTIVES

PAST AND PRESENT

ONE of the tasks which confront the officers of a railway, on the amalgamation of smaller concerns, is the consolidation of physical assets. The evolution, out of a heterogeneous collection of locomotives of all shapes and sizes, of a common locomotive policy, will absorb much time, thought and money. Much credit is due to those responsible for the inauguration of railway transport in Malaya, in that the advantages of standardisation were realised from the very-start. Although a few odd locomotives were at work for many years there was, nevertheless, introduced in 1885 the first standard type engine, which was adopted by both the Perak and Selangor States Railways, as well as by the Singapore Government Railway, and the Malacca Railway in later years. This type, known as the

"A" class in F.M.S.R. records, and of which there were 18 engines, was a 4-4-0 tank engine having cylinders 10" dia: × 16" stroke. The coupled wheels were 3'3" in diameter. The total weight was 20 tons, of which 14 tons 15 cwts. were carried by the coupled wheels.[12]

In 1890 a rather more powerful engine of the same type was put into service. The cylinders were 12" dia: × 18" stroke, and the total weight 24 tons. There were 7 in all, the last being built as late as 1911.

As route mileage increased, the want of an engine of greater capacity was felt. And here the liaison between the Perak and Selangor Railways appears to have broken down. Perak was content to add a tender[13] to the "B" class, thus increasing the fuel and water capacity. This type, ultimately known as the "C" class, was first introduced in 1893. Seven engines in all were built. In 1894 and 1895 Selangor put to work four 4 - 6 - 0 tender engines. This type appeared in F.M.S.R. records as class "D"; had cylinders 14" dia: × 20" stroke: coupled wheels 3'3" in diameter and a total weight of 42 tons. The tender was carried on 4 wheels.

In 1897 Perak retorted with two 4-6-0 ("E" class) engines having cylinders 14 ½" × 20" stroke, coupled wheels 4'3" diameter and a total weight, including the four-wheeled tender, of 43 tons. In the same year Selangor bought two 4-4-0 tender engines having cylinders 14" dia: × 20" stroke and the coupled wheels 4'3" diameter. The total weight was 40 tons.

It is not clear whether this multiplication of designs was due to rivalry or to the effect of the Federation of the States which took place in 1895. As these engines were very similar in detail, it is probable that the young Federal / department was experimenting prior to the adoption of a final locomotive policy. The point at issue was the general utility engine versus the more orthodox types of goods and passenger locomotives. Perak and the general utility engine won the day and in 1899 there was introduced what is now known as the "G" class. This was a 4-6-0 type, with cylinders 14 ½" × 20", 4'3" driving wheels,[14] and a total weight, including the six-wheeled tender, of 51 tons 15 cwts. The boiler pressure was 160 lbs. per sq. inch and the tractive effort at 85% of boiler pressure was 10,390 lbs. Thirty four of these engines were built between 1899 and 1904.

At this juncture it is convenient to place some general points on record. So far as is known the early Perak engines bore numbers, while the Selangor engines had names only, and classifications were not consolidated until after 1901 when individual State Management was abandoned and a General Manager appointed to supervise the united Railway. The Singapore Government Railway, as has already been mentioned, adopted existing types of locomotives from its opening in 1903 until its absorption by the Federated Malay States Railways in 1912. The Malacca Railway had no separate existence, but it is believed that some of the then standard locomotives were employed in its construction. The Sungei Ujong

Railway, constructed in 1891, was absorbed in 1908. With it there were taken over 3 "J" class engines and 1 "K" class. The "J" class was originally a 0-6-2 tank engine but was subsequently altered to 4-4-2. The cylinders were 10 ½" dia: × 18" stroke and the coupled wheels 2'9" diameter. The total weight was 23 tons 12 cwts. The "K" class engine had a similar wheel arrangement. The cylinders were 12" dia: × 18" stroke, the total weight 42 tons and the diameter of the coupled wheels 3'6".

The consolidation of the growing system had thus resulted in the adoption of the general utility locomotive, a policy which has never / been lost sight of, and is in force today.

In 1907 the first Pacific type engine was built. This type, known as the "H" class, was a considerable advance upon the "G" class, both in design and power. The cylinders were 15 ½" dia × 24" stroke and the coupled wheels were 4'6" diameter. The boiler had a wide firebox,[15] as being more suitable for burning firewood, the fuel then in use. The boiler pressure was 180 lbs per sq. in. and the total heating surface was 1235 sq. ft. The grate area was 18.5 sq. ft. The tender was carried by two four-wheeled bogies[16] and had capacity for 2,000 gallons of water and 315 cub: ft. of fuel space. The engine weighed 75 tons 6 cwts and the tractive effort was 16,293 lbs at 85% of boiler pressure. The axle load was 9 tons 15 cwts. In the later years the weight was increased to 78 tons, by the adoption of thicker frames.

The "I" class followed in 1908. This was a 0-6-4 tank engine, having cylinders 14 ½" × 20" and coupled wheels 4'4" diameter. The first 8 of these engines had water and fuel capacity of 800 gallons and 90 cub. ft. respectively, but in 1913 a further 8 engines were delivered having water capacity increased to 1,200 gallons. The axle load was 10 tons 10 cwts. All subsequent "I" class engines were of the larger type.

Standardisation was thus re-established. Apart from the earlier and smaller engines for which work could be found, there were now three types of locomotives; for main line work the "H" class, for short branches, banking and shunting, the "I" class, and for branch line and ballasting the "G" class. Between 1906 and 1914, sixty "H" class engines, and between 1908 and 1916, thirty-five "I" class engines were bought.

The Johore line, built and financed by the State of Johore, was completed in 1909. Its locomotive stock consisted of 12 engines. Six of these were "H" class engines built in 1908. They were painted a "Caledonian" blue. The remaining 6 engines, consisting of 2 "A" class, 2 "B" class and 2 "C" class, were purchased from the F.M.S.R. The whole stock were taken over by the F.M.S.R. in 1912, and were given F.M.S.R. numbers and painted the standard colours.

The growth of traffic made it difficult to find locomotives for construction purposes and between the years of 1912 and 1914, twenty secondhand engines (in separate lots of 5) were bought from Burma. These were known as the Burma

"E" and Burma "O" classes. The former was a 0-4-2 tender engine and the latter a 4-4-0. These engines, although obsolete, gave good service on construction, but the "O" class were found too light for open line use, and only a few were thus employed.

The extensive development by the Great Western Railway of the steam rail car led to the introduction of this principle in Malaya, and in 1914 designs were prepared and the construction locally of nine two-coach sets was commenced. The coaches are mentioned in another article. The engine with its vertical boiler was a close imitation of the G.W.R. design, but was carried on a six-wheel bogie. The cylinders were 11" dia: × 14" stroke. The coupled wheels were 2'9 ½" diameter. The boiler was pressed to 180 lbs. per sq. inch, the whole unit developing 7,737 lbs tractive effort. /

The boiler and main frames were purchased from England, but most of the details were manufactured at the Central Workshops. The outbreak, of the War, and the difficulty in maintaining existing locomotives in the face of increasing train mileage and decreasing facilities, led to considerable delays in manufacture and eventually to the abandonment of the scheme after four engine units had been completed.

In the meantime, superheated steam had been rapidly developed in England and Europe, and the economies to be effected by its use had been proved beyond doubt. In 1914 orders were placed in England for 20 superheated "H" class engines. The idea of the general utility engine was preserved, but the use of superheated steam necessitated considerable changes on boiler and cylinder design. The principal dimensions of this engine, known, as the "P" class, were as follows: –

> Cyls: 17" dia: × 24" stroke
> Cpld: wheels 4'6" diameter
> Bogie wheels 2'6" diameter
> Pony and tender wheels 2'9 ½"
> Boiler H.S. total 1000 sq. ft.
> Boiler Pressure 160lbs. per sq. inch
> Grate area 18.5 sq. ft.
> Tender Water capacity 2000 gls.
> Fuel 315 cub. ft.
> Total weight 78 tons 11 cwts.

It will be noticed that the wheel arrangement and diameters were similar to the "H" class, but the axle loading was increased to 10 tons 10 cwts. At that time locomotive engineers still looked askance at high pressures and it was a common practice to reduce the boiler pressure to counteract the increase in cylinder diameter required for the economic use of superheated steam. In this case the engines were supplied with steam at 160 lbs pressure, but the boilers were constructed to withstand 180 lbs per sq. in. Boiler maintenance had never been a serious problem in Malaya and it was not long before the pressure of the "P" class engines was raised to 180 lbs. per sq. inch. By this means, and with some reduction in the ratio of adhesion, a rather more powerful locomotive was obtained, the tractive effort of these engines now being 19,645 lbs.

Owing to the outbreak of War, the construction of these engines was temporarily suspended. The order was, however, finally completed as a war measure to make room for munitions work in British Workshops. Four engines only were delivered to Malaya in 1917, the balance being sent to the Bombay-Baroda and Central India Railway, where the shortage of locomotives was being acutely felt. Sixteen of this class were, however, put in hand on the conclusion of the War and delivered in 1920.

At the conclusion of the War, the Railway was handling a greatly increased volume of traffic with a stock of locomotives inadequate in numbers, and not a little depreciated in condition due to the necessarily restricted facilities for repairs.

In 1918 a number of American built Mallet compounds were offered to the Administration. The engines had a strange history. They were part of an order of 40 engines placed by the Russian Government with Messrs. Baldwin Loco. Works of Philadelphia in the early days of the War and were originally designed for a 3'6" gauge. Before delivery was effected, Russia collapsed and the engines / were left on the Makers' hands. Attempts were made to effect a sale by altering them to suit the metre gauge, the F.M.S.R. taking two and a number went to the then Mesopotamian Railways. These engines had a 0-6-0 – 0-6-0 wheel arrangement with an axle load of 8 tons. The principal dimensions were: –

> Cyls: H.P. 13" dia. *22"* stroke.
> Cyls: L.P. 19" dia. *22"* stroke.
> Cpld: wheels 3'8" diameter
> Boiler H.S. 1308 sq. ft.
> Grate Area 19.3 sq. ft.
> Total weight 71 tons 17 cwts.
> Tractive effort 18,250 lbs.

The tender mounted on a bogie and a single fixed axle, had water capacity of 2122 gallons and fuel space of 256 cub. ft.

Although relieving the situation at the time, the engines were not suitable for service on a railway the timetables of which were founded on the general utility principle and their use was largely confined to the Port Swettenham branch.

In 1919 an order was placed with Messrs. Baldwin & Co., for twelve 4-6-2 engines. These were of American design and the following principal dimensions: –

> Cyls: 17" dia 24" stroke.
> Cpld: wheels 4'6" dia.
> Axle load 10 tons 10 cwts.
> Weight 79 tons.
> Boiler grate area 24.9 sq. ft.
> Total heating surface 1403 sq. ft.

Boiler pressure 170 lbs. The steam was superheated and the total tractive effort was 18,553 lbs. The eight wheeled tender carried 2056 gallons of water and 5 tons of coal. These engines known as the "Q" class were the first in Malaya to be fitted with bar frames and steel fireboxes, a practice which has been found suitable for Malaya and developed in more recent British-built engines.

In 1920 further orders were placed with Messrs. Baldwin & Co. For open lines there were purchased ten 0-6-0 shunting tanks to replace the old "A", "B" and "C" classes which had either been condemned or turned over to Construction which was then being-pushed forward in Pahang and Kelantan. They were classified as the "R" class and had the usual American characteristics, with bar frames and steel fireboxes. The cylinders were 16" dia: × 20" stroke and the coupled wheels 3'6" in diameter. They were somewhat heavy and very powerful engines for their size, the driving axle load being 12 tons and the tractive, effort 17,554 lbs. For construction lines there were purchased ten 2-6-0 tender engines having cylinders 14" dia: × 18" stroke, and the coupled wheels 3'1" in diameter. The driving axle load was 9 tons 9 cwts. The total weight, including the eight wheeled tender, was 53 tons 8 cwts., the tractive effort being 12,257 lbs. These engines, known as the "M" class, did good work on the construction lines, but were of little value for open line work on account of the small size of driving wheel. The "R" and "M" class engines were delivered in 1921.

In the meantime, a want of a more powerful engine was being felt. The Singapore night mail trains were loading beyond the capacity of a single engine and "double-heading" [17] was the order of the day. The designs for an engine of greater axle load had been under discussion prior to the outbreak of the War, but it was not until 1920 that the matter was / again taken up and in that year an order for twenty 4-6-2 engines having a 12 ton axle load was placed in England. This class, known as the "L" class, had the following principal dimensions: –

> Cyls: 17" dia: × 24" stroke.
> Cpld: wheels 4'6"
> Bogie wheels 2'6"
> Boiler H.S. 1485 sq. ft.
> Grate area 24.3 sq. ft.
> Pressure 180 lbs.
> Tender water capacity 2500 gals.

Fuel 6 ½ tons.
Total weight 86 tons 10 cwts.
Tractive effort 19,645 lbs.

A Belpaire firebox was incorporated in the boiler design.

Owing to the somewhat conservative ratio of adhesion adopted, these engines gave but a small increment of power over the "P" class, the boiler pressure of which had been then advanced to 180 lbs. They performed most useful work however, and for a time were usually able to handle the night mails unassisted. They were fitted with the "Weir" system of feed water heating.

As a result of the financial depression of 1922, the locomotive stock of the Railway was more than adequate and it was not until 1926 that further locomotives were purchased. The need for a light shunting engine[18] was then felt, suitable for wharf work at Port Swettenham and other places where the track required a limitation of axle load to 8 tons. In that year, five 0-6-2 tank engines were bought. These locomotives have the following principal dimensions: –

Cyls: 13" dia: × 20" stroke.
Cpld: wheels 3'3" diameter
Boiler H.S. 422 sq. ft.
Grate area 9.6 sq. ft.
Pressure 170 lbs.
Water 750 gallons
Fuel 1 ½ tons.

They were the first British built engines to have a steel firebox and were delivered in Malaya fully erected, being landed at Singapore by the Tanjong Pagar sheerlegs.[19]

In 1926 an order was placed for seven Pacific type locomotives having an axle load of 12 tons. The five years which had elapsed since the "L" class had been put into service had shown the possibility of improvement in design, and the new "K" class, delivered in 1927, was a thoroughly modern engine in every respect. Standardisation, however, had not been lost sight of, as the principal dimensions will shew: –

Cyls: 17" dia: × 24" stroke.
Cpld: wheels 4'6" diameter
Pony & tender 3'0" diameter
Bogie 2'6"
Boiler H.S. 1445 sq, ft.
Grate area 24.6 sq. ft.
Pressure 180 lbs.'
Tender water 2,500 gallons
Fuel 7 tons.
Total weight 91 tons 5 cwts.
Tractive effort 19,645 lbs.

In addition to numerous small details which were common to the "L" and "P" class engines, the boiler itself was interchangeable with those of the "L" class. Plate frames were adhered to, but the steel firebox was adopted. Four more of these engines were bought in 1931. While adhering to the principle of inter-changeability, the boiler design was altered to include additional combustion space in the firebox, a provision which has been found economical in the consumption of Malayan coal. The heating surface was in consequence reduced to 1316 sq. ft. without impairing the efficiency of the boiler.

"Double-heading" was again the rule for the Singapore night mail trains, and it was felt that a still more powerful engine would cure this source of expense, and also effect more economical operation of freight traffic. There were, therefore, put into service in 1928 a three-cylinder 4-6-2 engine having an axle load of 16 tons. These locomotives, of which three were at first bought, had the following main dimensions: –

> Cyls: 17" dia: × 24" stroke.
> Cpld: wheels 4'6" diameter
> Bogie wheels 2'6" diameter
> Pony wheels 3'0" diameter
> Boiler H.S. total 2335 sq. ft.
> Grate area 35 sq. ft.
> Pressure 180 lbs.
> Tender water 3000 gallons
> Fuel 7 tons
> > Total weight 108 tons 9 cwts.

They had bar frames, steel fireboxes, the "Gresley" system of valve operation, and developed a tractive effort of 29,000 lbs. They are capable of handling 15 coaches on passenger service or 800 tons on freight trains. This represents an increment of power of practically 33%. /

Eight more were built in 1930 and five in 1932, the latter being fitted with the Rotary Cam Valve mechanism, roller bearing tender axle boxes and an increased water capacity of 4,000 gallons of water and 10 tons of coal.

In 1930 there was delivered a new type of tank engine known as the "C" class. They had the 4-6-4 wheel arrangement. The principal dimensions are: –

Cyls: 14 ½" dia: × 22" stroke.
Cpld: wheels 4'6"
Bogie 2'6"
Boiler H.S. 1026 sq. ft.
Grate area 23.6 sq. ft.
Water capacity 2000 galls.
Fuel 158 cub: ft.
> Total weight 73 tons
> Tractive effort 19,272 lbs.

These locomotives followed advanced practice, the boiler pressure having increased to 250 lbs. / while steam was distributed through the medium of the Caprotti cam valve gear.

To meet the demands of short branch lines, and pick up services, the Railcar system was again introduced, and in 1930 a Sentinel-Cammell Articulated Rail-car set was introduced. Five more were bought in 1931. These vehicles were to the well-known designs of the Sentinel-Cammell firm. The steam, generated in a vertical boiler, is delivered to the six-cylinder engine at 350 lbs. per sq. inch. The engine is single acting, the steam distribution being controlled by cam operated valve. The drive is by a 6-throw crank shaft coupled to a carden shaft driving the bogie axle by means of a reducing gear. The details of the coach work are referred to in another article.

In reviewing the locomotive practice of the F.M.S.R., the reader will realise, that although through circumstances over which the management had but little control, there are numerous types of engines, the principle of standardisation has never been lost sight of, as witnessed by the predominance of the Pacific type wheel arrangement and the now almost universal wheel diameters. To this might be added a host of smaller details common to all classes. At the same time, designs have advanced with the times and it may reasonably be claimed that the locomotives of the F.M.S.R., while conforming largely to economic standards of maintenance, are yet fully representative of modern locomotive engineering. /

LOCOMOTIVE MILEAGE

For some considerable time, railway locomotive engineers and operating officers all over the world have been endeavouring to increase the daily mileages of locomotives with the object of speeding up trains and reducing the number of locomotives required, and consequently capital costs.

No effort has been spared by the Federated Malay States Railways to effect improvements in this direction, and although handicapped by comparatively low speeds, limited distances and many other factors, the results have proved most satisfactory.

It is only on the mail trains, night mixed and goods trains running between Prai (for Penang) and Singapore, a distance of 488 miles, that long runs can be obtained in this country. Prior to 1934, the mail train engines were booked to work between Taiping and Kuala Lumpur, a distance of 184 miles, and between Seremban and Singapore, a distance of 199 miles, without a change, but in August that year, after effecting improvements to the locomotives, the mail train engine runs were extended between Kuala Lumpur and Singapore, a distance of 245 miles.

The extension of these runs and a similar extension of the locomotive runs of the night mixed and goods trains allowed the concentration of locomotives at Kuala Lumpur where the up-to-date Running Shed...and equipment facilitate the quick "turn-round" of engines, thus enabling them to be kept in a high state of efficiency.

In December 1934, after experience of this working had been obtained, five 3-cylinder express locomotives were selected to take up all the mail train workings between Taiping and Singapore. Four locomotives were employed daily on these runs and one reserved for relief purposes. Commencing from Kuala Lumpur with the day mail trains, the locomotives ran to Taiping and to Singapore, arriving there the same afternoon in sufficient time to leave on the night mail trains. They were thus back again in Kuala Lumpur the following morning in time to work the day mail trains. This programme continued day in and day out throughout the month, each locomotive being released for a day in turn by substitution of the spare to enable running repairs to be carried out.

During the month referred to above, the following mileages were run: –

Engine No.	238	S1	Class	10,354	miles.
"	246	S2	"	10,233	"
"	247	S2	"	11,141	"
"	250	S3	"	10,057	"
"	252	S3	"	10,465	"

52,250

Average per Engine 10.45

Although running over 1,600 miles daily during this period, none of the trains, which frequently consisted of 16 heavy coaches, were delayed by any engine defects.

Other exceptional mileages about the same time include 12,510 miles run by engine No. 245 in October 1934, and 13,267 miles by engine No. 241 in January this year.

These remarkable locomotive performances have not, it is believed, been equalled by any metre-gauge Railway throughout the world, and demonstrate the efforts which are being made to provide cheap and efficient railway transport in this country.

ALEXANDER, *BRITISH MALAYA: MALAYAN STATISTICS* (1928)

C. S. Alexander, *British Malaya: Malayan Statistics* (London: Malayan Information Agency, 1928), p. 94.

C. S. Alexander held the post of Financial Commissioner and Auditor-General of Johore for six years before becoming in 1921 Treasurer of the FMS. This extract from his 1928 compendium of Malayan statistics provides data on road mileage, motor vehicles, postal services, money orders and telegraphs and telephones.[1]

Notes
1. *Singapore Free Press and Mercantile Advertiser*, 29 March 1927, p. 3.

C. S. Alexander, *British Malaya: Malayan Statistics* (1928), extract

ROADS AND MOTOR VEHICLES. – FEDERATED MALAY STATES.

Compiled from the Annual Reports of the Director of Public Works, F.M.S.

ROAD STATISTICS.

Particulars.	Unit.	1914	1924.	1925.	1926.	1927.	1928.
ROADS.							
Metalled and Gravelled Roads.							
Total Mileage on the 31st December	Miles	2,16	2,515	2,537	2,565	2,600	2,672
Mileage Remetalled during the Year	"	*	517	528	425	461	510
Mileage treated with Bitumenous Compounds	"	*	364	511	697	904	1,135
Average Cost of Maintenance per Mile	S	1,012	1,284	1,308	1,432	1,476	1,483
Unmetalled Cart Roads.							
Total Mileage on the 31st December	Miles.	211	148	150	129	114	106
Bridle Paths and Roads.							
Total Mileage on the 31st December	"	1,641	1,951	1,878	1,942	1,972	1,952
MOTOR VEHICLES.							
Numbers Registered during the Year–							
Motor Cars (*a*)	No.	*	5,247	8,229	11,597	*	15,276
" Lorries	"	*	572	1,152	1,844	*	2,803
" Cycles	"	*	1,682	2,346	2,885	*	2,660

(*a*)   Includes buses.
*   Not available.

POSTS, TELEGRAPHS AND TELEPHONES –
FEDERATED MALAY STATES.

Compiled from the Annual Report of the Posts and Telegraphs Department, F.M.S.

Particulars.	Unit.	1913.	1924.	1925.	1926.	1927.	1928.
POSTAL SERVICES.							
Number of Post Offices (a) and Postal Agencies	No.	119	145	154	158	160	168
Correspondence Posted and Delivered.							
Letters	Thous.	11,006	20,028	21,072	23,933	29,416	31,369
Post Cards	"	777	1,253	1,450	1,312	1,433	1,193
Newspapers and Other Articles	"	2,766	3,639	4,001	4,551	5,702	6,106
Parcels	"	151	208	223	257	305	301
Total, excluding Registered Articles	"	17,700	25,128	26,755	30,053	36,856	38,969
Registered Articles	"	617	867	937	1,081	1,174	1,225
Money Orders.							
Issued –							
Number	Thous.	135·4	170·7	197·4	233·8	246·2	252·6
Value	$'000	4,845	8,935	11,724	14,570	13,747	12,719
Payable in –							
British Malaya	"	1,527	5,960	7,695	8,713	7,528	6,942
India	"	2,821	2,062	2,855	4,510	4,856	4,454
Ceylon	"	421	582	657	691	702	703
United Kingdom	"	34	227	280	372	450	453
Other Countries	"	42	104	237	284	211	167
Paid –							
Number	Thous.	12·9	80·8	84·3	88·5	93·4	100·9
Value	$'000	1,107	5,533	6,993	8,033	6,975	6,374
Drawn in –							
British Malaya.	"	1022	5,453	6,904	7,935	6,847	6,231
Other Countries	"	85	80	89	98	128	143 /
Cash on Delivery.							
Packets Posted –							
Number	Thous.	3·3	6·8	7·5	8·6	9·5	9·1
Trade Charges	$'000	27·6	65·5	71·8	91·3	104·8	99·0
Packets Delivered –							
Number	Thous.	7·3	23·8	32·0	38·5	46·3	48·5
Trade Charges	$'000	61·1	385·3	533·9	757·3	919·0	928·7
TELEGRAPHS AND TELEPHONES.							
Telegraph and Telephone System.							
Length of Overhead Line (a)	Miles	2,009	2,463	2,561	2,618	2,602	2,926
Length of Overhead Wire –							
Telegraph	"	2,349	3,290	3,365	2,989	3,233	3,136
Telephone	"	5,473	14,083	15,127	16,872	18,483	20,555
Length of Underground Cables	"	12	55	62	79	102	121
Length of Wire Single Line in Cables	"	1,074	5,502	5,959	7,774	9,908	11,428
Telegraph Business.							
Offices Open	No.	82	101	101	101	102	103
Telegrams Forwarded –							
Private and Press	Thous.	333·3	289·5	348·2	397·9	399·2	369·9

Particulars.	Unit.	1913.	1924.	1925.	1926.	1927.	1928.
Government	"	90·1	65·4	65·3	67·6	75·1	58·9
Total Forwarded	"	422·4	354·9	413·5	465·5	474·3	428·8
Telegrams Received –							
Private and Press	"	330·9	322·7	387·3	443·2	432·4	398·9
Government	"	87·1	66·9	64·2	66·3	73·8	55·5
Total Received	"	419·1	389·6	451·5	509·5	506·2	454·4
Total Forwarded and Received	"	841·5	744·5	865·0	975·0	980·5	883·2
Receipts from Private Telegrams Forwarded	$'000	150·8	310·6	342·0	455·6	498·4	466·3
Total Value of Business, including Government Messages	"	207·8	357·2	386·0	506·9	558·0	516·7

(*a*) Including places where postal business is transacted by station masters and others acting as Postal agents. For number of post and telegraph offices, see page 97

(*a*) Excluding Railway Department pole line used to carry post office wires – 46 miles on 31st December, 1928. /

POSTS, TELEGRAPHS AND TELEPHONES.

Particulars.	Unit.	1913.	1924.	1925.	1926.	1927.	1928.
Telephones.							
Subscribers	No.	993	2,536	2,827	3,450	4,003	4,534
Extension Lines, Extension Bells, Private Circuits, etc., Maintained	"	304	1,249	1,401	1,598	1,871	2,177
Public Exchanges	"	*	33	37	42	46	59
Estimated Number of Calls Originated –							
Local	Thous.	*	*	8,100	9,900	11,738·4	11,972·0
Junction	"	*	*	}1,220	210	292·0	817·6
Trunk[1]	"	*	*		1,200	1,314·0	1,255·6
Total	"		*	9,320	11,400	13.344·4	14,045·2
Average per direct exchange line per day	No.		*	11	12·0	12·3	11·3
Revenue –							
Total	$'000	136.7	560·4	696·8	904·5	1,062·6	1,196·9
Trunk	"		150·7	212·8	277·3	317·4	384·9
Wireless.							
Licences Issued –							
Temporary Licences for use of Receiving Apparatus (*a*)	No.		–	28	49	37	74
Experimental Transmitting Licences	"	–	–	–	1	4	2

(*a*) Licences first issued in April, 1925.

· Not available.

NANKIVELL, *A REPORT ON HIGHWAYS* (1936)

Kenneth Nankivell, *A Report on Highways* (Singapore: Government Printing Office, 1936), pp. 1–46.

Kenneth Nankivell's first post in Malaya was as an Assistant Engineer in the local Public Works Department. In 1935, the Executive Engineer of the Malayan Public Works Service, he was awarded a Carnegie Scholarship to study highway engineering in England. On his return to Malaya, he summarized all he had discovered in a report in which he discussed the administration and construction of highways in the UK, the advantages and drawbacks of various types of bitumen and the application of bitumen to road surfaces. In the extract below, he considers the use of rubber as an alternative to bitumen and the results of the experimental use of rubber coatings on roads in Kuala Lumpur and Singapore. Although rubber never replaced bitumen, in many countries rubber crumb is now mixed with asphalt to reduce road noise and the idea of using rubber as a road surface is again current.[1]

Notes
1. See Anon., 'Rubber Highway to Beat Congestion', available online at http://news.bbc.co.uk/1/hi/sci/tech/5034912.stm [accessed 1 April 2014]; Anon., 'Route to Peace and Quiet', available online at http://www.dailymail.co.uk/news/article-2320023/Recycled-rubber-soon-used-resurface-nations-busiest-roads.html [accessed 1 April 2014].

K. Nankivell, *A Report on Highways* (1936), extract

RUBBER ROADS IN MALAYA

[...]

2 Numerous claims have been made of the advantages of rubber over bitumen as a road material. These include: –

(*a*) Absorption of vibration and mitigation of noise.

(*b*) Evenness of surface.

(*c*) Freedom from dust.

(*d*) Cleanliness.

(*e*) Ease of maintenance.

(*f*) Anti-skid properties.

(*g*) Appearance.

(*h*) Durability.

In commenting on these claims comparison is made with bituminous materials which represent the most successful road surfacing material yet discovered.

(*a*) Absorption of vibration and mitigation of noise.

I have seen no evidence in the form of test results but although it appears likely that a thick rubber pavement, say 2" to 3", is capable of appreciably absorbing vibration it is very doubtful if a thin carpet of vulcanised rubber can do so. With the modern bituminous surfacing impact, percussion and resonance are reduced to a minimum and finally vibration is almost wiped out by improved springing of road vehicles. Foundation design is sufficiently advanced to resist destruction by these forces. On the thin carpets there is no appreciable diminution of vehicle noise. Noise is chiefly caused by loose connections of vehicles or by the engine. Provided a surface is free from corrugations then body rattle can only arise from faulty springing. This brings in the second claim of: –

(*b*) Evenness. Evenness can only be obtained by ensuring a stable foundation and rubber will conform to the shape of the foundation at least as readily as a bituminous carpet. Solid rubber tyred lorries are the noisiest vehicles on the road today. These tyres are from 2" – 4" thick. Can an additional ¾" on the road surface succeed where it fails on the wheels?.

(c) Dustiness is not a failing of bituminous surfaces. Dust must be conveyed to the surface either accidently or deliberately. The former may occur on any surface, the latter is only necessary with bituminous surfacing constructed by methods now abandoned in modern road construction.

(d) Cleanliness is surely a measure of efficiency of the scavenging department and not a monopoly of any particular surfacing material.

(e) Ease of maintenance is, in my limited experience, one virtue not possessed by rubber roads but possessed to a maximum degree by bituminous materials. Maintenance must include patching made necessary by excavation for access to ancillary services.

(f) During the brief life of the rubber surfacing at Bukit Timah Road it appeared to possess good anti-skid properties but oil drippings are not rapidly absorbed and this source of skidding is frequent in heavily trafficked city streets.

(g) Good appearance is not of first importance. If it is possible to produce a light coloured surface with good anti-glare properties in wet weather then the rubber road engineer will indeed have forestalled his bituminous surfacing rival.

(h) Durability. – Many years must elapse before this claim can be substantiated.

3 It is unfortunate for Malaya that one material, bitumen, which, with present day methods of construction, gives an almost perfect road surface, should be produced so cheaply and in such large quantities. But for this by-product of one of the worlds greatest industries there little doubt that rubber would ultimately find a world wide market as a road material. An unbiased analysis of the respective merits of the two materials shows only one in which rubber can claim an advantage and that is absorption of impact due to greater elasticity. By improvement in foundations and vehicle design the importance of this property is considerably decreased.

4 If rubber is unable to offer equal advantages as a surfacing material it can only establish itself as a cheaper substitute. The question of costs needs little consideration. Apart from the fact that bitumen is some 3 to 8 times cheaper than rubber, where the former can be utilised in small percentages to convey its properties to aggregate the latter must be used in much larger percentages. In carpet or thick pavement work where one can function as a binder the other must function largely as a matrix to utilise its useful properties. /

The use of rubber compound surfacing appears to have a very limited application because a better and cheaper material is available. Even for this limited application one thing further is required and that is a stable price. It is difficult to persuade authorities to embark on a rubber road programme whilst the price of the commodity is likely fluctuate 500%. Can a contractor accurately estimate for work when his raw material may increase in cost from 2*d* to 8*d* in a few weeks? The greatest advance in design has been made at a period when most estates were selling at or near cost and it was only this that permitted and encouraged increased experimental work. If the price again rises to 1/- per pound (and there is no guarantee that it will not) the application of methods developed during this period will be impossible.

5 It has been stated that provided the safety of the public demanded it, whatever the cost might be of providing a non-skid dressing County Engineers would be forced to adopt it. The snag in this is, of course, the proviso. In 1933, of 3297 accidents attributed to drivers, skidding was the sole or main cause in 161 cases. In that year there were 7001 accidents resulting in 7202 fatalities. Skidding, which may or may not be wholly due to road surface (faulty brakes are contributory causes) was responsible for less than 4.4% of the total accidents. Obstruction of view by corners or bends was responsible for 218 accidents and when it is remembered that most skids occur on corners and bends it is evident that heavy expenditure on elimination of these has a prior claim and may relegate skidding to a negligible potential danger. Further, it is logical to assume that these skids occured on surfaces laid when the skidding danger was not appreciated and surfacing technique was far below that of today.

EXPERIMENTAL RUBBER ROAD SURFACINGS IN KUALA LUMPUR, SELANGOR, F.M.S.

I. *Trade Name.* – "SILENT ROADWAYS".

Proprietors. – Messrs KENDALL, AND GRAHAM, Lahat, Perak, F.M.S.

Nature of surfacing. – 7/8" thick sheets in 3' 0" widths and lengths to order delivered ready for fixing to foundation. Weight about 59 lbs. p. sq. yd.

Percentage of rubber. – 30 per cent.

Position of trial. – Victory Avenue from Jalan Rajah, half width of road, east side.

Area laid. – 132 ft × 27 ft. = 396 sq. yards.

Intensity of traffic, 1935. – Approx, 4,800 tons per day.

Date laid. – 27th June, 1933.

Date opened to traffic. – 27th June, 1933.

Foundations. – The old asphalt grouted road swept clean.

Method of laying. – The sheets were freed of French chalk and then set loosely in position from centre to side of road with joints as small as possible. The material used for fixing the sheets was Socony Asphaltum "F" heated to 350°F. The sheets were fixed one at a time and by half lengths at a time by rolling them up to mid length and painting the foundation with the fixing material, and them unrolling evenly and slowly.

Approximate costs. – Sheeting f.o.r.[1] $6.50 per sq. yard. Rail freight averaged 24½ cents per sq. yard.

Labour and materials in laying 26 cents p. sq. yard.

Notes. – Labour soon became proficient in the work of laying which was carried out by the Public Works Department. The covering capacity of the asphalt used for fixing was 4 square yards per gallon.

Condition, end of 1935. – The sheeting is in very fair condition. The joints are not easy to control, and require resealing with bitumen about every 12 months.

II. *Trade Name* - None.

Proprietors. – Messrs. Gammon (Malaya) Ltd., Singapore, representing Messrs. Solar Rubber Processes Ltd. (Messrs. Solar Rubber Processes Ltd. have since been liquidated).

Nature of surfacing. – A ready made liquid referred to as 'Parafix', and the main materials of rubber latex and dry mix of fillers, vulcanising agents, etc.

Percentage of rubber. – Approximately 20 per cent.

Position of trial. – Victory Avenue from Jalan Rajah, half width of road, west side.

Area laid. – L shaped; leg 131' 4" × 28' 6'
toe 18' 0" × 35' 10"
Total area 488 square yards.

Intensity of traffic, 1935. – Approximately 4,800 tons per day.

Date laid. – July 25th to 31st, 1935.

Date open to traffic. – August 8th, 1933. /

Foundation. – The old asphalt grouted road freed of excess asphalt and whole surface cleaned with wire brushes.

Method of Laying. – The foundation was painted with 'Parafix' on to which was spread a definite mix of latex and fillers, etc. The mix was spread to a thickness of about 1½" by means of mason's trowels and then rolled progressively with a rolling pin, a 12" dia. concrete pipe, an 8' 0" dia. concrete pipe and a 10 ton steam roller. After rolling with the 12" pipe the carpet was covered to protect it from rain. Finally the surface was painted with 'Parafix', given a layer of fine sand and rolled with a 10 ton roller. The excess sand was removed before opening to traffic.

Approximate Costs. – Materials consumed in rubber carpet $2.70 p. sq. yd. Labour and laying 59½ cents. Supervision and miscellaneous charges extra.

Notes. – The consolidated carpet was about 1" thick. The mix begins to set as soon as it is poured. Rain caused some delay in the work. The laying was carried out by the Proprietors.

Condition, end of 1935. – The surface has generally failed, and in placed has been patched by the P.W.D.[2] with asphalt macadam. Messrs. Gammon (Malaya) Ltd. indicate that failure is due to insufficient anchorage.

III. *Trade name.* – (Not marketed).

Proprietors. – Prepared by The Rubber Research Institute of Malaya, Kuala Lumpur.

Nature of surfacing. – Rubber latex, fillers and vulcanising agents, etc.

Percentage of rubber. – Approximately 25 per cent.

Portion of trial – 4½ mile Petaling Road, full width.

Area laid. – 65' × 23' = 166 square yards.

Intensity of traffic, 1935. – Approximately 2,200 tons per day.

Date laid. – East side: April 30th to May 2nd, 1933.

West side: May 9th to May 12th, 1933.

Date opened to traffic. – East side: May 8th, 1933.

West side: May 18th, 1933.

Foundation. – Old asphalt painted surface scarified,[3] asphalt removed, new limestone laid, rolled and cement grouted, Limestone chips spread and rolled, except west side where tamping[4] was resorted to in place of rolling, giving a rougher surface.

Method of laying. – Took place 7 days after preparation of foundation on the East side, and 13 days after on the West side. The components were machine mixed on the site and laid in alternate bays of a maximum of about 12' × 7' and 1" thick. Frames were used to limit each bay and to act as templates for screeding[5] the mix. Frames were removed when coagulation had started. One bay on the West side was treated with an antioxidant "Oxynone", another surface painted with 'Colas' and sanded and another surface painted with 'Socony Asphaltum F' and sanded.

Cost. – Not known.

Notes. – No rolling was given. Consolidated carpet was one inch thick. Such work must be under the full authority of one person. Correct mixing is all important. Water must be at hand. Shade is required for the latex before mixing and for the actual mixing operations. Easy and speedy handling of the mix essential. Sufficient mix must be formed at one time to complete a limited area. The laying was carried out by the Rubber Research Institute with the co-operation of the Public Works Department.

Condition, end of 1935. – The West side was failing in 1934 and asphalt macadam patching had to be employed in March of that year. In August, 1935 half the West side had to be taken up and replaced with asphalt macadam and the remaining half similarly treated in October 1935. The East side is in very fair condition.

THE USE OF RUBBER FOR ROADWORK BY THE SINGAPORE MUNICIPALITY

The use of rubber roads in Singapore was first suggested in 1928 by Mr. R. J. FARRER, then President of the Municipality. A price was obtained from the Singapore Rubber Works of $36.25 per square yard for rubber paving blocks. This price included delivery at the site not laying. The proposal, which was to pave Elgin Bridge, was abandoned on account of the high cost.

The matter was revived in 1930 when it was suggested that the newly completed Read Bridge might be paved with rubber. [...]/

The high cost of even the cheapest form of rubber surfacing, the Cressonite block, was nearly ten times that of asphalt and an attempt was then made to obtain supplies of free rubber from the Rubber Growers Association for the work.

While negotiation were in hand, the Parry Davis process was brought to the notice of the Commissioners and an experimental area of 50 square yards was laid at Trafalgar Street in May, 1931 at a cost of f $15.22 per square yard [...]. From this test it was decided that the Parry Davis process would not be suitable for use of Read Bridge as it was felt that the difficulties of securing adhesion to the concrete decking and of getting rid of the water from the mix had not yet been overcome. A further area of 100 square yards of similar material was laid at Trafalgar Street in November and December 1931 [...] – at a cost of $9.86 per square yard. In May, 1932 the first area of 50 square yards laid in May, 1931 was taken up as its condition was very unsatisfactory owing to cracks and disintegration.

Later in 1932 the rights in Parry Davis process were acquired by Messrs: Gammon (Malaya) Ltd. and in September a strip of rubber ½ inch thick, 7 ft. wide and 50 ft. long was laid at their own coat at Trafalgar Street. In December, 1932 an area of 871 square yards of Raffles Place was paved with rubber of an average thickness of ¾ inch [...]. The subsequent history of this paving is given in the Annual Reports for 1933 and 1934 (Appendices IV & V). [...]

Early in 1935 Messrs. Gammon (Malaya) Ltd., laid several trial areas at Trafalgar Street of "rubber macadam", consisting of a layer of bitumen coated ¾ inch granite   inch thick after rolling, which was grouted in with a rubber paste known as Malaytex. This material was used to fill the voids in the stone base only and was finished off flush with the surface of the stone.

The results were encouraging and in March, 1935 the Commissioners placed a contract with Messrs. Gammon (Malaya) Ltd. to lay an area of 1,000 square yards of rubber macadam at a rate of $2.50 per square yard, in South Bridge Road opposite the Central Police Station. This area commenced to give trouble within a few weeks of having been laid and upon examination it was found that the bitumen coating was no longer adhering to the granite base and the stones were loose inside the matrix of rubber. Heavy braking by trolley buses pulled up large areas of the rubber leaving a layer of clean uncoated stone exposed. The rubber appeared to be of fair quality and there is little doubt that the result would have been satisfactory had the adhesion between the bitumen and the granite not broken down.

The areas at Trafalgar Street are in perfect condition after seven months service.

Mr. N. H. TAYLOR, Assistant Engineer Roads, of this Department carried out research work in a private capacity in order to ascertain a means of overcoming the adhesion difficulty and to improve the quality of the rubber. He has been successful in both lines of research and has not only secured perfect adhesion between the rubber, bitumen and stone but has increased the tensible[6] strength of the rubber by 500%.

Messrs. Gammon (Malaya) Ltd., have now undertaken to relay the area free of cost to Mr. Taylor's specification and it is anticipated that the results will be extremely satisfactory.

[...]/

APPENDIX IV
EXTRACT FROM MUNICIPAL ENGINEER'S ANNUAL REPORT FOR 1933

RUBBER ROAD PAVING

In my previous Annual Report I made reference to an experimental strip of Rubber Carpeting, made direct from latex and poured in situ, which was laid at Raffles Place under the supervision of H. W. COWLING, Managing Engineer and Director of Messrs. Gammon (Malaya), Ltd. Except for a few small areas adjoining the macadam parts of the road which loosened from the foundation, the paving as a whole is standing up well to traffic and has distinctly good riding qualities.

APPENDIX V
EXTRACT FROM MUNICIPAL ENGINEER'S ANNUAL REPORT FOR 1934

RUBBER ROAD PAVING

In my Annual Report for 1932 details were given of the experimental laying of Rubber Carpeting (871 square yards) made direct from latex and poured in situ at Raffles Place, under the supervision of Mr. H. W. COWLING, Managing Engineer and Director of Messrs. Gammon (Malaya), Ltd. In regard to its service during 1933 I reported that "the paving as a whole is standing up well to traffic, and has distinctly good riding qualities".

In March and June of 1934 about 207 square yards, or 24% of the carpeting, became detached from its foundation, and was replaced with asphaltic paving.

The damage was due to rain water, which penetrated a crack in a construction joint, and formed a blister. This blister was moved from place to place by traffic, thus extending the damage before it was observed by an officer of the Roads Department. The rubber paving cut out and removed was in good condition, but its adhesion to the macadam foundation was not sufficiently secure, since it was found that the adjoining sound paving could be pulled up by hand fairly easily.

After the detached rubber paving had been cut out and replaced with asphalt a few incipient cracks on the remaining area were made good, and the whole area was then given two coats of asphalt emulsion. This treatment has been very effective and there has been no further trouble.

At the present time (February, 1935) further experiments, but on somewhat different lines, are being undertaken by Mr. COWLING at Trafalgar Street Depôt, with encouraging results.

ANON., 'A PIONEER SHIPPING AGENCY. HISTORY OF MANSFIELD & CO.', *THE SINGAPORE FREE PRESS EXHIBITION SUPPLEMENT*, 2 JANUARY 1932 (1932)

Anon., 'A Pioneer Shipping Agency. History of Mansfield & Co.', *The Singapore Free Press Exhibition Supplement*, 2 January 1932, National Archives, CO 273/582/3, p. 4.

The following is a short article detailing the history of the shipping agency Mansfield & Co. Ltd and the associated shipping company the Straits Steamship Co. Ltd (see also the Transport and Communications thematic introduction). The Straits Steamship Co. was badly affected both by the early 1930s recession and the Second World War, but after each event recovered its former trading position. In the 1970s, it began to diversify into property, leisure, warehousing and distribution, and, in 1983, became a subsidiary of Keppel Corporation Ltd. Mansfield & Co. Ltd was also taken over by Keppel and, in 1992, was merged with National Car Rentals and SAFE Enterprises Pte Ltd.[1]

Notes
1. R. Lim, *Tough Men, Bold Visions. The Story of Keppel* (Singapore: Keppel Corp., 1993), pp. 66, 89; J. Chia, 'Straits Steamship Company', available online at http://eresources. nlb.gov.sg/infopedia/articles/SIP_1056_2008-01-05.html [accessed 28 March 2014].

Anon., 'A Pioneer Shipping Agency. History of Mansfield & Co.', *The Singapore Free Press Exhibition Supplement*, 2 January 1932 (1932), extract

The firm of W. Mansfield & Company, to give it the original name, was founded by Walter Mansfield, who came to Singapore in 1868. His family were shipbuilders of Teignmouth in Devon and he was in due course joined by his nephew G. J. Mansfield, who is still alive. The firm secured In 1868 the agency of The Ocean Steam Ship Co., Ltd. (The Blue Funnel Line), which had commenced its Eastern service two years previously and the steady growth of the latter, which in 1904 absorbed the "White Funnel" Line, as its chief rival the China Mutual Steam Navigation Co., Ltd., was known, ensured increasing prosperity to the agents.

Walter Mansfield died in 1873 and G. J. Mansfield took on T. C. Bogaardt as Partner. This able and enterprising man soon made his presence felt. Offices were opened in Penang and Sandakan (the latter since closed) and in 1890, with the experience he had gained in the coasting services then operated by Alfred Holt & Company to Bangkok, Borneo and Sumatra, he inaugurated the Straits Steamship Co., Ltd. in partnership with some of the leading Chinese of the day. For some years the connection between W. Mansfield & Co. and the Straits Steamship Co., Ltd. was very close, as called for in the original Articles of Association, but the rapid growth of the Straits Steamship Co., Ltd. and the increased work of W. Mansfield & Co., Ltd. (as it had become in 1902) in their own sphere of operations, caused the connection to be one of friendly co-operation rather than of intimate connection. The position was changed once more when in 1992 Mansfield & Co., Ltd. (as the firm is now styled) were appointed General Managers of the Straits Steamship Co., Ltd., a position which continues to this day.

STRAITS STEAMSHIP CO.

Space forbids any detailed history of the Straits Steamship Co., Ltd., but its progress has been as striking as it has been soundly planned, and will always be rightly associated with the names of D. K Somerville and H. E Somerville.

It will be sufficient to say that the problem of designing vessels suitable for the carriage of passengers in tropical waters, in perfect comfort and security, and at the same time catering for the endless different types of cargo, in spite of the many difficulties of draught and length imposed by small coastal harbours and rivers, has been completely solved. The famous express steamer "Kedah" will, for some years, represent the highest achievement of marine construction in these waters, whether as regards speed, comfort or efficiency.

The most recent event of importance in the Company's history has been a working arrangement with the Sarawak Steamship Co., Ltd. and the inauguration of a joint service to Kuching.

The period of development of the Straits Steamship Co., Ltd. has seen a no less striking progress on the part of the Blue Funnel Line.

The Blue Funnel Line has continued to Improve and extend its services on the main routes from Europe to the Far East, and from North Atlantic ports to the same areas, together with its coastal service to W. Australian ports. More frequent and faster regular services of first-class vessels specially designed to meet the ever changing demands of merchants have characterised its steady policy. The position of Alfred Holt & Company in the trades in which they operate, is eloquent testimony of the regard in which their services are held by exporters and importers, and by the travelling public, in their more recent development as first class passenger carriers.

NEW DEVELOPMENT.

Meanwhile Mansfield & Co. Ltd. have added to their original agency of the Blue Funnel Line, the China Navigation Co., Ltd., the Straits Steamship Co., Ltd., the Siam Steam Navigation Co., Ltd., the Sarawak Steamship Co., Ltd., the Sun Line, the Australian & Oriental Line and recently – a new development – have taken on passenger agencies for the F.M.S Railway and the Royal State Railways of Siam and the Royal Dutch Indian Airways.

The position of the Company here and its relations not only with the magnificent services of the Blue Funnel Line but the network of coastal and local services operated by the Straits Steamship Co., Ltd. and its associated Companies, made the incorporation of ordinary forwarding and shipping work in the normal activities of the firm an inevitable corollary. Agencies for the Liverpool & London & Globe and the Thames & Mersey Insurance Companies have been accepted and the Company is now in a unique position with all its local connections and its comprehensive scheme of agents and correspondents throughout the world, to handle the receiving, shipping, storage and insurance of cargo with the greatest possible efficiency and at the lowest possible cost. At the same time the firm is prepared to give intending passengers the benefit of its experience and advice in arranging passages home, locally, or round the world.

The branch office of the Company in Penang is prepared to handle similarly the requirements of merchants or travellers to its vicinity.

ANON., 'THE BRITISH INDIA STEAM NAVIGATION COMPANY MAIL AND INDIAN IMMIGRATION CONTRACT, 1923' (1923)

Anon., 'The British India Steam Navigation Company Mail and Indian Immigration Contract, 1923', John Rylands Library, Manchester, CO 273/582/16, pp. 1–4.

The British India Steam Navigation Company was founded in 1856 by the traders William Mackinnon and Robert Mackenzie of Mackinnon, Mackenzie & Co. as the Calcutta and Burmah Steam Navigation Co. to carry mail between Calcutta and Rangoon. Under the leadership of its Chairman, Lord Inchcape, in 1913 it became part of the P & O group of companies, though retained its own identity and organization. By 1922, when the contract was signed, it operated the largest merchant fleet in the world – 158 vessels of almost 1m gross tons – and ran services from India to Ceylon, the Bay of Bengal, Singapore, Malaya, Java, Thailand, Japan, the Persian Gulf, East Africa and South Africa. The one-year agreement details ports of call, the fees the company received for carrying mails and migrants from India to Malaya and the additional services it was expected to perform.[1]

Notes
1. Anon., 'A Short History of the British India Steam Navigation Co.', available online at http://www.biship.com/history.htm [accessed 21 March 2014].

Anon., 'The British India Steam Navigation Company Mail and Indian Immigration Contract, 1923', extract

This Agreement made the eighth day of March, One thousand nine hundred and twenty three (1923) Between His EXCELLENCY THE GOVERNOR OF THE STRAITS SETTLEMENTS acting herein for himself and his successors in office for the public service of the Colony (hereinafter called "the Government") of the one part and the BRITISH INDIA STEAM NAVIGATION COMPANY, LIMITED, (hereinafter called "the Company") of the other part WHEREBY it is agreed by and between the Government and the Company as follows: –

1. The term "State aided immigrant" means any adult labourer carried to the Colony of the Straits Settlements or to the Malay States on behalf of the Colony or of the Government of the Federated Malay States or of any of them or on behalf of any Committee constituted by the Government for the purpose of promoting immigration.

The term "minor" means a State aided immigrant under the age of twelve years.

The term "mails" means and includes all bags, boxes, baskets or other packages of letters and other postal packets including parcels (each parcel not exceeding the maximum weight of eleven pounds) without regard either to the country or place to which such packages may be addressed or to the country or place in which they may have been posted and also all empty bags, boxes, baskets or other receptacles and all stores and other articles used or to be used on the Post Office Service.

The term "postal packet" means any article for the time being transmissible by post and includes a parcel.

The term "parcel" means all such postal packets as by the regulations of His Majesty's Treasury in the United Kingdom made in pursuance of the Post Office Acts are defined to be parcels.

2. The date of the commencement of this agreement shall be deemed to be the 12th day of February, 1923, and it shall continue in force for a period of one year.

2a. If at any time during the term of this Agreement any law is passed either in India or in the Straits Settlements whereby the present capacity of the Company's steamers for carrying passengers is diminished the Government agree that the rates for passages as mentioned in Clause 7 hereof shall be proportionately increased.

Provided always that the diminution of such capacity is a necessary result of the passing of such law.

3. In consideration of the payment by the Government to the Company of a subsidy of Rs. 200,000 per annum payable quarterly at the end of each quarter and of the agreements on the part of the Government herein contained the Company shall while this agreement is in force provide: –

(a) a fortnightly immigrant service from Madras and Negapatam to Penang, Port Swettenham and Singapore;

(b) a fortnightly mail service from Singapore and Penang to India and *vice versâ* in connection with the Peninsular and Oriental Steam Navigation Company's mail service between Bombay and Europe in the week alternate to that in which the mail packets of that Company carry the mails to the Straits and China. /

4. – (1) The following provisions as to the time and place of starting and arrival shall apply to service (*a*) above mentioned: –

(i) The last port of call in India shall be Negapatam.

(ii) The hour of departure from Negapatam shall be not later than 9 A.M. on Sunday or as soon thereafter as the mails are on board.

(iii) The Superintendent of the Government Depôt at Negapatam shall have the option of delaying the steamer if she is being used for the mail service to wait for the mails from Europe on his giving 24 hours' written notice to the Company's agent at Negapatam before the schedule time of sailing.

(iv) The above hours are subject to alteration by agreement between the contracting parties.

5. The following provisions as to the place and time of starting and arrival shall apply to the fortnightly mail service (*b*) above mentioned: –

(i) The steamer carrying the mail to India shall leave Singapore not earlier than 4 P.M. on Wednesday and shall call at Penang and the Company shall then have the option of carrying the mails to Madras or Negapatam (with an option as to these ports) or by way of Rangoon to some port in India. By whatever route the mails are carried they shall reach India in time to connect with the mail train which conveys the mail for Europe to Bombay for shipment there on board the Peninsular and Oriental Steam Navigation Company's steamer to leave Bombay for Europe, on Saturdays at 1 P.M.

(ii) The Company shall have the option of carrying the mails from India from Madras or Negapatam (with an option as to these ports) or from some port in India by way of Rangoon. In case they shall be brought from Madras or Negapatam the provisions of Clause 4 (ii) shall apply but in any event the steamer carrying the mails shall call at Penang not later than 6 A.M. on Friday and shall arrive in Singapore not later than 8 a.m. on the Sunday unless the steamer's departure has been delayed by the Superintendent under Clause 4 (iii) when the hour of arrival may be extended by the number of hours for which the steamer was detained.

(iii) The Mail Steamer shall on its voyage from India to Singapore make a stay of 4 hours at Penang and shall make a like stay on the voyage from Singapore to India. On the voyage from India the 4 hours shall be 4 working hours of daylight, *i.e.* between 6 A.M. and 6 P.M.

6. The Government shall take from the Company during the continuance of this agreement 30,000 tickets for adult labourers (two tickets for minors counting as one ticket for an adult labourer) from any port in Southern India to Penang, Port Swettenham or Singapore upon the usual conditions the passage to begin and end on boardship. In case the Government shall take less than such 30,000 tickets they shall pay to the Company Rs. 12 net for each ticket taken short of the above number.

6a. State aided Immigrants shall be supplied with food according to a scale of diet to be mutually agreed upon.

7. The passage money payable for the said tickets shall be as follows: –

	From Madras.			From Negapatam.		
	R.	A.	P.	R.	A.	P.
To Penang or Port Swettenham	19	12	0	16	0	0
To Singapore	23	8	0	19	12	0

The rates for minors to be half the above rates. The above rates shall include food to be supplied by the Company.

In the event of the rate for ordinary passages falling below the rate mentioned in this clause (owing to any cause whatever) it is understood that the Government are to pay the rates above stated.

Provided that if either at the request of the Government or of the Company a weekly service is put in force with the consent in either case of the other party both the question of the number of tickets guaranteed under clause 6 and of the basic passage rate under this clause shall be reopened and re-discussed. /

8. The Company shall supply at the rates mentioned in the last clause as many tickets over the said 30,000 as the Government may requisition for.

9. The Government will not use any of the tickets purchased at the rates mentioned in Clause 7 except for *bonâ fide* labourers or artisans.

10. The passage tickets shall be provided by the Company and supplied to the Superintendent of the Depôt at Negapatam or the Government Agent at Madras and shall be paid for in cash on delivery of the tickets. The tickets shall be numbered consecutively, and shall be in counterfoil.

11. The Government shall not use more than 1,750 tickets for State aided immigrants for any one steamer unless space for more is available. Twenty-four hours before the time fixed for the departure of the steamer the Superintendent of the Depôt at Negapatam shall finally declare the number of tickets that he will require for that sailing, and after such declaration no additional tickets can be claimed. Passages so declared shall be paid for even if not used.

12. The Government agrees to forward by the Company's steamers all labourers from India in whom they are directly or indirectly interested.
Provided always if and when labourers in greater numbers than can be taken by the fortnightly contract steamer are presented for shipment at Madras or Negapatam, the Company will put on additional steamers as may be necessary.

13. The steamers shall go alongside the wharf at Madras for the embarkation of labourers if practicable.

14 All steamers performing service under this agreement shall: –
   (*a*) get medical examination immediately on arrival and preference for such inspection over all other steamers not being mail steamers;
   (*b*) be exempted inward and outward from the operation of Section 417 of Ordinance No. 125 (Merchant Shipping).
   (*c*) be liable to payment of half only of any light dues in force in the Straits Settlements, payment being made at the rate of $100 for each Rs. 175; and shall be exempt from payment of Port and Light Dues at Port Swettenham.

15. The Government shall provide adequate quarantine accommodation at Penang for 3,500 passengers irrespective of the port from which they arrive so that in case of any sickness among the passengers who may be landed at Penang the Company's steamers may not be detained to the detriment of the regularity of the service. In the event of steamers being quarantined at Penang and having to overcarry State aided immigrants to Singapore the Government guarantee the payment of return passages at Rs. 3 to Port Swettenham and Rs. 4 to Penang.

16. The Company's steamers shall at Port Swettenham receive a preference of railway tongkangs[1] and launches for the landing of passengers on the Company's Agent giving due date and time of arrival.

17. The Government will assist the Company in collecting all quarantine charges on account of State aided immigrants, but this clause should not be held to imply any responsibility on the part of the Government for the payment of such charges.

18. The Company shall convey all Government Post Office Officials and all Colonial and Federated Malay States Inspectors and Officers of the Indian Immigration Department travelling on duty free of charge on steamers performing service under this agreement.

19. The Company shall carry all mails which the Post master-General of the Colony shall require it from time to time or at any time to convey to and from India or from or to any ports from which the Company's steamers start or at which they call or arrive under the provisions of this agreement or for the purposes of the Company.

20. The Company shall at their own cost embark the mails at ports or places at which mails are to be embarked and shall also at the like cost immediately on the arrival of a steamer carrying any mail at any port or place at which mails are to be landed land the mails so carried and shall accordingly at their own cost provide suitable means and proper assistance and shall be responsible for the due embarking and landing of the mails./

21. The Company shall provide the following accommodation and assistance: –

(*a*) A separate room or rooms for the secure deposit of the mails under lock and key.

(*b*) A separate and convenient room of such dimensions as the Postmaster-General of the Colony shall require for the purpose of sorting and making up the mails between Penang and Singapore.

(*c*) Every such room shall be provided with all such furniture, lamps, fittings and other conveniences as are necessary for the purpose of sorting and making up the mails and all such furniture, lockers, lamps, fittings and other conveniences to be from time to time cleansed and kept in repair and the artificial light (including oil if used) to be supplied by the servants and at the cost of the Company.

(*d*) The services of the crew to be from time to time given in the conveyance of the mails between the mail room and the sorting room or rooms.

22. The Company shall be responsible for the loss or damage of any parcel or any registered postal article of any kind conveyed or tendered for conveyance under this contract (unless such loss or damage be caused or occasioned by the act of God, the King's enemies, pirates, restraints of princes, rulers or people, jettison, barratry,[2] fire, collision or perils or accidents of the seas, rivers and steam navigation provided that the expression "barratry" shall not be deemed to include any unlawful act in respect of the mails on the part of the master or officer having charge thereof) and in the event of any such loss or damage (except as aforesaid) the Company shall be liable to pay to the Government in respect of each parcel or registered postal article so lost or damaged such sums of money as shall be equal to the amount which may have been awarded and paid by the Govern-

ment at the sole option and discretion of Government (and though not under any legal obligation) to the sender or addressee of such parcel or registered postal article as compensation for the loss or damage thereof provided that such sum shall not in any case exceed rupees fifteen in respect of each parcel and rupees thirty in respect of each registered postal article.

23. In the event of the mails not being landed in India in time to connect with the mail train which conveys the mails for Europe to Bombay as provided by Clause 5 (1) of this agreement the Company shall (unless the default was due to *force majeure*[3]) pay to the Government as liquidated damages the sum of Rupees seven hundred.

24. In the event of the steamer carrying the mails not arriving at Penang at 6 A.M. on Friday or in Singapore by 8 A.M. on Sunday or by such later hour as is referred to in Clause 5 (ii) of this agreement the Company shall (unless the default was due to *force majeure*) pay to the Government as liquidated damages Rupees seventeen and a half per hour for each of the first twelve hours which elapse after the ship shall be in default, and Rupees seventeen and a half per hour or one hundred and seventy-five Rupees for each subsequent completed period of six hours in excess of the said first twelve hours but so that in no case shall the liquidated damages arising from the default of any steamer on any voyage from India amount to more than seven hundred Rupees.

ANON., *REPORT OF THE COMMISSION ON THE EASTERN SHIPPING OR STRAITS HOMEWARD CONFERENCE AS AFFECTING THE TRADE OF THE COLONY* (1902)

Anon., *Report of the Commission on the Eastern Shipping or Straits Homeward Conference as Affecting the Trade of the Colony* (Singapore: Government Publication, 1902), pp. 5–14.

As discussed in the Transport and Communications thematic introduction, the Straits Homeward Conference was established in 1897 by the shipping companies plying the route to Europe. Criticisms of its activities by Alexander Stuart, the Registrar of Imports and Exports of the Straits Settlements, and John Anderson, a director of Guthrie & Co. and the Chairman of the Singapore Chamber of Commerce, led the government in 1902 to establish a Commission of Enquiry. The Commission's inconclusive findings, partly reproduced below, were not shared by the 1907 Royal Commission on Shipping Rings, which condemned the secret rebate the cartel gave to certain trading companies as an 'undesirable expedient' and recommended its abolition. The conference eventually withdrew the rebate in 1911.[1]

Notes
1. C. H. Ding, 'The Early Shipping Conference System of Singapore, 1897–1911', *Journal of Southeast Asian History*, 10:1 (1969), pp. 260–1.

Anon., *Report of the Commission on the Eastern Shipping or Straits Homeward Conference as Affecting the Trade of the Colony* (1902), extract

[...]

17 [drawbacks of conferences] ... The purport of the evidence quoted is to the effect that trade was diverted from Singapore to Macassar,[1] and possibly to other ports, by the higher freights ruling at Singapore. The present state of the case is perhaps correctly put forward by MR. VON ROËSSING, p. 63, who, referring to freight, says of the rates from Macassar "At the beginning of the Conference I believe they were lower but present rates are about the same as from Singapore, and have been so for the last year" – that is to say that from the beginning of 1897 to say the beginning of 1901 freights from Macassar to Europe were admittedly lower than from Singapore.[*] The preference thus shown to Macassar has diverted trade from Singapore that is not likely to return unless the attraction offered be very considerable. In further support of this we may quote from a Return of the principal articles of produce shipped from Macassar from 1895 to 1901, Appendix 25. In 1896, 2,039,000 Kilos of Copra were shipped direct to Europe as compared with 6,615,000 sent to Singapore, while in 1901 the shipments direct to Europe and to Singapore were respectively 12,098,000 and 82,000 Kilos. Similar conditions will be seen to hold good in respect of other articles, *e. g.*, Gum Copal, Horns, Hides, Coffee and M. O. P. Shells.

(*d*) Ports in America and in Russia are exempted from the operations of the Conference. A consequence of this is that lower, much lower freights, are charged to Russian and American ports than to ports in Europe with the result that trade has been largely diverted from ports in the United Kingdom to Russian and American ports, more especially to certain of the ports of the United States of America – the United States of America importers and manufacturers being thus given a distinct advantage as compared with British manufacturers. This may be said not to have any direct bearing on the trade and prosperity of the Colony;[†] it is, however, undoubtedly in some degree at least one effect of the operations of the Conference.

[*]   See Appendices 10 and 12 [Appendices not reproduced].
[†]   See evidence of the HON'BLE C. STRINGER, M.L.C., p. 50. /

In support of the opinion expressed by us on this point we quote MR. JOHN ANDERSON, who, replying, p. 7, to a question as to whether the trade with the United States had very largely increased of late years, said "In my opinion that is due in great degree to the Conference", and p. 8, "I cannot say that the trade with the United States harms the Colony directly, but I have already stated my opinion that whatever harms the Empire harms the Colony, and it certainly harms the Empire to admit of the New York citizen getting his tapioca at a less price than our London citizens get theirs"; and, p. 10, "The rates of freight just now to America are 15/– for all sorts of cargo; * * * The effect of that is that you can ship cargo at 15/– to New York, and if it does not suit you to sell it there, you can keep it in bond and then ship it to Liverpool at less freight than you can ship it direct from here."

MR. G. PERTILE gave evidence to the same effect; he told us, p. 18, that "The freight is now 15/– to New York, 50/– to London, 57/– to Glasgow and 55/– to Liverpool. On cheap gums and other low priced things it makes a difference of 5 to 20 per cent. on the whole value of the produce. That is to say that the Englishman must pay 5 to 20 per cent. more for his raw material, and it is certainly most detrimental to the British manufacturer. In fact the changes in the export of Rattans during the last three years show the following figures: To the United Kingdom 61,000 piculs in 1899, and only 43,000 last year; to America 46,000 in 1899, 101,000 last year, – the one less by one-third, the other more than doubled. * * * the lower freight competes against England because it puts the manufacturer in America in the position of being able to pay a higher price."

MR. A. W. STIVEN, of STIVEN & Co., mentioned, p. 73, to us that "steamer rates are sometimes so low that it is possible to ship to America and send from thence to London cheaper than shipping direct".

MR. M. PUTTFARCKEN stated, p. 97, to us "I should like to point out, against the Conference, the cheap freights to America. The Americans are getting things much cheaper than the people in Europe".

We were told by Mr. W. A. GREIG, of MESSRS. BOUSTEAD & Co., that before the Conference came into existence there was a trade in Straits produce / to United Kingdom ports for shipment to the United States; and MR. LOVELL, of. McKERROW & Co., alleged, p. 22, that "The Conference has completely altered the status of the British buyer of our produce, from being able to buy cheaper than any other country, to the other extreme, which must have the effect of reducing the consumption, besides destroying the distributing trade of our own Country".

(*e*) Apart from the somewhat remarkable diversion of the trade to America we have formed the opinion from the evidence placed before us that the freights as fixed by the Conference give an undue preference in certain cases to Foreign ports as compared with some British ports at an equal or less distance from the Colony – that freights are, in fact, so arranged as to favour trade with Continental as compared with British ports. We have before us a copy of the Singapore

Exchange Market Report of June 2nd, a publication issued with the authority of the Singapore Exchange. In this we find a list of freights on different classes of goods "to London and Europe ports *en route*," and at the foot of this list we find it stated that to Glasgow an additional charge of 7/6 (a ton) will be made, and to Liverpool *viâ* London and London *viâ* Liverpool an additional charge of 5/–. Shipments to Leith and Belfast, we are given to understand, incur an additional charge of 13/6 a ton. Mr. Lovell brings this out clearly in his statement, p. 22, where he quotes the case of Tapioca which, as he says, costs 56/– a ton to Belfast or Leith and 50/– to Glasgow as compared with 42/6 to Continental ports, not merely the chief ports but such comparatively minor ports as St. Nazaire, Dunkirk, Rotterdam, Venice and Fiume. Again he points out that under Conference arrangements it is possible to ship directly or indirectly to Havre and/or Marseilles at one and that the lowest rate while shippers cannot obtain option of London and/or Liverpool except at 5/– extra. Mr. von Roëssing also informed the Commission, p. 68, that the companies represented by his firm, trading to Continental ports, gave options, *e.g.*, to Amsterdam and Hamburg.

It has been suggested that the higher rates to British out ports are due to the high charges in the United Kingdom for Light Dues, but we have not been able to elicit information as to Light Dues[2] that would support this theory, nor do we think it is compatible with the fact that, outside of the United Kingdom, the Conference gives options to ports of different countries without extra freight.

It is instructive to note, in this connection, that on the formation of the Conference the rates of freight first agreed to were: –

s.

London	20/–
Liverpool	22/6
Continental Ports with the exception of Havre, Bremen and Hamburg rates for which were to be fixed from time to time by the Committee	20/–

The first actual increase of rates appears to have been the putting the freight to Glasgow and Greenock at 5/– above London.*

In February, 1897, owing to Bag goods being shipped to Hamburg at 15/– by a non-Conference line, a supporter of the Conference represented to the Singapore Committee that he was unable to "work any business at the Conference rates." About the same time Mr. Laspe, of Messrs. Behn Meyer & Co., an active member of the Singapore Committee, drew the attention of the Committee to the fact that the Copra trade from Singapore was now practically being boycotted owing to the lower rates of freight charged from Manila.†

---

*   See Appendix 1. /
†   See Appendix 1. /

At the meeting of the Singapore Committee of February 18th, it was resolved to urge on London a reduction of the Conference rates to Havre and Hamburg to 15/–, while at the same meeting the rate to Glasgow and/or Greenock was fixed at 27/6.*

In June, 1898, MR. RITCHIE, the then Chairman of the Singapore Committee, pointed out to his Committee that up to that time those who had principally benefited from the higher rates on Tin had been the direct non-Conference lines to America, and suggested that they should be approached with a view to getting them to assimilate their rates as nearly as possible to the Conference rates; otherwise the Conference might have to consider the advisability of very materially reducing rates.†

The action of the Conference here referred to – reducing rates to Foreign ports and raising them to British ports, etc., would appear to justify MR. LOVELL'S expression of opinion, pp. 21 and 22, that the British lines in the Conference are "palpably concerned with the interests of their shareholders alone but the Foreign lines seem well to regard the trade and prestige of their country". /

(*f*) Another matter in respect of which complaint was made to the Commission is that not only were tramp steamers[3] excluded under Conference rules but that trade with Europe by means of sailing ships had practically been stopped. The transfer of the carrying trade from sailing ships to steamers is the natural course of events but yet there must be cases in which it might be to the interest of importers and shippers to make use of sailing ships. Coal has been and could undoubtedly still be imported cheaply in sailing vessels and there might be circumstances in which it might be, as instanced by MR. ANDERSON at pp. 8 and 9 of his evidence, more advantageous for exporters to ship their produce by sailing vessel than by steamship. The employment of sailing ships for the trade to the so-called Conference ports has been stopped with the one exception of Marseilles. But the grievance, if grievance it is, in this respect cannot be held to be of much moment seeing that during the six years, 1892 to 1897, only 32 sailing vessels cleared with cargoes from Singapore to the United Kingdom; and we understand that the exception made in favour of Marseilles is rarely availed of.‡

The fact that tramp steamers are excluded from a share of the trade is admitted by all, both by the supporters of the Conference and by those who expressed themselves in an opposite sense. Indeed the action of the Conference appears to have gone beyond this; it appears to have compelled lines whose owners wished to share in our trade with Europe in some instance to subscribe to the Conference terms, and in others, or at least in the case of one other Company, that did

---

*   See Appendix 1. /
†   See Appendix 1. /
‡   See Appendix 6. /

not or would not come into line with the Conference, the competing ships were acquired by lines connected with the Conference.

And there appears to be little or no doubt – indeed only one witness, MR. A. R. ADAMS, of MESSRS. MANSFIELD & Co., appeared to question it – the opposition of MESSRS. HUTTENBACH BROS., who proceeded to charter and run outside steamers, and of MESSRS. BRINKMANN & Co., ceased on their being allowed to share in the additional rebate granted to certain firms.

(*g*) This additional rebate forms another and, in our opinion, just cause of complaint. To all shippers by the Conference lines of steamers a rebate is granted, as has been already stated, of 10 per cent. of the freights paid. But over and above this 10 per cent. it seems that 5 per cent. of all the freights paid by shippers is pooled and divided among a certain limited number of firms. This was generally admitted but we need only refer to the evidence on this point of MR. VON ROËSSING, of MESSRS-BEHN MEYER & Co., pp. 66, 67, 69 and 70. This gentleman mentioned the following firms as sharing in the extra rebate: –

MESSRS. BOUSTEAD & Co.
MESSRS. GILFILLAN, WOOD & Co.
MESSRS. BEHN MEYER & Co.
MESSRS. PATERSON, SIMONS & Co.
MESSRS. HUTTENBACH BROS.
MESSRS. BRINKMANN & Co.

The justification of this was alleged to be the giving up in joining the Conference, by these firms of large profits from the chartering of steamers and the low rates at which they could obtain freight for the large quantities of produce shipped by them. This was aptly described by MR. W A. GREIG, of MRSSRS. BOUSTEAD & Co., as being "compensation for the deprivation of those facilities, which we have just been mentioning, in regard to chartering and in regard to making special rates". A larger share of the rebate is given to MESSRS. BOUSTEAD & Co., MESSRS. GILFILLAN WOOD & Co. and MESSRS. BEHN MEYER & Co., because these firms did a larger chartering business than the others. In what proportion the extra rebate of 5 per cent. is divided we did not learn; the local representatives of these firms who appeared before us expressed ignorance on this head and, with the exception of MR. VON ROËSSING, inability to supply the information required. MR. VON ROËSSING promised to look the matter up and to furnish details to the Commission, but wrote subsequently to say that he was unable to do so.

MR. VON ROËSSING stated that the profits from chartering lost to the firms in question by their adhesion to the Conference were very large, an opinion in which he was corroborated by other witnesses. It was also mentioned to us by several witnesses that before the institution of the Conference the firms who chartered made a large profit out of their transactions by charging higher rates of freight to those who were not so fortunately situated. /

(*h*) It has been alleged that the high, freights have restricted the imports of Coal and exports of Wood.

With respect to Coal we do not find that there has been any restriction; the direction of the imports only has changed. The table given in Appendix 24 shows that the total quantity of Coal imported into the Colony in 1901 was 668,000 tons as compared with 374,000 tons in 1891; but while in 1891 the imports from the United Kingdom amounted to 226,000 tons in 1901 they had fallen to 62,000 tons; the imports from Australia had also in the same period dropped from 65,000 tons to 38,000 tons; while Coal imported from Japan had risen from 57,000 tons, in 1891 to 476,000 tons in 1901, and from Bengal the imports had run up from 8,000 tons in 1891 to 77,000 tons in 1901.

The only witness who spoke to the export of Timber having been interfered with by high freights is MR. JOHN ANDERSON. He showed that with very low rates of freight he had successfully sent small experimental shipments of Wood to Europe and that with present rates this is no longer possible. But we had no evidence that the trade would develop into importance or that any appreciable loss to the trade of the Colony is entailed by the restriction in question.

(*i*) MR. D. W. LOVELL in his evidence attributed decreased production in certain articles of export to the action of the Conference in imposing high rates of freight, but though we sought information on this point from other witnesses well qualified to offer an opinion on this point, we did not elicit any corroboration of this statement. The decrease in production in such articles as have shown a decrease is due to causes other than rates of freight.

(*j*) Since the establishment of the. Conference there has been a very marked development in the number and tonnage of steam vessels trading with the ports of this Colony, flying foreign colours. In Appendix 21 will be found particulars of the number and tonnage of ships that cleared with cargo from Singapore during the ten years 1892 to 1901, British ships being therein distinguished from ships of foreign nationality.

These figures are instructive and go to show that influences have been at work in recent years leading to an extraordinary development of the carrying trade[4] in foreign bottoms.[5] Those who are opposed to the Conference allege that this development of the foreign carrying trade is at the expense of British shipping and that the existing condition of affairs is due to the operations of the Conference which enabled Foreign owners, merchants and companies to get a hold on the carrying trade of the Colony on terms that pay well, although their ships, being to a large extent mail steamers, are of a class more expensive to build and to run than British cargo steamers, and that being regarded as mail steamers they have to pay Suez Canal dues[6] at a higher rate than purely cargo steamers.

This development is especially noticeable in the case of ships of German nationality. If we compare vessels cleared from Singapore and Penang in 1901 with vessels cleared from these ports in 1896, we find that while the totals were: –

	1896.		1901.	
	No.	*Tons.*	*No.*	*Tons.*
From Singapore	4,554	3,993,605	4,924	5,453,999
From Penang	2,678	1,846,087	2,460	2,388,696

the number and tonnage of British and German vessels included in these totals were: –

	1896.		1901.	
	No.	*Tons.*	*No.*	*Tons.*
From Singapore – British	2,967	2,630,472	2,448	2,819,583
German	322	484,447	525	926,832
From Penang – British	2,313	1,442,219	2,034	1,579,299
German	85	142,668	192	463,966

Mr. von Roëssing, of Messrs, Behn Meyer & Co., Agents of the Norddeutscher Lloyd and Hamburg-America Companies, told the Commission, in reply to a question as to whether the operations of the Conference had led to the extension of the operations of the companies represented by him, that "they have availed themselves of its advantages to keep up a regular service and have by degrees / drawn regular supplies from outports, and I think the principal supporters have been the coasting ships which have been taken up by the North German Lloyds." He admitted that the business of his companies had materially improved during the last four or five years. In this connection it may be mentioned that the Norddeutscher Lloyd have during that period altered their sailings from monthly to fortnightly sailings; and among other vessels in the "coasting" trade taken up by them they acquired in 1899 the fleet of the Eastern Ocean Steamship Company plying between Singapore and Bangkok, a transaction that resulted in the transfer from the British to the German flag of eleven well equipped steam vessels of a gross tonnage of 13,559 tons. The same company acquired the vessels of the Scottish Oriental Steamship Company; and the evidence taken by us goes to show that these smaller lines absorb the trade with Siam, Sumatra and Borneo, acting as feeders for the vessels of the main lines.

Much of the remaining part of the so-called coasting trade is also carried on by ships flying the Dutch and other foreign flags.

So far, however, as the trade of the Colony is concerned, no loss has resulted from this; where the loss comes in is in the extension of the operations of foreign lines of steamers, trading direct to Europe, to ports which formerly sent their produce to Singapore for transhipment. This is the case in respect of Celebes,[7]

Borneo, Java and other ports a connection between which and Europe has now been further developed by German and Dutch lines of steamers.

18. We have now dealt, we hope sufficiently, with the disadvantages to the trade of the Colony alleged to arise from the operations of the Conference; and we come now to the advantages or benefits to trade, as they are termed, alleged by the supporters of the Conference to result from its operations.

(*a*) First, there is the partial elimination of speculation from the trade operations the Colony by merchants having fixed rates of freight. There is no doubt that in existing circumstances merchants do know beforehand what rates of freight they have to take into consideration and so far as this goes the knowledge would seem to be advantageous. But experienced witnesses expressed on this point different opinions, and it appears to the Commission to be a doubtful quantity in view of the fact that the bulk of the produce shipped from the Colony is said to be sold months ahead. It is further not clear – the evidence on this point also being conflicting – that even before the Conference came into existence it was not possible to book ahead, and unless this can be shown not to have been the case it cannot be claimed that the operations of the Conference have eliminated each element of uncertainty in this respect.

(*b*) Next it is claimed for the Conference that it provides a regular and satisfactory supply of tonnage. This MR. CHOPE, the Chairman of the Local Committee, told the Commission is the basis of the Conference, and this undertaking the Conference has, we believe, fulfilled. The one or two exceptions brought to our notice were unimportant, possibly unavoidable. MR. FRIZELL told us that formerly owing to delayed tonnage he had known instances of heavy advances having to be taken from the Banks against produce in the merchants' godowns; the present existing condition of affairs, "the regular arrival of tonnage at short and stated intervals relieves the market and largely does away with the necessity of storing produce in godowns for any length of time".

(*c*) Then it is asserted that the Conference ships are more suitable as carriers of produce than the tramp steamers that formerly took away most of the cargo exported from the Settlements. Only one witness, MR. D. W. LOVELL, alleged the opposite, his contention being that the Conference ships are "too big and do not carry their cargoes well". Other witnesses, notably MR. STRINGER, of MESSRS. PATERSON, SIMONS & Co., testified to the contrary. MR. STRINGER claimed for the Conference ships that they are "very much quicker" and deliver their cargoes in better order. As a result of the quicker despatch he said shippers got their money back more quickly and so increased their available capital; they are able to draw their bills at better rates of exchange, and get better rates of premium for marine insurances.

(*d*) Another of the benefits claimed for the Conference is that increased facilities are afforded of shipment to small Continental ports. About this there was no difference of opinion, the only question, being as to whether it is to the benefit of trade that it should be possible for merchants to send produce to these small Continental ports at lower rates than to many ports of the United Kingdom. With the objections to this we have already dealt; here, however, we might quote the opinion of an experienced and unprejudiced witness, MR. FRIZELL, who, while admitting that "Foreign shipping / has benefited by the Conference" stated that he did not see "how the fact of having contracted commercial ties with **** Continental port can adversely affect the trade or welfare of the Colony".

(*e*) Finally it is claimed for the Conference that under their rules and as a result of their operations equal treatment, in respect of freight and tonnage, is given to both large and small shippers. Nominally this is the case, in reality it is not so. All shippers are charged at the same rates and all, who confine their shipments to the vessels of the Conference, practically all concerned, receive a rebate of 10 per cent. If the transaction stopped here all would, we admit, be receiving equal treatment, but so long as a further 5 per cent. of the freights is pooled and divided amongst a certain number of Firms it cannot be held that the Firms excluded from participation in this extra rebate receive equal treatment with those who do so participate. With this matter of the extra rebate and with the reason alleged for its payment we have already dealt and we need not here further allude to it.

19. The Commission have been given to understand that Conference rules and rates are in force in Hongkong, Japan, Java ports and Macassar, but not in Colombo where the operations of a Conference would not be "practicable on account of the large and fluctuating supply of tonnage and the number of interests to get into line." A consequence of the non-existence at Colombo of such rules is that there occurs from time to time such cases as one quoted to us by a witness. In May, 1901, a homeward bound Conference steamer, which had passed through Singapore, remained at Colombo for two days filling up with Copra at 10/- to 12/6 a ton at a time when the rate from Singapore would not be less than 27/6. Ceylon is a large producer of Copra and it is manifest that the Ceylon article must have a distinct advantage in the markets if it can be carried for less than one half the freight that would be paid by the same produce shipped from Singapore.*

20. Copra is one of the articles of produce in respect of which most complaint has been made as to the adverse effect that Conference rates have had on its shipments, but it is not clear that the reduced quantities sent of late to Singapore for shipment may not have been due, in some part at least, to decreased produc-

---

* See Appendices 16 and 17.

tion; that a great part of the falling off is due to the higher rates of freight under Conference rules from Singapore and the lower rates with increased facilities from other ports does not appear to be open to doubt. It is to be regretted that no very reliable figures as to freight from Java ports are procurable; it seems clear, however, that as against Conference freights Java shippers find it to their interest now to avoid Singapore.

21. A remarkable illustration of the influence of high freight on a low priced article may be found in the statistics of Tapioca shipments for the two periods 1891 to 1895 and 1897 to 1901. A comparison of the two periods shows that while in the latter period there was a falling off in the exports to the United Kingdom of 35% and an increase to the Continent of 21 per cent. there was an increase to America of 71 per cent. Again Singapore during the three years preceding the formation of the Conference imported 19 per cent. of the Java Tapioca flour only; during the three years following the establishment of the Conference it imported only 15 per cent. This would obviously all be for re-shipment.*

22. Apart from the actual diversion of trade from Singapore that has taken or is alleged to have taken place, as a consequence of the operations of the Conference, it is asserted that there has been a further indefinite loss of trade that might have been, nay would have been attracted by low rates of freight, a loss that it is "impossible to estimate", to quote the words of one witness, or with another to say "that the Conference rates of freight have prevented us from getting the fullest possible share which otherwise would have accrued to the Colony of the general increase and development which in the last four or five years has taken place in the overall trade of the East".

23. The Conference was started when freights were ruinously low, and while it is impossible not to sympathise with the origin of the movement it cannot be denied that the influence of the Conference has not been satisfactory so far as regards the development of the Commerce of the Colony, and that had not the Conference been created the trade of the Colony might be greater than it now is. Had the same favourable conditions as to freight prevailed for European ports, especially for ports of the United Kingdom, as for American and Russian ports it may reasonably be surmised that the exports of produce to these ports would have developed in somewhat the same manner as the trade to the United States. Notwithstanding the opinion expressed by more than one witness that had not rates of freight been regulated by Conference / rules they would have fallen so low that tonnage would cease to be attracted to the port, the Commission experience some difficulty in believing that this would occur. Singapore is by its geographical position the natural collecting centre for the West Coast

---

*   See Appendix 18. /

of Sumatra, the Malay Peninsula, Java, Borneo, Moluccas, Celebes, and other Countries. If freights homeward from Singapore were on a low basis it would pay to send produce from outports for shipment here, while the geographical position of Singapore, the excellence of its harbour, its cheapness in the matter of supplies and labour, and its freedom from dues enable ships to make a profit on freights that would in other circumstances mean starvation.

24 In dealing with the subject of the trade of Singapore it has to be borne in mind that should it cease to be an *entrepot* for the produce of the outports it will be in danger of losing its position as a distributing centre for European and American manufactures. The local ships bringing produce to the Colony are in a position to carry manufactures to the outports at rates which would be generally unremunerative were it not that they get freight both ways. If the outports can get shipments to and from Europe at rates that will not allow of produce being shipped from Singapore the local ship-owning trade, under which heading must be included the owners of the smallest craft, may be expected to die out. The action and interaction of our trade with the outports was clearly shown by such witnesses as MR. MUHLINGHAUS.

25. In considering the effect of Conference rates of freight it must not be forgotten that they influence cargo not directly included in the Conference schedule. The Conference controls the amount of tonnage that may at any time be made available for the port, and at times when there is a large demand for freight room it is obvious that ships which can get other deadweight cargo at Conference rates are not anxious to take Rice at lower rates.

26. The majority of the Commission are disposed to think that the effects of artificially raised freights on the trade of the Colony are likely to be more felt in the near future than has been the case in the past. It may be assumed that the cessation of trouble in China and in South Africa has released and will release a good deal of tonnage. A portion of this released tonnage, not being able to find employment in the ports of the Colony may possibly find its way to the outports, and a marked condition of inequality between freights at the outports and Singapore, to the disadvantage of the latter, may arise. By inability to find cargo at Singapore is implied that merchants being tied to the Conference by the system of deferred rebates would be unable to load such steamers, any saving of freight on individual shipments being likely to be more than counterbalanced by loss of rebate and possible difficulties with regard to future, shipments.

27. Another Shipping Conference respecting the proceedings of which a representation was made to the Commission by a witness is the Bombay Conference – a Combination which we understand has been in force for some 7 or 8 years and to which the subscribing parties are the P. & O. Co., the Nippon Yusen Kai-

sha and the Rubattino line. This is a Combination of Shipping Companies only, not, as in the case of the Eastern Homeward Conference, of Shipping Companies and Merchants. The complaint was in respect of conditions imposed by one of these companies with respect to receipts for cargo. The matter appeared to us to be one in respect of which action by the Chamber of Commerce at Bombay or Singapore might be called for, if the grievance is a reasonable one...

W. T. TAYLOR.
W. J. NAPIER.
W. C. BROWN.
C. W. LAIRD.
A. GENTLE.

I qualify my concurrence by the rider attached.

J. M. ALLINSON.
23rd August, 1902. /

My first difference of opinion with the majority of the Commission arises out of clause (*c*) (page 4).

The opening paragraph in this Report acknowledges that "From its geographical position and natural advantages Singapore has come to be a great emporium and distributing centre for the products of the surrounding countries". Whilst it may be admitted that the higher rates of freight referred to in clause (*c*) may have accelerated the introduction of increased snipping facilities, these can have had no effect on the geographical position of Singapore; and ports that were out of the beaten track in the great trade route from West to East before the initiation of the Conference, retain their geographical positions.

The ports mentioned in clause (*c*) are Macassar, Manila, Batavia, and Bangkok; these ports were established in the years 1611, 1571, 1619, and 1769 respectively. When Sir Stamford Raffles selected Singapore, these ports had been in existence for centuries, and with the exception of Macassar they had fulfilled their purpose as ports of shipment for the Philippines, Java and Siam. What Sir Stamford Raffles foresaw was that a port on the "main line" was wanted at which ships of all nations must call, both outwards and homewards, and to which the products of the "surrounding countries" would be sent for distribution.

That important ports such as Macassar, Batavia, Manila, and Bangkok should in the ordinary evolution of trade expansion attract direct lines of steamers may be taken for granted, but this view the majority of the Commission altogether ignore. The port of Macassar is in a different position to the other ports, because like Singapore it is an "Emporium" and was such one hundred years before Singapore was even thought of.

For a great many years Copra was shipped from Macassar to Europe by small sailing ships, and an occasional steamer was chartered. With the enterprise that characterises our German friends, and which has brought their shipping to the front in all parts of the world (without the aid of the Straits Homeward Conference) they have for years kept in view the profitableness of increasing shipping facilities of the ports in the Celebes. The diversion of a small portion of the Copra trade has undoubtedly taken place, and this I attribute to direct shipment how available from Macassar. The opponents of the Conference and those that sympathise with them maintain that had there been no Conference there would have been no development in Shipping in the Eastern Archipelago. Mr. VON ROËSSING, who is frequently quoted from in the Report in support of-the views of the majority of the Commission, replied as follows, to a question asked by the Chairman: –

Q. – "You don't think a good deal of trade which used to pass through Singapore has been diverted to other neighbouring ports?"

Witness. – "To or from?"

Q. – "I am referring to produce that comes to the Colony and goes out again."

Witness. – "Well, as to produce formerly coming to the Colony, a very large part of such produce has through the development of the Dutch lines been diverted to and carried by them direct, but I don't see what this has to do with the Homeward Conference Singapore may have lost some part of the transhipments which used to pass through, but, on the other hand, has gained other transhipments. I suppose people attribute the decrease in the imports of Copra to the Conference. I may mention that the carrying of Copra direct from Celebes has been in view for a good many years, and the German Steamship Company which takes that part of the trade though a member of the Conference has not to rely upon the Conference. It is the action of the Dutch Steamship Companies which have taken up the carrying trade from the Celebes, Java and Sumatra ports."

I accept Mr. VON ROËSSING'S opinion on this point and I submit that there is no proof (unless the pious opinions of known opponents the Conference entirely unsupported by evidence is accepted as such) that

> "the higher rates that were for some time charged from these Settlements as compared with rates of freight from neighbouring and competing ports have contributed to the success if they are not primarily responsible for the establishment of new trade routes to which has been diverted trade that formerly came to this Colony".

And further I do not agree with the majority of the Commission

> "That the unfavourable effect on the trade of the Colony resulting from the development of these new routes is as yet only in the initial stage and may be expected / to increase with time unless the rates of freight from ports in these Settlements revert to their former relatively cheap basis as compared with rates from such ports as Macassar, Manila, Batavia and Bangkok,

My reasons are: –

That I deny that any new trade routes have been established. Direct shipments from all the Ports mentioned in clause (*c*) were established prior to 1896. To describe increased facilities from the Ports mentioned as the establishment of new "trade routes" is thoroughly misleading and incorrect. A line of German steamers now make Macassar a port of call, and the shipping facilities thus afforded have no doubt induced direct shipments; it may be noted chiefly of Copra. This point is of considerable interest, because the steamers that call at Macassar can give only direct shipment to say three ports, while the bulk of the articles exported other than Copra are articles that the whole world wants, and those continue to be sent to Singapore.

Singapore attracts produce from the surrounding countries because:

(*a*) It is on the "main line" and can give direct shipment to all parts of the world (which no other port can give).

(*b*) It is the largest and most representative Market in this part of the world.

(*c*) It finances the majority of the ventures in the surrounding countries.

I am of opinion therefore that the diversion of a portion of the Copra trade to Macassar is the outcome of increased shipping facilities and cannot be attributed to any recent action of the Straits Homeward Conference.

Whilst I agree with every word in clause (*e*), (page 6), this clause should have been prefaced by the statement that this unsatisfactory state of affairs was not initiated by the Conference, but only perpetuated by it. (*See* Appendix 1.) At the meeting of the Committee held on the 24th December, 1896, it was resolved

1. "That the rate to Glasgow and Greenock be 5/– over the London rate. Carried by 5 to 1. Mr. ADAMS advocated 7/– to 10/– respectively which had *hitherto* been obtained and wished to record a protest."

It is difficult to too strongly condemn the action of the British shipowners who refuse to British Ports, what Continental owners willingly grant to all Continental Ports. It may be here added that direct steamers to Liverpool take cargo at the London rate.

I cannot agree with the opinions expressed in the last paragraph on page 10, where it is stated "it cannot be denied that the influence of the Conference has not been satisfactory as far as regards the development of the Commerce of the Colony, and that had not the Conference been created the trade of the Colony would be greater than it now is. Had the same favourable conditions as to freight prevailed for European ports especially for ports of the United Kingdom, as for American and Russian ports it may be reasonably surmised that the exports of produce to these ports would have developed in the same manner as the trade to the United States."

If the last of these conclusions is correct then the opinion expressed in clause (*i*), (page 8), must necessarily be wrong. It is there expressed that: "The decrease in production in such articles as have shown a decrease is due to other causes than rates of freight."

If the decrease referred to were the outcome of natural causes, as is the opinion of the Commission, it is evident that there was only a given quantity of Produce available for distribution, and America with the cheap freights secured the lion's share. I do not deny the benefits to America, but I consider the assertion above quoted is not warranted by facts. The competition between America and Europe for what the Colony had to sell has been of the greatest advantage to the Colony as evidenced by the prices current in 1896 arid in 1901. The figures are: –

	1895.	*1901.*
Gambier	(December 1895) $ 8.20	(December 1901) $13.50
Black Pepper	(December 1895) $9 50	(December 1901) $31.75
Tapioca Small Flake	(December 1895) $3.65	(December 1901) $5.45
Sago Flour	(December 1895) $2.40	(December 1901) $3.60
Tin	(December 1895) $32.50	(December 1901) $65.75 /

To say that the trade of the Colony would have been greater than it now is, but for the creation of the Conference, is an assertion; pure and simple.

The prosperity of this port should be judged by: –

    (*a*) The volume of its trade.
    (*b*) The financial position of the Colony.
    (*c*) The value of land.
    (*d*) Tonnage Returns.

I cannot do more than reply to these headings in the briefest possibly way.

(*a*) *See* appendix No. 3.
    Total value of trade in 1895 $323,849,000
    Total value of trade in 1901 $528,152,000
an increase of over 60% since 1895.

(*b*) Colonial Revenue in 1895 $4,048,359
    Colonial Revenue in 1901 $7,041,686
    an increase of over 70% since 1895.

(*c*) So much has the trade prospered that the pressure for not only godown space but dwelling houses has so increased that it may without any exaggeration be said that the value of land has since 1896 been increased threefold.

(*d*) The tonnage of Merchant Vessels which entered and cleared from the ports of the Colony in the years 1895 and 1901 are given as:

1895	1901
–	–
Total Tons 11,684,795.	Total Tons 17,874.002.

The increase being 47%.

I am of opinion that the Conference has not in any way adversely affected the trade of this Colony in so much that the loss of a small portion of the Copra trade has been far more than made good by the greatly increased shipping facilities afforded by the Conference. I am also of opinion that the expansion of trade has been entirely satisfactory.

J. M. ALLINSON.

ANON., 'REPORT ON THE DEVELOPMENT AND PROGRESS OF CIVIL AVIATION IN MALAYA UP TO AND INCLUDING THE YEAR 1937' (1937)

Anon., 'Report on the Development and Progress of Civil Aviation in Malaya up to and including the Year 1937', National Archives, CO 323/1552/15, pp. 1–6, 9–11.

The following report covers every aspect of Malayan aviation in 1937 containing information on the administration of the sector, landing grounds and internal and international air services.

Anon., 'Report on the Development and Progress of Civil Aviation in Malaya up to and including the Year 1937' (1937), extract

GENERAL REVIEW

Considerable progress in all branches of Civil Aviation has been recorded during 1937.

Events of the past year calling for particular mention include the inauguration of the first internal Air service, the completion of Singapore Airport and the decision of the British and Dutch Governments to utilise air transport for the carriage of all first class mail matter without surcharge whenever possible.

The wide publicity accorded thereto throughout Malaya created a new interest in flying, and, by drawing attention to the many advantages to be derived from a wider use of air transport for commercial and private purposes, resulted in a marked increase during the latter part of the year in the loads carried by the regular air services and in the volume of private flying, as is indicated in Appendices 1 and 2.

A further development deserving of special notice is the completion during the past year of two private landing grounds, near Labis and Telok Anson respectively. This development is of particular interest, as it gives evidence of renewed interest in aviation on the part of owners of large estates and promises an early increase in the numbers of aircraft in private use.

ADMINISTRATION

The policy outlined in the last Report for the development of an administrative organisation has been adhered to and satisfactory progress towards the establishment of a unified technical control throughout the Peninsula has been made.

The adoption by the Federated Malay States of a revised Air Navigation Enactment in 1937 enabled their law on the subject to be brought into line with the Straits Settlements, and has paved the way for the issue of identical Regulations, which it is hoped will be promulgated early in 1938.

The appointment of Mr. A. NEWARK, formerly Chief Instructor to the Kuala Lumpur Flying Club, to the post of Airport Manager, Singapore, in March 1937, made it possible to commence training an Airport staff prior to the opening of the airport. This officer's wide experience of local flying conditions was of great value in this work, and ensured smooth operation of the aerodrome control from the opening date. His knowledge also will be of considerable assistance in the further task of training personnel for control duties at other aerodromes, which will be commenced in the new year.

A complete survey of all available seaplane alighting areas on the West Coast of Malaya was made during the year, in preparation for the new Empire Air Mail services, and all ground equipment required for the handling of the flying boats to be used thereon has been ordered.

A new Aviation Map of Malaya, drawn to a scale of 10 miles to one inch, was issued by the Surveyor-General, F.M.S., and S.S., in 1937. /

LANDING GROUNDS

Three new Civil Aerodromes have been added to the list published in the last annual report, and improvements have been effected to a number of those existing during the period under review.

Singapore Airport, the most important addition, was opened by His Excellency the Governor on 12th June, 1937, and on the following day all Civil Air activities in the Island of Singapore were transferred thereto. The aerodrome, situated 3 miles from the centre of the town with its modern buildings and complete equipment for land and marine aircraft, offers facilities equal to any in Asia for both aircraft and personnel.

Port Swettenham aerodrome, constructed partially from funds provided by the Royal Air Force, was opened to traffic on 17th September, 1937. This aerodrome provides two metalled runways,[1] each 700 yards long and is suitable for use by the largest of aircraft in all weathers. The position of this aerodrome, which is situated within two miles of the busy harbour of Port Swettenham will become of utmost value in future years.

Sitiawan, near the town and harbour of Lumut, was completed on 6th August, 1937. It is at present of little value commercially, but its presence adds greatly to the safety of aircraft following the coast route in bad weather.

A new hangar, capable of accommodating aircraft up to 100 feet in span has been constructed at Penang (Bayan Lepas Airport), the runway at Kuala Lumpur has been lengthened by 200 yards, and the approaches to Batu Pahat aerodrome have been improved.

Private landing grounds have been constructed on the Johore Labis Estate between Labis and Yong Peng by Messrs. Socfin, Ltd., and on the Jendarata Estate, 10 miles S.W. of Telok Anson, by Messrs. United Plantations, Ltd. Both Companies have given permission for the use of these grounds in emergency, and this public spirited action will be of great value, as these landing grounds are situated in districts otherwise devoid of open spaces suitable for forced landings.

A complete list of landing grounds now available in Malaya is given below.

State owned aerodromes. –
    Alor Star (Kedah)
    Batu Pahat (Johore)
    Ipoh (Perak)
    Kuala Lumpur (Selangor)
    Penang (Straits Settlements)
    Port Swettenham (Selangor)
    Singapore (Straits Settlements)
    Sitiawan (Perak)
    Sungei Patani (Kedah)
    Taiping (Perak)
Private Landing Grounds. –
    Dunlop Estate. Bahau (Negri Sembilan)
    Jendarata Estate. Telok Anson (Perak)
    Labis Estate. Labis (Johore)
    Ulu Bernam Estate. Bernam River (Perak) /
    Royal Air Force Aerodromes –
    Tengah. Singapore Island (Straits Settlements)
    Seletar. Singapore Island (Straits Settlements)
Marine Aerodromes –
    Glugor, Penang (Straits Settlments)
    Singapore (Straits Settlements)
Marine Alighting areas (with moorings) –
    Bass Harbour (Pulau Langkawi), Kedah
    Lumut (Dindings River), Perak
    Port Swettenham (Harbour), Selangor.

AIR SERVICES

INTERNAL AIR SERVICES

On the 28th June, 1937, Messrs. Wearne Brothers, Ltd., inaugurated Malaya's first internal air service, between Singapore, Kuala Lumpur and Penang. The machine used, a twin engined De Havilland "Rapide",[2] with accommodation for six passengers was flown out from England by the Company's Chief Pilot.

The service was operated thrice weekly at first but expanding traffic soon justified an increase in frequency, and as from the 25th September, 1937, a daily service (Sundays excepted) has been operated. The journey in each direction, including a stop of 20 minutes at Kuala Lumpur, is made in 3½ hours, and shows a saving of over 18 hours in comparison with other methods of transport.

Remarkable regularity has been achieved since the opening of the service and on only one occasion, when a tropical downpour flooded the aerodrome at Kuala Lumpur and caused a delay in departure of one hour, has a late arrival or departure been recorded.

For a new service traffic returns as shown in Appendix 3 may be regarded as satisfactory. Better results undoubtedly would have been achieved had it been possible to include Ipoh as a port of call, but unfortunately, owing to defective aerodrome foundations, it was not possible to permit heavy aircraft to use this aerodrome throughout the year.

The business was registered as a separate Company, under the name of Wearne's Air Services, Ltd., at the end of the year.

INTERNATIONAL AIR SERVICES

Imperial Airways and Associated Companies. – No change was made during 1937 in the services operated by Imperial Airways, Ltd., and its associated Companies.

Regularity on the Singapore Karachi section of the England Australia route, jointly operated by Imperial Airways, Ltd., and Indian Transcontinental Airways, Ltd., was much improved. On the Singapore–Sydney section Qantas Empire Airways, Ltd., as in the past, maintained a high standard of regularity. An increase in all classes of traffic carried to and from Malaya is reported.

The weekly Penang – Hong Kong service, operated by Imperial Airways (Far East), Ltd., also showed satisfactory results. As a result of the steady increase in loads carried, a twice weekly service is promised in the new year. /

At the end of the year the first flying boat survey flights, preparatory to the inauguration of the Empire Air Mail Service, were made. These flights aroused great interest locally, and the commencement of the accelerated service, carrying all first class mail matter without surcharge is eagerly awaited.

K.L.M. and K.N.I.L.M. – The decision of the Netherlands Government to transport all first class mail matter by air between Holland and the Netherlands Indies made it necessary for the Koninklijke Luchtvaart Maatschappij to replace their Douglas D. C. 2 aircraft[3] with the larger and more modern D.C. 3 type, and to increase the frequency of service from twice to three times weekly. The new schedule came into operation on 2nd October, 1937.

The marked increase in the number of passengers carried by this Company to and from Malaya show that the general public greatly appreciate the additional facilities provided.

The Koninklijke Nederlandsche Indische Luchtvaart Maatschappij maintained their weekly service between Singapore and Batavia throughout the year. An extension of this service to Australia is promised in the new year.

As from 24th October, 1937, this Company also operated a thrice weekly service between Medan and Penang, connecting with the K.L.M. main line service. This supplementary service was rendered necessary by the fact that the D.C. 3 machines were unable to use Medan aerodrome, as it proved to be too small for the safe operation of this type of aircraft.

FLYING CLUBS

The flying Club movement in Malaya continues to show satisfactory progress.

Membership, the number of hours flown and new pilots trained all show a marked increase over last year, and cross country flying is becoming increasingly popular.

A high standard of *ab initio*[4] instruction has been maintained and more attention has been given to tuition in night flying, instrument flying and other forms of advanced training, thereby raising the standard amongst qualified members.

Aircraft maintenance has been most satisfactory. No case of structural breakage or engine failure in flight occurred to Club aircraft during the year, in spite of the increase in hours flown and in cross country mileage.

Successful air rallies were held at Penang and Singapore. The opening of Singapore Airport was made the occasion for the latter, and the efforts of the Royal Singapore Flying Club and their visitors contributed largely to the success of the flying display which was held immediately after the opening ceremony.

The Royal Singapore Flying Club experienced the most successful year in its history during 1937, although handicapped by bad weather in the early part of the year and by the disturbances created by the move to the new Airport in June. Activities since its establishment in its new home indicate that even better results will be obtained in 1938. One new machine, a Miles Magister,[5] was purchased in June last and the Club now owns nine aircraft, all of which were in use at the end of the year.

The Kuala Lumpur Flying Club report successful results, in spite of several unfortunate accidents. Two new Tiger Moth[6] aircraft were / purchased, replacing the Gipsy Moths[7] which have now been written-off after six years satisfactory service. A second hand Spartan two seater was added to the Club fleet at the end of the year.

Although flying hours recorded by the Penang Flying Club show a slight decrease on last year, membership and numbers of pilots trained show an increase. The Club purchased another Gipsy Major Moth[8] during the year and now owns five machines.

The Perak Flying Club, in its first full year of operation, has achieved most gratifying results. Membership is already almost equal to that of the older Clubs and only one other Club succeeded in training more pilots daring the year.

Results achieved during the past year, in comparison with those of 1936 are given in Appendix 4. [...]

OTHER FLYING

Two privately owned aircraft have been registered in Malaya during the past year, bringing the number of such aircraft in active use up to a total of five.

The first machine to be operated solely for its own use by a public company in Malaya was also registered during the year. This machine, a twin engined De Havilland Dragonfly[9] was flown out from England in January, 1937, and has been in regular use since that date.

Private aircraft are visiting Malaya in increasing numbers. In addition to a number of visitors from the Netherlands East Indies for the opening of Singapore Airport, several tourist machines from Europe and Australia passed through the Peninsula. With the improved facilities now available this type of traffic is likely to show a steady increase in future. [...]

APPENDIX 1

Passengers Travelling to and from Malaya by Air

Year	Arrivals	Departures	Total
1934	–	–	896
1935	–	–	1,637
1936	–	–	2,095
1937	1,411	1,324	2,735

APPENDIX 2

Mails Despatched from Malaya by Air

1934	21,149 lbs.
1935	36,872 lbs.
1936	52,657 lbs.
1937	70,096 lbs.

APPENDIX 3

Internal Air Services*

Services scheduled	123
Services completed	123
Percentage regularity	100%
Total mileage flown	95,710
Passengers carried	818
Passenger-miles flown	221,735
Baggage and freight carried	14 tons.
Freight ton-miles	5,390
Mails carried	1,400 lbs.
Mail ton-miles	220 /

*   From 28/6/1937 only. /

APPENDIX 4

FLYING CLUB STATISTICS

Year	1936	1937
Flying membership	460	521
New licences issued	38	75
Hours flown	5,289	6,442
Aircraft owned	18	20

ANON., 'GROWTH OF THE POSTAL SERVICE. ILLUMINATING FACTS AND FIGURES', *THE SINGAPORE FREE PRESS EXHIBITION SUPPLEMENT*, 2 JANUARY 1932 (1932)

Anon., 'Growth of the Postal Service. Illuminating Facts and Figures', *The Singapore Free Press Exhibition Supplement*, 2 January 1932, National Archives, CO 273/582/3, p. 27.

The following text provides a thorough description of the postal service of Singapore in 1932. From 1949, under the Malayan Postal Union Agreement, the Postal Department was linked with that of the Federation of Malaya and standardised rules, regulations, procedures and postage rates were introduced.

Anon., 'Growth of the Postal Service. Illuminating Facts and Figures', *The Singapore Free Press Exhibition Supplement*, 2 January 1932 (1932), extract

The progress of a town is materially assisted or retarded by the postal facilities provided. No apology is offered, therefore, for this review of the growth of the postal service in Singapore.

In 1854 the Singapore Post Office was on the riverside near the Town Hall, as it was then called. The commercial quarter being on the other side of the river, business with the post office necessitated a river crossing until two years later, when a footbridge was erected and a toll of a quarter of a cent levied. Some years later it was moved to a portion of the site now occupied by Fullerton Building, its present home.

In the early days (1823 and thereabouts) letters from Europe usually arrived via Batavia.[1] The receipt within 10 months of an answer to a letter sent Home was a normal thing.

The practice of signifying by flags, the closing of the mails was initiated in 1853. A blue ensign referred to the Calcutta mail. A red to the mail for Europe, a white to the Australian mail and a yellow to the China mail.

Jardine Matheson and Co. and the Apcar steamers[2] began running between China and Calcutta in 1856, and share with the P. and O. the honour of being the first regular callers at Singapore. On Nov. 21, 1862, the first of the Messageries Imperiales[3] arrived from Suez with mails from London that had been 33 days in transit. The first German mail arrived in Singapore in August, 1886. The German mail called monthly, coming out and returning, and became a fortnightly service in 1899.

The notification regarding the approximate dates of arrival and departure of mail steamers was first issued in October 1891 and, with the exception of the break during the period of the Great War, has been continued until the present day.

FIRST P. AND O. MAIL

The first P. and O. mail arrived here on August 4, 1845, in pursuance of a contract made in 1844 for the conveyance of Home mails to China via Ceylon. The contract provided for a period of 140 hours from Ceylon to Penang and 45 hours from Penang to Singapore. The average number of days occupied in the transit of mail from England to Singapore was 43 in 1845, 33 in 1846, 44.75 in 1849, 23 in 1923, 24 in 1924, 22.5 in 1928, 23.5 in 1929 and 22.5 in 1930. From the beginning of 1853 the P. and O. mail service became a bi-monthly one.

For an annual contribution of $6,000 by the Colony, a fortnightly mail service between India and the Straits via Burmah was maintained. It was discontinued in 1884. The mails had come via India, as well as by other routes, since the days of Sir Stamford Raffles.

The Homeward British India Service from Singapore was begun in 1902 and in 1904 the outward European mails were also carried.

A parcel post service between Singapore and the United Kingdom by the P. and O. line was inaugurated by 1875. In 1917 this service was supplemented by a contract with the Holt line of steamers and with the British India line, the parcels in the last names instance being carried overland through India. The total number of parcels posted, delivered and in transit to and from Singapore during the year 1930 was 272,726. Registration of letters came into operation in Singapore in 1872. The fee was 12 cents. This was reduced to eight cents and in 1890 to five cents. It was raised in 1904 to 10 cents. The present fee is 15 cents per letter. Registered articles dealt with in Singapore during the year 1930 totalled 1,168,964.

Mail exchanges with Johore were by coach until 1903, when the Singapore – Kranji railway was opened. With the completion of the Johore railway in 1909 nearly all the mails between Singapore and the central and western portions of the Peninsula were conveyed by rail. The mail line was linked up with the Siamese system, and the mail service to Bangkok on this section was begun on Nov. 1, 1918. A month after the opening of the East Coast railway in August 1931, mails for Kelantan were sent by rail.

Having in mind the large part the Chinese have played in the development of Singapore, it is of interest to record that correspondence between Chinese in Singapore and their relatives and friends in China and remittances of money to the family in some remote China village lay in the hands of a few Chinese merchants until the year 1876. Notice of the position had been taken three years earlier, but there was considerable correspondence between Singapore and the Imperial authorities, the British Minister at Pekin, the Consuls in China and the authorities at Hong Kong before finally a "Chinese Post Office" was opened in Market Street, Singapore, on Dec. 15, 1876. The monopoly which the Chinese letter collectors and money remitters had built up was broken by insistence that all letters to China and from China, from and to Chinese in Singapore, should pass through the post.

The number of such letters despatched through the Market Street post office in 1880 was 80, 000. In 1889 Chinese letters jumped to 280,000, in 1914 the number was over a million and in 1930 reached a total of 1,670,135. In 1887 the Chinese sub-post office in Market Street was removed to the General Post Office with no resulting disorganisation, and the post of Chinese sub-postmaster was abolished in 1920. The letters still reach the General Post Office largely through licensed Chinese letter shops, of which there were 198 in Singapore in 1930 as compared with 16 in 1891.

The first money order service from Singapore was with the United Kingdom and was inaugurated in 1871. A money order service within Malaya was introduced the same year, a service with Hong Kong, China and Japan in 1878, a service with Ceylon in 1882, with Australia, Labuan and North Borneo in 1885, and, from Jan. 15, 1885, arrangements were made for the use of the United Kingdom as intermediary for the transmission of money orders to a great many countries with which the United Kingdom has exchanges. Siam and Sarawak entered into agreements for the exchange of money orders in 1888, Kelantan in 1907, Kedah in 1910 and the Netherlands East Indies in 1911.

A telegraphic money order service with the rest of Malaya was introduced in 1910. This was extended to the United Kingdom in 1916.

The public, accustomed to walking up to a post office counter and despatching a money order as a matter of course, hardly realise that such privileges and aids to trade and industry were gradually introduced as the country developed. Money sent away from Singapore by money order in 1930 amounted to $3,679,958 and money arriving through the same channel amounted to $1,576,654.

Those who have had occasion to send postal orders to Britain may be interested to learn that this service was introduced in 1885, and that it was not until 1904 that British postal orders could be cashed in Singapore.

Who has not at some time or other bought goods from Home on the cash-on-delivery system? In 1909 insured and uninsured parcels began to be exchanged between Singapore and the United Kingdom and certain British Colonies and Protectorates. The following year the service, having evidently revealed a keen demand, was extended to the Federated Malay States, Johore, Kelantan and Sarawak, and in 1913 to Kedah and British North Borneo. A similar service with India was inaugurated in 1912. That the convenience of being able to telegraph from some up-country station "Please send such-and-such an article C.O.D." [4] is being taken full advantage of is indicated by the fact that during 1930, 23,486 such parcels were sent away from Singapore on the cash-on delivery system. The value was $268,587. The corresponding figures for arrivals were 9,386 and $213,723.

It was not until the year 1891 that it was possible to insure parcels sent through the post from Singapore, and then the privilege applied only to exchanges with England. The following year the system was applied to all descriptions of articles sent by post to wherever there was service from Singapore.

With the facilities now available for sending letters by air mail, messages by wireless, and for telephoning to Kuala Lumpur, Ipoh and Penang, it is difficult to realise that there was a time within comparatively recent memory when there was no telegraph office in Singapore. But such indeed is the case. The Singapore Government Telegraph Office opened in 1909 the line from Singapore to Kuala Lumpur and Penang being opened for public traffic on May 17 and June 17 respectively of that year. Since June, 1930, it have since been possible to send from Singapore to Kuala Lumpur and Penang and receive from those towns telegraphic messages throughout the night.

Wireless communication between Singapore and the outer world was established in 1915, and Sarawak was brought into communication in 1917. In 1930, 13,008 wireless messages were sent from Singapore and 12,664 were received. Wireless messages from the aeroplane "Spirit of Australia" on its way from Australia to London were received by the Paya Lebar Wireless Station on Nov. 7, 1928. It was the first time short wave signals had been received from an aeroplane by a Malayan Government wireless station.

In 1929 Singapore was made the collecting office for air mail correspondence from Malaya for the internal Australian air service via Perth. On August 2 of the same year a fortnightly air mail service was begun from Penang to London via Karachi, and on Nov. 30 the service became a weekly one. At first the average time occupied in transit was over 19 days, but towards the end of the year there was an improvement. Beginning from October, 1929, a direct mail was made up at Singapore for Basle, Switzerland, containing air mail correspondence for Switzerland, France, Italy, Germany and Continental Europe generally. A weekly air mail service between Singapore, Palembang and Batavia was inaugurated in March 1930, Singapore being made the collecting office for air mail correspondence from Malaya. A fortnightly air mail service to Europe was begun in October, 1930. By utilising the Dutch service from Medan to Amsterdam, and this has now become a weekly service as from October 16, 1931.

The Singapore Post Office Savings Bank was inaugurated in 1877. During 1930 deposits numbered 17,200 to the value of $3,338,136.

Beginning with one postmaster, seven clerks, and 19 other subordinates including postmen in 1867, the Singapore General Post Office has grown with the service it has had to give until to-day the total staff numbers 800, including 11 senior officers and 310 clerks.

HUMAN CAPITAL

From 1891 to 1940, Malaya experienced rapid population growth; numbers rising from 1.7m in 1891 to 5.9m in 1947 (owing to the war there was no 1941 census) (see Table 1). The rise was partly related to falling death rates caused by improvements in infant welfare and the use of anti-malarial drugs, but mainly the result of Chinese and Indian immigration, the nature of which is discussed in the General Introduction. Indian migrants were recruited through the indenture, Kangani and free labour systems. From 1844 to 1910, approximately 250,000 indentured labourers arrived in Malaya. Plantations employed one of the recruitment companies in Madras or Nagapatnam or sent their own agents to South India, who would travel to cities and villages and enlist those wishing to emigrate. In return for an advance of the cost of travelling to Malaya, those engaged signed an indenture contract in which they agreed to work for a named employer for a fixed wage and for a fixed period of five years, and, from 1904 and the Labour Ordinance of that year, three years. Once they had signed, they were sent to a government transit camp, where they were shaved and bathed and then despatched in grossly overcrowded ships to Penang. Here, they were kept at a quarantine station for one week or longer and, if judged healthy, forwarded to their employer's estate. They were released from their contract on the completion of the indenture period, though only if they had paid off their travelling expenses. As they were forced to purchase food and other essential items from a shop owned by their employer at grossly inflated prices (the truck system), many failed to repay the advance and had to remain until the debt had been worked off. At the end of the indenture period, most returned home, though some signed a further contract.[1]

Table 1: Southeast Asian populations, 1891–1947 (000s).

Countries	1891	1911	1931	1947
Burma	7,772	12,115	14,667	19,051
Malaya	1,710	2,651	4,348	5,900
Thailand	6,670	8,266	11,506	17,443
Indonesia	33,800	–	60,727	–
Indochina	13,400	16,395	21,450	31,397
Philippines	7,635	8,835	13,405	19,234

Source: G. Huff, 'Gateway Cities and Urbanisation in Southeast Asia before World War II',
    University of Oxford Discussion Papers in Economic and Social History, 96 (2012), pp.
    1–45, on p. 38.

Indenture recruitment was abandoned by estates long before 1910 when the Malayan administration, under pressure from the British and Indian governments and Indian nationalists, abolished it. Over time, its drawbacks had begun to outweigh its main advantage, low-cost labour. The recruitment companies found it increasingly difficult to obtain the number of workers needed and charged ever higher fees and those recruited often lacked agricultural experience or were physically unable to undertake heavy manual labour. Others rebelled against the low wages/truck system and either refused to work or ran away, finding employment on other estates. Between 1902 and 1910, 13 per cent of Indian migrants absconded, even though the penalties were severe; deserters could be fined or jailed, and, when they were returned to their employer, were usually severely beaten. Most, not surprisingly, returned home once the indenture period had been served, despite numerous inducements to stay. Penang Sugar Estates Ltd, for example, offered those who signed new contracts a house and garden plot and permitted them to undertake paid seasonal work for Malay rice farmers.[2]

Kangani recruitment was a variant of the indenture system in that workers were indebted to and employed by Kanganis, estate overseers, who travelled to India, engaged members of their own families, village, tribe or caste and hired those recruited to their plantation owners at a given day rate. The system, under which 62 per cent of the Indian migrants who came to Malaya from 1844 to 1938 were engaged, was approved by the British government, as the labourers were theoretically 'free', and by the estates. To maximize their returns, Kanganis recruited large numbers of good quality workers, which over time enabled plantations to cut day rates, and, through social ties and monetary and other obligations, ensured that they worked hard, did not abscond and remained in Malaya for as long as they were needed. However, the system was regarded by Indian nationalists as exploitative and in 1938 it was banned by the Indian government.[3]

The proportion of Indians making their own way to Malaya as wage labourers rose from 12 per cent in 1920 to over 91 per cent by the 1930s. The increased flow was partly related to the existence of formal and informal networks between India and Malaya, which allowed workers to obtain employment before they left their villages, and support from plantation owners, who often found such migrants cheaper to employ than those recruited through the Kangani system, though many complained that they were far more difficult to control. A more important factor, however, was the Indian Immigration Fund established in 1908 when it became apparent that the increased demand for labour brought about by the expansion of rubber cultivation threatened to raise wages. The Fund paid the travelling expenses of all migrants, plus quarantine charges and the cost of repatriation to

India, and was financed via obligatory quarterly fees paid by all employers of Indian labour, the size of which were related to the number of workers employed. Administered by an Indian Immigration Committee, comprising government and planter representatives, and an Emigration Commissioner and Assistant Emigration Commissioner stationed respectively in Madras and Negapatam, the Fund by 1912 had funded 73,761 passages at a cost of $8m.[4]

Like their Indian counterparts, Chinese migrants were at first employed on indenture contracts. The recruitment system was controlled by Chinese brokers, often Penang merchants with financial interests in mining, who via agents and recruiters in Xiamen, Shantou and Hong Kong, obtained workers for the mines of Perak and Southern Siam and the plantations of Sumatra. The men recruited were sent to coolie depots at the main ports of demarcation and then herded onto junks or steamships that transported them to their destination. Initially, migrant travelling costs were paid by the owners of these ships, who then recovered the money from the contractors (the 'credit ticket system'). Later, after criticism from the Qing Governor of Liang Guang, the expenses were directly met by the contractor (the 'borrow fare system'). On arrival in Singapore or Penang, the migrants would be locked in a compartment of the vessel or in a Chinese lodging house to prevent them absconding, and, after the broker had received the sum owed, moved to the mine/plantation. Here, the contractor would place them in a Kongsi House, owned by himself, where they would be supervised for the duration of their time at the mine/estate by a further employee, the Kongsi headman, who would supervise their work, maintain discipline and pay them.[5]

The indenture contracts were slightly different from those signed by Indian migrants. Labourers agreed to work for a fixed wage until the advances they had received had been paid off. Unskilled labourers who cleared land and constructed and repaired waterways were paid on a piecemeal basis (the Nai-Chiang system) and others according to the number of days or hours worked (the Kong-si-Kong and Tai-Ki-Tsai systems, respectively). Food, opium and other necessities were provided by the Kongsi headman, who also operated the local gambling house. Once or twice per year, he would deduct the cost of the articles supplied plus any gambling debts from his coolies' wages and give them the balance, from which they would pay a portion of their travelling costs. As food was provided at a mark-up of 30 to 60 per cent and opium at a premium of 200 to 300 per cent and most of the gambling house games were rigged, many workers received no or minus wages, never repaid the money they owed and remained at the mine/plantation for decades.[6]

For the miner/estate owner, the system had both benefits and drawbacks. The advantages were that the management of workers was undertaken by Kongsi headmen, especially important for European entrepreneurs, turnovers were low and labour easily replaced. Drawbacks were ever-increasing recruitment fees,

contractor fraud and, after the expansion of rubber cultivation and a corresponding increase in employment opportunities, greater worker indiscipline, riots
breaking out at tin mines in Rasa and Rawang in respectively 1902 and 1904,
and high levels of desertion, despite tough sanctions. Eventually, the system's
deficiencies outweighed its benefits and mines and planters began to employ
free labour employed on a tribute or share-wage basis. On discovering that these
alternatives were feasible and concerned at the exploitation of workers, the Perak
administration in 1894 made indenture recruitment illegal, followed in 1895 by
Selangor and Negri Sembilan. In 1908, the truck system was prohibited, and in
June 1914 indentured labour was terminated across the whole of Malaya.[7]

Chinese migrants began to pay their own travelling expenses, obtaining the
money from family and friends who had migrated earlier. Those who worked on
established rubber estates received a normal wage and those employed on new
rubber plantations signed six to eight year share-wage contracts. In return for
the cultivation of catch crops and the planting, weeding and tending of rubber
trees, they received a fixed monthly payment, a portion of the net revenue from
the sale of the catch crops and a per acre bonus for clearing the land at the end
of the agreement after which they became wage labourers. If they were to enter
the mining sector, they would band together with other migrants and the group
would sign an agreement with a financier, who would supply foodstuffs, provisions, clothes and opium, and a tribute contract with a mine owner. The latter
would establish the mine, covering the cost of obtaining the lease, clearing the
land and installing living accommodation and basic equipment, and the group
would be responsible for mining the tin in return for a proportion of the output,
usually 10 to 20 per cent. After extraction, the group's share of the ore would be
sold either by the mine owner, who would give the group the proceeds (from
which the financier would be repaid), or by the financier himself, who would
pass onto the group the sale price minus the cost of the supplies plus interest.
Such arrangements proved highly popular in the early twentieth century; by
1908, the number of tribute workers in the FMS had reached 118,864, 60 per
cent of the country's total mining labour force.[8]

The experiences of migrants once they had arrived in Malaya varied according
to race. The working conditions of Indians were initially poor. Heavy workloads,
insanitary living accommodation and the absence of medical care led to high
mortality rates, particularly among new recruits with little or no immunity to disease. Protests from humanitarian groups and a realization that new arrival death
rates of up to 80 or 90 per cent increased production costs and discouraged future
migration, prompted the Malayan government to introduce various regulations
that were consolidated in 1902 into the Labour Code, which laid down basic
requirements relating to pay, hours of work and accommodation and was later
supplemented by further legislation. To ensure that employers conformed to the

Code, a Labour Department was established headed by a Controller of Labour, who arranged the inspection of premises and to whom migrants could address complaints. Businesses breaching its conventions could be prosecuted and even closed down. Although generally successful, the Code was criticized by Indian nationalists, and, in 1923 following the passage of the Indian Emigration Act of the previous year, regulation was passed to the Indian government. A new set of stringent rules were framed that set a minimum wage, limited the working week to six days and the working day to six to nine hours and defined working conditions, living accommodation and the provision of medical and educational facilities. An agent was stationed in Malaya with full access to all places of employment, which were additionally regularly inspected by Indian leaders.[9]

No similar regulation was introduced for Chinese migrants. As coolies were employed by Kongsi rather than plantations/mines, they were not covered by the Labour Code and the Malayan government was reluctant to provide alternative protection, fearing that it would prompt a great influx of migrants that would threaten the social and political fabric of the country. Supervision of working conditions was thus undertaken by the Secretary for Chinese Affairs, who appointed a Protector of Chinese Migrants, along with several deputies. Unfortunately, the various holders of the post had insufficient resources to perform their role and the conditions of migrant workers were often dire. Workers were beaten if they failed to complete the work assigned to them, forced to live in insanitary accommodation, worked in unsafe environments and were denied medical care. The result was annual death rates of between 50 and 250 per 1,000. In an attempt to improve such conditions, many migrants from the early 1930s formed themselves into trade unions. Initially suppressed by both employers and by government officials, convinced that they were led by communists, their right to exist was gradually accepted and, after widespread strikes in 1937, basic trade union and industrial relations legislation was enacted.[10]

In Burma recruitment of Indian workers was through the Maistry and free labour systems. Maistries, labour contractors, would agree to deliver to an estate, mill or business a given number of Indians on a specified date, the work of whom they would manage, paying the employer a deposit as security. They would then use agents in India to recruit the workers, who would agree to work for the Maistry until their travelling costs were repaid, and to move them to an emigration depot, where a government appointed Emigration Agent and Medical Inspector would ensure that they were healthy and migrating of their own free will. From there, they would be transported to Burma, either by sea or overland from Bengal to Arakan, where Head Maistries would divide them into work gangs of between ten and twenty migrants headed by Charge Maistries. Gangs would then be sent to employers, who would refund the Maistry's security and pay him the agreed commission. As with Malayan Kangani recruitment, over time the power of the

Maistry dissipated. Shipping companies, such as the British Indian Steam Navigation Co., which transported migrants to Burma, began to act as labour recruiters both for Maistries and for employers. More significantly, Indians began to pay for their own transport and arrange their own employment, obtaining loans and contacts from relatives and friends already working in Burma.[11]

Note: Information on human capital can also be found in the following sources/ themes:

Topic	Source	Volume/Theme
Mine Labour conditions in Malaya and Burma	Anon., *Golden Raub*; G. E. Greig, *Mining in Malaya*; Anon., *Report on the Mineral Production of Burma 1939*.	Volume 2/Mining
Occupations, Malaya (1921)	Anon., *The Manufacturing Industries of the British Empire*	Volume 2/Industry
Occupations, British North Borneo (1921)	Anon., *The Manufacturing Industries of the British Empire*	Volume 2/Industry
Transport of Indian migrants to Malaya	The British India Steam Navigation Company Mail and Indian Immigration Contract, 1923'	Volume 3/Transport and Communications

Notes

1. A. Kaur, 'Indian Labour, Labour Standards, and Workers' Health in Burma and Malaya, 1900–1940', *Modern Asian Studies*, 40:2 (2006), pp. 425–75, on pp. 443–4; R. K. Jain, 'Tamilian Labour and Malayan Plantations, 1840–1938', *Economic and Political Weekly*, 28:43 (1993), pp. 2636–70, on p. 2367; J. Hagan and A. D. Wells, 'The British and Rubber in Malaya, c1890–1940', in G. Patmore, J. Shields and N. Balnave (eds), *The Past is Before Us: Proceedings of the Ninth National Labour History Conference* (Sydney: University of Sydney, 2005), p. 4. There were also a number of speculator recruiters, who would offer the men they enlisted to estates (M. Periasamy, 'Indian Migration into Malaya and Singapore', *Biblioasia*, 3:3 (2007), pp. 4–11, on p. 5).

2. L. H. Lees, 'International Management in a Free-Standing Company: The Penang Sugar Estates, Ltd. and the Malayan Sugar Industry, 1851–1914', *Business History Review*, 81:1 (2007), pp. 27–57, on pp. 48–9, 51; A. Gordon, 'Contract Labour in Rubber Plantations: Impact of Smallholders in Colonial South-East Asia', *Economic and Political Weekly*, 36:10 (2001), pp. 847–60, on p. 854; Periasamy, 'Indian Migration', pp. 5–6; Jain, 'Tamilian Labour', p. 2365; Hagan and Wells, 'The British and Rubber', p. 4. Some argued that the recruiters deliberately restricted the supply of labour in order to raise fees (Kaur, 'Indian Labour', p. 443).

3. Kaur, 'Indian Labour', pp. 443–5; Hagan and Wells, 'The British and Rubber', p. 4; Jain, 'Tamilian Labour', p. 2365; J. Lim, 'Chinese Merchants in Singapore and the China Trade, 1819–1959', *Chinese Southern Diaspora Studies*, 5 (2011–12), pp. 79–115, on

p. 84. See also S. S. Amrith, 'Indians Overseas? Governing Tamil Migration to Malaya 1870–1941', *Past & Present*, 208:1 (2010), pp. 231–61.

4. Jain, 'Tamilian Labour', p. 2365; W. T. Yuen, 'Chinese Capitalism in Colonial Malaya, 1900–1941' (DPhil. dissertation, University of Hong Kong, 2010), pp. 1–450, on p. 202; W. G. Huff and G. Caggiano, 'Globalization, Immigration, and Lewisian Elastic Labor in Pre-World War II Southeast Asia', *Journal of Economic History*, 67:1 (2007), pp. 33–68, on p. 43; A. Gordon, 'Colonial Surplus and Foreign-Owned Investment in South-East Asia', *Economic and Political Weekly*, 39:4 (2004), pp. 371–8, on p. 377. Until 1910, the Fund was named the Tamil Immigration Fund.

5. Hagan and Wells, 'The British and Rubber', p. 4; Lees, 'International Management', p. 50; T. Tojo, 'Chinese-Operated Tin Mining in Perak during the Late Nineteenth Century: A New Style of Labour Employment and the Problem of Absconding', *Chinese Southern Diaspora Studies*, 3 (2009), pp. 204–15, on p. 6.

6. Tojo, 'Chinese-Operated', p. 6, 10; Huff and Caggiano, 'Globalization', p. 40; Yuen, 'Chinese Capitalism', p. 109.

7. W. G. Huff, 'Sharecroppers, Risk, Management, and Chinese Estate Rubber Development in Interwar British Malaya', *Economic Development and Cultural Change*, 40:4 (1992), pp. 743–73, on p. 747; Yuen, 'Chinese Capitalism', pp. 107, 111, 152; Lees, 'International Management', p. 50. From 1885, those who absconded in Perak faced fines, prison and eighteen strokes of the lash.

8. Huff and Caggiano, 'Globalization', pp. 40–1; Yuen, 'Chinese Capitalism', pp. 112–13.

9. Jain, 'Tamilian Labour', p. 2364; C. Z. Guilmoto, 'The Tamil Migration Cycle, 1830–1950', *Economic and Political Weekly*, 28:3/4 (1993), pp. 111–20, on p. 116; Hagan and Wells, 'The British and Rubber', p. 4; Kaur, 'Indian Labour', pp. 441, 453–4.

10. Hagan and Wells, 'The British and Rubber', p. 4; Yuen, 'Chinese Capitalism', p. 107; C. A. Trocki, 'Opium and the Beginnings of Chinese Capitalism in Southeast Asia', *Journal of Southeast Asian Studies*, 33: (2002), pp. 297–314, on p. 7; J. N. Parmer, 'Trade Unions in Malaya', *Annals of the American Academy of Political and Social Science*, 310 (1957), pp. 142–50, on p. 142.

11. Kaur, 'Indian Labour', pp. 430, 434–5; Huff and Caggiano, 'Globalization', p. 45.

VLIELAND, *BRITISH MALAYA: A REPORT ON THE 1931 CENSUS* (1932)

C. A. Vlieland, *British Malaya: A Report on the 1931 Census* (Singapore: Government Publication, 1932), pp. 246–51.

Charles Archibald Vlieland (1890–1974) began his career as a lowly Malayan civil servant, but rapidly rose to become a District Officer, the Superintendent of Census (1930–2), the Financial Commissioner and Auditor General of Johore and the Malayan Secretary for Defence (1938–41). The tables extracted from his 1931 Census report detail employment by occupation in the Straits Settlements, the FMS and the UFMS and in the States that made up each territory and reflect the dominance of the rubber and tin mining sectors. Occupation data from the 1921 Census can be found in *The Manufacturing Industries of the British Empire Overseas* in the Industry section of Volume 2 of the collection.

C. A. Vlieland, *British Malaya: A Report on the 1931 Census* (1932), extract

TABLE 118.
STRAITS SETTLEMENTS. – ALL RACES BY INDUSTRY.

Category.	Order.	Group.	No.	Singapore Municipality. Males.	Females.	Singapore Remainder. Males.	Females.	Penang. Males.	Females.	Malacca. Males.	Females.	Colony. Males.	Females.
A. AGRICULTURE AND FISHING.	I. Fishing	1. Fishing	1.	1,723	14	3,393	29	7,727	100	3,004	40	15,847	183
	II. Agriculture	1. Rice Cultivation.	1.	2	–	417	265	7,204	2,278	944	343	8,567	2,886
		2. Rubber Cultivation	2.	871	49	5,440	680	13,111	4,056	25,906	6,835	45,328	11,620
		3. Coconut Cultivation	3.	82	–	315	143	2,076	276	395	13	2,868	432
		4. Oil Palm Cultivation	4.	37	2	6	–	13	7	4	–	60	9
		5. Market Gardening	5.	1,667	258	4,209	222	3,852	173	2,502	371	12,230	1,024
		7. Stock-rearing and Poultry Farming	6.	739	72	628	46	1,758	378	160	58	3,285	554
		8. Forestry and Wood-cutting	8.	183	1	417	4	433	11	695	17	1,728	33
		9. Other or Multifarious Agricultural Industry	9.	3,598	67	4,957	146	11,954	2,560	3,747	424	24,256	3,197

Category.	Order.	Group.	No.	Singapore Municipality.		Singapore Remainder.		Penang.		Malacca.		Colony.	
				Males.	Females.	Males.	Females.	Males.	Females.	Males.	Females.	Males.	Females.
B. EXTRACTION AND PREPARATION OF, AND WORK IN, MATERIAL SUBSTANCES AND ELECTRICITY SUPPLY.	III. Mining and Quarrying and Treatment oil Non-metallicerous Mine and Quarry Products.	1. Tin Mining	11.	60	–	49	–	156	3	52	4	317	7
		2. Other Mining and Quarrying Industries	12.	162	–	1,346	–	540	40	264	17	2,312	57
		3. Treatment of Non-metalliferous Products.	13.	360	5	106	1	77	9	19	–	562	15
	IV. Manufacture of Bricks, Pottery and Glass.	1. Manufacture of Bricks, Pottery and Glass.	14.	235	1	181	2	233	7	61	–	710	10
	V. Manufacture of Chemicals, Dyes, Explosives, Paints, Oils, Grease.	1. Manufacture of Vegetable Oils and Soap	15.	211	8	16	–	149	3	15	3	391	14
	VI. Manufacture of Metals, Machines, Implements, Conveyances, Jewellery, Watches.	1. Tin Smelting	16.	5	–	8	–	469	1	–	–	482	1
		2. Foundry Work	17.	110	1	2	–	76	–	3	–	191	1
		3. Forge Work	18.	856	21	64	–	420	–	127	2	1,467	23
		4. Motor Car and Cycle Repair	19.	1,083	7	83	–	423	1	191	1	1,780	9
		5. Tin, Brass and Copper Smithing	20.	523	3	175	–	190	1	99	2	987	6
		6. General and Undefined Mechanical Engineering	21.	4,281	17	660	–	1,017	1	245	–	6,203	18
		7. Gold and Silver Smithing and Electro-plating	22.	1,604	15	78	–	1,611	19	643	3	3,936	37

Category.	Order.	Group.	No.	Singapore Municipality.		Singapore Remainder.		Penang.		Malacca.		Colony.	
				Males.	Females.	Males.	Females.	Males.	Females.	Males.	Females.	Males.	Females.
		8. Watch and Clock Manufacture and Repair	23.	250	8	4	–	122	1	60	–	436	9
		9. Electrical Work	24.	1,169	5	220	–	533	–	97	–	2,019	5
		11. Other Industries	26.	101	–	10	–	104	–	1	–	216	–
	VII. Manufacture of Textiles and Textile Goods (not dress).	1. Weaving	27.	5	8	5	7	99	124	2	3	111	142
		2. Rope and Net Making	28.	43	–	34	1	46	4	–	–	122	5
		3. Dyeing	29.	199	1	–	–	33	–	5	–	237	1
		4. Other Industries	30.	247	9	21	–	24	43	22	23	312	75
	VIII. Preparation of Skins and Leather and Manufacture of Goods of Leather and Leather Substitute (not clothing or foot-wear)	1. Tanning	31.	43	1	–	–	103	1	–	–	146	2
		2. Other Industries	32.	22	2	–	–	–	–	–	–	22	2
	IX. Manufacture of Clothing (not knitted).	1. Manufacture of Boots, Shoes and Clogs	33.	1,756	132	43	2	601	14	147	2	2,547	150
		2. Manufacture of Other Articles of Clothing	34.	3,400	506	222	20	1,445	225	581	121	5,648	872
	X. Manufacture of Food, Drink and Tobacco.	1. Manufacture of Food	35.	1,920	64	429	20	862	74	294	14	3,506	172
		2. Manufacture of Drink	36.	81	22	15	–	161	1	62	–	320	23
		3. Manufacture of Tobacco	37.	85	62	6	–	91	38	5	–	187	100

Category.	Order.	No.	Group.	Singapore Municipality. Males.	Females.	Singapore Remainder. Males.	Females.	Penang. Males.	Females.	Malacca. Males.	Females.	Colony. Males.	Females.
	XI. Wood Working; Manufacture of Cane and Basket ware, Furniture, Fittings (not elsewhere enumerated).	38.	1. Timber-sawing	1,739	8	33	–	212	–	136	–	2,120	8
		39.	2. Carpentry, Joinery and Furniture Making	8,071	66	990	7	3,545	347	1,228	786	13,834	1,206
		40.	3. Basketry	936	194	62	15	366	12	63	50	1,427	271
		41.	4. Boat and Ship Building	335	–	7	–	130	–	14	–	486	–
	XII. Paper Making; Manufacture of Stationery and Stationery Requisites, Printing, Bookbinding and Photography.	42.	1. Printing and Bookbinding	994	5	18	–	339	–	47	–	1,398	5
		43.	2. Photography	263	9	6	–	86	5	16	–	371	14
	XIII. Building, Decorating, Stone and Slate Cutting and Dressing and Contracting.	44.	1. House Building, Painting, etc.	4,458	188	583	2	1,710	20	534	9	7,285	219
		45.	2. Contracting	376	4	43	–	205	–	82	1	706	5
	XIV. Other Manufacturing Industries.	46.	1. Rubber Goods Manufacture.	802	838	730	85	323	17	158	1	2,013	941
		47.	2. Other Industries	45	26	3	–	37	3	3	–	88	29
	XV. Gas, Water, Electricity	48.	1. Gas, Water and Electricity Supply	7	–	1	–	3	–	–	–	11	–
C. TRANSPORT AND COMMUNICATION.	XVI. Transport and Communication	49.	1. Railway Transport	506	1	275	3	743	6	134	4	1,657	14
		50.	2. Road Transport	18,276	21	2,051	91	7,745	10	3,745	3	31,817	125
		51.	3. Water Transport	20,792	59	1,875	1	5,632	13	548	2	28,847	75

Category	Order	Group	No.	Singapore Municipality. Males.	Females.	Singapore Remainder. Males.	Females.	Penang. Males.	Females.	Malacca. Males.	Females.	Colony. Males.	Females.
		4. Post, Telegraph and Telephone Service	52.	467	45	142	9	335	12	81	10	1,025	77
		5. Other Industries	53.	2,272	6	301	–	1,125	1	223	–	3,921	7
D. COMMERCE AND FINANCE.	XVII. Commerce and Finance	1. Banking	54.	336	2	22	–	103	–	30	–	491	2
		2. Insurance	55.	144	4	4	–	15	–	2	–	165	4
		3. Broking and Agency	56.	1,174	10	92	–	453	3	70	–	1,789	13
		4. Auctioneering and Valuing	57.	16	–	4	–	69	–	13	–	102	–
		5. Moneylending, Pawnbroking, Money changing	58.	734	8	8	–	697	2	291	–	1,730	10
		6. Wholesale and Retail Dealing	59.	33,765	972	3,592	37	16,879	333	6,056	276	60,292	1,618
		7. Street Vending and Peddling	60.	19,651	848	2,201	25	9,218	515	3,081	182	34,151	1,570
		8. Other industries	61.	179	2	11	–	100	6	13	1	303	9
E. PUBLIC ADMINISTRATION AND DEFENCE.	XVIII. Public Administration and Defence.	1. Central Government	62.	1,645	211	271	24	911	45	369	13	3,196	293
		2. Municipal Administration	63.	790	22	85	1	292	4	85	2	1,252	29
		3. Navy	64.	8	–	28	–	–	–	–	–	36	–
		4. Army	65.	996	–	521	–	8	–	2	–	1,527	–
		5. Air Force	66.	22	–	279	–	–	–	–	–	301	–
		6. Police	67.	1,626	1	334	–	1,385	2	494	–	3,839	3

Category	Order	Group	No.	Singapore Municipality. Males.	Females.	Singapore Remainder. Males.	Females.	Penang. Males.	Females.	Malacca. Males.	Females.	Colony. Males.	Females.
F. Professional Occupations.	XIX. Professions	1. Religion	68.	423	150	48	4	359	71	164	10	994	235
		2. Law	69.	305	–	11	–	152	2	31	–	499	2
		3. Medicine, Dentistry and Veterinary Surgery	70.	4,333	790	354	77	1,518	547	607	290	6,812	1,704
		4. Education	71.	2,086	1,137	461	85	2,275	619	1,134	208	5,956	2,049
		5. Accountancy	72.	206	1	25	–	75	–	6	–	312	1
		6. Engineering, Architecture and Surveying	73.	646	7	178	–	253	2	161	–	1,238	9
		7. Other Industries Professional in Nature	74.	417	63	33	–	128	12	34	–	612	75
	XX. Entertainments and Sport	1. Entertainments and Sport	75.	1,280	287	35	78	537	23	80	–	1,932	388
G. Personal Service.	XXI. Personal Service (including Hotels and Catering but excluding Government and Local Authority).	1. Domestic Service	76.	14,792	7,055	1,728	559	6,607	3,113	2,260	1,708	25,387	12,435
		2. Hotels, Lodging-Houses, Restaurants and Clubs	77.	1,623	101	225	4	1,652	35	589	9	4,089	149
		3. Laundries	78.	1,800	357	137	19	657	77	208	34	2,802	487
		4. Hairdressing, etc.	79.	2,036	53	229	–	1,035	11	447	–	3,747	64
		5. Other Personal Service	80.	–	43	–	–	–	8	–	–	–	51

TABLE 119.
FEDERATED MALAY STATES. – ALL RACES BY INDUSTRY.

Category.	Order.	Group.	No.	Perak. Males.	Perak. Females.	Selangor. Males.	Selangor. Females.	Negri Sembilan. Males.	Negri Sembilan. Females.	Pahang. Males.	Pahang. Females.	Federated Malay States. Males.	Federated Malay States. Females.
AGRICULTURE AND FISHING.	I. Fishing	1. Fishing	1.	5,567	61	4,505	61	621	14	2,518	32	13,211	168
	II. Agriculture	1. Rice Cultivation	2.	28,188	15,025	3,128	1,337	7,655	7,564	16,277	13,152	55,248	30,078
		2. Rubber Cultivation	3.	80,175	27,224	65,346	27,388	52,943	11,051	20,874	4,134	219,338	69,797
		3. Coconut Cultivation	4.	7,026	1,776	9,889	1,539	178	4	507	83	17,600	3,402
		4. Oil Palm Cultivation	5.	1,131	630	1,081	518	1	–	34	1	2,247	1,149
		5. Market Gardening	6.	12,964	4,472	8,015	2,115	3,900	912	1,220	553	26,099	8,052
		6. Stock-rearing and Poultry Farming	7.	2,044	737	2,477	489	2,193	2,133	306	48	7,020	3,407
		7. Forestry and Wood-cutting	8.	5,980	297	2,404	195	1,608	45	1,589	22	11,581	559
		8. Other or Multifarious Agricultural Industry	9.	18,725	4,798	14,471	3,115	4,639	1,690	2,908	1,192	40,743	10,795
EXTRACTION AND PREPARATION OF, AND WORK IN, MATERIAL SUBSTANCES AND ELECTRICITY SUPPLY.	III. Mining and Quarrying and Treatment of Non-metalliferous Mine and Quarry	1. Tin Mining	10.	44,486	7,021	18,633	2,088	1,801	39	3,142	138	68,067	9,281
		2. Other Mining and Quarrying Industries	11.	856	101	2,027	219	465	8	803	220	4,151	548
		3. Treatment of Non-metalliferous Products.	12.	402	17	280	4	102	–	7	2	791	23
	IV. Manufacture of Bricks, Pottery and Glass.	1. Manufacture of Bricks, Pottery and Glass.	13.	239	5	327	8	111	3	31	3	708	19

Category	Order	Group	No.	Perak Males	Perak Females	Selangor Males	Selangor Females	Negri Sembilan Males	Negri Sembilan Females	Pahang Males	Pahang Females	Federated Malay States Males	Federated Malay States Females
	V. Manufacture of Chemicals, Dyes, Explosives, Paints, Oils, Grease.	1. Manufacture of Vegetable Oils and Soap	15.	37	22	33	–	4	–	3	48	77	70
	VI. Manufacture of Metals, Machines, Implements, Conveyances, Jewellery, Watches.	1. Tin Smelting	16.	19	–	33	–	1	–	1	–	54	–
		2. Foundry Work.	17.	383	2	134	–	20	–	27	–	564	2
		3. Forge Work	18.	959	–	675	–	184	1	105	–	1,923	1
		4. Motor Car and Cycle Repair	19.	914	7	982	–283	1	49	1	2,228	8	–
		5. Tin, Brass and Copper Smithing	20.	308	–	321	–	116	–	52	–	797	–
		6. General and Undefined Mechanical Engineering	21.	2,963	–	3,317	1	379	–	255	1	6,914	2
		7. Gold and Silver Smithing and Electro-plating	22.	1,267	19	880	1	322	4	187	–	2,656	24
		8. Watch and Clock Manufacture and Repair	23.	231	–	159	–	61	–	42	–	493	–
		9. Electrical Work	24.	658	2	847	1	113	–	59	–	1,677	3
		11. Other Industries	26.	213	–	281	–	6	–	32	–	532	–
	VII. Manufacture of Textiles and Textile Goods (not dress).	1. Weaving	27.	14	36	5	21	1	4	1	65	21	126
		2. Rope and Net Making	28.	8	9	234	6	2	–	–	6	244	15
		3. Dyeing	29.	8	–	6	1	1	–	1	–	16	1
		4. Other Industries	30.	45	–	–	–	3	19	5	329	53	348

Category	Order	Group	No.	Perak. Males.	Females.	Selangor. Males.	Females.	Negri Sembilan. Males.	Females.	Pahang. Males.	Females.	Federated Malay States. Males.	Females.
	VIII. Preparation of Skins and Leather and Manufacture of Goods of Leather and Leather Substitute (not clothing or footwear).	1. Tanning	31.	1	–	4	–	–	–	2	–	7	–
		2. Other Industries	32.	–	–	1	–	–	–	–	–	1	–
	IX. Manufacture of Clothing (not knitted).	1. Manufacture of Boots, Shoes and Clogs	33.	598	9	511	2	188	5	134	–	1,431	16
		2. Manufacture of other Articles of Clothing	34.	2,326	317	1,867	290	709	110	358	32	5,260	749
	X. Manufacture of Food. Drink and Tobacco.	1. Manufacture of Food.	35.	725	55	488	60	226	16	163	47	1,602	178
		2. Manufacture of Drink	36.	58	3	18	1	12	1	18	–	106	5
		3. Manufacture of Tobacco	37.	405	248	107	30	22	45	3	–	537	323
	XI. Wood Working; Manufacture of Cane and Basket ware, Furniture, Fittings (not elsewhere enumerated).	1. Timber-sawing	38.	1,707	–	707	–	364	10	215	–	2,993	10
		2. Carpentry, Joinery and Furniture making	39.	5,088	6	3,878	6	1,387	25	1,504	164	11,857	201
		3. Basketry	40.	351	85	132	278	108	36	39	1	630	400
		4. Boat and Ship Building	41.	36	–	52	–	1	–	13	–	102	–

Category.	Order.	Group.	No.	Perak. Males.	Females.	Selangor. Males.	Females.	Negri Sembilan. Males.	Females.	Pahang. Males.	Females.	Federated Malay States. Males.	Females.
	XII. Paper Making; Manufacture of Stationery and Stationery Requisites, Printing, Bookbinding and Photography.	1. Printing and Bookbinding	42.	198	2	468	2	40	–	–	–	706	4
		2. Photography	43.	144	3	102	–	34	–	11	2	291	5
	XIII. Building, Decorating, Shone and Slate Cutting and Dressing and Contracting.	1. House Building, Painting, etc.	44.	1,824	–	2,189	54	613	6	363	1	4,989	61
		2. Contracting	45.	269	2	500	–	46	–	6	–	821	2
	XIV. Other Manufacturing Industries.	1. Rubber Goods Manufacture	46.	44	–	24	–	21	4	11	–	100	4
		2. Other Industries	47.	76	19	56	2	21	–	43	3	196	24
	XV. Gas, Water, Electricity	1. Gas, Water and Electricity Supply	48.	19	–	–	–	–	–	–	–	19	–
	XVI. Transport and Communication	1. Railway Transport	49.	2,904	45	3,723	65	1,201	28	694	38	8,522	176

Category.	Order.	Group.	No.	Perak. Males.	Perak. Females.	Selangor. Males.	Selangor. Females.	Negri Sembilan. Males.	Negri Sembilan. Females.	Pahang. Males.	Pahang. Females.	Federated Malay States. Males.	Federated Malay States. Females.
C. TRANSPORT AND COMMUNICATION.	XVI. Transport and Communication	1. Railway Transport	49.	2,904	45	3,723	65	1,201	28	694	38	8,522	176
		2. Road Transport	50.	9,496	19	7,641	5	3,080	7	1,165	47	21,382	78
		3. Water Transport	51.	3,109	17	1,737	1	76	–	364	–	5,286	18
		4. Post, Telegraph and Telephone Service	52.	535	17	494	50	137	–	82	–	1,248	67
		5. Other Industries	53.	888	3	1,162	–	222	–	128	–	2,400	3
D. COMMERCE AND FINANCE	XVII. Commerce and Finance	1. Banking	54.	83	–	179	2	37	–	6	8	305	10
		2. Insurance	55.	14	–	23	–	5	–	1	–	43	–
		3. Broking and Agency	56.	80	6	113	–	18	–	3	–	214	6
		4. Auctioneering and Valuing	57.	141	–	37	–	8	–	5	–	191	–
		5. Moneylending, Pawnbroking, Moneychanging	58.	635	1	559	1	223	–	65	–	1,482	2
		6. Wholesale and Retail Dealing	59.	20,887	750	16,567	474	5,333	260	2,720	99	45,507	1,583
		7. Street Vending and Peddling	60.	9,588	829	7,772	640	1,005	74	440	99	18,805	1,642
		8. Other Industries	61.	125	18	38	1	33	1	24	–	220	20
E. PUBLIC ADMINISTRATION AND DEFENCE.	XVIII. Public Administration and Defence.	1. Central Government	62.	2,160	180	2,185	91	645	64	458	165	5,448	500
		2. Municipal Administration	63.	–	–	–	–	–	–	–	–	–	–
		3. Navy	64.	–	–	–	–	–	–	–	–	–	–
		4. Army	65.	744	–	9	–	7	–	4	–	764	–
		5. Air Force	66.	–	–	–	–	–	–	–	–	–	–
		6. Police	67.	1,986	–	1,848	1	633	–	511	–	4,978	1

Category.	Order.	Group.	No.	Perak.		Selangor.		Negri Sembilan.		Pahang.		Federated Malay States.	
				Males.	Females.	Males.	Females.	Males.	Females.	Males.	Females.	Males.	Females.
...ESSIONAL ...JPATIONS.	XIX. Professions	1. Religion	68.	668	79	296	22	137	3	73	5	1,174	109
		2. Law	69.	97	–	70	–	17	–	–	–	184	–
		3. Medicine, Dentistry and Veterinary Surgery	70.	585	221	591	96	230	38	179	47	1,585	402
		4. Education	71.	1,445	344	904	261	605	73	326	31	3,280	709
		5. Accountancy	72.	16	5	37	3	3	–	4	–	60	8
		6. Engineering, Architecture and Surveying	73.	93	–	100	–	96	–	94	–	383	–
		7. Other Industries Professional in Nature	74.	52	–	31	2	49	–	15	2	147	4
	XX. Entertainments and Sport	1. Entertainments and Sport	75.	571	103	477	80	501	38	95	31	1,644	252
...ONAL ...CE.	XXI. Personal Service (including Hotels and Catering but excluding Government and Local Authority).	1. Domestic Service	76.	9,985	5,052	9,367	5,035	3,034	505	1,533	292	23,919	10,888
		2. Hotels, Lodging-Houses, Restaurants and Clubs	77.	2,742	179	2,077	109	933	57	534	39	6,286	384
		3. Laundries	78.	934	137	1,054	139	300	77	116	10	2,404	363
		4. Hairdressing, etc.	79.	1,902	19	1,285	10	530	6	308	3	4,025	38
		5. Other Personal Service	80.	366	201	154	17	30	647	26	660	576	1,525

TABLE 120.
OTHER MALAY STATES. – ALL RACES BY INDUSTRY.

Category.	Order.	No.	Group.	Johore. Males.	Johore. Females.	Kedah. Males.	Kedah. Females.	Kelantan. Males.	Kelantan. Females.	Trengganu. Males.	Trengganu. Females.	Perlis. Males.	Perlis. Females.	Brunei. Males.	Brunei. Females.
A. AGRICULTURE AND FISHING.	I. Fishing	1.	1. Fishing.	5,005	131	2,731	27	6,249	378	10,028	379	480	2	921	15
	II. Agriculture	2.	1. Rice Cultivation	7,706	431	68,424	38,706	67,193	42,162	23,661	14,585	11,640	8,520	3,306	2,997
		3.	2. Rubber Cultivation	95,299	12,666	28,898	12,794	7,520	2,548	2,477	113	262	55	1,047	63
		4.	3. Coconut Cultivation	8,210	303	174	14	1,582	307	774	63	1	7	22	3
		5.	4. Oil Palm Cultivation	559	364	1	–	–	–	7	–	–	–	–	–
		6.	5. Market Gardening	6,373	897	3,501	290	932	448	890	213	206	6	111	43
		7.	6. Stock-rearing and Poultry Farming	8,646	805	961	505	1,649	176	255	30	27	2	18	3
		8.	7. Forestry and Wood-cutting	2,326	21	581	9	168	12	390	32	25	–	144	7
		9.	8. Other or Multifarious Agricultural Industry	17,432	1,365	3,747	320	2,741	825	1,228	163	86	–	514	27
B. EXTRACTION AND PREPARATION OF, AND WORK IN, MATERIAL SUBSTANCES AND QUARRY PRODUCTS.	III. Mining and Quarrying and Treatment of Non-metalliferous Mine and Quarry Products.	10.	1. Tin Mining	693	76	574	93	1	–	131	8	184	6	– (125 Oil)	–
		11.	2. Other Mining and Quarrying Industries	2,320	10	265	32	36	4	95	2	843	–	–	–
		12.	3. Treatment of Non-metalliferous Products	115	1	27	2	14	7	27	2	8	–	3	1
ELECTRICITY SUPPLY.	IV. Manufacture of Bricks, Pottery and Class.	14.	1. Manufacture of Bricks, Pottery and Class	125	12	124	9	16	9	16	3	7	–	6	–

utegory.	Order.	Group.	No.	Johore.		Kedah.		Kelantan.		Trengganu.		Perlis.		Brunei.	
				Males.	Females.	Males.	Females.	Males.	Females.	Males.	Females.	Males.	Females.	Males.	Females.
	V. Manufacture of Chemicals, Dyes, Explosives, Paints, Oils, Grease.	1. Manufacture of Vegetable Oils and Soap	15.	16	4	21	–	1	8	14	31	–	–	–	4
	VI. Manufacture of Metals, Machines, Implements, Conveyances Jewellery, Watches.	2. Foundry Work	1.	1	–	–	–	2	–	–	–	1	–	15	–
		3. Forge Work	18.	309	–	300	1	248	2	148	–	39	–	35	–
		4. Motor Car and Cycle Repair	19.	355	3	116	–	40	1	79	–	12	–	9	–
		5. Tin, Brass and Copper Smithing	20.	178	1	57	1	55	14	221	–	6	–	46	–
		6. General and Undefined Mechanical Engineering	21.	362	–	174	3	79	–	128	–	10	–	66	–
		7. Gold and Silver Smithing and Electroplating	22.	785	8	800	20	325	39	192	5	61	1	59	3
		8. Watch and Clock Manufacture and Repair	23.	13	9	39	1	17	–	15-	1	–	6	–	–
		9. Electrical Work	24.	145	–	117	1	27	–	3	–	3	–	15	–
		11. Other Industries	26.	66	–	81	–	4	–	–	7	1	–	–	87

tegory.	Order.	Group.	No.	Johore.		Kedah.		Kelantan.		Trengganu.		Perlis.		Brunei.	
				Males.	Females.	Males.	Females.	Males.	Females.	Males.	Females.	Males.	Females.	Males.	Females.
	VII. Manufacture of Textiles and Textile Goods (not dress).	1. Weaving	27.	30	127	13	23	36	798	1,600	1,884	–	–	2	106
		2. Rope and Net Making	28.	1	4	9	38	89	157	68	394	–	–	1	149
		3. Dyeing	29.	7	–	5	–	–	3	17	3	–	–	–	–
		4. Other Industries	30.	10	6	5	62	25	32	67	1,394	–	–	6	14
	VIII. Preparation of Skins and Leather and Manufacture of Goods of Leather and Leather Substitute (not clothing or foot-wear).	2. Other Industries	32.	–	–	–	–	–	–	–	–	–	–	130	–
	IX. Manufacture of Clothing (not knitted).	1. Manufacture of Boots, Shoes and Clogs	33.	232	3	156	12	42	–	24	1	3	–	4	–
		2. Manufacture of other Articles of Clothing	34.	1,152	106	445	141	263	263	135	327	51	3	49	20
	X. Manufacture of Food, Drink and Tobacco.	1. Manufacture of Food	35.	721	34	407	46	161	93	300	199	22	–	69	56
		2. Manufacture of Drink	36.	163	–	131	–	3	–	4	1	–	–	5	–
		3. Manufacture of Tobacco	37.	83	17	185	79	4	3	12	6	2	–	–	–

Category	Order	Group	No.	Johore. Males.	Females.	Kedah. Males.	Females.	Kelantan. Males.	Females.	Trengganu. Males.	Females.	Perlis. Males.	Females.	Brunei. Males.	Females.
	XI. Wood Working; Manufacture of Cane and Basket ware, Furniture, Fittings (not elsewhere enumerated).	1. Timber-sawing	38.	403	3	196	2	68	–	46	–	31	–	5	–
		2. Carpentry, Joinery and Furniture-making	39.	2,740	76	1,485	64	1,518	199	1,354	429	107	–	386	121
		3. Basketry	40.	280	14	104	7	80	19	69	63	4	–	–	–
		4. Boat and Ship Building	41.	24	21	–	19	–	91	–	–	–	12	–	–
	XII. Paper Making; Manufacture of Stationery and Stationery Requisites; Printing, Bookbinding and Photography.	1. Printing and Bookbinding	42.	120	–	43	–	32	–	14	–	–	–	–	–
		2. Photography	43.	52	1	30	8	–	10	1	2	–	2	–	–

Category.	Order.	Group.	No.	Johore. Males.	Females.	Kedah. Males.	Females.	Kelantan. Males.	Females.	Trengganu. Males.	Females.	Perlis. Males.	Females.	Brunei. Males.	Females.
	XIII. Building, Decorating, Stone and Slate Cutting and Dressing and Contracting.	1. House Building, Painting, etc.	44.	984	15	654	2	575	6	242	1	22	–	7	–
		2. Contracting	45.	43	–	48	–	18	–	22	–	1	–	–	–
	XIV. Other Manufacturing Industries.	1. Rubber Goods Manufacture	46.	29	–	6	–	3	1	–	–	–	–	–	–
		2. Other Industries	47.	95	–	62	2	43	46	31	23	1	1	21	35
	XV. Gas, Water, Electricity	1. Gas, Water and Electricity Supply	48.	1	–	4	–	–	–	–	–	–	–	–	–
C. TRANSPORT AND COMMUNICATION.	XVI. Transport and Communication	1. Railway Transport	49.	800	26	362	5	1,112	15	75	–	142	7	14	–
		2. Road Transport	50.	5,263	22	2,395	10	857	4	547	1	123	–	42	–
		3. Water Transport	51.	1,178	3	1,016	7	443	6	1,728	–	24	–	95	–
		4. Post, Telegraph and Telephone Service	52.	253	1	185	–	34	–	29	–	4	–	20	–
		5. Other Industries	53.	296	–	207	2	138	–	43	–	21	–	64	–

Category	Order	Group	No.	Johore. Males.	Females.	Kedah. Males.	Females.	Kelantan. Males.	Females.	Trengganu. Males.	Females.	Perlis. Males.	Females.	Brunei. Males.	Females.
D. COMMERCE AND FINANCE.	XVII. Commerce and Finance	1. Banking	54.	39	–	10	–	6	1	2	–	–	–	–	–
		2. Insurance	55.	3	–	–	–	–	–	9	–	–	–	–	1
		3. Broking and Agency	56.	27	–	2.1	–	13	5	–	–	–	–	–	–
		4. Auctioneering and Valuing	57.	21		4	–		–	1	–	–	–		–
		5. Moneylending, Pawnbroking, Moneychanging	58.	306	1	193	–	30	–	18	–	9	–	–	–
		6. Wholesale and Retail Dealing	59.	11,329	499	9,006	590	3,624	3,143	11,766	1,677	750	66	426	27
		7. Street Vending and Peddling	60.	2,132	66	881	124	517	1,164	565	1,268	26	2	147	94
		8. Other Industries	61.	97	3	16	1	10	1	8	–	–	–	–	–
E. PUBLIC ADMINISTRATION AND DEFENCE.	XVIII. Public Administration and Defence.	1. Central Government	62.	1,464	233	745	54	335	38	372	9	72	3	62	1
		2. Municipal Administration	63.	8	–	2	–	4	–	–	–	2	–	–	–
		4. Army	65.	755	–	–	–	–	–	–	–	–	–	–	–
		5. Air Force	66.	–	–	–	–	–	–	–	–	–	–	4	–
		6. Police	67.	1,402	4	809	1	482	–	320	1	75	–	73	1

ry.	Order.	Group.	No.	Johore. Males.	Johore. Females.	Kedah. Males.	Kedah. Females.	Kelantan. Males.	Kelantan. Females.	Trengganu. Males.	Trengganu. Females.	Perlis. Males.	Perlis. Females.	Brunei. Males.	Brunei. Females.
FIS-AL UPA-IS.	XIX. Professions	1. Religion	68.	282	15	563	–	218	1	102	3	36	–	12	–
		2. Law	69.	57	–	15	–	12	–	9	–	5	–	1	–
		3. Medicine, Dentistry and Veterinary Surgery	70.	546	134	185	96	153	114	95	130	17	12	9	10
		4. Education	71.	581	124	840	60	552	66	190	19	80	17	21	4
		5. Accountancy	72.	6	–	1	–	6	–	–	–	1	–	–	–
		6. Engineering, Architecture and Surveying	73.	288	–	213	–	76	–	69	–	6	–	1	–
		7. Other Industries Professional in Nature	74.	7	–	1	–	1	1	4	–	–	–	–	–
	XX. Entertainments and Sport	1. Entertainments and Snort	75.	379	90	250	60	133	70	77	23	24	11	4	–
ᴸ ᴬᴸ ᴵᶜᴱ.	XXI. Personal Service (including Hotels and Catering, but excluding Government and Local Authority).	1. Domestic Service	76.	4,957	1,271	2,161	763	1,136	807	636	357	183	136	143	36
		2. Hotels, Lodging-Houses, Restaurants and Clubs	77.	1,933	128	1,242	74	225	24	349	111	137	9	18	2
		3. Laundries	78.	449	108	242	70	107	24	71	14	10	3	11	2
		4. Hairdressing, etc.	79.	1,413	18	676	–	147	2	90	4	29	–	17	–
		5. Other Personal Service	80.	434	2,265	51	1,549	71	2,126	4	798	17	383	5	288

ALEXANDER, *BRITISH MALAYA: MALAYAN STATISTICS* (1928)

C. S. Alexander, *British Malaya: Malayan Statistics* (London: Malayan Information Agency, 1928), pp. 121–5, 128.

The tables list average retail prices for a range of foodstuffs and the daily wage rates earned in the most important occupations for the years 1926 to 1928, providing some indication of living standards. As reflected in the 1923–8 Post Office Savings statistics, a surprisingly large number of workers managed to save a proportion of their earnings. Living standards are also discussed in W. L. Blythe, *Methods and Conditions of Employment of Chinese Labour in the Federated Malay States* reproduced below.

C. S Alexander, *British Malaya: Malayan Statistics* (1928), extract

Retail Food Prices.

Kuala Lumpur Cold Storage and Market Prices and Ipoh Market prices of Rice, 1926–1928.

Means of twelve monthly quotations of "Average Market Prices"

Extracted from Monthly Price Lists published in the F.M.S. Government Gazette.

Particulars.		1926.		1927.		1928.	
		$	c.	$	c.	$	c.
KUALA LUMPUR COLD STORAGE							
Beef –							
Fillet Steak	Per lb.	1	0·25	1	10·0	1	05·9
Sirloin, Roast			65·0		65·0		64·8
Mutton –							
Leg	"		77·9		70·0		69·7
Shoulder	"		57·9		50·4		50·1
Lamb, Leg	"		87·9		80·4		80·1
Fowl	"		85·0	1	07·9	1	05·9
Butter, Fresh	"	1	10·0	1	02·9	1	03·5
KUALA LUMPUR MARKET.							
Beef –							
Bullock	Per-Kati(*a*)		56·3		58·7		55·0
Buffalo	"		56·4		57·7		55·0
Mutton	Per lb.		58·4		57·0		60·0
Goat Flesh	"		58·4		57·0		60·0
Pork –							
Lean	Per Kati (*a*)		87·8		89·7		88·0
Fat and Lean	"		69·6		69·3		64·0
Poultry –							
Fowls	each	1	57·4	1	61·2	1	43·9
Ducks	"	1	00·1		99·2		95·7
Chickens			67·5		70·7		64·8
Fish –							
Bawal Puteh (Pomfret)	Per Kati(*a*)		52·2		48·3		47·1
Kurau (Indian Salmon)	"		65·5		65·8		60·7

Particulars.		1926.	1927.	1928.
		$ c.	$ c.	$ c.
Lidah-lidah (Sole)	"	50·3	46·4	47·0
Prawns (sea)	"	52·4	51·9	53·5
Selangin	"	50·2	46·0	43·0
Tenggiri (Spanish Mackerel)	"	50·1	49·3	46·6 /
Vegetables –				
Bombay Onions	Per Kati (*a*)	13·0	12·6	12·2
Brinjal	"	08·4	09·2	07·2
Cabbage, Bengal	"	28·0	21·0	21·0
Cucumbers	"	07·3	06·9	06·1
French Beans	"	32·0	29·4	27·5
Long Beans	"	09·0	09·6	08·8
Potatoes	"	11·4	11·0	11·2
Tomatoes	"	40·2	46·0	37·9
Carrots	"	30·7	31·1	25·0
Beetroot	"	33·8	30·2	27·4
Fruit –				
Bananas	Each	01·5	01·5	01·5
Pineapples, Straits	"	08·0	07·3	05·3
Oranges	Per Kati (*a*)	35·8	35·0	36·1
Bread, large loaf	Each	09·0	08·8	09·0
Eggs, Ducks	"	04·0	04·4	04·1
" Fowls	"	05·6	05·2	04·9

IPOH MARKET.

Rice (*b*) –				
" Siam " – 1st quality	Per Gantang (*c*)	60·7	66·5	62·0
" " 2nd	"	57·1	62·7	55·6
" " 3rd	"	47·5	55·5	49·7
Parboiled	"	47·1	50·2	43·7

(*a*) 1 kati = 1 1/3 lbs.
(*b*) Rice is not included in the Kuala Lumpur price lists.
(*c*) 1 gantang = 1 gallon. /

POST OFFICE SAVINGS BANK – FEDERATED MALAY STATES.
Compiled from the Annual Reports of the
Posts and Telegraphs Department, F.M.S

Particulars.	Unit.	1923.	1924.	1925.	1926.	1927.	1928.
Deposits during the Year –							
Number	No.	19,450	44,448	55,156	63,728	60,223	67,210
Amount	$'000	792·6	1,994·6	2,906·3	3,434·6	3·096·2	3,103·5
Withdrawals during the Year –							

Particulars.	Unit.	1923.	1924.	1925.	1926.	1927.	1928.
Number	No.	6,885	21,854	22,586	27,589	30,138	32,229
Amount	$'000	762·0	1,649·4	2,040·7	3,033·9	3,174·4	2,937·7
Interest Paid	,,	21·9	52·0	63·8	87·3	92·2	97·0
Accounts open 31st December –							
Number	No.	8,036	21,651	25,620	29,803	32,595	37,036
Amount	$'000	842·2	2,199·4	3,128·7	3,616·8	3,630·9	3,943·8
Average Amount per depositor	$	1·05	101	1·22	1·21	111	106
Amount to credit of Depositors of different Nationalities –							
Europeans	$'000	*	215	269	237	272	267
Eurasians	*	*	95	135	225	229	236
Malays	*	*	176	428	464	436	379
Chinese	,,	*	211	301	334	342	361
Indians	,,	*	1,170	1·509	2,027	1,985	2,320
Ceylonese	,,	*	246	364	131	158	159
Other nationalities public accounts etc.	,,	*	86	123	199	209	222

·   Not available. /

WAGES OF LABOURERS – FEDERATED MALAY STATES.

Compiled from the Annual Reports of the Labour Department.

Particulars.	Daily Rates of Wages.		
	1926.	1927.	1928.
	Cents.	Cents.	Cents.
Indian Agricultural Labourers: –			
Perak –			
Stores and Factories	50 – 100	50 – 80	50 – 80
Tappers (Men)	45 – 50	45 – 55	45 – 55
" (Women)	35 – 45	35 – 50	35 – 50
Field (Men)	40 – 50	40 – 50	40 – 50
" (Women)	30 – 35	30 – 45	30 – 45
Selangor –			
Stores and Factories	50 – 60	50 – 60	50 – 60
Tappers (Men)	40 – 50	45 – 52	45 – 52
" (Women)	35 – 50	40 – 50	40 – 50
Field (Men)	40 – 45	40 – 45	40 – 45
" (Women)	30 – 40	30 – 40	30 – 40
Negri Sembilan –			
Stores and Factories	60 – 65	60 – 65	60 – 65
Tappers (Men)	45 – 50	45 – 50	45 – 50
" (Women)	45 – 50	45 – 50	45 – 50
Field (Men)	40 – 50	40 – 50	40 – 50
" (Women)	30 – 40	30 – 40	30 – 40

Particulars.	Daily Rates of Wages.		
	1926.	1927.	1928.
	Cents.	Cents.	Cents.
Pahang –			
Stores and Factories	60 – 65	65 – 75	60 – 65
Tappers (Men)	55 – 60	55 – 60	50 – 65
" (Women)	50 – 60	50 – 60	50 – 65
Field (Men)	50 – 55	55 – 60	50 – 65
" (Women)	45 – 50	45 – 50	40 – 50
Indian Unskilled Labourers, Public Works and Railway Departments	40 – 60	40 – 50	(*a*)
Javanese Indentured Labourers, Men	45	45	45
" " Women	35	35	35
Free Javanese and Malay Labourers	50 – 65	50 – 60	50 – 60
Chinese on Contract	80 – 200	80 – 210	70 – 200

(*a*) Minimum rates of 50 cents for men and 40 cents for women in all Government Departments.

GERRARD, *ON THE HYGIENIC MANAGEMENT OF LABOUR IN THE TROPICS. AN ESSAY* (1913)

P. N. Gerrard, *On the Hygienic Management of Labour in the Tropics. An Essay* (Singapore: Methodist Publishing House, 1913), pp. 14–8, 61–4. 3697 LSE, Historical Statistics, 595 (HA161)

Dr Percy Nettervill Gerrard (1870–1915) was District Surgeon at variously Ula Selangor (1896), Klang (1898), Kuala Lumpur (1900, 1902), Raub (1904), Taiping (1904) and Petit Buntar (1906). The extracts from his 1913 pamphlet describe migrant worker living conditions and medical provisions in the FMS and Sumatra.

P. N. Gerrard, *On the Hygienic Management of Labour in the Tropics. An Essay* (1913), extract

Ventilation of Lines.[1]

Ventilation of lines, etc. The question of ventilation involves little extra expense, as obviously the less we place between ourselves and "God's good fresh air" the less it will cost us in houses, and yet the better we shall be.

One of the best types of lines which I have ever seen was a converted sugar factory. The building consisted of a large expanse of roof, tiled and with brick drains round the building.

In this–after the quallies etc., had been removed–partitions were erected forming rooms 12' x 12'. A space at the floors of about 6" was left open and between the rooms, which were back to back, a passage of about 4' existed.

The air circulated over and through the rooms and the expansive roof rendered the lines cool.

Lines built on some similar plan and say 3' raised from the ground would I believe be satisfactory.

One of the most important points about all buildings in the Tropics is a large expanse of roof.

Brick drains are usually insisted upon by the Health Department F.M.S. in the case of permanent lines. Even on estates where no revenue can be expected for some years I think they are advisable from a Health standpoint.

If brick drains are not put in the earth between the lines is used to dump stale rice and remnants, and the soil becomes saturated with decomposing vegetable matter and consequently exceedingly offensive.

Some of my planting friends will realise that the above statement is a change from my previous attitude towards the brick drain, as I have in past years expressed the opinion that if the surroundings of the lines were kept sanded and sloped, brick drains were not necessary, I now consider that the brick drain is a necessity and I could point to estates where they had not been put in which, from the flies and stench at the lines, would rapidly convince one of the necessity for a drain which could be flushed out clean.

With regard to temporary lines which may be advisable in some cases for the proving of the healthiness of a particular site or again on young estates may be necessary from a financial standpoint, the simpler they are the better. A large roof area is always advisable and if earth drains are permitted they should be well graded and the out fall[2] carried to say 50'.

The rooms should be raised off the ground I consider in such types of lines to a height of say 5'. /

A Jack roof[3] will not materially increase the cost and will undoubtedly assist ventilation.

The lines should not as a rule face the west as coolies frequently hang dirty sacking and such-like in front of their rooms and fire places to keep off the afternoon sun.

The ventilation of lines will depend principally on the area of open land round them and as much open space as can be spared should be spared for this purpose.

I submit through the courtesy of the F.M.S. Government in an appendix [not included] the plan of lines approved by the F.M.S. Government; variations of this plan have been erected on many estates, and personally I think the type with verandah outside the rooms, well raised off the ground and cemented underneath, is as good a labourer's quarters as one is warranted in expecting in the F.M.S. at present. Examples of these lines may be seen amongst other estates on Sungei Rengam (manager G. H. Bennett, Esq.) and on Bukit Jelutong (manager C. R. Harrison, Esq.).

I am not sure whether a more permanent type than even the present Government lines will not in time be adopted by the Planters. When the absolute soundness of rubber becomes proven, "when the markets cease from bubbling and rubber is at rest."

The F.M.S. Railways have adopted a permanent type which may well insinuate itself on the estates when the present period of "paying out" becomes converted into one of plenty and fixed prices.

Through the courtesy of the General Manager for Railways* I am enabled to state that the cost of the Railway type of lines is $462.50 per room, and the upkeep, $5 per room, including lime wash, etc.†

In discussing lines I find I have wandered somewhat from my heading "ventilation."

On many estates the health of the labour force has suffered owing to the lack of air-circulation round the lines; rubber, vegetable gardens, and even jungle surrounding the living rooms acts as a wet blanket, the damp never leaves the lines,

---

*   "G.M.R. 532/12."

†   I can see no objection to detached rooms which are in use on some estates, provided the drainage of each is good.

the sunshine is cut out and thus nature's greatest purifier–which costs nothing–
is prevented from oxidising and destroying noxious material.

Since 1894 the Casier Sanitaire of Paris have been carefully considering the
question of darkness and absence of air circulation in dwellings in their relation
to consumption, and the conclusion come to by the Chief of the Dept: Mr. Juil-
lera is this. "The darkness and absence of air in inhabited rooms is the enemy to
be "fought against and pursued without mercy."

"All the other factors in the propagation of consumption; "however grave
these may be; are not as murderous as the absence "of the light of the sun." /

It would be unfair of me to state that consumption is a common cause of the
general debility, inability to work, or even a cause of the high death rates which
occur now amongst labour forces, but I must state that I believe investigation of
the point very advisable.

It will be advisable perhaps to epitomise[4] rather than to dilate upon this ventilation question. I shall submit therefore some "Laws for lines" as a companion
for my "Don'ts for Drainage."

Laws for Lines.

a. Lines should not be nearer to jungle than 600 yards.

b. All lines should be provided with a jack roof for purposes of ventilation.

c. Lines should be provided with latrines at a convenient distance, in the proportion of 10 "places" for every 100 coolies; arrangements for the convenience
of females should be made.

d. All lines should be provided with brick or half pipe or concrete drains.

e. All drains should be connected with either a main drain which flows, or with
a rough septic tank, continuation of the brick, half pipe or concrete drain to
the main drain or tank is necessary.

f. Lines sweepers are a necessity and their work should be supervised.

g. It is advisable to build rooms 12' x 10' at least.

h. A dresser should visit all lines daily to render first aid in all cases of illness or
wounds.

k. An excessive height of the ground (over 7') is a mistake. Frequent inspection
will be necessary to prevent the under part being used as a hen house, store
or even additional living room.

Lines on the ground should be cement-floored, this becomes imperative
near Plague Foci and large towns.

Some Managers seem to have no difficulty in keeping the under part of
lines clear, and on some estates, where cooking underneath is permitted, and
the erection of unsightly, dark cubicles prevented, the labourers seem content and the ventilation of the lines is not interfered with.

l. Remember storm water when putting in your drains.

m. The best surroundings for lines is gravel I think, open, swept clean, and if the lines lie low the surroundings can be drained by a cheap modification of the anti-malarial subsoil drains described above. In my original paper written in 1906 I described what are called French drains for lowlying places, a series of which were put in at Parit Buntar and Bagan Serai Hospitals about 1905. These French drains are merely graded trenches filled to about 12" deep with very coarse metal; over this finer metal is put, and then earth, covered by grass turfing, sand / or gravel. These rough and cheap drains acted well in the Krian district hospitals and caused the storm water to dry up in a period which was short enough to prevent mosquitoes breeding out.

n. Lines near rivers may be provided with tidal gates on their drains for flushing purposes, but the water should be under control by the gates, as spring tides may flood the whole compound, which is not desirable.

o. The planks of the bed benches should be loose, i.e. not nailed to their supports.

Sanitation at the Lines.

We now come to the question of *Sanitation at the lines.* Everyone who has had anything to do with the Tamil coolie is aware of his roaming habits under certain circumstances, his love of variety and the fields, or preferably the road or pathway, but that Tamil coolies or Chinese coolies or any other coolies cannot be gently but firmly educated I absolutely decline to believe!

Now, under existing Sanitary arrangements on many estates. in this country, I submit that the unfortunate coolie who gets "a tummyache" at say 1 a.m., should not be blamed by the inspecting doctor or agent the next day, in the garish sunlight, for filthy habits; in other words "until proper sanitary accommodation becomes a feature of every coolie lines in the country and a special coolie be detailed to look after the matter, disease must continue to exist amongst the whole class."

The type of latrine to be erected is of the simplest, an attap-roofed shed elevated above the surrounding ground level, with a trench or pit to be filled in with a mixture of dry earth and lime daily to a depth of about three inches, the trench protected from storm-water by means of ordinary earth drains around it, and sufficiently removed in its situation from the main water supply to prevent contamination–this will suffice to prevent contamination of the lines area. [...]

A type of Latrine is in action on one Estate in Kuala Langat which consists of a cemented trench with sloping sides (also cemented).

At one end is a pump to the river, and about the middle a sluice gate of wood.

Twice daily water is pumped into the trench until fairly full, the sluice opened and the whole trench flushed into the river,–the washings however should I consider be led to a cesspit or Septic Tank in every case and only permitted to enter the stream after natural purification has taken place.

Another type which I am informed is in use on a Selangor estate is on wheels on rails and fresh pits or trenches can be dug as necessary, the old ones being filled up.

In common with all other measures concerning the health of a labour force, constant iteration of orders to enforce the use of latrines on an estate is necessary, and fines which are now legal / under the labour code should be inflicted where breaches of Sanitary rules occur.

It is an unfortunate fact that very little mutual visitation of estates occurs at present amongst the Planting community, so that Managers do not get the experience which some Government Officials do, of what can be, and is being done on Estates within moderate distances of their own charge.

The result of this is "Grooviness" and one frequently hears on inspections, the statement of one Manager that an arrangement or regime which is actually being carried out efficiently on an estate in the neighbourhood is "impossible" on his estate.

With respect I commend to the P. A. M. the establishment of a system of interestate visitations, with a view to enlarging the purview of the stop-at-home, hard worked Managers, who in some instances have never seen "First Class" lines, well kept compounds, anti-malarial measures, nor Sanitary arrangements, in operation, and many of whom would not only learn valuable lessons but–if I know anything of the hospitality of Planters–would enjoy a hearty welcome from their brethren.

Too much stress cannot be laid upon the system of facilitating all sanitariness amongst coolies. At present they are blamed as altogether bestial; they have no opportunity of being otherwise unless the European places every convenience within their reach.

First Aid Treatment.

Every estate of over 100 coolies should in their own interests employ an estate dresser who should go round the lines after muster time and send the sick to hospital. He should be made responsible for the proper condition of the lines and should report to the manager and to the Estate Visiting Medical Practitioner any lines found in a bad state.

No sick should be permitted to remain in the lines under any circumstances.

Discipline and system should be the passwords, but in the race for output when prices rule high, I fear both are sometimes lost sight of and overworked managers are prone to consider their coolies health after the factory, and store, which is not really "the Game."

Principal Diseases on Estates,
with Especial Regard to the Labour Force.

For obvious reasons it would be improper of me to write a full description of the methods of treatment and diagnosis of disease in this paper, nor would it be possible to do so within the limits of an ordinary essay, but in the interests of both parties I may perhaps sketch briefly the principal symptoms which lead one to suspect serious disease, and suggest a sound amateur treatment to be adopted in such cases.

The following notes will I trust be of use to Dressers also. /

MALARIAL FEVER.

The principal disease to which the coolie is liable is Malarial Fever, but if the attacks of this disease remain discrete–by which I mean so long as the attacks are separated by a day or days–one may safely deal with him on the estate by the administration of quinine in 10gr. doses twice daily. If, however, the attacks overlap, and the disease becomes continuous, then an hospital is the proper place for the case. Where it is found that the fever yields to quinine the drug should be continued in 5 gr. doses daily for two (2) months, but neglect of this most important "regime of prophylaxis"[5] is the reason for the relapse cases which cause so much invaliding and disturbance of estate work quite unnecessarily. The 20 grs. per day might be stopped in 7 days.

It is inadvisable if the attacks be acute, i.e. accompanied by high fever, prostration, or added symptoms, that the fever stricken cooly be kept on the estate, as the danger of collapse is serious in such cases.

The use of mosquito curtains could, I still believe, be introduced amongst Tamil coolies, although the majority of Managers have given the task up as hopeless. When we read of coolies on certain estates demanding their quinine mixture, as has undoubtedly occurred (their quinie education having been commenced in this country) I cannot believe that it is "impossible" to get them to use curtains! Almost all of the lowest class of Chinese Sinkehs use curtains, and it is I believe a matter of meeting Eastern lethargy with western insistance and persistence, to solve the question, and thus reduce the malaria say by 20% which would be a consideration.

In dealing with the question of fever the mosquito naturally comes under notice, and although I have dwelt upon the means to be adopted to combat the existence of this pest, I must make my peace with some planters who still believe that this insect is not the only means of propagation of malaria, by stating that the malarial parasite has been constantly found in the stomachs of certain mosquitoes, but it has not been found in decomposing granite, nor in any of the other earths and clays, etc., which have been blamed as distributors or propagators of the disease. Experiments with infected Anophelines have been positive, and I am quite willing to guarantee or gamble on the result of the experiment of infecting any new-comer to this country by the means of infected Anophelines,[6] provided the doubting planter will make the necessary arrangements with his newly-arrived assistant.

Mosquito houses were the only means adopted by the commission sent out by the London School of Tropical Medicine to that hotbed of malaria the Roman Campagna, and no cases occurred amongst the members of the expedition; and again, the European who submitted himself to the bites of Anophelines which were infected 48 hours previously in Rome, still occasionally gets fever (Mr. WARREN, assistant in the London Tropical School who had an attack while I was studying there). /

[...]

APPENDIX A.

By Dr. Charles Vere Nichol.

Medical Arrangements on Estates in Sumatra.

In March 1911. I had the pleasure of seeing several of the Estate Hospitals in Sumatra. I have nothing but praise for the excellent and up to date Hospitals we found everywhere we visited. The splendid results obtained as regards health are best exemplified by the fact that in many instances the death rate was as low as 10.21 per 1000. The Hospitals we visited were chiefly those maintained and supported by large Tobacco growing companies. In every instance a large central Hospital, of about 200 beds, is established for a group of Estates, the patients being brought by means of *special spring bullock cart ambulances.*

If a coolie does not work in Sumatra, he is promptly forwarded to Hospital, when he is kept under observation for two days, and then if found to be malingering he is sent on to the Magistrate. This simple and very efficient plan insures all cases of sickness being promptly dealt with and much assists the managers of Estates in their control of malingerers.

The Hospital is in charge of a fully qualified medical man, often a German, he lives close by and personally sees and treats every case, often he has a European assistant. He never goes out to visit Estates nor does he do any private practice, and is paid a salary of over £1000 a year. Even Europeans on Estates are obliged to come direct to Hospital, and are not attended on the Estate by the Company's doctor, but come to the European Ward, which is close by the Native Hospital.

The equipment is all quite up to date in these Hospitals, quite as good as that found in London Hospitals. I saw tiled operating theatres with basins arranged so that the water is turned on by means of a pedal, similar to those seen at home. X-Ray and other electrical apparatus for treatment in the large Hospitals are frequently found. Salvarsan[7] is given regularly to cases of Syphilis, and the results were very good. Most of the Sumatra doctors give / 606 by the intravenous method. (Salvarsan is not allowed in F.M.S. Government Hospitals. P.N.G.)

On the arrival of a new batch of coolies for an Estate *they are first sent to Hospital for a fortnight, and kept under observation treated with Quinine if indicated by an examination of the blood, and by a course of thymol8 if ankylostomiasis9 is present.*

At Medan there is a large Institute for Medical Research, to which all pathological specimens are forwarded for diagnosis. A large number of animals are kept for inoculation purposes, and there are two horses specially kept for procuring serum for the treatment of Dysentery. This Laboratory is entirely supported by funds received from the Planting companies. Before employing labour, every company must make known to the Government, what medical arrangements it has made. *The Planters all seemed to be entirely in sympathy with the Government on medical matters, and realised that good health and efficient work on the Estates were only to be obtained by having the very best Hospital arrangements.* The only thing they grumbled at was the expense of the Hospitals, but they always explained that the latter were so good, that nothing more could be said about the expense.

The Wards are large lofty and well ventilated with, in most cases, doors all along the sides or with large expanded metal windows. The roof is tiled or of corrugated iron. The floors are white washed every day. Separate rooms are provided for dressing and treating septic cases. Separate wards are provided for special cases, and Small-pox is treated in a separate ward in the Hospital.

Shower and needle baths were seen in most of the Hospitals. Mosquito and fly proof wards are used for Malaria and Dysentery.

The Ward has a latrine at the end of it, with buckets of disinfectant in it.

A Laboratory with apparatus for pathological examinations, and often a very efficient Chinese attendant doing blood examinations, and Widal's reactions. Typhoid Fever seems more common in Sumatra than the F.M.S. In all cases where 606 was given, Wasserman's reaction[10] was done.

A barbed wire fence of about 8 feet high, surrounds the Hospital.

Estates. One of the most striking features about Estates in Sumatra, are the beautiful *well kept surroundings of Bungalows and Coolie Lines.* Round every manager's and assistant's bungalow one finds close cut lawns and padangs with shrubs and palm trees. The mowing machine is much more used than the sythe for keeping the grass cut.

The Estates are visited by the Health Officer and not by the Estate doctor. *Sick coolies are not found in the Lines during working hours,* as they are with the doctor or the magistrate. [...] /

The country is very open and flat, and not so difficult to drain as the F.M.S. Tobacco is only replanted in the same place, after several years interval. During this interval lalang[11] etc. grows up over the old planted area, and is not cleared again until the ground is to be replanted. One goes along the road for miles with patches of tobacco alternating with patches of lalang etc. on each side.

The following statistics are interesting and show the good results obtained. There are very few Tamil coolies in Sumatra, nearly all are Chinese or Javanese. Tamils as a rule are employed only for the care of cattle. When I was in Sumatra Malaria was less common than in the F.M.S., and Typhoid more common.

Death Rate per Thousand.

Hosp. A.		Hosp. B.		Hosp. C.	
Year 1907	21	Year 1890–1898	33.06	Year 1909	14.93
" 1908	16	" 1908–1909	10.21		
" 1909	–				

Hosp. D.		Hosp. E.		Hosp. F.	
Year 1909	14.6	Year 1909	14.1	Year 1907	21.17
				" 1908	19.49
				" 1909	16.89

To introduce the Sumatra methods into the F.M.S. in toto, would, I think, be very difficult. The coolie is not under such complete control and in many cases it is very difficult to get him into Hospital especially when dealing with free Javanese. They much prefer when sick to go off to their kampong, and very few of them have faith either in the European methods or the Tamil dresser, who on most Estates carries out the treatment. On going round some Lines (in Selangor) where there were Javanese coolies, I discovered a man with signs of Phthisis[12] and advised the manager to send him to Hospital, so that we might examine his sputum for tubercle. Directly I left he gave the manager a month's notice, and said he would prefer to pay up a month's wages than go to Hospital. A mandor on another Estate who the manager tells me has complete excellent control over the coolies, persistently teaches them that to go to Hospital is quite contrary to the religious ideas they ought to hold.

The Chinese appreciate Hospital more than any other class of Native, and the Tamil is fairly easy to control in this respect. I think also that however keen a manager may be to carry out the requirements of Government and send the sick to Hospital, he often has at the back of his mind, when the Javanese coolie objects, that perhaps after all he is as well looked after by his own people in his own Kampong, as in a Hospital looked after by people in whom he has no faith.

A great step towards the remedying of this state of affairs would be to get more Malays and Javanese trained as dressers, and also to have throughout the country separate Hospitals for separate nationalities. If you have all in one

Hospital, it is difficult to both separate the different diseases and the different nationalities, and / the question of Staff and of feeding is difficult. Moreover I would have large Hospitals and a European doctor constantly in charge of each. Excellent in many ways as the dresser is, or perhaps tries to be, he is far better if under constant European supervision.

Some method of teaching hygiene the benefits of proper food etc., is sadly needed among Estate coolies if the death rate is to be lowered. Notices printed near the lines explaining the elementary principles of hygiene etc., would I think be useful, and managers and assistants might do much to help educate the coolie in these respects. Of course in Sumatra there is no question as to whether a coolie shall or shall not go to Hospital etc., but here (F.M.S.) with free coolies, if you coerce, in many instances you lose your labour, which moves on to another Estate, and Labour is often as we know, very hard to get.

CHARLES VERE NICOLL,
Medical Officer,
Group of Estates,
Federated Malay States.
July 19th, 1912.

APPENDIX B.

The Septic Tank.

The Septic Tank in its elemental form consists merely in a hole in the ground into which drains bring sewage and such like material and wherein continual multiplication of the organisms of putrifaction eventually cause a breaking up of such material and render it odourless and eventually innocuous.

The form most appropriate for estate would consist in a tank of say 6'x6'x6' – the depth to vary as the subsoil water level– made of concrete, filled about ¼ of the depth with coral rock or coarse metal.

The overflow should be ærated and filtered by being allowed to pass by Herring bone[13] ½ pipe drains on to the soil before entering any river or drain. The distance of safety from the River or drain of the Tank will vary with the constitution of the soil over which the watery material has to pass, but I should be inclined to advise 100 as the lowest limit of safety.

It is important to keep such tanks clear of grease and coarser refuse, but the ordinary washings of lines drains such as rice-refuse etc. will be dealt with by the tank.

The sludge which accumulates after a time should be removed occasionally and it will be found to be a highly nitrogenous manure suitable for use only at a distance from lines and buildings. /

Flooding of Septic Tanks by storm water should be provided against as far as possible and the area liable to be affected by such flooding restricted by a band.

I am quite convinced that the system of leading lines drains into the ordinary road drain is a fertile source of disease in this country and that any tank which would allow of sufficient delay for some purity to take place before the contents of the drains reach the Road or estate main drain would be an improvement on the present system which is dangerous.

More elaborate and efficient septic tanks can be seen in action at Singapore and Kuala Lumpur, and a complete sewage system on a large scale at Rangoon. /

MARJORIBANKS AND MARAKKAYAR, *REPORT ON INDIAN LABOUR EMIGRATING TO CEYLON AND MALAYA* (1917)

N. E. Marjoribanks and A. K. G. Marakkayar, *Report on Indian Labour Emigrating to Ceylon and Malaya* (Madras, 1917), pp. 1–43.

Sir Norman Edward Marjoribanks (1872–1939) was variously an Indian magistrate, the Madras Commissioner of Salt and Excise, a member of the Madras Board of Revenue and of the Executive Council of the Governor of Madras, and, from 29 June to 11 November 1929, the acting Governor of Madras. In 1916, protests by Indian independence movement activists prompted the Indian government to establish a Commission chaired by Charles George Todhunter to investigate the conditions of Indian indentured migrants working on the plantations of Ceylon. In October, the Madras government replaced Todhunter with Marjoribanks, who widened the scope of the investigation to cover Indian labour in Malaya. He and A. K. G. Ahmad Thambi Marakkayar arrived in Penang on 27 December and spent the following month collecting information and visiting arrival depots, quarantine camps and estates throughout the country. Their extremely thorough report provides a history of Indian migration to the region and describes the recruitment, payment and living conditions of workers and the operation of the Immigration Fund. Published in India in 1917, it was severely criticized by Indian nationalists, who claimed that it was insufficiently wide-ranging.[1]

Notes
1. P. Peebles, *The Plantation Tamils of Ceylon* (London: Continuum International Publishing Group, 2001), pp. 110–13.

N. E. Marjoribanks and A. K. G. Marakkayar, *Report on Indian Labour Emigrating to Ceylon and Malaya* (1917), extract

II. Strength, distribution and sufficiency of the labour force. – 3. The peninsula having been under the Government of India till April 1st, 1867, migration between India and Malaya has gone on for a long time past. In the main, there are three classes of Indians employed in Malaya: (1) traders and petty shop-keepers mostly Muhammadans of the Marakkayar community and Chettis, (2) Sikhs and Pathans (locally called Bengalis) who are employed as cart-drivers, policemen and watchmen and (3) Tamil, Telugu and Malayalee labourers. It is with the last class alone that this report is concerned.

4. At the census of 1911, the Indian population of the whole of Malaya totalled 267,170 (204,220 males and 62,950 females). Of this number 5,659 were in Johore, 6,074 in Kedab, 731 in Kelantan, 114 in Perils, and 61 in Trengganu. In the Federated Malay States and the Colony proper, the Labour Code is administered by one and the same department under the Controller of Labour. There are also Health Officers for each district under the Principal Medical Officers, Federated Malay States, and Straits Settlements, respectively. No particulars as to the occupation of the Indian population in the non-federated States is available, nor is the Indian labourer in these States under the care of the labour department of the Colony and the Federated Malay States. The Johore State, however, has a British adviser and has a specially appointed State official (a Malay officer) as Superintendent of Indian immigrants and the Johore Immigration Ordinance is similar to the law in force in the Colony and the Federated Malay States. In Kedah, the State Surgeon (a British officer) is the Health officer and the Superintendent of Indian immigrants. Indian labourers in Kedah also petition the Deputy Controller of Labour at Penang who goes into their cases in consultation with the State Surgeon. There appear to be no special arrangements in Trengganu and Perlis where the Indian labour population is insignificant.

5. In the Colony proper, the Indian population in 1911 was 82,055 (62,330 males and 19,725 females). Separate figures are not given for the labour pop-

ulation on estates. But the total Tamil, Telugu and Malayalee population was 67,443 only (52,075 males and 15,868 females). These figures include the large Tamil Muhammadan (Marakkayar) population in Penang, Singapore and other towns. These people do not, as a rule, bring their womenfolk from India but contract alliances with Malay women. Taking only the rural districts in Province Wellesley, Dindings and Malacca, the total Tamil, Telugu and Malayalee population in 1911 was 25,369 (18,845 males and 7,024 females); deducting 6,869 as an estimate of the population engaged in trade and under Government on the railway and other public works, 20,000 may be taken as approximately the estate labour population. The annual reports of the Controller of Labour give the number of working labourers only; and the number of Indian workers in the Colony on the 31st December 1910, including statute and free immigrants, was 12,054, Province Wellesley contains a number of large estate properties of many years standing, and there is on these estates a much larger proportion of non-working women and children than in the more recently-established estates in other parts of the Colony and Federated Malay States. For example, on the Caledonia group of estates there are 1,077 non-workers among the total Indian estate population of 4,484 and on Prai estate there are 364 non-workers among the total estate Indian population of 845.

6. In the Federated Malay States, the Indian population in 1911 was 172,465 (131,865 males and 40,600 females.) Of these 156,730 (117,856 males and 38,874 females) were Tamils, Telugus and Malayalees. The total estate population was 159,638 (127,144 males and 32,494 females); of these 94,950 (70,208 males and 24,742 females) were Indians, 93,462 being Tamils, Telugus or Malayalees. As in the case of the Colony, the annual reports of Controller of Labour give only the number of the working labourers on estates; the number of Indian working labourers / on the 1st January 1911 was 85,268; as the estate Indian population over 12 years of age at the Census was only 82,490, it would follow that there are fewer non-workers in the estates in the Federated Malay States than in the Province Wellesley. This is also the result of our personal observation.

7. It will be noted that only 60 per cent of the estate population was Indian. Of the remaining 40 per cent, 25 per cent is Chinese and the remainder consists of Malays and allied races. The employment of Chinese labour on estates was quite recent in 1911. Also, the estate Indian labour population in the whole of Malaya at the Census was only about 130,000, out of a total Indian population of 267,170, the great majority of whom were from the Madras Presidency.

8. The following table exhibits the numbers of arrivals and departures between Madras and Penang from 1900 to 1916. In 1910, the last batch of immigrants executed indentures and the last indenture expired in 1913. The figures in columns 2 to 5 (*b*) inclusive represent labourers alone. Those in columns 6 and 7 include traders, domestic servants, etc., but the Controller of Labour in his annual report estimates that two-thirds of the numbers in columns 6 and 7 represent labourers otherwise than those recruited by registered licensed kanganies. Unfortunately no information is available to differentiate the returning labourers from others in columns 9 and 10. /

STATEMENT of arrivals and departures between Madras Presidency and Malaya.

Year.	Statute adult labourers.		Non-statute recruited labourers with free or assisted passages.		Other third-class passengers		Total.	Departures from Malaya. (All third-class passengers.)		
(1)	Males. (2)	Females. (3)	Adults. (4)	Minors. (5)	Adults. (6)	Minors. (7)	(8)	Adults. (9)	Minors. (10)	Total. (11)
1900	5,676	1,939	7,365	1,542	20,371	1,636	38,529	10,739	512	11,251
1901	1,883	902	3,871	1,356	18,701	1,546	28,259	15,434	770	16,204
1902	1,849	581	1,757	260	14,488	1,307	20,242	17,219	964	18,183
1903	385	97	1,994	155	18,080	1,319	22,030	16,868	964	17,832
1904	2,333	337	3,556	331	22,665	1,479	30,701	18,649	901	19,550
1905	3,854	969	8,049	1,099	24,179	1,389	39,539	18,799	955	19,754
1906	2,937	737	20,498	2,149	24,419	1,301	52,041	21,144	735	21,879
1907	4,555	934	24,882	2,066	28,345	1,482	62,274	29,631	891	30,522

Year. (1)	Statute adult labourers.		Arrival in Malaya. Non-statute recruited labourers with free or assisted passages.				Other third class passengers.				Departures from Malaya. (All third-class passengers.)		
	Males. (2)	Females. (3)	Adult Males. 4 (a)	Adult Females. 4 (b)	Minor Males. 5 (a)	Minor Females. 5-(b)	Adult. Males. 6 (a)	Adult Females. 6 (b)	Minors. (7)	Total. (8)	Adults. (9)	Minors. (10)	Tot (11)
1908	4,506	950	17,157	3,124	875	685	24,041	1,714	1,419	54,471	29,774	1,146	30,920
1909	3,557	562	17,286	3,163	841	673	20,910	1,686	1,139	49,817	30,284	1,090	31,374
1910	2,289	234	46,506	9,586	2,338	1,917	17,969	1,773	1,111	83,723	37,829	1,251	39,080
1911			64,718	13,658	3,259	2,754	21,533	1,309	1,240	108,47	46,464	1,639	48,103
1912			60,083	13,610	3,327	2,818	23,330	2,222	1,538	106,928	61,350	2,535	63,885
1913			67,957	15,892	4,056	3,331	22,776	2,962	1,609	118,553	66,695	3,395	70,090
1914			27,991	6,256	1,489	1,169	12,076	1,486	750	51,217	60,408	2,665	63,073
1915			42,174	9,104	2,005	1,598	17,470	1,776	1,196	75,323	48,137	2,183	50,320
1916			51,611	13,562	3,955	2,963	19,262	2,549	1,674	95,566	52,397	2,082	54,479
Total from 1911 inclusive.			314,534	72,082	18,091	14,633	116,437	12,304	8,007	556,088	335,451	14,499	349,950 /

9. Since the beginning of 1911 to the end of 1916, there has been an excess of immigrants over emigrants of 206,138. But it is not possible to estimate with accuracy what proportion of these are labourers. The annual medical reports of the Colony do not give separately for Indians the births and deaths in each year. Only a portion of the excess appears to consist of estate labour as the number of working labourers at the beginning of 1916 was 129, 396 in the Federated Malay States and 19,829 in the Colony. This is an increase of 44,128 and of 7,775 respectively on the corresponding figures at the beginning of 1911. The excess of deaths over births among the whole Indian population in the Federated Malay States during the five years 1911 to 1915 inclusive was 31,719.

The total estate Indian population, workers and non-workers, might perhaps now (January 1917) be estimated at 150,000 in the Federated Malay States and 30,000 in the Colony.

In Johore, the estate Indian working population on estates of over 100 acres was 9,399 in 1915 and the corresponding figure for Kedah and Kelantan was 6,505. The total Indian estate population in these non-federated States at present may therefore be pat at 20,000.

Thus the total Indian estate population in the whole of Malaya, workers and non-workers, may be estimated to number at present 200,000 and the total Indian population to be about double that number.

Outside the rubber estates, Indian labour is employed chiefly under Government on public works, roads, railways and canals. The working Indian labour force under Government in the Federated Malay States at the end of 1915 was 15,803 and in the Colony proper 3,678. Few Indian labourers are employed on the tin mines which are worked almost entirely by Chinese labour.

10. The report of the Agricultural Department for 1915 gives the statistics of labour and acreages under rubber, etc., for the Federated Malay States and the non-federated States only, i.e., the figures for the Colony proper are not given. Moreover the statistics are only for estates* over 100 acres in extent. The following statement shows the present (1915) acreages under rubber in those areas and the available labour force (workers) thereon. The areas under products other than rubber (cocoanuts, coffee, etc.) being insignificant, they have been left out of account.

---

*   Under the Labour Code, an estate is defined to mean any agricultural land exceeding twenty-five acres in extent upon which agricultural operations of any kind are carried on or upon which the produce of any plants or trees is collected or treated or any mine to which the provisions of the code have been declared to apply. /

Province or State.	Number of estates.	Area planted. ACS.	Area producing. ACS.	Indian.	Others, i.e., Chinese, Malaya and Javanese.	Total.
Selangor	324	211,704	125,261	64,568	10,779	75,347
Perak	365	166,248	91,069	51,707	18,609	70,316
Negri Sembilan	166	109,723	59,934	10,373	20,476	30,849
Pahang	31	11,804	4,866	1,461	2,422	3,883
Total, Federated Malay States	886	499,479	281,130	128,109	52,286	180,395
Johore	153	131,396	47,609	9,399	20,350	29,749
Kelantan and Kedah	151	70,049	19,011	6,505	16,169	22,674
Trengganu	8	2,611	Nil.	18,	4,543	4,561
Grand total	1,198	703,535	347,750	144,031	93,348	237,379

The header above the Indian / Others / Total columns reads: "Labour force (workers only) – Men, women and children."

Thus, counting women and children, there is one labourer to every 1.46 acres in bearing and to every 3 acres planted.

III – History of labour immigration from India, present system of recruitment, immigration fund, legal status of labourer. – 11. As in the case of Ceylon, the history of / immigrant labour to Malaya has been intimately connected with that of the planting industry. A brief account of such immigration, up to the passing of India Act V of 1877, is given in the report of a commission that sat in the Straits in 1890-91... At all times there appears to have been a considerable number of free immigrants but it is doubtful how far these comprised estate labourers. Till about 1887, the chief planting industry was sugarcane cultivation in Province Wellesley and, up to 1885, Indian labourers were recruited for work on these plantations on indenture under the provisions of India Act V of 1877. The increase in the number of immigrants not coming under the Act led to the question being raised as to the need for such a law in India. Mr. (afterwards Sir) E. C. Buck, Secretary to the Government of India, and Colonel Bowness Fischer were deputed to visit Malaya and as a result of their report, the Straits Government passed an Indian Immigration Ordinance in 1884, and the Government of India repealed Act V of 1877 in 1885. Recruitment in India was under the new arrangement freed from legal restrictions, but, under executive rules, recruiters sent over by persons in the Straits to recruit labourers in India were registered and granted licences by the Straits Immigration agent: such licences did not, however, confer on the recruiter any legal powers or rights whatever. Persons engaged under these rules were also registered and on arrival in the Straits came under the provisions of the Indian Immigration Ordinance, 1884; and all persons who had received advances as defined in the Ordinance were bound to execute three-year contracts on arrival at the Straits or to repay the advances received together with "smart" money. No recruiter was to receive any commission for any labourer not registered as emigrating under "advances."

12. These rules and the contract labour system were apparently devised to meet the requirements of the sugar plantations. When coffee-planting developed and extended, coffee-planters found that the conditions enabled them to dispense with long contracts and to recruit free labourers and the number of free labourers emigrating from India continued to increase notwithstanding the executive rules above referred to. In 1897, these executive rules were cancelled and the Government in India ceased to exercise any direct control over emigration to Malaya whether the emigrants went as free or as contract labourers.

13. From about 1900, rubber began to displace both sugar and coffee and the area of the plantations increased rapidly. The demand for estate labour became great and complaints were rife that labourers recruited by employers at considerable cost from India, were crimped[1] by their unscrupulous neighbours. At this period there were three kinds of immigrant labour, viz., indentured or contract labour, kangany-recruited labour, and the so-called independent labour. The indentured or contract labour was engaged under the provisions of the Indian Immigration Ordinance VI of 1904 (which superseded Ordinance VII of 1899 which had in its turn superseded the Immigration Ordinance of 1884). These indentured labourers were mainly for the sugar estates, Government departments (Roads and Railways) and a few of the rubber estates where the conditions were such that other labourers were reluctant to go there. The kangany-recruited labour formed the bulk of the labour on the rubber estates. These labourers were recruited by kanganies or gang headmen chosen by estate managers and sent over to India to recruit labourers under licences issued by the Superintendent of Immigrants. The labourers recruited received free passage tickets but did not enter into any indenture on arrival in Malaya. They were expected to pay back the advances they had received; but the complaint was that they were enticed away by other employers before they had paid back their advances. The independent labourers were men recruited in India at the instance of the proprietors opening up new estates. Such proprietors having no labour force from which to send recruiters were compelled to have recourse to professional labour agents or recruiters in India, and the class of labourers supplied is said to have been generally most unsatisfactory, both in character and physique.

14. In the interests of the development of the country, the Straits Government took up the question of the labour supply. The control and supervision of immigration was in 1907 vested in an Immigration Committee consisting of the Superintendent of Immigrants (now Controller of Labour) as Chairman,

the Principal Medical / Officer of the Federated Malay States, the Director of Public Works of the Federated Malay States and four or five non-official gentlemen, members of firms of estate agents or managers of estates. This committee after consulting the Planters' Association of Malaya recommended that the cost of importation of Tamil labourers should be distributed amongst all those who employed them, and the Indian Immigration Fund Enactment (incorporated in the Federated Malay States Labour Code of 1912) was subsequently passed. Similar enactments or rules passed by the States concerned are in force in the non-federated Malay States. In the colony, the law relating to Indian labourers has not yet been codified, but for practical purposes it may be taken to be identical with the provisions of the Federated Malay States Labour Code (1912).

15. Under these laws, an assessment on the amount of work done by their labourers is levied upon all employers of labourers native to the Madras Presidency (described as "Indian labour") and the proceeds are paid into a fund styled the Immigration Fund. Employers are required to send in to the Labour office, Penang, on printed forms which may be obtained free, certified returns of their Indian labour for every quarter... The returns must be sent within a month of the expiration of each quarter, i.e., in April, July, October and January and should be addressed to the Deputy Controller of Labour, Penang. These returns are assessed according to the rates published for each quarter in the Government gazette and each employer is duly sent a notice informing him of the amount of assessment he is required to pay. The amount each employer is assessed at should be forwarded to the Deputy Controller of Labour, Penang, within 21 days of the posting of the notice and for payments made after such period, the employer is charged interest at the rate of 8 per cent per annum on the amount assessed.

All such payments are credited to the Immigration Fund, which forms no part of the general revenue of the Government, but is administered by the Controller of Labour under the authority of the Immigration Committee solely in the interests of importers of Indian labour. The Government is in fact the largest single contributor to the Fund through the assessments which it pays on all Indian labour employed in the Railways, Public Works Departments, Municipalities, Sanitary Boards and other departments.

16. The law (section 156 of the Federated Malay States Labour Code, 1912) provides for the levy of two rates, one, ordinary, on all Indian labourers employed, and the other, a special, or extra rate on the Indian labourers employed over and above the number recruited from India by the employers within the last 24 months: the maximum assessment per labourer per quarter may not exceed three dollars. A special or extra rate was proposed during 1911-14, but gave rise to dissatisfaction and was finally abandoned on the ground that it bore too heavily on

small estates in comparison with large ones. With a large labour force, a shortage of labour can be tided over pending recruitment from India without resorting to local engagement of labour, while a small estate cannot do without or wait. The ordinary rate has varied from two dollars* to ½ a dollar and has from 1st January 1917 been fixed at 1 ½ dollars per quarter. The assessment is calculated in the following manner. The total amount of work done by all the Indian labourers under an employer in the quarter is reduced to so many days' work in accordance with [certain] rules..., and the result is divided by 78, this being taken as the standard number of days' work a labourer may be expected to do in a quarter. The number of work units thus arrived at is multiplied by the rate (now 1 ½ dollars) and the result is the quarter's assessment.

17. The terms, employer and Indian labourer, are defined (section 150 of the Federated Malay States Labour Code) so as to include in the scope of the law –
(1) Agriculture including the treatment of produce and its porterage[2] to the place of treatment.
(2) The making and upkeep of roads. /
(3) The construction and maintenance of canals.
(4) Railway construction, maintenance and working.
(5) The construction, maintenance and working of all works of a public nature or for the public good.
(6) Mining and work in mines.
(7) Quarrying and stone breaking.
(8) Brick-making.
(9) The treatment in mills and factories of padi, rubber and other agricultural produce, including porterage in connection with such treatment.
(10) Any other kind of labour to be notified by the High Commissioner (Governor) except administrative or clerical work or work in private gardens attached to residences.

18. When an estate manager or other employer wishes to recruit Indian labour, he selects his own recruiters from amongst his labour force and applies to the Indian Immigration Committee at Penang for a licence.

Licences...to recruit labourers in the Madras Presidency are then issued to these persons (kanganies so-called) on the authority of the Chairman of the Immigration Committee and are granted free of charge. Blank licence forms are sent to any employer on application to any of the Labour offices, and when the required details have been filled in the licences should be sent to the Deputy Controller of Labour, Penang, for registration and signature. Such licences are not issued to persons under the age of 21 years. The Controller and Deputy Controller of Labour have full powers to refuse licences or to cancel licences.

---

*   One dollar = one rupee twelve annas. /

19. At Madras and at Negapatam emigration offices have been established by the Colonial Government under the charge of their officers. The agent at Madras, Mr. Bathurst, is an officer of the Colonial Civil Service. The agent at Negapatam. Dr. Ford, is an officer of Straits Medical Service. There are also fourteen recruiting inspectors stationed at various places* in the Madras Presidency, whose duty it is to assist kanganies, help in forwarding their recruits and to pay their train fares.

The kangany on receipt of his licence proceeds to Madras or Negapatam, and has his licence registered in the office of the emigration agent.

The licence is valid for six months only but the emigration agent may renew it for further periods of three months at a time if he is satisfied that the kangany is likely to recruit the number specified in his licence if given more time. The number of recruits is limited in any licence to 50. After his licence has been registered, the kangany has to go to either Messrs. Binny & Co., Madras, or Messrs the Madura Company, Negapatam. These firms are the British India Steam Navigation Company's agents, and generally act as financial agents in India for employers in the Straits. In addition there is the Malay Peninsula Agricultural Association Agency in Madras and Negapatam who also act as financial agents for certain estates in the Straits. The employer when sending his kangany to recruit therefore makes arrangements with such agents to finance the kangany, and according to the instructions received these agents make advances to the kanganies and pay commission for each labourer actually produced by the kanganies and shipped.

By this system the risk is avoided of giving to the kangany large advances in cash in Malaya which he might very likely squander. The firms mentioned above have agents in Malaya to whom they cable on the occasion of every shipment the number of labourers shipped for each estate; the local agents inform the employers and it is thus possible for each employer to know before arrival of the steamer the number of labourers shipped for him.

20. After receiving an advance (usually about Rs. 20) from the financial agents, the kangany proceeds to find labourers willing to emigrate. When he has succeeded in getting together as many as he thinks it practicable to obtain at the time, the kangany takes them to the nearest railway station and thence to the Straits Government camps or depots at Avadi (near Madras) or Negapatam, where the intending / emigrants are accommodated and fed until shipment. The

*

Waltair.	Katpadi.
Bezwada.	Tindivanam.
Gudur.	Negapatam.
Tanjore.	Trichinopoly.
Manapparai.	Kodikānal Road.
Erode.	Tirur.

emigrants are examined medically before embarkation but the examination is not of a searching character. Cases of enlarged spleen[3] and poor physique are rejected. Women are not examined at all.

The trainage[4] of the emigrants to Madras or Negapatam is paid for by the Recruiting Inspector (if there happens to be one at the station where the emigrants are first entrained) or advanced by the kangany and afterwards recovered by him from the Emigration Agent (Madras) or Superintendent of the Emigration Depot (Negapatam). After the emigrants are shipped, the kangany receives his commission, less the advance already received, from the financial agents of his estate and again looks for recruits: or he returns to the estate if he has got his complement, or thinks he cannot get more within the time allowed him on his licence.

21. The emigrants are carried by the British India Steam Navigation Company's steamers weekly. The company has contracted to run a weekly service from Madras and Negapatam to the Straits Settlements and to provide extra tonnage if necessary. The rate charged per emigrant is Rs. 12 from Madras and Rs. 10 from Negapatam. This rate includes charges for food during the voyage which may last as long as eight days from Madras and six days from Negapatam. The company employs a sufficient number of cooks on board the steamers to supply suitable meals to passengers twice a day. Two to three inspectors (Indians) are employed by the Immigration Bund Committee to look after the health and comfort of the emigrants during the voyage and to deal with all complaints.

22. All immigrant labourers are quarantined, usually for a week, on arrival at Penang and Port Swettenham. The quarantine camps have been built and are maintained at Government expense but the cost of feeding the immigrants in quarantine is borne by the Fund. After quarantine, immigrants are removed to two large depots at Penang and Port Swettenham, and from thence removed by the employer or his agent to their place of employment. Each employer is notified previously as to the day his labourers will be ready for removal from the depot.

23. Of the expenditure involved in the arrangements above described the following items are borne by the Immigration Fund: –
(*a*) The salaries of the inspectors of recruiting.
(*b*) The train fares of recruits (where advanced by an inspector) from the place of recruitment to Avadi or Negapatam.
(*c*) The cost of feeding the intending emigrants at the camps at Avadi and Negapatam; and at the quarantine camps after their arrival in Malaya.
(*d*) The cost of transporting the emigrants from Avadi or Negapatam to their first place of employment in the Federated Malay States, Straits Settlements, Johore, Kedah, Perlis or Kelantan, including all boat hires, steamer, train and motor-bus fares and the cost of telegrams by estate agents to employers stating the number of labourers received in the immigrant depots.

24. The Government bears all the expenses of administering the Fund, paying the salaries of officials and clerks; maintains the camps or depots at Madras and Negapatam where labourers recruited by kanganies are housed pending shipment; provides officials in India (the Emigration Agent at Madras and the Superintendent of the Emigration Depot at Negapatam) who superintend these camps and generally assist in matters connected with recruiting; provides detention depots in Penang and Port Swettenham and grants a large annual subsidy to the steamship company which maintains the weekly service from India to the Straits.

25. Other charges that are met from the Fund are: –
(1) the cost of maintenance of a Home for decrepit Indian labourers
(This Home, which is in Kuala Lumpur, was opened in November 1913... The
    Home is under the supervision of a Medical Superintendent and is visited
    periodically by members of a Board of Visitors appointed for the purpose);
(2) the payment of interest upon moneys borrowed by the Indian Immigration
    Committee; /
(3) the payment of recruiting allowances (since the starting of the fund a
    recruiting allowance has been paid to employers in respect of each labourer
    imported by them from the Madras Presidency under the Committee's
    licences. This allowance has varied from $3 to $5 a head, and now stands at
    the latter figure); and
(4) the payment of the cost of preparing registers of locally engaged Indian
    labourers.

26. The whole sum collected for the Immigration Fund is thus spent either in meeting the expense of recruiting or in encouraging employers to recruit. The cost of administration is only to a small extent charged on the fund, namely, the cost of salaries of Inspectors above referred to, that of the clerical labour employed on the compilation of the register of local engagements, and the upkeep of the Home. All direct cost of recruiting is met from the fund, except the commissions the employer may pay his recruiters, the charges made by his financial agents and the cost of meals supplied to immigrants discharged from quarantine and awaiting removal in the detention depots at Penang or Port Swettenham. Where commissions are kept low, these expenses should be nearly met by the recruiting allowance, at its present figure. An account of receipts and expenditure of the immigration fund is published half-yearly... The fund has a credit balance of over half a million dollars.

Practically the only expenses a kangany recruiter has to meet out of his commission are the possible settling of any of the village debts of the intending emigrant, a small gift to any dependants of the emigrant left behind and the cost of the usual little farewell feast. The total of such expenditure need not amount to more than 3 or 4 rupees per head.

A few years back when demand for labour in Malaya was keenest, large commissions were undoubtedly paid by employers in the hope that they would thereby more quickly get labour. The results were uniformly unsatisfactory. The kangany simply used the money to buy recruits from a professional recruiter and brought back a large number of persons to his estate who were not proper agriculturists. They could not do the work expected, earned little, fell ill and many died, The reports of the Labour Department for 1911 and 1912 quote several instances of this kind and contain warnings to employers on the subject.

The matter is better understood now and the commission to a kangany per recruit rarely exceeds Rs. 12. Estates in the healthy coast districts of Selangor find a commission of Rs. 7 or even Rs. 5 to be ample to secure as much labour as they need.

27. The Straits Government officers at Negapatam and Avadi take several precautions to ensure that recruiting is properly done. The recruiting kangany is warned on arrival that any irregular practices on his part, such as dealing with professional recruiters or enticing away minors without their parents' consent will involve the loss of his licence. The locality in which he is to recruit, namely, the village he himself belongs to, is noted on his licence and if any of the recruits he brings to the depot are found to come from other localities they are rejected. Boys under 16 years of age are rejected unless they are accompanied by their parents or adult near relative and the relationship is substantiated by separate cross-examination of the parties. Minor girls are rejected unless they are accompanied by their parents: an immature girl is not allowed to emigrate with her husband unless her parents also are going. Single women are rejected unless they are accompanied by male relatives who can look after them. Twice a day at Avadi and every morning at Negapatam, all petitioners who have come in search of lost relatives are allowed into the camp, and if they find the persons they are seeking they remove them without let or hindrance.

In all cases where intending emigrants are rejected for any of the above reasons (except where the only reason of rejection is the objection of relatives) their railway fare is paid back to their villages, and the amount together with any expenditure already incurred (e.g., for food) on their account is debited to the financial agents of the estate to recover or not as they may see fit from the kangany. If the case discloses any misbehaviour on the part of the kangany his licence is endorsed or cancelled as the circumstances may warrant. /

28. It will be seen from the statement in paragraph 8 that the system of controlled recruitment and assisted immigration above described has been very successful in increasing the numbers of immigrants to Malaya. The figures have risen every year from 1907 to 1913. In 1914 there was a considerable falling off owing partly to economies on rubber estates and partly to the war. Since 1914,

the figures have increased again each year. The number of recruiting licences issued was 10,806 in 1913, 5,732 in 1914 and 5,436 in 1915. The number of emigrants recruited by kanganies in each of these three years was 88,486, 34,735 and 52,572, respectively. This gives an average of about eight recruits per licence issued: but many licensees (one-seventh of the total number, it is estimated) do not succeed in getting recruits at all.

The numbers in columns 4 and 5 of the statement in paragraph 8 include for each year a certain number of emigrant labourers who were not recruited but who presented themselves voluntarily as emigrants and were given free passages as being emigrant labourers. The number of such emigrants for the six years 1910 – 1915 was as follows, 1,327, 2,187, 1,467, 2,750, 2,170 and 2,309, respectively. Most of these were going out to join relatives or friends who had been recruited and had emigrated previously. These voluntary emigrants are free to go where they please after their quarantine is over.

29. The system of indenture having been discontinued after 1910 and the last indenture having expired in 1913, all Indian labourers are now employed on monthly parol agreements and are entitled to leave their employer after a month's notice or on the payment of a month's pay in lieu of notice, whether they are immigrants imported from India or are engaged locally. The law prohibits the Indian immigrant from entering into a written contract to serve as a labourer (section 61 of the Labour Code). No deductions may be made from their wages for any sums advanced to them or expended in their recruitment before their arrival at their place of employment (section 98 of the Labour Code). Nor may a labourer be made liable for the debt or default of another (section 97). The Labour Code contains other provisions regarding work and wages, housing, and sanitary and medical care of labourers which will be noticed in dealing with these subjects.

30. The Code and the similar Ordinances in the colony proper are administered by the Controller of Labour and his deputies and assistants with the aid of the various district medical or health officers. All these officers systematically inspect estates and other places where labourers (Indian and others) are employed. The form of a labour officer's report…shows that all matters in any way concerning the labourer's health and welfare receive notice. Besides the Controller, there are at present seven labour officers of whom three are stationed at Penang for supervision of Indian labour employed in Province Wellesley, the Dindings and Perak, two at Klang for the greater part of Selangor, one at Seremban for Negri Sembilan and Malacca and one assists the Controller at the headquarters, Kuala Lumpur.

All these officers know to speak Tamil and to read petitions in Tamil.

The officers of the Labour Department also receive petitions and complaints from labourers and enquire and take action thereon. Indeed, apart from health and sanitation, the most useful work of the labour officers lies in settling disputes and misunderstandings between employers and labourers and in promoting harmonious relations between them. The annual reports of the Controller give details of such work. Generally speaking, trouble between an estate manager and his Indian labourers is mainly due to the inability of the former to communicate readily with the latter in their own language. Besides leading to actual misunderstanding, the inability of a manager to speak directly with his labourers allows of the gang head – men and other subordinates (kanganies or mandors) getting too much influence over the labourers – a state of things that does not conduce to the benefit either of the labourer or of the estate.

31. The Indian labourer in Malaya does not start in debt as in Ceylon. His wages also are considerably higher than in Ceylon. Yet there appears to be considerable restlessness among the labour force. In 1915, 40,028 Indian labourers deserted, i.e., left their employers without notice, and 58,848 Indian labourers were engaged / locally and of these engagements only 32,917 were notified at the time they occurred to the labour offices as required by section 66 of the Code. A labourer intending to return to India usually gives notice. It is only where a labourer is dissatisfied with a particular estate whether because of its unhealthiness (a sudden increase in malarial attacks usually causes numerous departures), or because of quarrels with other labourers or with his employer, or because he has been offered some special inducement to go elsewhere, that he appears to feel shy about giving notice and prefers to depart silently as soon as he has got his last month's wages. It is doubtful, however, if all cases of desertion can be accounted for in this way. We heard no complaints that there was a practice among kanganies or mandors (as they are locally called) of moving labourers from one employer to another to benefit themselves, though some of our cooly informants said this was sometimes done. But an annual movement of about one-third of the labour force from one employer to another would seem to indicate that some such influence must be at work. In any case, any employer paying to get labourers in this fashion could not recover what he paid or even debit it against the labourers.

IV – Work, wages, and punishments. – 32. On the rubber estates, where much the greater portion of the Indian labourers in Malaya are employed, the work consists chiefly of tapping and weeding and factory work. Tappers begin work at daybreak and bring in the latex to the factory about 11 a.m. By noon their regular day's work is over. They can, if they like, do weeding or other odd jobs in the afternoon for which they are paid extra. Weeding is usually done on contract at from one dollar to 15 cents an acre according to the state of the land. The task for men tappers is from 300 to 400 trees according to the nature of the ground (as hilly or level). Wages vary within a margin of about 10 cents between the coast districts of Selangor and the more remote and less healthy districts in Negri Sembilan and Perak. Tappers thus begin at 25 cents to 35 cents a day and rise as they become efficient to 35 or 45 cents a day. Women tappers usually get 25 cents to 30 cents a day and boys and girls 10 to 15 cents. Weeding where done by task is paid for at about 30 to 35 cents for men and 25 to 30 cents for women. On many estates a sliding scale of pay is in force, e.g., if a labourer works 20 days in the month he is paid 35 cents a day; if 24 days in the month, he gets 40 cents a day; if 28 days, then 45 cents a day. The number of days and the rate varies on different localities and on different estates.

Factory labourers get 50 to 60 cents a day and overtime. Kanganies are paid at the same rate as ordinary labourers plus 2 cents (paid by the estate) per day per labourer of their gangs that turns out to work.

By law no labourer shall be bound to work on more than six days in a week or more than six consecutive hours or more than nine hours a day. If he works for and at the request of his employer more than nine hours in any one day, he is entitled to be paid extra at the rate of not less than one-eighteenth part of his ordinary daily wages for each half hour of overtime work (section 99 of the Labour Code).

33. Wages must be paid at least once a month and that not later than, in the case of Muhammadan labourers, the second Thursday and, in the case of other labourers, the second Saturday of the next month.

Only the cost of rice and food (not intoxicating liquor) advanced by an employer may be recovered from a labourer's wages which must otherwise be paid in legal tender. No interest may be charged and no deductions are admissible on account of fines for bad work or for injury to the materials or other property of the employer. Employers may establish shops for the sale of rice or, if the place of employment be more than two miles from any town or village, for the sale of provisions generally to his labourers. But in the latter case the scale of prices must be approved by the Labour Department. The labourers moreover shall not be compelled to buy either rice or any other provisions at such shops.

We heard no complaints about the supply of rice or other provisions. Rice alone is usually advanced at the rate of two gantangs* a week to men and two gantangs one week and one gantang the next to women. It is charged as a rule at cost price and sometimes at under cost price in localities to which the cost of transport is considerable. There are usually several shops in the neighbourhood of large estates. /

34. Some estates pay weekly as they find that this conduces to thrift on the part of their labourers and serves to prevent their getting into debt with the bazaar men or spending their money in the toddy shops on pay days. By law the keepers of liquor-shops are prohibited under severe penalties from selling spirits to Indian labourers. A special commission is now sitting on the question of the

*   8 Gantangs = 1 bushel.[5]

purity and wholesomeness of the toddy supplied to estate labourers. The right to sell toddy is sold under licence but the supply is not at present regulated by any system of licensing the right to tap trees (coconut palms). The general consensus of opinion is that drunkenness amongst the Indian labourers has diminished in recent years. The great improvements effected in sanitation and housing and the high wages now paid would naturally tend to produce this result.

35. As regards the cost of living of an Indian labourer, a dollar does not perhaps go much further than a rupee in India, but it certainly goes as far: and any surplus dollars are worth Rs. 1-12-0 to bring home to India. One of the most experienced and sympathetic of the Labour Officers we met, who had been Emigration agent in India for some years and knew the Indian cooly and his language well, told us he had several times worked out the monthly cost of living of the Indian labourer on an estate and estimated it at six dollars on the average, rather less on the coast of Selangor and rather more on the out-of-the-way estates inland. This estimate allows not only for food but for little luxuries such as cigarettes or cheroots and occasional drinks.

In appendix XV [not included] will be found a number of statements showing the actual number of days a month Indian labourers worked and the actual wages they earned on estates situated in different parts of the colony and the Federated Malay States. In these statements men, women and children workers are all reckoned and accordingly the average wage is lower in Province Wellesley generally and on estates (such as Estate B) where there are a large number of women and children workers than it is in Malacca where the labour population is nearly all adult male. On the other hand family earnings will be high where the number of women and children workers is large. The statements moreover omit the head money usually paid to kanganies and amounts earned on contract and piece-work.

36. There is ample reason for believing that the average Indian labourer not only can, but does, save money during his employment in Malaya. In the first place, every week large numbers of Indian labourers return from Malaya. They must have saved at least their passage money, Rs. 22-8-0. Next, the post office returns of the Federated Malay States show that 84,410 dollars were on 31st December 1915 held on account of 1,500 Indian labourers in the savings bank. No doubt the classification is approximate, and the labourers may be, and probably are, kanganies, as the ordinary Indian labourer hoards his savings and remits them or brings them home with him, and does not put them into the post office savings bank. Still, it should be remembered that the kangany is of the same class as the labourer, and that any labourer of intelligence and enterprise may become a kangany. The post office returns further show that the amount remitted to India by money order in 1915 was over 35 lakhs of rupees in 46,866 orders. Traders and merchants as a rule use hundis[6] and bills for remittance, not the post office: a great part of these remittances were undoubtedly those of Indian labourers.

Lastly, there is the evidence of the returning labourer himself. On S.S. *Thongwa* on the 21st and 22nd, Mr. Marjoribanks questioned many of the returning labourers (who were to have been, but could not be landed at Negapatam on the 22nd) and, later, we questioned many labourers on board outward bound who had been to Malaya before. We also questioned several labourers on the return voyage. Practically every man said he had saved something, the amount varying from 30 dollars to 200 dollars. Mr. Ahmad Tambi Marakkayar mustered the labourers returning home on the S.S. *Teesta*, about eleven hundred in number, and found that they had no complaints to make against their late employers and that they all had savings of varying amounts and that all appeared to be in good health.

37. The Labour Code contains several penal provisions, some directed against the employer, and others against the labourer. The chief offences an employer may be guilty of under the code are assaulting or molesting a labourer, crimping and failure to pay wages within the time required by law or to send in the returns prescribed. The labourer may offend by neglecting or refusing to work, absconding (or leaving / without notice), unlawful disobedience or insolence. In appendix XVI [not included] is printed a complete return of the cases brought against employers and labourers in the Federated Malay States during 1915 and a return for the first half of 1916. It will be seen that the commonest offence of employers was crimping (102 cases in 1915) and that of labourers was absconding (964 cases in 1915). The number of offences is small in comparison with the total labour population.

In the colony, the only cases taken to court were under section 14 of Ordinance I of 1882. Under this law disputes as to wages and complaints of disobedience, negligence, carelessness, or other misconduct, may be laid before a magistrate, who may after enquiry adjudicate thereon, and levy a fine not exceeding 25 dollars. Imprisonment is awardable only in default of payment and may extend to 30 days for such default. Appendix XVII [not included] contains a complete statement of the cases taken to court during the first half-year of 1916 for the Straits Settlements. There were only 21 cases concerning 38 labourers.

38. Under the Labour Code an employer who wishes to lay a complaint against any labourer in his employment for disobedience to lawful orders, neglect of duty or neglect or refusal to work may, if the labourer is in the estate or place of employment, apprehend and take him forthwith to the magistrate, but he has not the power to arrest a labourer who has absconded or to detain any labourer in custody. As noted in paragraph 33 an employer is prohibited by law from fining a labourer and the officers of the Labour Department have taken pains to make this generally known.

All the managers of the estates we consulted considered that employers would be well advised to refrain from using the penal provisions of the code if they possibly could, and nearly all were of opinion that there would be no practical objection to their abolition at any rate so far as the penalty of imprisonment was concerned.

V. – Housing, sanitation and medical care. – 39. With the large influx of labour, much of it unsuitable for agricultural work, consequent on the opening of fresh land for rubber (see paragraph 13), high death-rates prevailed and special laws were passed to deal with the matter. Ordinance VII of 1911 (The Estate Labourers Protection of Health Ordinance) the provisions of which are reproduced in the Federated Malay States Labour Code provides (*inter alia*)[7] that it shall be the duty of every employer to provide for every labourer employed by him on an estate who resides on such estate

(*a*) sufficient and proper house accommodation;
(*b*) a sufficient supply of wholesome water;
(*c*) sufficient and proper sanitary arrangements;
(*d*) hospital accommodation and equipment;
(*e*) medical attendance and treatment including diets in hospital;
(*f*) a sufficient supply of medicines of good quality (section 189 of Labour Code).

An employer is liable to a fine that may amount to 100 dollars if he houses any labourer in a building the state of which or the surroundings of which is such as to endanger the health or safety of the labourer. Separate lines must be provided for labourers of different nationality or race. The controller has power to condemn lines as insanitary or to order alterations therein. New lines must be in accordance with approved type-designs.

An employer who wishes to engage labourers on a newly-opened place must first satisfy the controller of the adequacy and suitability of the arrangements made for the residence and employment of labourers and obtain a permit. The controller has power to prohibit the employment of additional labourers unless proper arrangements are made: and the Government (Chief Secretary) may prohibit the employment or retention of labourers on any place where the arrangements to protect them from ill-treatment or ill-usage are insufficient.

40. All the lines we saw were commodious and comfortable. Those of recent construction were excellent. There are two main types. In one type, the sets of rooms are on a wooden floor raised from 4 to 8 or 10 feet above the ground on masonry pillars. The roof is lofty and well ventilated. It is sometimes of asbestos but usually of corrugated iron, in both cases with an inner ceiling of planking. The partitions do not extend up to the roof, but each room is covered with wire netting which / prevents access or peeping over the partition. Each room is 12 feet by 10 feet or 10 feet by 10 feet and is allowed either to a married couple or to not more than three adults. In the space below the superstructure the labourers

cook, stow firewood, keep fowls, etc. This type of dwelling raised above ground level is universal in Malaya. It is due apparently partly to the dampness of the soil and partly to the prevalence of white ants. In the other type the rooms are on a cement floor provided with drains and wooden walls are raised an inch or two above the floor to permit of flushing. In the lines of the latter type cooking is done in the verandahs. Separate cooking places have been experimentally tried but the labourers would not use them. The lines are usually built in blocks and in large estates practically constitute a village. In old estates the lines are sometimes of brick in lime very much of the type of the ordinary domestic servants' godowns in Madras but with broad sheltered, verandahs in front for cooking, etc. The immediate neighbourhood of all lines is kept free of all vegetation.

The water-supply on nearly all large estates is by pipes from a protected reservoir. On smaller estates protected wells are used. Health officers have power to order the provision of fresh sources of water-supply both for drinking and bathing and to prohibit the use of any existing source. Latrines of the pit or trench type are provided, but it cannot be said that their use is as general as it might be. The Tamil labourer has yet much to learn in the matter of cleanliness in person and habits. The Controller has power at the instance of the Health officer to order the provision of latrines and to fix their sites.

41. The powers referred to in paragraph 39 have been used where necessary by the Controller on the reports of the Health officers: in one case the Chief Secretary exercised the powder of prohibiting the employment of labour on an estate where malaria was very bad and prompt remedial action was not being taken. Generally, however, those responsible for the management of estates recognise that their best interests lie in maintaining their labour force in health and comfort.

42. For the general population, including labourers on estates which do not possess hospitals of their own, there are, in the Federated Malay States, 43 Government hospitals, excluding two lunatic asylum hospitals, nine gaol hospitals and two leper hospitals. The number of Indians treated at these hospitals during 1915 was 30,028 and the death-rate amongst them was 77·2 per mille[8] of admissions. There are 15 Government out-door dispensaries, but the number of Indians treated thereat is not available. In addition there were 169 estate hospitals serving 349 out of 809 estates. At these hospitals 70,506 labourers (all classes) were treated and the death-rate was 20·42 per mille of admissions.

In the colony there are outside the towns of Penang and Singapore, three Government and eight estate hospitals in Province Wellesley, two estate hospitals in the Dindings, and four Government and six estate hospitals in Malacca. The number of Indians treated in the Government hospitals is not given separately in the medical reports: nor the number of patients treated in the estate hospitals in Province Wellesley. In the Malacca estate hospitals 4,450 persons were treated and the death-rate was 31 per mille.

43. Under the Labour Code, the Controller has power to order an estate to establish and equip a hospital and to provide a qualified resident medical practi-

tioner. The power to require hospitals to be established on estates has been fully used and most of the estate hospitals appear to have been started in this way. The requirement of a qualified medical practitioner has not been insisted on to the same extent owing to the lack of qualified men. The latest rules...made under the code require, however, that there shall be one resident "dresser" for every 36 patients for whom there is accommodation, and a dresser must possess a certificate as a hospital assistant from the Medical School, Singapore, or as a dresser in the Federated Malay States Medical Department, or a certificate from a health officer to the effect that he holds qualifications similar to the above.

44. The hospitals vary from very fully equipped institutions of the most modem type in charge of resident fully-qualified European doctors to barn-like structures with a scanty equipment in charge of men of the sub-assistant surgeon class. All estate hospitals are however visited once a week usually (but sometimes less often) by fully qualified private practitioners employed by the estate: and these practitioners are telephoned for in all serious cases. /

The number of estate hospitals and their equipment and staffing has greatly improved during the last few years, and their further improvement and extension is being steadily pressed by the Labour Department. Attempts have been made to obtain qualified assistant surgeons and sub-assistant surgeons from Madras, but the result has been generally disappointing. Persons who have been dismissed from service in India, and drunkards, have largely composed the class of applicants: so much so that the local medical officers have come to prefer the men locally trained of whose character and steadiness they can be sure. The salary paid to a qualified man of the sub-assistant surgeon class is about 90 dollars a month. One hospital we visited was in charge of a Brahmin sub-assistant surgeon who was getting 120 dollars a month. The Labour Department is ready and willing to find employment for any competent and trustworthy men from Madras.

The Government hospitals are all in charge of qualified officers and those institutions we saw compared favourably with rural local board hospitals in Madras.

VI. – Vital statistics. – 45. The compilation of vital statistics is the concern of the Government Medical departments both in the Federated Malay States and in the Colony. But the published statistics do not in all cases differentiate Indians from other classes of the population or Indian labourers from others. The population is also very diverse and fluctuating, and the birth and death rates accordingly are of little or no value for purposes of comparison. The most accurate figures are those for the estate population given in the annual reports of the Controller of Labour. These are of deaths only: the figures given for births are for the whole Indian population, large sections of which, e.g., the Sikhs and the Marakkayar community, live under conditions totally different to those of the Indian estate labourer. The information about deaths in the Controller's reports is abstracted in the following statement for the five years 1911 to 1915. The figures for Johore are taken from the reports of the Superintendent of Indian Immigrants for 1913 to 1915. /

District.	1911				1912				1913				1914				1915			
	Average population.	Death-rate per mille.	Number of estates with population over 200 and death-rate over 50 per mille.	Maximum death-rate on estates with population over 200.	Average population.	Death-rate per mille.	Number of estates with population over 200 and death-rate over 50 per mille.	Maximum death-rate on estates with population over 200.	Average population.	Death-rate per mille.	Number of estates with population over 200 and death-rate over 50 per mille.	Maximum death-rate on estates with population over 200.	Average population.	Death-rate per mille.	Number of estates with population over 200 and death-rate over 50 per mille.	Maximum death-rate on estates with population over 200.	Average population.	Death-rate per mille.	Number of estates with population over 200 and death-rate over 50 per mille.	Maximum death-rate on estates with population over 200.
FEDERATED MALAY STATES –																				
Perak	30,605	49.8	14	193.1	41,090	34.3	12	110.6	47,646	25.5	12	172.1	49,277	25.9	14	97.7	48,084	17.9	5	55.8
Selangor	53,613	60.3	44	189.4	59,396	37.2	27	215.1	72,829	29.7	24	110.5	66,938	28.5	22	89.2	60,970	20.3	6	74.9
Negri Sembilan	11,378	195.6	18	527.1	11,639	114.0	19	362.8	11,802	53.2	12	143.9	11,313	58.4	11	125.0	9,825	37.9	7	84.2
Pahang	639	109.5	2	147.0	600	78.3	1	97.1	794	46.6	1	105.2	972	24.7	1	41.2	1,311	33.5		43.9
Government Departments	8,060	16.5		46.5	13,877	14.9	3	68.6	20,383	14.2	1	55.7	21,519	12.4		44.9	16,618	11.1		42.2
Total	104,295	68.9	78	527.1	126,602	41.1	62	362.8	153,455	28.3	50	172.1	150,019	28.9	47	125.0	136,808	19.8	21	84.2
STRAITS SETTLEMENTS PROPER –																				
Singapore					582	12.0		4.1	659	15.1		9.6			Not available.		754	9.3		6.6
Penang					214	4.7		237		8.4					Not available.		210			
Province Wellesley	7,677	36.6	5	72.6	9,060	18.7	5	47.9	8,366	17.0		30.3			Not available.		8,566	14.6		36.5
Dindings	609	50.9	1	56.3	947	14.8		19.3	1,249	17.6	13.4				Not available.		1,364	12.5		27.6
Malacca	3,103	121.2	3	299.5	4,895	53.9	4	115.7	5,852	41.0	3	154.8			Not available.		6,711	30.6	2	67.2
Government Departments									1,606	11.8		46.0			Not available.		3,745	1.9		2.3
Total	11,389	59.7	9	299.5	15,698	28.4		115.7	17,969	24.3	4	115.7			Not available.		21,350	17.0	2	67.2
Johore		59.7				28.4	Not available.		6,678	37.8		92.5	5,807	68.9	7	213.7	7,558	57.6	10	111.5 /

It will be seen that, in 1911, the death-rate per mille varied from 195·6 in Negri Sembilan to 49·8 in Perak and that it exceeded 50 per mille in 78 estates, the average labour population of each of which was over 200. The rate has fallen till in 1915 it varied from 37·9 in Negri Sembilan to 17·9 in Perak and exceeded 50 per mille on 21 estates only of average population over 200. In the colony, the rate varied in 1911 from 121·2 per mille in Malacca to 36·6 in Province Wellesley and in 1915 varied from 12·5 in the Dindings and 14·6 in Province Wellesley to 30·6 in Malacca. It was over 50 per mille in nine estates (of average population over 200) in 1911 and in two estates in 1915.

The comparatively low rates entered against Government departments are rather misleading, as Government labourers who fall ill and leave their employment and go into hospitals in the towns and die there are not reckoned in the returns.

These figures refer to workers only, i.e. the labour force on the employer's check roll. All children capable of doing any work and all adults except those incapacitated by old age are, as a general rule, entered on the check roll. Infants and aged people and deaths among them are thus not included in the above statement. There were only 1,112 persons over 55 years of age on estates in the Federated Malay States in 1911. But the infantile mortality there is much reason to believe to be high though statistics on the point are not available. On one large group of estates the manager found that nearly two out of every three children born died and took special measures to have the children regularly inspected by the estate doctor and fed with suitable infant foods at the estate expense. But small estates possess neither the organization nor the money to take such action.

The death-rates must therefore be considered still high in some localities especially in Negri Sembilan and Malacca. They appear to be even higher in Johore.

46. Though exact figures are not available to show the causes of death amongst Indian labourers, local enquiry and the general hospital returns leave no doubt that malaria and anchylostomiasis[9] are answerable for much the largest number. According to the medical reports of the Federated Malay States, malaria has been the cause of from 35 to 45 per cent of the total deaths in the years 1911 to 1915 while to anchylostomiasis is attributed from 10 to 15 per cent of the deaths.

47. Much attention is being given to combating malaria. In November 1911 a Malaria Advisory Board was appointed to direct a general campaign against this disease. Before the establishment of the Board many attempts were made in various localities to reduce malaria. But except in the flat land estates near the coast where drainage and clearing over a sufficient area proved entirely effective, in no case was the improvement completely maintained. We visited an estate where 30,000 dollars had been spent on anti-malaria drainage two or three years ago.

There had been no malaria after this till recently when it had broken out again, and on the morning of our visit to the hospital 93 labourers or about 6 per cent of the whole labour force of the estates served were in hospital with malaria. Quinine prophylaxis[10] is tried but with varying results as no organization exists to ensure its systematic application. The Board aims at the extermination of anopheline[11] mosquitoes in all thickly populated centres and wherever economically possible in rural areas. The means followed are (*a*) land drainage and clearing of drained areas; (*b*) reduction of breeding in lakes, rivers and other large bodies of water by removal of weeds and algae from shallow places; (*c*) removal of bottles, tins, boxes, shells, or any other waste articles likely to hold water and the screening of all tanks, wells or water containing vessels; (*d*) periodical use of oil or larvicides[12] on breeding places not otherwise dealt with; and (*e*) efficient upkeep of all anti-malarial works. An Entomologist, Dr. Strickland, has also been at work for the last two or three years on researches into the epidemiology of malaria and the biology of the malaria-carrying mosquitoes. Action is also being taken to educate by pictorial cards the population generally in regard to malaria, and elementary lessons on the subject are given in schools.

The Indian labourer suffers more from malaria than the Chinese labourer because the latter always drinks tea (and so boils his water) and uses a mosquito curtain at night. The Indian will net as a rule do either. Even where curtains are provided as in hospitals, there is great difficulty in getting the Indian patients to use them. /

48. As regards anchylostomiasis no regular campaign appears to have been instituted as yet; but the disease is treated regularly in the estate and Government hospitals with the chennopodium[13] oil, and estate dressers are taught how to look for and recognise the ova.

49. *Suicide.* – Particulars of suicides amongst Indian labourers have been collected only since 1915. In 1915 there were 16 suicides in the Federated Malay States and two in the Colony proper. This makes 18 cases among an estimated population of 180,000 or a rate of 100 per million, but such a rate for one year has clearly no statistical value or significance having regard to the distribution and fluctuation of the population. The causes of suicide so far as ascertained or indicated by the circumstances were illness bodily or mental in seven cases, drink in three cases and jealousy in three cases.

VII. – Miscellaneous – 50. Education. – Schools of varying degrees of efficiency are maintained on nearly all estates. The better class of schools (these are usually in the larger estates) are recognized by Government and receive grants-in-aid when the managers apply for such grants. There are also a few Government schools. The average attendance at the Government schools during 1915 was 1,796 out of an enrolment of 2,275 children The attendance at estate schools (not recognised by Government) is variable and depends chiefly on the personal interest taken in the schools by the estate managers. Parents usually are more anxious that their children should earn money or do household work or run errands than that they should attend school. We did not hear of any secondary or higher schools for Indian children: there is at present neither any demand nor need for such institutions. The Indian labourer has not yet made Malaya his home to anything like the same extent as in Ceylon.

51. *Repatriation.* – -The Labour department estimates that the majority of the Indian labourers return to India after a stay of not more than two years. Those who keep fair health and are ordinarily industrious have no difficulty in finding the money necessary for a return passage. For those who break down in health, a Home has been established as noted in paragraph 25 and they are repatriated if fit to bear journey. Besides these, eases of destitute Indians are constantly being investigated by the labour officers who repatriate at the expense of the estate (if the relation between employer and labourer can be established) or at the expense of the Immigration Fund those unlikely to be able to earn a living in Malaya. In this manner, 593 persons were repatriated in 1913, 671 in 1914 and 1,096 in 1915. The British India Steam Navigation Company granted free tickets in many of these cases.

52. *Settlement on land.* – -So far as we could ascertain there is no positive bar to the acquisition of land for cultivation as their own holdings by Indians; but with the exception of some areas of rice cultivation on the flat land near the coast which is almost entirely in the hands of Malays, there seems to be no land suitable for small holdings; nor does the Indian labourer evince any disposition to settle in the country as a cultivator on his own account. On the old estates in the north (North Perak and Province Wellesley) the estate labourers often cultivate small patches of estate land with vegetables or *ragi.*

53. *Sex proportion.* – The exact numbers of males and females among the Indian labouring population in 1911 cannot be ascertained as, at the census, the Muhammadan Marakkayar community which consists chiefly of traders and shop-keepers was enumerated as Tamil, while both they and Malays were reckoned as Muhammadans: and under the category Hindu came the Sikhs, Pathans and Chetti community as well as Tamil, Telugu and Malayalee labourers. Making allowance for these factors, it may be estimated that there were 5 males to every 2 females in the Indian labouring population in the Colony; and in the Federated Malay States the proportion was 3 males to 1 female. The proportion of women to men was higher among the Telugus (4 to 7) and much lower (1 to 10) among the Malayalees who do not generally take their womenfolk with them. /

The following table gives the proportion of women to men among the immigrant labourers arriving from India each year from 1908 to 1916: –

PERCENTAGES of females to males among the immigrant labourers in Malaya.

Year.	Number of arrivals among labourers.		Proportion of females to 100 males.
	MALES.	FEMALES.	
1908	22,538	4,759	21·1
1909	21,684	4,398	20·3
1910	51,133	11,737	22·9
1911	67,977	16,412	24·1
1912	63,410	16,428	25·9
1913	72,013	19,223	26·7
1914	29,480	7,425	25·2
1915	44,179	10,702	24·2
1916	55,568	16,525	29·8

It will be seen that the proportion before 1911 was only about 1 female to 5 males, but it has gradually improved and now is about 1 female to 4 (rather less) males.

Whatever may have been the case some years ago before the Straits Government appointed its officers to supervise the recruitment of labour in India, female emigrants now consist of married women and girls accompanying, or going to, their husbands or parents respectively. In the old established estates in Province Wellesley and the Selangor Coast districts the labourers live in families; there are almost as many women as men, and children abound. Many of the families have settled down permanently and have no intention of returning to India save perhaps for a short visit. In the other parts of the country, there are many more single men, but the women are either living with their husbands or are minor girls living with their parents. Some prostitutes there no doubt are, but we certainly could find no indications of any general immorality nor was the existence of any such conditions locally alleged.

It is in the cooking of his food that the single Tamil labourer most feels the want of his womenfolk. He, however, has no intention of remaining in the country for more than a year or two.

54. Caste of emigrants and facilities for exercise of religious rites. – The great majority of Tamil emigrant labourers are of low caste – Pariahs, Pallas, Padayachis and Goundans. Among the Telugus there are some Telegas as well as Malas and Madigas. The Malayalee labourers are mostly Tiyas, but some Nayars and Moplahs also go.

No restrictions are placed on the labourers in regard to the exercise of any of their customary ceremonial rites. There are temples on most estates though they are usually not so elaborate or well built as in Ceylon.

APPENDIX 1

(See paragraph 4 of Ceylon Report.)
ARRIVALS AND DEPARTURES OF INDIAN LABOURERS.
From 1855 *to* 1915.

Note. – The figures for years previous to 1900 include third-class passengers other than labourers.

Percentages of arrivals.				Arrivals.				Departures			
Men.	Woman.	Children.	Year.	Men.	Women.	Children.	Total.	Men.	Women.	Children.	Total.
89·23	8·61	2·16	1855	51,979	5,018	1,270	58,267	23,131	573	313	24,017
87·16	9·32	3·52	1855	59,263	6,342	2,399	68,004	32,148	1,502	659	34,309
86·63	10·06	3·31	1857	60,048	6,974	2,298	69,320	36,887	2,278	772	39,937
78·26	16·83	4·91	1858	75,172	16,172	4,718	96,062	45,747	3,277	1,416	50,440
80·79	14·45	4·76	1859	32,397	5,797	1,911	40,105	43,900	3,722	1,196	48,818
79·16	16·89	3·95	1860	41,906	8,946	2,093	52,945	21,279	1,874	721	23,874
80·70	15·30	4·00	1861	43,147	8,175	2,110	53,432	32,636	3,487	1,079	37,202
75·28	18·14	6·58	1862	51,859	12,503	4,534	68,896	35,577	4,691	1,641	41,909
76·13	16·76	7·11	1863	53,828	11,858	5,032	70,718	50,334	7,804	3,627	61,765
77·13	17·37	5·50	1864	63,087	14,214	4,499	81,800	54,724	8,526	4,029	67,279
73·66	18·80	7·54	1865	66,007	16,831	6,759	89,597	51,504	8,478	4,555	64,537
66·21	26·87	6·92	1866	58,488	23,723	6,117	88,328	38,997	6,717	3,515	49,229
60·04	35·69	4·27	1867	31,688	18,836	2,255	52,779	35,507	7,293	3,198	45,998
74·87	20·32	4·81	1868	41,499	11,510	2,682	55,691	44,820	7,524	2,182	54,526
76·29	19·33	4·38	1859	43,998	11,150	2,523	57,671	43,826	8,330	2,175	54,331
79·20	16·61	4·19	1870	51,614	10,835	2,735	65,214	44,787	8,035	2,260	55,082
79·17	17·48	3·35	1871	70,090	15,471	2,968	83,529	55,603	9,660	3,347	68,610
79·90	15·25	4·85	1872	64,018	12,216	3,887	80,121	59,005	10,783	4,247	74,035
79·42	15·91	4·67	1873	70,687	14,166	4,159	89,012	63,238	12,075	5,316	80,629
76·43	17·10	6·47	1874	95,659	21,400	8,097	125,155	73,210	10,699	5,818	89,727
76·87	16·56	6·57	1875	66,659	14,358	5,695	86,712	77,074	11,808	6,637	95,519
73·87	17·39	8·74	1876	121,743	28,670	14,384	164,797	73,668	11,532	6,770	91,970
65·93	23·52	10·55	1877	117,181	41,786	18,614	177,581	72,791	10,458	5,360	88,609
84·65	10·74	4·60	1878	170,247	21,584	9,262	201,093	72,148	13,512	5,528	91,188
84·15	7·98	7·57	1879	149,423	14,110	13,364	176,897	63,431	12,162	5,157	80,750
79·16	13·78	7·06	1880	36,092	6,286	3,222	45,600	54,410	12,524	6,749	73,683
79·58	14·45	5·97	1881	42,679	7,789	3,419	53,887	48,686	9,776	4,778	63,240
80·35	14·34	5·31	1882	40,901	7,301	2,705	50,907	44,725	8,814	4,281	57,820
81·05	12·14	6·81	1883	31,778	4,759	2,667	39,204	41,137	8,148	3,677	52,962
79·47	13·55	6·98	1884	36,381	6,203	3,193	45,777	39,365	7,083	3,637	50,085
77·79	14·53	7·68	1885	37,181	6,943	3,670	47,794	38,695	6,592	3,576	48,863
79·19	13·84	6·97	1886	31,602	5,525	2,780	39,907	36,009	6,190	3,051	45,250
77·88	16·09	6·03	1887	56,582	11,696	4,382	72,660	45,266	6,796	3,059	55,121
77·70	16·20	6·10	1888	64,170	13,376	5,041	82,587	48,878	6,441	2,486	55,805
77·10	16·11	6·79	1889	47,597	9,947	1,191	61,735	44,103	6,405	2,111	52,619

Percentages of arrivals.				Arrivals.				Departures			
Men.	Woman.	Children.	Year.	Men.	Women.	Children.	Total.	Men.	Women.	Children.	Total.
73·10	18·19	8·71	1890	61,484	15,300	7,322	84,106	39,450	5,078	1,228	45,756
72·83	18·47	8·70	1891	75,121	19,051	8,977	103,149	51,959	6,761	1,322	60,042
71·70	18·45	9·85	1892	83,504	21,494	11,474	116,472	57,604	8,163	1,849	67,616
71·75	16·52	11·73	1893	65,782	15,149	10,745	91,676	52,086	16,048	5,047	73,181
74·25	15·50	10·25	1894	63,310	13,200	8,735	85,245	46,840	14,977	4,575	66,392
70·70	16·40	12·90	1895	87,385	20,272	15,954	123,611	59,260	15,809	5,604	80,673
72·03	16·91	11·06	1896	92,452	21,711	14,187	128,350	70,755	16,988	5,538	93,281
69·71	17·92	12·37	1897	106,722	27,434	18,919	153,075	77,584	19,888	11,741	109,213
73·89	13·70	12·41	1898	97,484	17,943	16,487	131,914	83,796	17,634	4,276	105,706
82·30	10·70	7·00	1899	56,488	7,320	4,585	68,393	59,930	16,388	5,311	81,629
64·00	17·00	19·00	1900	132,183	40,827	34,984	207,994	76,231	24,493	12,212	112,936
69·00	19·00	12·00	1901	83,526	22,386	14,691	120,603	84,465	23,888	9,990	118,343
76·91	12·15	10·94	1902	73,580	11,475	9,377	‖ 94,432	†	†	†	77,197
69·30	16·81	13·89	1903	44,067	10,668	8,711	63,446	†	†	†	47,715
68·72	17·33	13·95	1904	52,892	13,340	10,733	‖ 76,965	†	†	†	56,246
63·80	17·93	18·27	1905	110,510	31,053	31,610	*173,173	†	†	†	65,513
66·26	17·30	16·44	1906	82,620	21,573	20,496	‖ 124,689	†	†	†	59,659
61·23	21·99	16·78	1907	34,122	12,247	9,355	55,724	†	†	†	63,671
61·39	21·87	16·74	1908	53,042	18,897	14,462	§ 86,401	† 76,396	†	† 2,344	78,740
59·62	22·94	17·44	1909	47,593	18,321	13,931	79,845	† 59,188	†	† 2,099	61,287
58·77	23·52	17·71	1910	69,701	27,908	21,004	‖ 118,613	† 62,626	–	† 2,034	64,660
59·52	22·71	17·77	1911	58,052	22,156	17,328	97,536	–	–	–	58,916
58·21	22·04	19·75	1912	68,638	25,983	23,289	117,910	–	–	–	77,840
58·19	22·36	19·45	1913	69,961	26,880	23,389	120,230	–	–	–	90,374
59·37	22·12	18·51	1914	46,310	17,253	14,441	78,004	–	–	–	49,031
57·05	21·69	21·26	1915	54,092	20,565	20,152	94,809	–	–	–	38,298
73·45	16·75	9·80	Total	4,369,908	996,931	584,149	5,950,988	2,688,806	442,727	190,550	4,208,233

* This is according to Master Attendant's return. The Principal Collector of Customs gives the total as 160,080 only.

† Separate figures for men, women and children not given; the totals under these columns are only up to 1901.

‡ Adult men and women only.

§ This is as per Principal Collector of Customs' return, but it is less than the total number of coolies who passed through the Ragama Camp.

‖ For 1902, 1904, 1906 and 1910, the customs returns give 87,763, 77,302, 88,915 and 112,202 respectively.

ANON., 'INDIANS IN MALAYA' (1926)

Anon., 'Indians in Malaya', National Archives, CO 273/534/11, pp. 96–9.

The *Swadesamitran* was a Tamil language newspaper founded in 1882 by the journalist and politician G. Subramania Lyer. Published weekly, and, from 1889, daily, its editorial line was highly critical of the actions of the British government both in India and elsewhere in the Empire. In March 1926, it printed three articles on the conditions of Indians working on Malayan rubber estates, which are summarized in this Colonial Office memo. As discussed in the General Introduction and thematic introduction, such revelations fuelled nationalistic opposition to migration and contributed to ever-tighter Indian government controls.

Anon., 'Indians in Malaya' (1926), extract

<u>Swadesamitran, Madras, 23rd, 26th and 27th March 1926.</u>

The Swadesamitran publishes, from the pen of a correspondent, an article on the educational, medical and other facilities afforded to the Indian coolies working in the rubber plantations in Malaya, in which the following observations find place among others: – There is a provision in the Labour Code that free education should be imparted; to satisfy this condition, a school is maintained in every plantation. But these schools do not commence work in the morning as in other places. There are no separate teachers in these schools. One of the persons who tap the rubber trees will also look after the work of teaching. The educational qualifications of such a person and the instruction which he can impart to others may better be imagined. Unless the Government secure the services of really competent teachers from India and employ them in the schools maintained in the plantations, the education imparted will not be satisfactory. Why should not the anxiety evinced in the matter of recruiting coolies be evinced also in the matter of imparting education to the children of these coolies? The Government should, instead of stopping with imparting primary education, try to afford the necessary facilities to those who have the aptitude for higher education. As regards medical facilities, when even in veterinary hospitals straw is spread on the floor for sick animals to lie down at night., in the plantations hospitals only large planks are provided for the Indian coolies to lie down. Our benign Government who send coolies from here should urge that the Controller should look after these things. All the dressers or doctors employed in the plantation hospitals have not secured a good medical training. If good dressers are / not available in Malaya, why should not the services of persons who have been trained in the medical schools in South India be requisitioned? They want only coolies from India and not teachers or doctors. Why this obstinacy? The same paper elsewhere observes: Though hospitals and schools are maintained in the plantations trained teachers and efficient doctors are not found there. It is not proper to engage as a teacher a labourer whose educational qualification is very poor. It is said that the bedding facilities afforded in the hospitals are not satisfactory. It is surprising to hear that the teachers or doctors who have studied in India and secured degrees here are not given employment in Malaya. Why should not Indian teachers and Indian doctors be employed? The argument that only coolies are wanted from India and that Indians are not wanted for fostering the intellect and the body of these coolies, does not appear to be just. We do not know what the Controller of Labour is doing. The Swadesamitran (26th) publishes an article on this subject, from the pen of a correspondent, wherein he refers to the questions asked by Mr. Uppi Sahib in the Madras Legislative Council regarding the hardships experienced by the coolies during embarkation at the Negapatam harbour in December last and the reply given thereto by the Hon'ble the Home Member and observes: – When the steamer, which was to start from Negapatam in the first week of November last, started on its voyage, the waves ran so high that even the mail bags could not be brought to the steamer and the bags in the boats got completely drenched. This steamer arrived at Malaya without the Indian mail. When there were such high waves that even the mail bags could not be brought to / the steamer, the boats that conveyed the coolies to the steamer could not but have experienced a rough sea. Let us consider the facilities afforded to the coolies in the matter of food in the steamer which started from Negapatam at the end of December last. Four persons died during the voyage and about thirty persons died while they were in the inspection camp after disembarking. What other reason can there be for these deaths, than the lack of proper facilities in the matter of food? It is only the fear of the coolies owing to the rough seas, the lack of proper facilities in the matter of accommodation and food and the absence of any facilities for bathing, etc. that accounts for the deaths referred to above. It is stated that for five months in the year the sea is not rough in the Negapatam harbour and that, for the rest of the year, the passengers and coolies are put to great trouble owing to the high waves in the sea. Hence the Negapatam harbour should be closed for seven months in the year. The B.I.S.N. Company[1] should stop their steamers Tara and Teesta from plying and ply Takkaniva and another steamer wherein similar facilities are provided. As the middle class people are travelling in large numbers, arrangements should be made for employing Brahman cooks on the steamer, so as to provide facilities for these people in the matter of food. If it is stated that it will take time to provide all these facilities, licences for the recruitment of coolies should not be issued until these facilities are provided. The same paper elsewhere observes: – If we look into the details furnished by our correspondent, it is evident that the Hon'ble the Home Member has tried to gloss over the whole affair instead of admitting the true state of things. It is not proper on his part to have taken advantage of the reference made by. Mr. Uppi / Sahib to a steamer that sailed in the midst of December and to say in reply that he thinks that Mr. Uppi Sahib refers only to the steamship Taksiva. For, of all the steamers that go to Malaya, the Taksiva may be said to be the best. Besides this there are two other steamships known as Tara and Teesta. Why should not the Home Member think that Mr. Uppi Sahib referred to these two ships? Nobody can deny that, for a period of seven months in the year, embarkation at the Negapatam harbour is dangerous to passengers. But we do not know what meaning is given to the word 'danger' in the dictionary of the Government. Our correspondent says that about thirty persons died on board a steamer bound for Malaya. What is the reason for this? Is it due to any defect in the steamer itself, or to anything bad in the food, or to the incapacity of the doctor in the steamer who is serving on a low salary? Why should not efficient doctors be engaged on high salaries? Why should the coolies be allowed to die during the voyage without any help being rendered to them? The Swadesamitran (27th) publishes another article, from the pen of a correspondent, on the condition of Indian labourers in Malaya, in which the following observations find place among others: – Those who exercise control over the labourers are Kanganis, Manduras and Kranis. The Kanganis and Mandurus are mostly Tamils, while 99 per cent of the Kranis are Jaffnese.[2] The hardships to which the labourers are subjected by Kanganis and Manduras under the instructions of Kranis, are indescribable. In every plantation, there are one or two Mariamman temples. In some plantations, taxes are imposed on the coolies in proportion to the wages earned by them and poojas[3] performed in these temples. In some plantations it is said that poojas are performed / with the profits derived through toddy shops. Monthly and annual festivals also take place in these temples. On such occasions, special taxes will be levied and the Krani, Manduru and Kangani constitute themselves into a board of trustees and celebrate the festivals. In these festivals, potfuls of toddy and other things are offered as oblations and are then distributed to the coolies. The coolies avail themselves of this opportunity and get themselves fully drunk. Moreover, there is none to see whether all the money collected for these festive occasions has been spent or not. The Indian coolies have become habituated to being duped like this. Again, these Kranis, Mandurus and Kanganis join together on the occasion of Dipavali, buy cloth suitable for the Indians from a town near by and saying that, out of a desire to help the coolies, they have got cloth direct from India at a cheap price and that those who want cloth can purchase it from them and pay the cost in two or three instalments, carry on a highly profitable trade. The poor coolies believe this trickery, buy the cloth and pay its price in two or more instalments. These are matters causing great regret. Similar to this is the money-lending business carried on in the plantations. If a coolie borrows from the Krani, Manduru or Kangani one or two dollars for his expense before the date on which the pay is disbursed, the rate of interest is 25 cents per dollar for a month. If the coolie fails to pay back this amount as soon as he gets his wages, the Manduru and the Kangani will enter his house, and, beating him with a cane in the presence of his wife and children, come back only after recovering the amount from him. These things do not generally reach the ears of the Manager, and even if they reach his ears, he would not accuse the Manduru / and the Kangani as they are essential to him. Hence, though these coolies are not indentured coolies, their position is in fact worse than that of the latter. It is very important that Indian leaders should pay attention to this matter, agitate and take the requisite steps to see that the Government do not issue licences for recruiting coolies. Remarking that its correspondent has made it clear whether the coolies in Malaya are benefited or inconvenienced through the temples in Malaya, the same paper observes: – It appears that not only the European planters but also the Kranis, Mandurus and Kanganis are exploiting the submissive nature of the Indian coolies. The Chinese are independent persons; but the Tamils are not like that. Hence the European planters desire to have only Tamil coolies to a large extent. This is but natural. But who is there to urge the claims of the Tamil coolies in Malaya? Even God has not shown them mercy. It is said that the Kranis from Jaffna have no sympathy for the Tamil coolies. Why should those who have no sympathy for the coolies, be appointed as maistris and Kranis, when these coolies are Tamils?

BLYTHE, *METHODS AND CONDITIONS OF EMPLOYMENT OF CHINESE LABOUR IN THE FEDERATED MALAY STATES* (1938)

W. L. Blythe, *Methods and Conditions of Employment of Chinese Labour in the Federated Malay States* (Kuala Lumpur: Government Publication, 1938), pp. 1–53.

Wilfred Lawson Bythe (1896–1975) joined the Malayan civil service in 1921 and ended his career as Colonial Secretary of Singapore (1950–3). Unlike the previous two sources, his voluminous report concentrates on the recruitment and employment of Chinese migrant workers.

W. L. Blythe, *Methods and Conditions of Employment of Chinese Labour in the Federated Malay States* (1938), extract

INTRODUCTION

This report is the result of a tour of inspection of Chinese labour in the Federated Malay States which occupied some two months from 4th October, 1937. It is concerned mainly with labour on rubber estates and mines, because these occupations absorb incomparably larger numbers of labourers than any others. The following figures are taken from the 1931 Census and, although they are not up to date, they may serve to illustrate the outstanding importance of these two industries in the Chinese labour market of the Federated Malay States:

Chinese.	(F.M.S. figures.)		
	Males.	Females.	Total.
Rubber cultivation	84,342	16,447	100,789
Mining	64,628	8,948	73,576
Agriculture – Fruit and vegetable growers	24,984	7,637	32,621
Agriculture – Others and multifarious	13,256	2,859	16,115
Carpenters, joiners and cabinet makers	10,287	14	10,301
Tailors, dressmakers and seam-stresses	4,269	566	4,835
Makers of boots, shoes and clogs Sawyers	2,910	–	2,910
[…]			

Investigations were also conducted in other industries, foundries, sawmills, rubber factories, match factories, tobacco factories, brickkilns, and in some of the shop-industries such as carpentry, shoemaking and tailoring.

The most striking general impression received during the course of these inspections is the noticeable change in the outlook of the large bulk of the labourers. It is true that for the past sixty years there has been steady progress in the emancipation of the Chinese labourer from the days of indentured labour and widespread debt-slavery. But this process has been remarkably accelerated during the last ten years and perhaps even more remarkably during the last five years. Ten or fifteen years ago it was not unusual to find that the labour force on an estate or a mine consisted of a number of labourers who had been recruited in China by a labour contractor engaged by the management of the place of employment. The contractor paid all the expenses of the journey from the native village in China to the place of employment. It would frequently be found that the majority of the labourers were from the / same Chinese village as the contractor or from neighbouring villages. On their arrival here, they were debited in the contractor's account book with a sum of money purporting to represent the cost of their recruitment. These sums were frequently grotesquely exaggerated and it was impressed upon the labourers that until this debt had been worked off they were not free to leave their employment. The repayment of the debt was made more difficult by a variety of methods – exorbitant charges for food and goods supplied by the contractor through his shop, the supply of chandu[1] by the contractor at high prices, the running of "crooked" gambling by the *kepalas*[2] and the charging by the contractors of monthly sums for clerk's wages, sleeping accommodation, interest on advances and other items.

It was to deal with these abuses that Chapters IV and XI of the Labour Code were introduced, and a good deal of the work of the Chinese Protectorate lay in the eradication of these abuses. One of the main difficulties encountered was the frequent unwillingness of labourers to complain because of their acceptance of what they understood to be old-established customs. There were also family and village ties which bound them to the contractor and reinforced his power of control.

Already ten years ago the system was beginning to disintegrate. Labourers who had been in Malaya for some years had worked off their debts and were increasingly aware of their legal rights, and contractors warned by the prosecution of their fellows for infringements of the Labour Code were inclined to be more careful in their conduct towards the labourers, but fresh batches of new recruits were constantly arriving from China offering the temptation of exploitation which it was well nigh impossible for the contractor to resist. The death blow was given to this system by the introduction into the legislation of the Straits Settlements of the Aliens Ordinance, whereunder power was given to the Governor-in-Council to limit the number of aliens landed in the Colony. The immediate result of this limitation was a big increase in the cost of recruitment of labourers from China for, in addition to the higher passage rates charged by the shipping companies to reimburse their losses due to limitation of the number of immigrants, the opportunity of profiteering was seized by the passage brokers at China ports who were aware of the large demand forand the limited supply of passage tickets and raised the prices of the tickets accordingly. This fact, coupled with an adequate supply of labour already in Malaya made it far cheaper to recruit labour locally than in China.

During my tour I have not met with a single instance of the survival of the old system, and enquiries from Protectors and from Chinese employees have confirmed my belief that this system has vanished. The average present-day labourer is not indebted to the contractor for the expenses of his recruitment from China. Recruitment takes place through local lodging-houses where labourers live when unemployed, or else from among squatters living on vegetable gardens in the vicinity, and the labourers have not the same feeling of being bound to the contractor. Recruitment from lodging-houses sometimes entails the payment of an advance to the labourer to cover the expenses incurred by him for board and lodging, but this amount at present is only from $3 to $5.

Concurrently with this development of freer labour forces in Malaya there has been in China a growing labour emancipation movement. The first Chinese National Labour Conference was held in Canton in 1922. The movement was later stimulated by Dr. Sun Yat Sen[3] who urged the / promotion of labour unions, by the Russian influence in China (1924-27), by the student movement and by the growth of "proletarian literature" with its emphasis on the oppression of the worker and the evils of capitalism. It is true that the labour union movement – as distinct from the older guild system embracing masters and men – has for the most part been confined to industrial labour in the towns – mechanics, printers, builders, transport and factory workers, but it is important to note that the stronghold of this movement is the province of Kwangtung from which the majority of the labourers on estates and mines in Malaya are drawn. Similar labour unions have become established among the Chinese in Malaya, and although these too are at present chiefly associated with town industries they have had a leavening influence throughout the whole of Chinese labour.

And this leads to the mention of another widespread change – the tremendous increase in ease of communication – which during the last few years has been brought within the reach of labourers by the introduction of the cheap (usually Japanese) bicycle. The bicycle is now ubiquitous where, only a few years ago, it did not exist at all. In almost every kongsi-house[4] one now finds lines of bicycles. Squatters, men and women, ride to work on them; labourers living on estates and mines ride to the nearest village to buy food and necessaries; the daily newspaper is frequently to be found in kongsis; there is continuous contact and intercourse between the labourer and his fellows in the vicinity.

Another, and a very remarkable phenomenon, is the extraordinary increase in the employment of Chinese women on estates. There have always been estates which made use of adjacent squatter labour, but there are now many estates – particularly in Negri Sembilan and Selangor – where the labour force is largely composed of families living in kongsi-houses which have been partitioned into rooms to provide for this development. And some estates have groups of women without husbands or families housed in rooms in kongsi-houses. During the last three or four years shiploads of Cantonese women (mostly from the Shun Tak and Tung Kwun districts) have been coming to Malaya in search of work. Their ages have ranged between 20 and 40 and they invariably claim to be widows. This spate of female immigration is probably due (*a*) to the poor economic state of China and, in particular, the slump in the silk industry due to the widespread use of rayon fabrics, and (*b*) to the exemption of women from the operation of the immigration quota. This exemption means that passages for women are much cheaper than for men, so that it is easier for the women than for the men to emigrate. This tendency has been stimulated by the action of ticket brokers at the China ports who have habitually refused to sell quota tickets unless three or four non-quota tickets were bought by the lodging-houses for each quota ticket bought. It has therefore been to the advantage of the lodging-houses and their agents to encourage the emigration of women to take up these non-quota tickets.

The 1931 Census figures of Chinese adults (over 15 years old) in Malaya were:

Male.	Female.	Proportion of F. to M.
901,274	374,097	41.5%

The gain or loss by migration as shown by the Malayan Migration Statistics from the Census date (1st April, 1931) to 30th June, 1937, is as follows – adults:

Male.	Female.
– 36,082	+105,634 /

Neglecting those who reached the age of 15 while in this country we thus have mid-1937 figures of:

Male.	Female.	
865,192	479,731	55.4%

The 1921 Census figures were:

Male.	Female.	
727,836	216,730	29.7%

The majority of women whom I saw employed on estates and mines were living with husbands. Whether they originally came here as widows it is impossible to say. But the future of the Chinese labour forces on estates will undoubtedly witness a transition from bachelor to family labour. In these family units the marketing and cooking is invariably done by the family and not by the contractor. A further result of this infiltration of female labour to estates has been the application of section 72 of the Labour Code – dealing with maternity benefits – to these women. This is a very recent development to which I shall refer later.

A further general observation is that there is now far less smoking of opium than there used to be. One Chinese mine manager went so far as to estimate that whereas ten years ago 70 per cent. or 80 per cent of the mining labourers were opium smokers, to-day only some 10 per cent. smoke. Some mines refuse to employ opium smokers. Those labourers who do smoke almost always have individual chandu cards and obtain their supplies personally from the Government chandu shop and not, as previously, through the contractor or *kepala*.

Finally, there is considerably more direct contact between the management of European estates and their labour forces than there used to be. This is far from being general but it is developing. The proportion of labourers who can speak a little Malay is increasing and systems of direct employment are being tried – almost invariably with complete success – to the exclusion of the contractor and to the benefit of the labourer and of the estate.

In addition to these developments there has been a considerable amount of propaganda among the labourers during the last ten years by the Malayan Communist party[5] and by its subsidiary organisations, in particular the Malayan General Labour Union. But it is quite incorrect to suppose that any large numbers of the labourers have any conception of communism as a political or economic creed. In general I think the labourer mistrusts the political agitator, he is mildly amused at the fantastic slogans. He may be persuaded to favour any movement which promises less work and more pay but he regards such promises sceptically, and would rather stand by and see others do the arguing. There are, of course, groups of labourers who are deeper in communism than this, but by comparison with, the more fundamental forces which as mentioned above, have been at work for some years, the influence of the Malayan Communist party has been slight.

In general, the conditions of employment of Chinese labourers in the Federated Malay States to-day are very much better than they were ten or fifteen years ago. The labourer is free in fact as well as in law and he is far more aware of what is happening in the world around him. /

Section I.

ESTATES – METHODS OF EMPLOYMENT.

Contractors.

The traditional method of employment of Chinese – whether tappers or weeders – on rubber estates is the contractor method, and this method is still the most usual on European-managed estates. Chinese-managed estates do not always employ this system; the labour force is sometimes managed by *kepalas* employed by the owner.

Under the contractor system the manager engages a Chinese contractor to recruit and employ labourers on the estate. Contracts for tapping are usually in terms of a rate per lb. of dry (smoked) rubber produced. On Chinese estates payment is usually per *katty*[6] of dry (smoked) rubber: This rate may be the same for the whole estate or it may vary for different "divisions" or even for different "fields" on the estate according to whether the known yield is high or low, the ground steep or flat, the tapping cuts easily accessible or laborious to reach owing to their nearness to the ground or to their height above the ground – necessitating the use of a ladder. The manager will also usually stipulate that a certain number of men be employed, for he has already been over the ground and calculated the size of the labour force necessary to do the tapping, by dividing each field into "tasks" – equivalent to the tapping capacity of one man per day. These tasks may vary from 250 to 500 trees.

The contractor engages his men and allots them to the tasks. He arranges to pay each man at a certain rate per lb. of dry (smoked) rubber produced. This rate is usually – though not always – lower than the rate per lb. received by the contractor from the manager. It varies with different tasks – again depending upon the terrain, the height of the tapping cuts, the yield, etc., and in order to induce tappers to undertake the more difficult or unproductive tasks it may be necessary for the contractor to offer a higher rate per lb. than the all-in contract rate which he himself receives, but this he adjusts by cutting down the rates paid to tappers on the easier and more productive tasks.

The tapper having tapped all the trees in his task carries the latex collected therefrom to the kongsi or to the factory in buckets. Here the latex is weighed and the weight in *katties* is entered in the contractor's book under the name of the tapper. A sample of the latex (usually five *chis*) is taken by the contractor or his *kepala* by means of a small tin "dipper". This sample is at once coagulated by the addition of acid and hung on a board to dry. This board has a number of projecting nail points – each is numbered so that the sample on any nail may be identified with the tapper who bears that number. The latex is usually brought in – and the samples taken – between 12 noon and 2 p.m. In the evening when the samples have had time to dry, each sample is weighed on a small Chinese balance (rod and daching). The tappers are present at the weighing which is done by the contractor or one of his *kepalas*. The weight of the sample in *chis* is entered in the book under the tapper's name. The bulk weight of the latex brought in by one tapper (in *katties*) is multiplied by the dry weight of his sample (in *chis*) and the result is entered as the dry smoked weight of the bulk in lbs [...]

Under this system the manager, as a rule, has no knowledge of the rates of wages paid to the labourers. The latter are, as one manager phrased it, "just so many coolies". The manager is able to work out a figure by dividing the amount paid to the contractor by the number of tasks. This gives him a gross rate of daily pay for each task. But this rate includes contractor's profits and expenses (wages of clerk and *kepala*); furthermore, it is quite customary for the contractor to vary the tasks given to the labourers, there may be more or fewer than the number originally allotted by the manager. So that the manager's figure, in such cases, is of no use in the investigation of wage rates.

I have, however, been struck during this tour with the interest shown by some more enterprising managers and assistants on estates which still use the contractor system. On one estate some of the assistants regularly went through the contractor's day-book to acertain the daily wages credited to each labourer. They were able to do this because they had learned the very simple "running hand" Chinese numerals, and although they were unable to investigate the accounts in detail they could read the daily figures of wages earned. The recent agreements in Negri Sembilan and Selangor for the payment of a "minimum" or "average" wage of 75 cents to tappers have probably had the effect of stimulating the interest of the management in the actual wages received by the labourers. But there are still many estates where the manager concerns himself only with the gross figure paid by him to the contractor.

Under the contractor system the estate invariably provides a kongsi-house – usually of attap or plank construction – for the accommodation of the labourers. On estates whose labour force is obtained from squatters from nearby villages or settlements such kongsis are usually unnecessary. Under the traditional system the contractor employs a cook, a clerk and *kepalas* – their number depending upon the size of his labour force. He supplies food – either full diet or part diet – to the labourers at a fixed daily charge to cover the cost of the food, kerosine oil for lighting, and cook's wages. Additions to the diet are brought from the contractor's shop which is in the kongsi-house at prices fixed by the contractor. These amounts are debied to the labourer's accounts together with any cash advances made to the labourer and a monthly balance is struck. Wages are either paid monthly or credit balances are left with the contractor until the labourers wish to draw them or wish to remit money to China. Interest on advances made to labourers is still frequently charged – each $1 advanced being debited as $1.10 even if the advance is given just before the end of the month.

But there are now considerable variations of this system. It is very usual now to find that the labourers (whether married or bachelors) receive frequent advances of money, buy their own food either from the kongsi shop or more frequently, if near a village, from the village or from hawkers and cook it themselves. And the charging of interest on advances although frequently to be found is by no means universal. It has always been the policy of the Protectorate to oppose the charging of interest on advances and the charging of high prices for food supplied by the contractor. Chapter XI of the Labour Code would appear to give powers to deal with these matters but, as will be shown later in this section, its validity when applied to contract labourers on estates is doubtful. /

DIRECT EMPLOYMENT.

One of the most encouraging features of the changing conditions of employment on estates is the adoption by several European-managed estates in Negri

Sembilan and Selangor of systems of direct employment of Chinese tappers. These systems have not usually been applied on estates employing exclusively Chinese labour, but on estates with mixed Indian-Chinese labour forces.

A very simple system of payment at fixed daily rates (Kung-sz-Kung) was tried out for some months on an estate in Negri Sembilan but, at the time of my visit, it had been decided to abandon it because the in-turn of latex under the system of fixed daily pay was too low. There was no incentive for the tapper to do a fair day's work and it is a practical impossibility to have sufficient supervision to ensure that each tapper taps each tree in his task daily.

But the more usual system is to pay on piece rates – as is done by contractors – without the intervention of a contractor. The names of all the tappers are entered on the estate check-roll. The manager fixes the task for each man and the rate per lb. of rubber to be paid to him. This usually varies with the yield of the task. One manager varied his rates as often as twice a month. He found that tappers on higher rate tasks showed a tendency to bring in increasing quantities of latex whereas those on lower rates brought in steadily diminishing quantities. This he believed to be due to the transfer of latex from the latter to the former in order to obtain payment at higher rates – to be followed by a private adjustment between the tappers concerned. To check this he reduced the high rate and increased the low and kept up a perpetual see-saw of rates to compensate for this tendency. Another manager kept to his fixed rates unless it was apparent that the yield was insufficient to ensure the basic wage. He then put a "test tapper" on to the task. He had six of these men on daily pay (90 cents daily). They were good tappers, trusted men who had been on the estate for years. Normally they were kept for replacing sick labourers or tapping odd tasks. When put on to test tapping the manager noted their in-turn and decided whether to increase the rate to the tapper usually employed on that task or whether to dismiss him for inefficiency. A third manager gave a fixed rate per lb. over the whole of the estate but arranged his tasks so that each tapper had either two moderate yielding tasks or one good and one poor yielding task, in an attempt to achieve a rough uniformity of wages – preference being given of course to the better tappers. All three methods were declared to work satisfactorily.

The latex when brought in is weighed and sampled by staff employed by the estate. In some cases the contractor has been retained but transformed into a *kepala*. In any system of direct employment the estate must employ additional staff – *kepalas* and clerk – to do the work previously done by the contractor. his *kepalas* and his clerk. In some cases the provision of food and advances for the labourers is left in the hands of the chief *kepala*, the cost being debited to each labourer and deducted from his wages before payment by the manager. In one case the manager sold rice to the labourers at cost price and prohibited the *kepala* from keeping a shop or making advances. He had found that the *kepala* allowed labourers to overdraw, thus hampering the manager's freedom of action in the dismissal of incompetent labourers. Advances were made direct from the estate to the labourers weekly. As there was a village nearby there was no need for shops on the estate. The labourers all cooked their own food. On another estate advances were / made direct to the labourers every two days. No rice or provisions were sold on the estate, all supplies being obtained by the labourers from shops in a nearby village or from hawkers.

The methods of estimating the dry weight of rubber equivalent to the bulk latex brought in by each tapper varied. I found the following four methods employed:

(*a*) Usual Chinese method – *see* Appendix "A" [not included]
(*b*) Improved "Hawthornden" method – *see* Appendix "B" [not included]
(*c*) "Metrolac" } – *see* Appendix "C" [not included].
(*d*) "Simplexometer" }

Of these methods I was at first most impressed with the "Metrolac" used in the bulk latex with water added up to a known volume. The volume in gallons as shown by a measured scale in the container multiplied by the reading of the "Metrolac" floating in the latex gave the number of lbs. of dry (smoked) rubber to be credited to the labourer. Every labourer could read the figures and work it out for himself. There are, however, drawbacks to any system of calculation by specific gravity which is the basis of the "Metrolac" and "Simplexometer" methods. It is possible for the labourer to adulterate his latex – by the addition of flour or urine so that a higher reading will be given by the instrument, and cases have occurred in Selangor of difficulties between the labour force and the manager because of this.

The best system that I have seen is described in Appendix "B". I have called it the Hawthornden system because it was on that estate that I saw it. I understand that it was thought out by the manager there. It seems to me to be so excellent and fool-proof that I have given a detailed description of it.

Under all these direct systems, advances of wages and final monthly settlements are made at the estate office – the money being paid direct to the labourer. Where village shops are accessible – and the advent of the bicycle has greatly effected this accessibility – the payment of frequent money advances and the abolition of the supply of food and advances by the *kepalas* is ideal. On more remote estates it may be necessary to permit the supply of food by the *kepala*, but I should like to see a shop kept by the management of the estate where foodstuffs would be supplied at reasonable prices. I have not anywhere seen such a shop.

I understand that the Negri Sembilan Planters' Association has discussed the question of the introduction of systems of direct employment of Chinese tappers and has come to the conclusion that such systems are only suitable for small labour forces. I know, however, that some managers in Negri Sembilan who employ direct labour do not agree with this view. The largest direct labour force that I met with was 126. All managers of direct labour were unanimous as to the savings effected by the direct system. The usual estimate of this saving was "at least 10 cents per task per day". If this is so – with a month of say 26 days' work – the saving is at least $2.60 monthly per man or $260 monthly for a labour force of 100. From this must be paid the additional staff – and it is emphasized that there must be adequate additions to the staff – but there is still a balance in hand, and it has been represented to me that on estates with large Chinese labour forces the savings would be sufficient to allow for the employment of a European assistant to supervise the working of the system. /

It appears certain that, in general, under direct systems the tappers receive higher wages, and the estate gets better results (through the elimination of incompetent tappers) at lower costs. It is admitted that there are possibilities of malpractices – favouritism by *kepalas* in allotting tasks or by the staff in charge of weighing but these malpractices are more readily detected and remedied under the direct system than under the contractor systems. There is access by the tapper to the manager, even though this be through the office clerk, but an increasing number of tappers can talk a little Malay and thus converse direct. Some managers have told me that it took a good deal of hard work to introduce the system – particularly when the contractor had been retained as a *kepala* and probably tried to wreck the system which threatened to reduce his income. But in view of the success of direct employment it seems highly desirable that it should be tried with larger labour forces, though it is probably advisable to have such forces split up into kongsis of about fifty tappers.

Weeders, Etc.

The introduction of forestry methods in rubber cultivation has resulted in less weeding on estates, and this weeding – when done by Chinese – is invariably done through contractors. The contractor is usually paid at piece rates and pays his labourers either at piece rates or at daily rates. Labourers for felling and clearing new areas, for planting, road making and drain digging are also employed by contractors on the usual traditional contractor system, though the practice of labourers buying and cooking their own food is increasing in popularity.

Accommodation, Sanitation and Health.

Under the contractor system the contractor is the employer for the purposes of the Labour Code. He is responsible for the provision of lines, etc., as required, by section 168 of the Code. These requirements are:

(*a*) sufficient and proper house accommodation,
(*b*) a sufficient supply of wholesome water,
(*c*) sufficient and proper sanitary arrangements,

(*d*) hospital accommodation and equipment

(*e*) medical attendance and treatment including diets in hospital,

(*f*) a sufficient supply of medicines of good quality.

He is also required, subject to exemption by the Controller of Labour, to set aside land for allotments or grazing lands for the use of labourers employed on the estate who have worked on the estate for not less than six consecutive months and who have dependants.

In practice, lines, water supply and sanitary arrangements are invariably provided by the management of the estate. It is usually not within the capacity of the contractor to provide hospital accommodation, medical attention or land for allotments. In view of these facts and of the increasing incidence of the direct employment of labour by estates, it appears reasonable to suggest that the legal responsibility for the provision of these items should be removed from the contractor to the estate management. Managers who employ direct labour have, by removing the contractors, themselves become the employers and are, therefore, responsible for the provision of these items just as are the managers of estates employing Indian check-roll labour. To retain the law as it stands may operate as a deterrent to the transition from contract to direct labour; for managers retaining the contract system escape the responsibilities imposed by this section of the Code. In any / case the laying of these responsibilities on the contractor has never been satisfactory.* It has resulted in lack of attention by managers to the conditions under which their Chinese labour forces lived while the contractor has frequently been a man of no substance against whom it would be inequitable to attempt to enforce compliance with these requirements.

The type of lines provided varies from old attap sheds in filthy condition and disrepair to excellent modern plank kongsis. During this year there appears to have been a considerable improvement in the provision of lines. In west Pahang

---

* It is indeed doubtful whether it was intended that the Labour Code should have this effect. The original draft of the Labour Code (*G.N.* 3296/23) contained the following definition of "employer":

"Employer" includes any person, and any body of persons, corporate, or unincorporate, who or which enters into an agreement or contract with any labourer as hereinafter defined, and the duly authorised agent or manager of such person or body of persons, and a person (*other than the Government*) *who makes payments for work executed by labourers shall be deemed to be the employer of such labourers if such work is done in the conduct of any trade, business, undertaking or industry carried on by him or on his behalf.*

Had that definition been retained, the estate management would have been responsible for all housing, health and sanitation. The latter half of the definition was withdrawn not because of its effect upon the employment of estate labour but because of the possibility of collusion and fraud between labourers and contractors in other occupations, *e.g.*, the building trade. /

the Health Officer informs me that he has had a great number of plans submitted this year – principally by the owners of Chinese estates – for good up-to-date lines. In Negri Sembilan and Selangor too, improvement is noticeable – doubtless due to the demands of labourers during the strikes and to the pressure of inspecting officers. If the Labour Code is amended to fix the responsibility upon the estate management there should be no difficulty in ensuring the provision of decent lines on all estates.

I have already referred to the amazing increase in the number of women employed on estates. Where these women are resident upon estates they are invariably housed with their families or, where unmarried, in groups in the old kongsi-houses roughly partitioned-off into rooms. These rooms are necessarily dark and unsatisfactory. In a few instances new and well-designed lines are being erected for their accommodation. One estate tried the experiment of moving some plank bungalow-lines formerly occupied by Tamils to the Chinese area for occupation by Chinese families. The experiment was an instant success – each family having its own house and cooking place. Not only was it welcomed by the married people, but a few of the houses left over after their accommodation were eagerly sought after by bachelors who lived two or three in a house. It would appear to be good policy for estates in future to provide for their labour forces lines constructed in rooms or bungalows which could be used for either Indians or Chinese. Type plans should be drawn up and made available to managers, and Planters Associations should be informed.

The provision of hospital accommodation is a more difficult because of the preference of the average Chinese labourer for treatment by Chinese medicine, but it is not unreasonable to insist on medical supervision and medicines. On some estates such supervision of the Chinese labour force by qualified doctors is already carried out. It should be required on all estates.

It will probably be some years before the supply of land for allotments will be necessary generally. Nevertheless the tendency undoubtedly is towards the more settled family labour force and this tendency may be strengthened by the provision of land for vegetable / growing. Some small proprietary estates make such provision for some of their employees who have been with them for some years, and at Ladang Geddes an experiment is being conducted on a larger scale by the allocation of plots of land to Chinese labourers.

MATERNITY ALLOWANCES.

The Increase in the employment of women on estates has brought forward the question of the payment of maternity allowances in accordance with Section 72 of the Labour Code. The payment of such allowances to Chinese women was practically unheard of before the early part of this year when it formed part of the demands of the strikers. The provisions of the Code are now well-known in north Negri Sembilan and south Selangor, but elsewhere no action appears to be taken for the claiming or payment of these allowances. Even in Negri Sembilan and Selangor it is not unusual to find that some estates disregard these provisions. Planters point to the difficulty of identification, to the possibility that the woman may only have worked on the estate for a month or a week before her confinement, to the tendency for the woman to clear off as soon as she has received her benefit, to the fact that the wages of a Chinese woman are higher than those of a Tamil and the maternity benefit correspondingly greater, and to the fact that where the labourers are engaged through a contractor, the latter is the responsible employer who is liable for the payment of the allowance. It is also pointed out that Chinese squatter women employed but not resident on estates will probably work elsewhere during their benefit periods.

I have no doubt that in course of time most of these difficulties can be dealt with. Some estates have already introduced a system of identification by cards. A card is kept for each woman employed showing the date of her engagement and bearing her name and thumb-print. On this card is kept a record of her wages month by month so that at the time of confinement the amount of her benefit can be calculated. It is admittedly more difficult to do this with contract labour than with direct labour but it is being done. With regard to the responsibility of the contractor, here again I think that this responsibility should be shifted to the estate management. But the whole question of the payment of maternity allowances to Chinese women on estates might with advantage be discussed with representatives of the Planters' Associations. At the time when these provisions were enacted there was practically no regular female Chinese labour on estates and these allowances in practice applied to the more settled Indian labour forces usually resident on the estate. We are now applying these provisions to female Chinese labourers who are differently circumstanced.

THE TRUCK SYSTEM AS APPLIED TO ESTATES.

Chapter XI of the Labour Code is entitled "Provisions as to the Truck System". It requires that wages shall be paid entirely in legal tender and that no employer shall make any deduction by way of discount. Interest or any similar charge on account of advances of wages. It also permits the establishment by the employer of a shop for the sale of rice and provisions – with the approval of the Controller of Labour. In the same Chapter occurs Section 111 which reads "Nothing in this Chapter shall be held to apply to any body of persons working on an agreement of co-operation". In 1924 the then Secretary for Chinese Affairs informed Government that it was considered that *inter alia* contractors' labourers on estates came within this exemption and proposed that it be clearly stated that such labourers were protected by the Truck provisions. This proposal did not meet with approval, but experience since that date confirms its wisdom. /

The system of charging interest on advances is pernicious. It encourages the contractor to advance money so freely that the labourers are overdrawn and remain indebted to the contractor and the rate of interest charged is scandalously high, the method of computation being that $1 advance is reckoned as $1.10 no matter at what date the advance is made. But with the changes now taking place in methods of employment the Truck provisions should be made even wider. It should be provided that "No employer *and no person in charge of or supervising labourers* shall make any deduction, etc.". I have already mentioned a case where the labour was directly employed by the estate but advances were made by the *kepala* – the *kepala* in this instance receiving advances from the estate – free of interest to advance to the labourers. That is likely to be a very general practice in the transition from contract to direct labour.

PAYMENT OF WAGES.

Section 55 of the Labour Code coupled with the presumption contained in Section 53 (ii) appears to mean that wages should be paid not later than the seventh of the month following that in which the work was done. This is by no means the general practice. Under the traditional contract system credit balances are left with the contractor to be drawn against as required. The contractor does not pay interest on these credit balances. It is usually explained that the labourer can take his balance whenever he wants it. This may well be so, but I far prefer the full settlement made monthly. This is in operation with some contractors though settlements may be deferred until the fifteenth of the month. Under the direct employment system it is usual to find wages paid in full within the proper period.

GENERAL.

It has frequently been remarked to me that if estates are required to undertake the responsibility for housing, medical attention, maternity benefits and the like for Chinese labourers as they have in the past done for Indian labourers, the tendency will be for Chinese labour to be displaced by Indian. In fact it is pointed out that this is already taking place on some estates in Negri Sembilan.

It is probable that there will be some turn over from Chinese to Indian labour, but there is no guarantee that Indian labour will always be satisfied with its present wage-level or that it too may not paralyse the industry by striking. To my mind the solution lies not in dispensing with Chinese labour but in organising it under the more economical system of direct employment.

SECTION II.

MINES – METHODS OF EMPLOYMENT.

[...] The annual report of the Senior Warden of Mines, Federated Malay States, gives the following figures showing the numbers of labourers employed in the Federated Malay States by the different methods of mining in 1936;

Open cast.	Underground.	Hydraulic.		Bucket dredging.
		Gravel pump.	Sluicing.	
10,951	6,742	42,197	4,822	15,506

The total labour force of 80,218 is grouped by race as follows:

Europeans.	Chinese.	Malays.	Indians.	Others.
498	66,552	3,964	9,019	185

DREDGES.

The typical labour force on a dredge or group of dredges is composed as follows:
  A. Artisans.
  B. General labourers (transport of tin, fuel, earthwork, etc.)
  C. Dredge coolies.
  D. Ore treatment coolies.
  E. Amang[7] washing coolies.

Classes "A" and "B" are on the direct check-roll of the company. They receive their pay monthly in person at the company's office – receive advances once a month – say on the 20th, with final payment on the 5th of the following month. Class "B" may however be employed through a contractor.

Classes "D" and "E" are employed by contractors who are paid at piece rates by the company – so much per pikul of ore recovered, with bonuses for high assay values. The labourers are usually paid by the contractors at daily rates varying with their skill and experience, but they may be paid at piece rates sharing the money received by the contractor after the deduction of a percentage for his profit and of charges for food and various other items or some may be on piece rates and others on daily rates. An example of the complicated working of accounts for one of these mixed gangs is given below:

Received by contractor from company			$3,543.87
[...]			
"	Miscellaneous disbursements	2.70	
"	Bonuses to coolies	40.00	
"	Food for daily paid coolies @ cents daily	181.20	
"	Wages of daily paid coolies	234.00	
"	Overtime of daily paid coolies	51.88	
"	Overtime of other coolies	154.05	

"	Cost of newspapers	1.50
"	Paid to women for bag-stitching	73.45
"	Percentage for *kepalas*	114.00
		1,207.16
		$2,336.71

Number of day's work done by share coolies = 1645

$$\text{Rate per Kung} \qquad \frac{\$2,336.71}{1645} = \$1.42$$

Cost of food per day .40
Balance per Kung to be paid to share coolies $1.02 /

In this instance the main body of workers was composed of piece work (or share) coolies. Extra hands were employed to speed up work required urgently. Daily rates were also paid to new hands not proficient. The "Kung" was a working day of 8 hours. Overtime was paid to the share coolies at 80 cents for 2 hours and to the daily paid coolies at 25 cents for 2 hours. The *kepalas* receive free food and, in addition to their percentage payment received, counted their days as Kungs for the division of the final amount. They also received part of the bonus money. This was allotted by the contractor and head *kepala* as they thought fit. to those who had worked well. All the labourers paid the contractor a flat rate of 40 cents daily for food.

Class "C" may be employed directly on cheek-roll, or through a contractor or on a pseudo-direct system. When employed directly they differ in no way from the artizans. Their names are entered on the check-roll and they are paid at the company's office, with advances once monthly. When employed through a contractor, the contractor is paid at a rate per man-day. He engages the labourers and pays them at a lower rate per Kung. He also supplies food and may keep a shop. He makes advances as required, frequently charging interest at the usual rate – $1 debited as $1.10. In one case in Selangor I found that the contractor charged 40 cents monthly to each man for workmen's compensation premium. A similar case has been found by the Protector of Chinese. Perak, where the charge was 1 per cent. of salary.

The pseudo-direct system appears to be the most usual. Dredging companies habitually say that their labourers are on check-roll but this does not necessarily mean that payment is made to the labourer direct. Under this system the name of each labourer is entered on the check-roll and the number of Kungs done monthly is also entered. At the end of the month payment is made to the *kepala* who supplies food to the labourers and makes advances to them. He also engages fresh labourers when required. He may pay the labourers at the same rate as is shown in the company's check-roll or he may pay them at lower rates. For all practical purposes he is a contractor. One company goes so far as to put each man's pay into a separate envelope and then hands these envelopes to the *kepala* who deducts money for food, advances, etc., and pays the balance to the labourers.

The following is an example of the working of the contractor system. In this instance the contractor provided free food for all the labourers – two meals of rice and one of congee[8] daily. The rice meal consisted of rice (Siam Grade III), salt-fish and vegetables. Meat, pork or fresh-fish were supplied on festival days only:

Employed.	Wages paid by contractor.	Wages paid to countractor by company.
1 Clerk	$30 monthly	nil
1 *Kepala*	$2.70 daily	$2.70 daily
1 Assistant *kepala*	$1.28	nil
3 Shift *kepalas*	.98	$1.35
6 Jigmen[9]	.76	$1.00
6 Bucket coolies	.60	.90
3 Sampan coolies[10]	.60	.90
24 General	5 @ 68 cts. / 10 @ 63 cts. / 2 @ 58 cts. / 7 @ 53 cts.	.80
1 Cook	$34 monthly	$27 monthly /

The food supplied may have been worth 16 cents per head daily – though on the figures given to me by the contractor he appeared to manage to provide it for about 10 cents per head. This contractor supplied labour for six dredges and employed 260 labourers. I calculated his profit at $800 to $1,000 monthly. He admitted this but said he had to give half to his head *kepala*. This may have been true for the contractor had other business interests in a sundry shop and a pawn shop and did not live at the mine or supervise the labour.

QUARTERS, ETC.

At all the dredges that I visited quarters are provided free of charge by the companies. They vary from ramshackle huts to excellent plank and iron lines. Artisans are usually housed in separate houses or in rooms in lines and have their families with them.

HOURS OF WORK.

Work on dredges is continuous and is done in three shifts – four hours on and eight hours off. Usually overtime is only necessary on the dredge itself to replace sick or absent labourers temporarily. Such overtime is paid at the same rates as ordinary work.

GENERAL.

The labour forces on dredges are invariably racially mixed. Among the artisans – fitters, Boilermakers, etc., one finds Chinese and Tamils. Engine drivers are frequently Malays or Tamils and there is often one or more gangs of Indians – Tamils or Sikhs – employed on earth-work, pushing trucks, fuel supply or ore transport. There appears to be no differentiation of wage rates among artisans of various races. Indian manual labourers are normally paid at lower rates than Chinese.

Open Cast and Hydraulic Mines.

These types may be grouped together for the purpose of considering their labour organisation. The traditional system employed follows the following pattern:
Employed direct by the company:

Kepala (Kung Thau),
Assistant *kepalas* (Yi Kung),
Third *kepalas* (Saam Kung),
Croup overseers (Kwun Paan),
Skilled workmen (Pong Shau), Grades I, II and III,
Miscellaneous workmen (Tsaap Kung), Grades I, II and III,
General labourers (Kung-Sz-Kung).

All the above receive free board and lodging. The skilled workmen (Pong Shan) may be employed supervising work done by contractors' labourers, repairing palongs,[11] making drams, fitting pipes, etc. Miscellaneous workmen (Tsaap Kung) may be employed on palong and dram work, on building or on manning the monitors. It is difficult to distinguish clearly between the types of work allotted to each. From the general labourer (Kung-Sz-Kung) up to the skilled workman there are several grades distinguished by increasing rates of pay. The long-service and capable employees ascend the ladder. The system works as a buffer or expansion-joint between the company and its directly / employed labourers. Should a man complain that his pay is inadequate he may be moved up one step – this will not necessitate an all-round increase of wages. Additional elasticity is provided by the system of overtime (Ka han). Normally the day's work (Kung) is eight hours and overtime is reckoned at 3 hours or 2 ½ hours = ½ Kung. But if there is urgent work to be done or if in wet weather the labourers are loth to turn out, the management may offer a full Kung or two or three Kungs for a specific piece of work, or a full Kung for two hours' work, with the result that it is not unusual to find such labourers credited with an average of 50 to 60 Kungs in a month with a maximum of 70 or more.

In addition to the above there will also probably be the following types employed directly by the company with free lodging but no board: Pump attendants, electricians, excavator-drivers (where excavators are used), electric motor attendants and foundry staff. They make their own arrangements for food either by buying and cooking their own or by themselves employing a cook to cook for all the occupants of a kongsi.

There will also be various contracts on the mine:

(*a*) *Engine drivers* – Diesel or Steam. – There is usually one contractor for attendants for all the engines on the mine. His contract rate depends upon the horse-power of the engines. He engages all the engine drivers, pays them at monthly rates and provides them with food. They normally sleep at or close to the engine sheds.

(*b*) *Winchmen.* – On open-cast mines where trucks are hauled up inclines it is usual for a contractor to undertake to supply all the winch attendants. He is paid at different rates for different types of winch, and pays the attendants monthly wages. He may or may not provide food.

(*c*) *Trucking.* – On open-cast mines the earth is filled into trucks at the face and trucked by hand power to the inclines. These truck-pushers are employed by a contractor who is paid a price per filled truck, the price varying with the distance of the face from the incline. The contractor takes a percentage (10%) of the total receipts. Some contractors supply food and charge or divide the total cost of food and cook's wages among the labourers in proportion to the number of Kungs done by each. Other contractors do not provide food. After deduction of contractor's percentage, food money, and any other charges the balance is divided among the labourers in proportion to the number of Kungs done by each.

Finally there may be contractors for excavation of earth by changkol.[12] In this category I include too the nai-cheng thau, called in Section 149 of the Labour Code a "mining headman".

An account of the changing nature of the nai-cheng system prepared by Mr. Middlebrook, Protector of Chinese, Perak, who has during this year had considerable contact with nai-cheng labour is attached to this report as Appendix "D" [not included]. Translations of typical nai-cheng agreements are also attached as Appendices "E-1"* and "E-2".* Briefly the original system was based upon an agreement between the management and the nai-cheng than for the removal of earth (either over-burden or tin-bearing Karang) at a stated price per "cheng" (50 cubic feet) over a marked area, the price for Karang being higher than that for over-burden. Accounts were not made up until the area was completed which / usually took from three to six months. Meanwhile advances were made by the management to the nai-cheng than who engaged the labourers to do the work, provided their food, employed a clerk and a cook and, in the old days, the planking for the beds in the kongsis, and made advances of pay to the labourers. On completion of the work it was measured by the management and the nai-cheng thau. This business of measurement has always been a fruitful source of trouble between the labourers and the management. The measurement of earth excavated from irregular-shaped patches is rarely a straightforward matter even for trained engineers. The Chinese method of measurement is at times liable to lead to very inaccurate results. [...]

*   Not printed

When a satisfactory figure had been agreed upon, the nai-cheng than was paid the amount owing to him, i.e., the total value of work done less the amount of advances and cost of tools if supplied by the management. Under the original system the "advancer" to the mine was usually a shopkeeper and the advances consisted largely of goods supplied. This system of a separate advancer has practically disappeared.

The nai-cheng than then deducted a percentage for himself to cover supervision charges (*kepalas'* wages), cost of tools if supplied by the nai-cheng thau, and provision of nipah rain coats. The cost of food supplied would also be deducted. The balance would be divided by the total number of Kungs done by the gang and the answer would be the rate per Kung to be credited to the labourers. From each man's total would then be deducted advances made – with interest at the usual rate – a charge for bed planks and a charge for clerk's wages and the balance would be paid at the rate of 98 cents to the dollar. This reduced payment was known as "Kaau Paat" or "nine-eight". Another term for this reduced payment is "lui shui" or "exchange profit" sometimes / referred to as "commission". It was sometimes deducted from the lump sum after the deduction of the nai-cheng thau's percentage but before the deduction of anything else. The following is a recent example of a nai-cheng wage calculation. In this case the nai-cheng thau did not supply food: Period of agreement 3 months 20 days.

Deductions:

(A) 14% for nai-cheng thau for supervision, changkols, baskets and raincoats.

(B) $2 per $100 "lui shui".

(C) Actual cost of tea leaves and firewood supplied by the nai-cheng thau.

Received from management	$7,209.93
Deduct (A)	1,009.39
	$6,200.54
Deduct (B)	124.01
	$6,076.53
Deduct (C)	111.50
	$5,965.03

Total number of Kungs 8,812 ½.

Wage per Kung 67.7 cents (the nai-cheng thau adding $1.03 to the total to make it a divisible figure).

Then deduct –

(i) Cook 2 cents daily,

(ii) Clerk 1 cent daily,

(iii) Extra food supplied by nai-cheng thau on festival days – 3 at 50 cents – $1.50 per man.

There are innumerable variations of the nai-cheng system now existing, the most usual probably being the payment of a fixed rate per Kung during the period of agreement and the distribution of any balance as a bonus at the end of the period. The nai-cheng than is developing into a contractor or even into a *kepala* in the pay of the management. Nai-cheng agreements are still made but many of the terms of the agreements are regarded as inoperable.

Early this year strikers on the Hong Fatt and Sungei Besi Mines in Selangor demanded the abolition of charges for interest and for bed planks. Later in the year nai-cheng labourers on a mine at Temoh. Perak, complained of the charging of interest and of other items paid the Perak Chinese Chamber of Mines recommended its members to see that such charges were not permitted. The whole system is now becoming discredited. A leading Chinese miner in Perak informed me that he proposed to abolish the nai-cheng system on his mine and adopt a system of direct employment with pay at Kung-Sz-Kung rates. This can be done successfully on mines because it is possible to supervise the labour closely and to eliminate lazy workers whereas on estates such close supervision of tappers is not possible. There is no doubt that the direct employment of Kung-Sz-Kung labourers will become much more prevalent in the future. It is the / custom where nai-cheng or pseudo nai-cheng labourers are employed to destroy all the nai-cheng thau's account books a few days after final settlement is made, thus conveniently destroying all evidence of the details of the final settlement. This is a thoroughly reprehensible practice.

On large open-cast mines it is not unusual for parts of the work, at some distance perhaps from the main mine, to be let out to a tributor who conducts the whole of the mining operations including the treatment of the ore, and sells the ore, paying to the lessee a tribute – which may be 20% of the selling price of the ore if quota-coupons are supplied by the lessee. Such a tributor will employ a labour force on the same general plan as other open-cast mines but will probably have no contractor or nai-cheng labourers. He may provide his own kongsi and lines for the labourers and will post up a notice stating the rules which apply to labourers working there. [...]

For the working of small areas among rocks or otherwise inaccessible "landchute" gangs are occasionally employed. The gang consists of 12 or more labourers with a headman. The "landchute" or sluice-box is the property of the headman or its cost may have been shared by all the gang. The headman undertakes to work the ground on payment of tribute to the lessee. The wages of the labourers may be fixed by the headman at Kung-Sz-Kung rates or the proceeds may be shared proportionately to the number of Kungs done with an extra percentage for the headman. There are comparatively few labourers employed, in this way and the system is not worth more than passing reference.

The old style of tribute labourer as defined in Section 149 of the Labour Code may be said to have disappeared. The advent of modern machinery and the formation of companies and groups with large capitalization have squeezed out the old-fashioned advancer – tribute-labourer system.

Female labour on mines is mainly confined to grass cutters, though they are sometimes found on bunding[13] work for the retention of tailings and even on truck-pushing work. Such women do not live on the mine. [...] Grass cutters are paid at piece rates – so much per pikul or load of grass cut and brought to the mine. The grass is used for binding the mud in bunding and for thatching the slopes of some open-cast mines to prevent wash. Women working on bunding work or as truckers are paid at daily rates. On some mines in Perak women, and in particular Malay women, are employed to do the raking of the palongs and to wash the concentrate in the palongs by means of "dulangs" or wooden "pans". These women are paid at Kung-Sz-Kung rates. On some Chinese mines there may still be found a few Chinese women employed on "foot-stamps" – crude wooden mechanical hammers which are worked by two women, each with one foot on the "tail" of the pivoted hammer, alternately putting their weight on these feet and then releasing it. These women are paid at Kung-Sz-Kung rates.

Indian labourers – both Tamils and Northern Indians – are to be found on many open-cast mines usually employed on general odd-job work at daily rate. I have also found one gang of Sikhs working on a Chinese mine as nai-cheng labourers with their own Sikh "nai-cheng thau". The Chinese manager reported that they worked well and were not as much trouble as the present-day Chinese labourers. /

Underground Mining

The three underground mines in the Federated Malay States are at Sungei Lembing, Pahang (Pahang Consolidated Company, Ltd.), Raub, Pahang (Raub Australian Gold Mining Company, Ltd.) and Batu Arang, Selangor (Malayan Collieries, Ltd.), and produce tin, gold and coal respectively. Each of these companies is possessed by lease or concession of large areas of land – Pahang Consolidated 182,400 acres; Raub Gold 12,000 acres; and Malayan Collieries 8,000 acres and each employs a very large labour force – Pahang Consolidated 3,000; Raub Gold 1,200; and Malayan Collieries 5,000. The labour force in each case is composed mainly of Chinese. The labour organisation on all three mines is necessarily intricate, but a broad general classification is possible. Artisans in the workshop and, at Sungei Lembing and Raub, labour employed in the crushing mill and for the treatment of ore are employed on direct check-roll by the companies. Those engaged in actual mining are employed through contractors at Sungei Lembing; partly through contractors and partly on a direct "party system" at Raub; and partly through contractors and partly on a direct system at Batu Arang.

The artisans, etc., on direct check-roll follow the ordinary system. An eight-hour day is the rule. Overtime is rarely necessary except perhaps for boilermakers when the work is frequently given to them at piece rates. Advances of pay may be made once monthly with final settlement monthly – the date of settlement varying between the fifth and the sixteenth of the succeeding month. The labourers provide their own food. There is nothing specially worthy of comment in this method of employment except the provision of accommodation which as it concerns all the labourers employed on these mines will be referred to later. At all three mines the main interest of the labour investigator centres round the methods of employment of the labourers employed in the actual mining operations.

SUNGEI LEMBING

At Sungei Lembing these labourers are all employed through contractors of whom there are twenty nine. Contracts may be for development work (driving galleries by blasting), stoping (removing the blasted rock to chutes for extraction later), filling old workings with refuse rock, removal of rock from the stopes, and timbering.

Development work is done either by hand-drilling or by machine drills worked by compressed air. The company arranges a price per fathom[14] advanced provided that the gallery is not more than 6 feet wide. For wider galleries the contract is for cubic yards of development work. From this contract price the contractor pays for explosives and drill-steel (both bought from the company's store), tools and labour. Where machine drills are used the company provides these machines. The value of the work done is computed at the end of each month. The contractor employs a gang of labourers. The rule is that after deducting the cost of explosives, the contractor takes 10 per cent. to cover administration expenses [wages of "tai kong" (overseer), clerk, tools, etc.] and the balance is divided equally among the members of the gang. The gangs are usually small – 4 or 5 men but one contractor will have / a number of such contracts and may employ 200 or 300 labourers in all. In practice the sharing of the profits varies with different contractors. Here, for example, is an extract from one of the contractor's books:

Gang of 4 men. Total value of work paid to contractor		$324.79
Deductions made by contractor:		
Cash, advance	$1.10 ($1 + 10% interest)	
Carrying tea	.63	
Cash advance	2.20 ($2 + 10% ")	
" "	1.10 ($1 + 10% ")	
Payment of substitute workers (6 days)	21.66	
Payment of substitute workers	3.50	
Carrying steel	1.50	
Supply of congee	8.14	
Carrying congee	6.90	
Explosives 16 pkts. @ $3.50	56.00	
Fuses, 18 @ 75 cts.	13.50	
Detonators 100	2.70	
		118.93
		205.86
Further deductions by contractor:		
10% contractor's profit }	15 % of $205.86	
5% for wages of tai kong and tools		30.88
	Balance	$174.98
= $43.74 per man.		

Some other contractors appear to be satisfied with a 10% profit + interest on advances. This charging of interest is general at Sungei Lembing, though some of the contractors allow $5 or $10 monthly free of interest. This, they say, was done at the under of the manager in March or April last. The most flagrant case of all was that of a contractor whose labour force comprised 143 men (Hailams 70, Kwangsi 60, Cantonese 13). Of these no fewer than 112 were overdrawn, many to the extent of $70–$80 and a few to the extent of $125. I did not work out the average indebtedness per man, but if it were $40 – and I think it was probably more – the interest earned would be perhaps $4 monthly per man or $450 monthly for 112 men. The acting manager informed me that these were the hardest working labourers on the mine and their monthly earnings were certainly higher than those of other contractors, ranging from $35 to $60 as against $25 to $40 for other contractors' labourers. In this case too the contractor's deduction for profits was lower than usual, but this he could well afford on account of his large interest-earnings.

Other underground contracts are for stoping (removing the broken ore to chutes from which it is drawn off in trucks as required) filling of disused cuts with refuse rock, and trucking. These are contracts in terms of cubic yards removed, the contractor giving a lower contract price to the gang than that received by him from the mine. There are also timbering labourers employed by contractors, the rates varying with the size of timber put in. /

Work underground is conducted in 4-hour shifts but is not limited to 8 hours daily. In fact the general custom appears to be a 12-hour day underground. This the company does not control. It is left to the individual gangs to determine how long they shall work, the company requiring of course that a certain rate of progress be maintained. The timbermen – whose work is heavy – work shorter hours – probably about 6 hours daily and draw higher rates of wages than most of the others.

RAUB.

At Raub most of the mining is done through contractors. The contracts for development work are in terms of footage driven, for ore blasting in terms of tons of ore blasted and for sloping in terms of cubic yards. The contractor provides explosives, takes a percentage (10%) of the balance of the contract money – after the deduction of the cost of explosives – and divides the balance among the labourers in proportion to the number of shifts worked. In some cases pay may be reckoned by shifts and not by sharing, but the management encourages the sharing or piecework system. The management endeavours to fix its contract rates to allow minimum wages of 80 cents daily for unskilled labour and $1,20 for experienced labour working at a fair rate, and the contractors are instructed to pay these minima. On pay day each contractor is required to submit a pay-sheet showing the wages paid to each labourer. European assistants select labourers at random and enquire what wages have been received by them, and every endeavour is made to see that contractors' labourers do actually receive the amounts shown on the pay-sheets. Payment of wages is made every four weeks.

Early this year experiments with a new system, referred to as the "Party System", were begun. This system eliminates the large contractor. Small contracts are given to gangs of four men who divide the nett proceeds (after deduction of the value of explosives, etc., used). The experiment began with five parties, and two more parties have since been added. The manager informed me that the difficulty in extending the system lay in finding men as "gangers" of the parties who were competent to undertake these contracts.

This system, as far as it goes, is excellent. It establishes close contact between the individual labourer and the European assistant who is in charge of payments and eliminates all possibility of deductions. This is the easier because at this mine – and at Sungei Lembing – the contractors have not been in the habit of providing food for their labourers. Each labourer fends for himself. The system involves, however, the splitting up of the work into very small contracts and, apart from the difficulty of finding suitable "party heads" the work involved in thus splitting the contracts might well prove burdensome at the larger mines of Sungei Lembing and Batu Arang. An outstanding feature of the method of employment at this mine is the limitation of work underground to 8 hours daily. It is the contention of the manager that longer hours than this underground result in diminishing returns.

BATU ARANG.

The actual mining at Batu Arang is done partly underground and partly in open cuts. Until recently all this work was done by contract labour. Shortly before my visit (November, 1937) a new system had been introduced, whereby all the underground labourers are now paid directly by the company. At present some 2,000 labourers are paid direct and it is proposed, to extend the system to the open-cut labourers who at present work under contractors. /

Each labourer is given a permanent brass identity disc on which is engraved his number. His name, thumb print and other personal details are entered on individual cards and indexed. The labourers live in kongsis as they did when they worked under contractors. The contractors are now termed Kung Thaus (Headmen) and are paid a monthly wage equivalent to a percentage of the total monthly wages of the labourers under their control. The clerk and the cook in each kongsi are now employed and paid direct by the company. Allotment of work at piece rates to each Kung Thau follows the same system which was in operation when these men were contractors – rates per cubic yard of earth and shale and per ton of coal. Apparently the men themselves decide which shall work at the face and which shall work at filling and removing trucks. The number of trucks removed each day by the labourers in one kongsi is given by an overseer to the clerk of the kongsi and is entered by him on a work sheet which is kept posted in the kongsi. The work sheet also shows against each man's name the days on which he worked – as on an ordinary Kung phaai (working board) kept at all mines. At the end of the month the amount to be paid by the company is divided by the number of Kungs done and the rate per Kung obtained. In addition to the work sheet, the clerk is responsible for another sheet which is kept posted in the kongsi. This shows "agreed deductions". On this sheet is entered the cost of the food supplied to the labourers by the Kung Thau and the cost of tools, etc., supplied by him or by the company. These amounts are also divided by the number of Kungs and a rate per Kung for "agreed deductions" obtained. Finally the clerk keeps an account book in which are shown advances of money made through the Kung Thau to the labourers.

At the end of the month a duplicate of the work sheet and the "agreed deductions" sheet together with a statement of advances is taken to the mine office by the kongsi clerk. There a pay-slip is made out for each man showing gross earnings, agreed deductions, advances received and credit balance. These pay-slips are given to the kongsi clerk for distribution to the labourers who can then see exactly how they stand. On pay-day – between the 5th and 7th of the succeeding month the labourers parade at the mine office where a special pay counter with entrance and exit to allow of orderly filing past has been constructed. The pay of each labourer has already been put into a tin bearing his number by the accountant's staff. As each labourer files in he hands in his identity disc and his pay-slip. The money from the corresponding tin is given to him, the pay-slip retained and the identity disc returned to him.

There is no deduction from wages for the payment of the Kung Thau. His percentage is an additional payment made to him by the company. The labourer is in possession of his pay-slip for a day or two before pay-day so that he has ample time to lay any complaint either before or at pay time.

This appears to me to be an excellent development from the contractor system. Close supervision of the Kung Thau's "agreed deductions" is necessary and this is provided for on this mine by the engagement of a European assistant whose main duty is the supervision of the labour force. His work includes the registration of all the labourers on the mine with their living places, the care of the quarters and kongsi houses of the labourers, investigation of their wages, food supplied, etc., the hearing of any complaints, the allotting of houses and of market stalls and shops in the village, the control of market prices and general supervision of sanitation. He has Chinese clerks and overseers on his staff who are available for interpretation and investigation of accounts. /

The creation of this post of "Labour Assistant" and the introduction of the system of direct payment are both recent innovations but I think they cannot fail to be successful. Before introducing the direct payment system the greatest care was taken to see that every detail was correct beforehand, for it was realised that a hitch on the first pay-day might completely discredit the system. This is the most interesting and intelligent large scale experiment of adjusting methods of employment to changing conditions that I have seen and its development should be of the greatest importance.

The open-cut labourers employed by contractors follow the usual contractor system. Food is supplied by the contractor, its cost being divided among the labourers. Two cents a day per man is charged for the cook's wages and the cost of tools supplied by the contractor – changkols and baskets – is deducted monthly. The contractor, whose contract with the company is in terms of cubic yards of earth and shale and weighed tons of coal, pays the labourers at fixed prices per truck each of earth, shale and coal. The price paid to the labourers for earth was higher than the contract rate; the prices paid for shale and coal were lower.

One curious feature is the payment of timbering labourers on the same basis as the other labourers, i.e., according to the number of trucks of rock removed, and not according to the size and amount of timber used. It is explained that in coal mining in friable shale the amount of timbering required is fairly constant and has a reasonably steady ratio to the amount of rock removed whereas in tin and gold mining the ratio is not constant as mining takes place in less friable rocks.

Batu Arang has a number of subsidiary industries – plywood factory, brick kiln, paid wood-distillation. The labourers in these industries are either on or are about to be brought on to the direct payment system.

Accommodation and Sanitation on Mines.

Chapter XVI of the Labour Code is headed "Sanitation and Hospitals upon Mines". Section 159 begins as follows:

"Every employer who has agreed or contracted to provide house accommodation for his labourers shall supply and maintain such accommodation as shall fulfil all reasonable sanitary requirements."

Section 161 reads:

"Every employer who is bound to provide house accommodation for his labourers shall also be bound to provide for them a sufficient quantity of wholesome water."

In practice – with the exception of Sungei Lembing and Raub Gold – the managements of mines throughout the Federated Malay States provide house accommodation for their labour forces. A minor exception to this rule occurs when a tributor himself provides a kongsi house for his labourers, but such cases are rare. But whether this general provision of accommodation can be presumed to be evidence of agreements to provide accommodation is very doubtful.

It is true that section 160 reads: "Should the accommodation upon any mine be insanitary or otherwise unsatisfactory, it shall be lawful for the Controller or a Magistrate to order that no labourers shall be admitted to such mine until the necessary improvement has been effected," but this presumably can only be taken to apply to mines which have an agreement to provide accommodation. /

Chapter XVII of the Labour Code deals with house accommodation, and, though it is not so specifically stated, it is obvious from the phrasing of this Chapter that it is intended to apply to estates. Section 166, within this Chapter, reads:

"It shall be lawful for the Resident upon the recommendation of the Controller, to declare by notification in the *Gazette* that the provisions of this Part or of such Sections thereof as may be specified in such notification shall apply to any mine or other place of employment and be complied with by the owner, lessee or occupier thereof."

These powers have been used to apply the provisions of Part IX or of portions thereof to two mines in Selangor (*G.N.* 5041/80 and 6413/31) and to various other places of employment, e.g., rubber factories, tile works and brickfields in all States (*G.N.* 299/27).

The accommodation provided on mines varies from old filthy attap shacks with primitive sanitary arrangements to up-to-date plank and iron or concrete buildings with ceilings and concrete floors, piped water supply and flush latrines. In general the type of quarters provided and the provision of latrines and general sanitary arrangements leave ample room for improvement. This is particularly so on the smaller Chinese mines.

It has frequently been represented to me that it is unfair to expect miners to erect permanent quarters because most unmined areas adjacent to mines may later be required for mining, or because of the necessity of moving labour forces from place to place on large dredging properties, or because of the short life of some mines. Nevertheless some of the large mines – open-cast and dredges – have excellent permanent quarters. One dredging company has a type of semi-permanent quarters which are dismantled and moved on to new concrete foundations as required. On smaller mines it may be inadvisable to erect permanent quarters. In fact a well-constructed faily new attap kongsi kept in clean condition is frequently cooler and better-ventilated than some of the more permanent buildings of plank with iron roof and without ceilings and jack-roofs. But the attap building is invariably allowed to outlive its wholesomeness.

At Sungei Lembing, with the exception of a new block of quarters which will house a few of the artisans, practically no living accommodation is provided by the company. Labourers live in groups in rooms in shop-houses in the village (which is on the company's property) or, with the permission of the company, build themselves iron or attap huts on the company's property and grow a few vegetables and keep fowls or pigs.

Raub Gold follows a similar system except that when permission is given to erect a hut a fee of $2 is charged and a document is prepared purporting to vest the ownership of the hut in the company.

I consider that this system is open to grave objection. The labourer must live on the company's property for there is no other property sufficiently near to his work. His only alternatives are to build himself a hut – which may cost $40 or $50 – or live in the company's village where accommodation is limited. As a bachelor he may, by sharing a room with others get his lodging reasonably cheaply, but when he marries and needs a room for himself and his wife it becomes more expensive and may cost him $3 to f 5 monthly. He prefers, if allowed, to build himself a hut. But when he has done that his position is that, should he lose his employment, he will also lose his house and the capital invested therein without compensation. He is therefore not a free agent in his dealings / with the company. The scales are unfairly weighted in favour of the employer. If the huts were built by the company, the man's dismissal would only involve the partial sacrifice of his immature crop of vegetables or of his part-grown pigs.

It is difficult to see why mines of this size and permanence should not provide quarters for their labourers, the more so because permanent family populations are growing up there. Excellent quarters are provided at Batu Arang, kongsi houses for bachelors and huts for approved married men. Tenancy of a hut is prized, and applicants are selected from those with good service and good conduct.

I consider that the provision of quarters, sanitary arrangements and water supply should be a duty laid upon all mine owners or occupiers by the Labour Code. Such lines should not necessarily be permanent but should be to the satisfaction of the Controller or Health Officer. If thought necessary, power could be given to the Controller to permit exemption in special cases but the general principle should be clearly stated.

THE TRUCK SYSTEM AS APPLIED TO MINES.

A general feature of many contract and nai-cheng systems is the charging of items such as interest on advances, clerk's and cook's wages, rent for bed-planks, etc., and payment, of balances at 98 per cent. All these practices are part of the traditional mining customs of the country. They are not so universal as they used to be but they are still very frequently encountered. The charging of interest on advances also extends to the pseudo-direct system on dredges where the *kepala* may be found to be making advances and charging interest. All these practices are contrary to the provisions of the Truck Chapter (Chapter XI), but here again section 111 referring to "agreements of co-operation" has been interpreted as exempting nai-cheng labourers and piece-work contract labourers from these provisions. This point too was raised in 1924. It should be made quite clear that all such labourers are subject to the truck provisions. This could probably best be clone by repealing section 111. I imagine that its original intention was to exempt "tribute labourers", who, as I have said, have now practically disappeared. The provisions should also be extended to prohibit *kepalas* who are not "employers" From making such deductions. But care must be taken to permit the supply of food either by the employer or the *kepala*. This is still the usual practice, though it is being gradually displaced on the initiative of the labourers themselves.

GENERAL.

Reference has already been made to nai-cheng agreements or "notices". Although the terms and conditions of these notices are subject to the approval of the Controller of Labour it is the exception to find that such notices are brought to the Protectorate for such approval by the Protector – who is a Deputy Controller of Labour. And, until the application of the truck provisions to such labourers has been made clear, it would be unwise to insist upon this. Such notices invariably contain provisions for the charging of interest, etc. It is not clear at present that these charges are illegal yet no Protector would wish to approve a notice containing provisions for such deductions.

In addition to nai-cheng notices it is customary for contractors of all kinds to post notices containing regulations governing the employment of their labourers. The management too may post similar notices. [...]

SECTION III.

ESTATES. WAGES AND COST OF LIVING.

At the time of the beginning of my tour (4th October, 1937), the price of rubber was 28 ⅝ cents a lb. At the end of the tour it was 24 7/8 cents a lb.

It is not true to say that tappers employed through contractors always receive lower wages than tappers employed direct by the estate, but, as far as my observation went, it is true to say that the lowest rates are paid on estates with contract labour.

The lowest rates I found were in Perak among squatter labour employed through a contractor on a European-managed estate. The rate paid to the contractor by the estate was fixed every ten days and was worked out in poundage on a basis of paying the contractor 68 cents per task. The manager informed me that it did not exceed 69 cents per task. From this the contractor had to make his profit. His tappers' wages varied from 48 cents daily upwards to a maximum of 75 cents. Most of these tappers were women. The next lowest area appeared to be the southern half of Negri Sembilan where group averages of wages for September were at times down to 70 cents daily. In the northern half of Negri Sembilan wages ranged from 89 cents to $1.21, along the railway line in Pahang between Mengkuang and Mengkarak from 75 cents to 92 cents. Some of these estates –

Chinese-owned – paid tappers at the rate per katty (dry, smoked), which included tapping and processing, coagulating, sheeting, mangling and smoking. This is a very usual system on small Chinese estates. Further north on the Kuala Lipis road (Budu Estate) a group average for September was as high as $ 1.27. That however was exceptional. The estate is somewhat remote, very precipitous and has been unhealthy so that it is necessary to pay high rates to attract the labour. Throughout the country considerable variation and fluctuation was evident.

Wage levels have certainly increased since the beginning of the year. The following figures of a Negri Sembilan estate employing direct labour are typical

1936.		1937.		1937.	
October	50 *cts.*	January	57 ½ *cts.*	June	84 *cts.*
November	45 "	February	60 "	July	88 "
		March	63 "	August	87 "
		April	80 "	September	87 "
		May	81 "		

During November I found that, on account of the fall in the price of rubber, there was a tendency to reduce wage rates. This does not, so far, appear to have caused any labour trouble. Managers who had reduced rates informed me that the labourers realised that lower prices would result in lower rates. This has always been typical of the Chinese labour force in Malaya generally but it has its corollary, that when prices of the products rise, a higher wage rate is expected.

I did not meet with any instance of a sliding scale, varying wage rates with the price of rubber, as applied to tappers, though I understand that one exists on an estate in Johore. On the Kepong group of estates (Kepong Malay Rubber Estates Limited), there is a sliding scale in force as between the management and the contractors. [...]

The method of payment for scrap[15] and lump rubber[16] varies considerably. Some estates pay nothing but require a certain poundage of scrap to be brought in daily in default of which the tapper is fined or dismissed. Other estates pay varying amounts – 1 cent to 3 ½ cents per lb.

WEEDERS.

Weeders' wages varied from 55 cents to 80 cents daily per man employed on Kung-sz-Kung (daily rates), the corresponding figures for women being 50 cents to 60 cents. Group averages of wages paid to weeders employed under contractors worked out at 65 cents to 73 cents daily for men and 55 cents for women.

The rates quoted above for both tappers and weeders are the money wages. Some managers have pointed out to me that the method of calculation – dividing the amount credited to the tapper by the number of days worked results in a figure which is lower than that actually earned because, on wet days, the tappers may only work for part of the task and earn low wages but these days are nevertheless, shown as working days. The error however is not. I think, of any great extent.

A comparison of money wages does not necessarily give a fair picture of real wages. Where contractors supply food the price of the food to be deducted from the wages varies considerably with different contractors – even in the same vicinity. On one large estate in Negri Sembilan one contractor sold rice to his labourers at 45 cents a gantang and another at 50 cents. The rice cost about 35 cents a gantang[17] delivered to the estate.

As regards expenditure of a Chinese tapper who supplies his own food (the prices quoted are those ruling at Seremban at the time of my visit):

		$	c.
Siamese rice	5 gantangs @ 42 cents	2	10
Pork	3 catties @ 44 cents	1	32
Groundnut oil	1 catty @ 30 cents		30
Fish	3 catties @ 36 cents	1	08
Vegetable	10 catties @ 7 cents		70
Sauce	1 bottle (small) @ 10 cents		10
Ginger	3 tahils[18] @ 2 cents		02
Garlic	3 tahils @ 8 cents		03
Salt	½ catty @ 3 cents		03
Sugar	1 catty @ 10 cents		10
	Carried forward	5	78 /
		$	c.
	Brought forward	5	78
Native tobacco	8 packets (2 tahils) @ 10 cents		80
Cigarette paper	20 packets @ 1 cent		20
Salt egg (duck's)	10 eggs @ 3 cents		30
Bean curd	15 pieces @ 2 cents for 3		10
Barber			25
Matches	20 boxes @ 1 cent		20
Rubber shoes	1 pair @ 60 cents for 2 months		30
Tapping knife	30 cents each for 2 months		15
Knife sharpener	45 cents each for 3 months		15
Soap	3 pieces @ 5 cents		15
Wooden clogs	.10 cents a pair		10
Clothing	$1.20 a suit for 4 months		30
Towels	30 cents each for 3 months		10
Face towels	12		04
Tooth brush	12		04
Singlets	60		20
Socks	45		15
Mat, mosquito net, blanket, etc.			20
Tea, cigarettes, travelling expenses		1	49
		$11	00

This budget does not allow for amusements, opium or remittances to China, and is the budget of a bachelor. It will be seen that rice, pork and fish combined form about 45 per cent. of the expenditure.

The price of rice is liable to very considerable fluctuations, but in addition to this there is the usual difference between the price at which it is bought by the contractor and that at which it is sold to the labourer. The usual price charged for Grade II Siamese rice by contractors during October was 40 cents a gantang. The lowest price I found was on a European estate which sold rice direct to the labourers at 35 cents. The highest price was 50 cents. I think it would be fair to say that the average contractor makes a profit of from 5 to 10 cents a gantang on rice sold to the labourers. This is a profit of from 14 per cent. to 28 per cent. monthly – for rice stocks are invariably bought monthly. The effect on the labourer consuming 5 gantangs monthly is a loss in real wages of 50 cents to $1 a month. This appears to be an inconsiderable amount, but a further source of profit is the supplying of Grade III rice under the name of Grade II or of Grade II instead of Grade I. This is a not unusual practice. The difference in market price between Grade III and Grade II rice may be 4 to 6 cents a gantang. There is, of course, considerable variation in the amounts charged by contractors for rice and foodstuffs. There is variation in the cost of the same / articles at various centres in the Federated Malay States. The following Table I shows variations in prices of some staple articles at some of the places visited.

Table I.

Foodstuff Prices.

–		Kampar.	Batu Gajah.	Ipoh.	Teluk Anson.	Seremban.	Raub.	Bentong.
		$ c.	$ c.	$ c.	$ c.	$ c.	$ c.	$ c.
Rice: gantang, Siamese	I	40	38	36	38	42	39	38
" "	II	38	36	34	34		37	36
" "	III	34	32	32	28		35	34
	Rangoon	32	32	31	31	44	44	44
Pork: katty {	lean	50	56	44	52			
	fat	24	24	26	24			
	mixed	30	32	36	40			
Groundnut oil: katty (5 kati tin)		1 15	1 15	1 05	95	1 50		
Dried bean curd: katty		18	14	13	13			
Wooden clogs: pair		09	10	08	09			
Rubber shoes: pair		48	47	45	48	60	49	48
Fish: fresh, katty		32	48	56	32	36		
" Dried „		34	40	36				
Duck eggs: fresh, each		03	03	03	02 ½	03		
" salt „		03	03	03	02 ½	03		
Tobacco: 2 tahils		09	09	09	09	10		
Sugar: katty		06	06	06	06	10		
Vegetables; katty {		06 to 14	06 to 14	06 to 12	07 to 12	07 to 12		

[...]

But the regional differences of market prices are not usually so great as the differences caused by contractors' charges, particularly in respect of rice and, sometimes, of pork. These differences vary with the remoteness of the estates from villages, though in the case quoted above where rice was sold at 50 cents a gantang a further item helped to bolster up the price, namely, a charge of 2 cents a day levied on those labourers who did not buy their rice from the contractor. This was said to be "tea money" to pay for tea supplied by the contractor to labourers, but those who bought their rice from the contractor were exempt from this charge. But in general, with the greater ease and cheapness of / individual transport, the abuse caused by the charging of high prices by contractors on estates is not as great as might be expected. A stricter control of exorbitant charges can be enforced if it is made clear that the truck provisions of the Labour Code apply to contract labour on estates, but the provisions prohibiting the keeping of shops without the approval of the Controller should be extended to include supervisors of labour.

At times contractors charge a sum of 13 to 15 cents daily to cover cooked rice, cook's wages, lighting of kongsi (kerosine), tea and salt instead of selling these individual items to the labourers.

As a matter of general interest I include Table III, consisting of extracts from a list prepared by the Pahang Consolidated Company, Limited, showing fluctuations in prices of some of the principal articles at Sungei Lembing from 1926 to 1937.

TABLE III.
FOODSTUFFS.

	1926.	1927.	1928.	1929.	1930.	1931.	1932.	1933.	1934.	1935.	1936.	1937.
	$ c.	$ c.	$ c.	$ c.	$ c.	$ c.	$ c.	$ c.	$ c.	$ c.	$ c.	$ c.
Rice – Siam No. 1, per katty	10	11	11	10	10	06	06	05	04½	06	05	05
Sugar – per katty	12	12	11	11	09	09	09	11	10	10	09	09
Tea – Leaf, Chinese (4 tahils), per lb. packet		18	18	19	19	13	13	11	11	09	09	09
Fish – Fresh No. I, per katty	28	28	28	28	26	26	22	22	22	22	25	25
" – Salt No. 1 " "	37	37	37	37	32	32	20	20	20	20	26	26
Pork – Shoulder " "	64	64	64	64	60	52	46	46	36	36	36	40
Eggs – Fowl, each	05½	05½	05½	05½	04½	03½	03½	03½	03½	03½	03½	03½
Duck "	04½	04½	04½	04½	03½	03	03	03	03	03	03	03
PCCL. godown fowl eggs each	05	05	05	05	05	05	05	05	05	03	03	03
Bean oil – per 10 katty tin	4 00	3 80	3 80	3 47	3 80	2 25	2 77	2 14	2 14	2 69	2 69	2 69

Section IV.

MINES. WAGES AND COST OE LIVING.

The following are typical wage rates in force on dredges:

Directly employed staff

Head fitter	$90–1100 monthly
Second fitter	$80 monthly
Fitters	$1.20–$2.15 daily
Apprentice fitters	45 cents–$1 daily
Improvers	$1.20 daily
Boilermakers	$1.50–$2.25 daily
Welders	$1.30–$2.25 daily
Apprentice welders	75 cents–90 cents daily
Blacksmiths	$1.75–2.50 daily
Blacksmiths' strikers	$1.00–$1.25 daily
Turners	$1.30–$2.70 daily
Carpenters	$1.50–$2.20 daily
Winchmen I	$2–$2.40 daily
" II	$1.10–$1.90 daily
Greasers	$1 daily
Engine drivers I	$1.40–$1.50 daily
" II	$1.25 daily
Firemen	$.1.10 daily
Painters	75 cents daily /

Engine drivers I, II, Firemen, Painters } often Indians or Malays {

Electrical. –

Fitters	$1.40–$1.75 daily
Apprentice fitters	60 cents.–80 cents daily
Wiremen	$1.0–$2.70 daily
Overhead linesmen	$1.75 daily
Apprentice linesmen	55 cents–70 cents daily
General labourers	85 cents. $1.10 daily

All the above type make their own arrangements for food. Lodging and lighting is provided by the company.

Dredge staff –

Kepala	$2.70 daily
Assistant *kepala*	$1–$1.28 daily
Jigmen	76 cents daily
Bucket coolies	60 cents daily
Sampan coolies	60 cents daily
General coolies	44 cents–70 cents daily

} plus lodging, light and food.

The above are usually supplied with free food by the *kepala* or contractor. The food usually consists of two meals of rice and one of congee. Pork is supplied infrequently – say, once a week, and fresh fish rarely. If employed direct by the company and not receiving free food the above rates would be about 5 per cent.

higher. Similarly higher rates may be paid by a contractor who, instead of providing free food, supplies food the cost of which is deducted from the labourers' wages. These food charges usually amount to 21 cents to 25 cents daily.

Ore Treatment and Amang-washing Labourers.

An example of wages paid to ore-treatment labourers has already-been given.

Amang-washers are paid by the contractor at Kung-sz-Kung (daily) rates, the contractor providing free food. Rates are from 50 cents to 11 daily for men – with a usual wage of 65 cents and 50 cents daily for women. The Kung is 8 hours with overtime at the rate of 6 hours = 1 Kung.

Open Cast and Hydraulic Mines.

Typical wage rates are as follows:

Kepala (Kung Thau) – may be as high as	$270 monthly
Assistant *kepalas* (Yi Kung)	$150 "
Third *kepalas* (Saam Kung)	$120
Group overseers (Kwun Paan)	$ 38 "
Skilled workmen (Pong Shau) –	
Grade I	42 *cts.*–55 *cts.* daily
„ II	41 *cts.*–50 *cts.* daily
„ III	40 *cts.*–48 *cts.* daily
Miscellaneous workmen (Tsaap Kung) –	
Grade I	40 *cts.* daily
„ II	89 "
„ III	38 "
General labourers (Kung-sz-kung)	33 *cts.*–36 *cts.* daily

Free food, lodging and lighting is supplied by the company. /

Engine Drivers.

Wages $18 to f 50 monthly with free food supplied by the engine contractor. Company provides lodging and lighting. Work in shifts – 6 hours on, 12 hours off.

Winchmen.

Wages $24 to $26 monthly. No food supplied. Work in shifts – 4 hours on, 3 hours off.

Trucking.

Paid by the contractor at a rate per truck. Group averages for September showed wages at 87 cents a Kung plus food, lodging and lighting, with average of about 22 Kungs monthly – fewer in wet weather. Kung of 8 hours worked in shifts – 4 hours on, 8 hours off.

Nai-cheng Labourers.

It is difficult to estimate an average wage. One example has already been given and worked out at $1.50 daily with no food. Rates vary considerably according to the difficulty of the work.

Underground Mines.

(a) – DIRECTLY EMPLOYED LABOUR.

"A" – Sungei Lembing. –

Head fitter	$94 monthly
Fitters	90 cents–$1.80 daily
Apprentices	30 cents-80 cents daily
Loco fitters	$1.05–$2 daily
Apprentices	30 cents–85 cents daily
Welders –	
Head	$50 monthly
Others	$1.40 daily
Apprentices	30 cents–75 cents daily
Tinsmiths	$1.15 daily
Turners	$1.20–$2.10 daily
Apprenties	30 cents–50 cents daily
Blacksmiths	$1.25–$1.90 daily
Strikers	70 cents daily
Motor fitters –	
Head	$60 monthly
Others	30 cents–50 cents daily
Boilermakers –	
Head	$95 monthly
Others	$1–$2 daily
Apprentices	30 cents–$1 daily
Moulders	50 cents–$1.70 daily
Carpenters	$1.25 daily
General labourers	40 cents-$1 daily
Normal wage is –	
Chinese men	70 cents daily
" women	60 "
" youths	40 "
Malay men	60 "
Sikh men	65 " /
Masons	70 cents–$1 daily
Lorry drivers	$1.10 daily
Engine drivers	$40 monthly
" attendants	65 cents–$1.20 daily
Firemen (Malays)	75 cents daily
Furnace coolies (Malays)	60 "
Gardeners (Tamils)	60 "

Sanitation coolies	60 "
Mine. –	
Timbermen (on special work)	$1.30–$1.60 daily
Plotmen (on the hoists)	70 cents–90 cents daily
Tallymen[19]	80 cents daily
Carpenters	$1.10–$2.20 daily
Sample boys	$1–$1.20 daily
Surface coolies –	
Women	60 cents daily
Men	80 "
Battery men[20]	80 cents–$1.20 daily
"B" Raub. –	
Fitters	$1.75–$2.60 daily
Apprentices	65 cents–$1.40 daily
Turners	$2.30–$2.75 daily
Apprentices	$1.60 daily
Electric fitters	$1.65–$2.20 daily
Apprentices	60 cents–$1.50 daily
Moulders	$2.20 daily
Pattern makers	$2.20 "
Boilermakers	$1.90–2.20 daily
Apprentices	$1.20 daily
Blacksmiths	$2.20 daily
Carpenters	$1.65 "
General labourers –	
Chinese male	80 cents daily
" female	45 "
Indian male	65 "
"C" – Batu Arang. –	
Chargemen –	
Turners	
Moulders	} $2.55–$3.50 daily
Fitters	
Carpenters	$1.80-$2.50 "
Fitters –	
Grade I	$1.65–$2.50 '
" II	$1.40–$1.60
" III	$1–$1.35 daily /
Turners –	
Grade I	
" II	
" III	
Moulders –	
Grade I	$1.65–$2.50 daily
" II	$1.40–$1.60 "
" III	$1–$1.35 daily
Blacksmiths –	

Grade I	$1.50–$2 daily
" II	80 cents–$1.40 daily
Pattern makers	$2.30–$2.60 daily
Electricians –	
Grade I	$2–$3 daily
" II	$1–$1.90 daily
Welders –	
Grade I	$1.65–$2.50 daily
" II	85 cents–$1.60 daily
Carpenters	$1–$1.50 daily
Masons	$1–$1.50 daily
Painters	80 cents–$1.20 daily
Brickmakers	$1–$1.25 daily
General labourers –	
Chinese men	72 cents daily
Tamil men	52 "
" women	40 "

(*b*) – CONTRACT LABOUR – MINING.

Sungei Lembing. –

It is extremely difficult to reach any conclusion as to the average wage of drillers, stopers[21] and truckers. The variation of rates and of hours worked is very complicated. $23 t Tallymen o $38 for stoping, filling and trucking and $30 to $50 for drilling would appear to be the usual ranges for a full month's work (30 days), with a probable average of 12 hours' work daily. No women are employed underground. Contractor's labourers provide their own housing and food.

Raub. –

Examination of the contractors' books gave the following averages from sample groups:

	Average days worked.	Average wage per day.
Drillers	21 ¼	$1.66
Mullockers[22]	19 3/5	.98
General: (Timber, etc.)	21	1.40
Truckers	–	.80–$1

All labourers provide their own food and make their own arrangements for housing.

Batu Arang. –

Sample groups taken from the contractors' books showed wages of 75 cents and 76 cents daily for mining labourers. Free housing is provided. Food is supplied by the contractor at a charge of 15 cents daily. /

(c) – DIRECT EMPLOYMENT – MINING

At Sungei Lembing all the mining is carried on through contractors.

Raub. –

The "party system" for three consecutive periods of 28 days gave the following wage results:

Party.	Period I. Average days per man.	Period I. Average wage per day. $ c.	Period II. Average days per man.	Period II. Average wage per day. 1 c.	Period III. Average days per man.	Period III. Average wage per day. $ c.
A. Ore boring and blasting	22 ¼	1 30	20	2 62	21	2 33
B. Handling ore	20	1 08	22	1 03	18 ¼	92
C. Fitting stopes	18	1 23	22	1 63	19	1 60
D. Machine development (boring and blasting)	22	2 10	17	2 70	18	1 77
E. Mullocking (shifting the broken rock)	22	1 38	21	1 22	17	1 28

Batu Arang. –

The average figure for underground miners was $1.65 daily gross. The amounts to be deducted from this for "agreed deduction" (cost of food and tools), varied with different Kung Thaus. Cost of food varied from 20 cents to 23 cents daily. The system will need to be tried for a longer period before a true picture of the earnings can be obtained.

It should be borne in mind that at Sungei Lembing and at Raub no living quarters are provided for the labourers. At Batu Arang free living quarters and lighting are provided for all labourers. It should also be remembered that at Sungei Lembing and at Batu Arang the number of hours worked per day by the miners is not restricted. At Raub it is limited to eight hours.

The following is a typical budget for a mining labourer, prepared at prices ruling in Ipoh at the time of my visit (December). It represents the cost of living of a labourer providing his own food, and allows nothing for remittances or opium. In practice, however, it is far more usual to find that food is supplied to mining labourers either free or at a charge. Notable exceptions to this practice are Sungei Lembing and Raub. Food supplied by a contractor would be on a lower scale – one katty of pork would be nearer to the usual scale and no fresh fish would normally be supplied. /

A Mining Cooly's Average Monthly Budget.

		$	c.
Siamese rice	6 gantangs @ 32 cents	1	82
Pork	2 ½ katties @ 44 cents	1	10
Groundnut oil	2 ½ katties @ 30 cents		75
Fish	1 katty @ 36 cents		36
Salt fish	2 katties @ 12 cents		24
Vegetables	12 katties @ 6 cents		72
Sauce	½ bottle @ 5 cents		05
Ginger	2 tahils		02
Garlic	2 tahils		03
Salt	½ katty @ 4 cents		02
Sugar	1 katty @ 6 cents		06
Salt egg (duck's)	10 eggs @ 3 cents each		30
Bean curd	15 pieces @ 2 pieces for 3 cents		10
Native tobacco	8 packets (2 tahils @ 4 cents)		64
Tobacco paper	10 packets @ 1 cent		10
Matches	15 boxes @ 1 cent		15
Barber			25
Rubber shoes	1 pair @ 60 cents for 6 months		10
Soap	3 pieces @ 5 cents		15
Wooden clogs	10 cents a pair for 2 months		05
Clothing	$1.20 a suit for 6 months		20
"	$1,20 two suits for 6 months		40
Towels, red	30 cents each for 6 months		05
Face towels	12 cents each for 6 months		02
Tooth brush	12 cents each for 6 months		02
Singlets	60 cents each for 3 months		20
Socks	20 cents each for 3 months		07
Tea, cigarettes and travelling expenses		1	30
Mat	80 cents one		
Mosquito net	$2.80 one to last 3 years, i.e., 36 months		
Basin	50 cents one		
Blanket	$1.50		
	$5.60=16 cents a month		16
Sun hat	35 cents each for 4 months		09
		$9	72

I have already referred to the noticeable decrease in the number of opium smokers among the Chinese labour forces on mines. Few can afford to smoke to any extent. An ordinary smoker requires at least two or three tubes daily. Government chandu costs 28 cents a tube. In Perak, at present, purchase of Government chandu other than from the Government shop, e.g., through another licensed purchaser, costs 50 cents a tube. Most of the labourer-smokers appear to have permits to purchase one tube daily and are said to eke out this allowance by swallowing dross.[23] /

GENERAL.

Any attempt to summarise the rates of pay on mines must be liable to serious criticism. Rates vary a good deal even between mines of similar type and size, and the contractor's charges also vary with different individual contractors. Furthermore there is constant fluctuation of rates on some mines according to the price of tin. One mine in Perak has even introduced a sliding scale under which wage rates fluctuate, within limits, with the price of tin. But any such sliding scale must be prepared individually by each mine. As an illustration of the extraordinary way in which wages may fluctuate over a period of years, a leading Chinese miner in Perak informed me that in 1926, when the price of tin was for a considerable period between $90 and $150 a pikul, the wage rate of a trucking coolie was $2.40 daily.

SECTION V.

FACTORY AND SHOP LABOUR AND MISCELLANEOUS EMPLOYMENT.

It is impossible to frame any useful generalisations to cover the methods of employment in factories and shops. Processes are so varied, and methods of employment differ greatly in individual factories. I have therefore merely included in this section summaries of methods and conditions of employment at certain factories, etc., representing some of the more important of such industries. There are, of course, many (mostly minor) industries which are not here included. In particular reference should be made to the timber cutting panglongs, especially those on the East Coast rivers of Pahang. These are difficult of access and have, for some years, been the subject of special reports. As I have had no personal knowledge of these places for the past ten years I have not presumed to make any detailed reference to them.

A feature of some of the newer industries, e.g., match factories, rubber goods factories, cigar factories, is the employment of labour forces consisting mainly of young Chinese women, who seem to be particularly suited to such employment by reason of their nimble manipulation.

It is probably advisable to attempt to standardize certain features of factory employment such as hours of work, overtime periods and rates of pay, dates of payment of wages, space and ventilation of factories, provision of facilities for refreshment, etc. The Labour Code was not designed to deal with these matters and a factories Enactment should be introduced for this purpose. Such an Enactment should be of considerable flexibility, particularly in its definition of "factory", and it is probably advisable that it should only apply to such places of employment as are from time to time notified in the *Gazette* by the British Residents on the advice of the Controller of Labour. Many of the provisions of such an Enactment would probably be automatically observed as they became known to employers and employees, but others, such as the limitation of hours of labour of piece-workers, may eventually require the appointment of an inspecting staff.

The tendency of workers in these industries is undoubtedly towards the establishment of fair conditions through the organisation of workers' associations in individual industries, and the time would therefore seem to be ripe for the legal acknowledgment of this progressive tendency by the introduction of a Factories Enactment. /

FOUNDRIES AND ENGINEERING SHOPS.

The workers in these industries are normally better organised than those in other industries. They have their fitters' or mechanics associations which are, on the whole, well controlled and which too can usually be relied upon to be truly representative of the workers. For some years now these associations have been the bodies with which settlements as to wage rates, conditions of labour, holidays, etc., in these industries have been arranged, and there is little fear of any real grievance of labourers in these industries being allowed to go unannounced.

All workmen, except boiler-makers, are employed direct by the management. Boiler-making is invariably given to contractors employed at the company's premises at piece rates. They engage their own workmen and pay them at daily rates. An eight-hour day is universal with extra payment, usually at the rate of 1 ½ times the normal rate for overtime and double rate for Sundays and holidays. At times, the overtime pay is at double rate, or it may be at the 1 ½ rate up to midnight and at double rate from then to 7 a.m. Food and lodging are not supplied by the management. Workmen working away from the shop, e.g., fitting up machinery on mines, receive an extra allowance of 50 cents or 70 cents daily and food and drink money. Wages may be paid in full twice or thrice monthly, or may even be paid weekly. Notice of dismissal or resignation may be 24 or 48 hours.

The agreed holidays in Selangor are:

Western calendar –

January 1st-3rd – New Year.
March 12th – Death of Dr. Sun.
March 29th – 72 Martyrs Anniversary.[24]
May 1st – Labour Day.
August 15th – Anniversary Day of the Mechanics' Association.
October 10th – China's National Day.
November 12th – Birthday of Dr. Sun.
December 25th – Anniversary of Yunnan Rising.
December 31st – New Year's Eve.

In practice work does not stop on 31st December, but a day's holiday is given at Chinese New Year instead.

The agreed holidays in Perak are:

Western calendar –

March 12th – Dr. Sun's Death.

March 29th – 72 Martyrs.

May 1st – Labour Day.

August 27th – Confucius' Birthday.

October 10th – China's National Day.

Chinese Calendar –

I Moon – 1st, 2nd and 3rd.

Tshing Ming Festival.

V Moon – 5th day. Dragon Boat.

VIII Moon – 15th day. Moon Festival.

Winter Solstice.

XII Moon – Last day.

There are no holidays with pay. /

It is usual for the company to pay the hospital expenses of workmen injured at work. Such workmen are treated in the second-class wards and half wages are paid. In cases of sickness no hospital treatment is paid for unless the disease, e.g., malaria, was contracted while at work for the company, e.g., while working at a mine or on an estate.

The following are typical wage rates:

	Federated Engineering Company.	Chinese Foundries.
Head fitter	$100 per mensem	$90 per mensem
Fitters 1	$2.72-$2.96 daily	$2.68 daily
„ 2	$1.60-$2.08 „	$2.34 „
„ 3	$1.04-$1.44 „	$1.50-$2 daily
Improvers	–	$1.24-$1.50 daily
Apprentices	–	34 *cts.*-65 *cts.* daily
Turners 1	$8.44 daily	$2.82 daily
„ 2	$3.12 „	$2.40 daily
„ 3	$2.48-$2.72 daily	$1.70-$2.80 daily
Pattern makers 1	$3.84 daily	$2.75 daily
„ „ 2	$2.48-$2.88 daily	$1.75 daily
Apprentices	40 cents daily	–
Moulders 1	$2.88 daily	$2.80 daily
„ 2	$1.60-$2.54 daily	$1.80-$2.20 daily
General labourers	80 cents daily	80 cents daily

Wage rates paid at the Central Workshops of the Federated Malay States Railways are shown in G.M.R. Circular No. 6 of 1937, a copy of which is attached to this report as Appendix "I". All the Federated Malay States Railways staff in receipt of daily pay of $1 and under are eligible for free quarters if available, but no allowance is paid if quarters are not available. A large percentage of the staff works on piece rates which enable them to earn bonuses varying from 20 per cent. to 30 per cent. above the basic wage rates.

FACTORIES FOR THE MAKING OF RUBBER ARTICLES.

I inspected three of these factories at Klang. At one factory (Bata) rubber shoes only were made. The others turned out a variety of goods – mats, cycle tyres and tubes, sheeting, etc., in addition to rubber shoes. At all factories the labour force was composed mainly of young Chinese women. Each factory had a different method of employment.

BATA FACTORY.

This is a newly-established factory. The basis of the method employed is an endless movable line of iron lasts[25] which passes from woman to woman, each woman performing her part of the process on each shoe while the line is moving. The rate at which the line moves can be varied with the average proficiency of the workers or to control production. At the time of my visit the output was 1,600 pairs of shoes daily. The manager was of opinion that when the labour force was more experienced the output could easily be raised to 2,200 or 2,400 pairs daily. Throughout the entire processing, the greatest use is made of the most modern specialised machinery. The building is of very recent construction and is well lighted and ventilated. The layout of the machinery follows the sequence of the processes in a well-planned manner. A coffee-shop has been built close to the main building and is / rented to a Chinese keeper. Later, it is proposed to erect a hostel for those of the girls who wish to live there. The factory is 3 ½ miles from Klang and the company runs its own bus service for its employees, charging a daily fare of 7 cents.

Work on the sewing machines, cutting machines and on the assembling line is done in two shifts of 7 hours each, daily. The shifts are (1) 7 a.m.-10.30 a.m.; 11 am-2.30 p.m. and (2) 2.30 p.m.-6.30 p.m.; 7 p.m.-10 p.m. For each shift 35 women are employed. No woman may work more than one shift a day except under exceptional circumstances, e.g., when one asks to be allowed to work an extra half shift in place of her sister who is absent. But this is not encouraged. The staff of 35 per shift allows of three women who can replace absentees and who otherwise are employed at odd jobs.

The mixing and rolling machines and the vulcanizers are tended by men. At present the factory is under-equipped with vulcanizers and three shifts are worked – 7 a.m.-1 p.m.; 1 p.m.-7 p.m.,; and 7 p.m. -12 p.m.

The wages of all the manufacturing staff, except the tenders of mixing and rolling machines, are calculated at piece rates and are paid weekly. There is a minimum wage for competent women of $4 weekly (six days). Wages for the men tending machines range from $8 to $12 weekly with overtime at 20 cents an hour; the normal factory hours for these men are from 7 a.m. to 12 a.m. and from 1.30 p.m. to 5 p.m.

MALAYAN RUBBER WORKS.

Women are employed for the manufacture of rubber shoes and for part of the tyre making process (fitting wire edges and cutting canvas). Some of the mixing machines are also tended by women. All these women, except those tending the mixing machines, are employed at piece rates but the speed of production is not mechanically controlled. There is no assembling line, Goods are taken from one department to another by hand.

The normal factory hours are from 7.30 a.m. to 11.30 a.m. and from 12.30 p.m. to 4.30 p.m. Overtime at the rate of 15 cents an hour is paid for work after 4.30 p.m. These hours do not apply to piece-work labour or to the mixing machines. Piece-work labourers may continue to work as long as there is work to do – which may be ten, twelve or even fifteen hours – receiving pay at ordinary piece rates. The mixing machines are kept going from 7 a.m. to 3 a.m. with, shifts as follows:

7 a.m.-1 p.m.

1 p.m.-7 p.m.

7 p.m.-9 p.m. – tended by foreman only

9 p.m.-3 a.m.

The attendants of these machines work in alternate shifts as follows:

Attendant "A" 7 a.m.-1 p.m.

9 p.m.-3 a.m.

„ "B" 1 p.m.-7 p.m.

7 a.m.-1 p.m.

"A" 1 p.m.-7 p.m., etc.

Each attendant works 12 hours a day which is reckoned as 1 ½ Kungs, no additional overtime rate being payable. /

The following are examples of monthly wages of machine attendants, all of whom, are paid at Kung-sz-Kung (daily) rates:

Tyre vulcanizers	$26 monthly
Rubber sheet machine	$14-$23 monthly
Rolling machine	$18-$24 „
Bleaching and dyeing	$22-$24 „
Miscellaneous	$18-$25 „

A normal wage for a mixing machine attendant is about $26 for 30 Kungs. As these workers usually put in 1 ½ Kungs daily a normal monthly wage for 30 days of twelve hours each would be about $39.

Typical group-average monthly wages of piece-rate workers are as follows:

Canvas upper cutters (women)	$30.00 monthly (max. $35)	
Gumming dept. (women)	35.00 ,,	(„ 60)
Tyre making (women)	18.50 ,,	(„ 30)
,, (men)	34.00 ,,	(„ 37)
Tube testers (women)	32.00	
Pillow makers (women)	35.00	
Tube joiners (two men)	38.00	

There is, however, no means of ascertaining what number of hours have been worked for these wages. The following are the piece-rate prices paid by the company for some of the principal processes:

	$ c.
Sewing tops	80 per 100 pairs
Cutting tops	47 ,, ,,
Fixing eyelets and lacing	39 ,, ,,
Gumming soles	1 26 ,, ,,
Smoothing soles	82 ,, ,,
Roughening tubes for joining	21 ½ per 100
Wiring tyres	30 ,,
[...]	

Wages are paid on or before the 5th of the succeeding month. Advances may be had at any time up to approximately the amount earned.

The factory is close to Klang town and no quarters for the workers are provided. The general impression received is that the piece-rate workers – in particular the women – are working at intensive pressure. The layout is not well arranged, every odd corner seems to be occupied. In this factory I found women tending the mixing machines after 11 p.m. – an infringement of section 65 of the Labour Code.

SHUM YIP LEUNG FACTORY.

The distinctive feature of the method of employment at this factory is that all employees are paid at daily rates. The factory hours are 7.80 a.m.-11.30 a.m. and 12.30 p.m. to 4.30 p.m. for six days a week. Work after these hours or on Sundays is paid for at a 50 per cent. additional rate except in the engine shop where all overtime is reckoned at double rates. All the men employees are provided with free food. The women are supplied with food (two meals daily) at a charge of $3 monthly. /

There are quarters for about 200 of the 275 women employed. The quarters consist of one line divided into rooms each of which accommodates 10 women. There is a line of fire-places at which the occupants may cook any additional food they may require. This is the only factory I have seen where accommodation on anything like this scale is made for women workers. There is no accommodation for the men workers – most of whom are mechanics and machine-tenders. Wages are paid in full on the 5th of the succeeding month. Advances are made on the fifteenth of the month.

Women workers begin as learners at 80 to 35 cents daily, rising to 40 to 86 cents when proficient. Typical rates for male employees are:

Carpenters	76 cents-$1.58 daily
Fitters	$1-$1.68 daily
Apprentices	20 cents-90 cents
Electricians	41 cents-$1.50 daily
Engine drivers	$1.21-$2.11 daily
Greasers	50 cents-$1.65 daily
Blacksmiths	50 cents-$1.68 daily
„ strikers	90 cents daily

MATCH FACTORIES.

There are two match factories in the Federated Malay States – one at Port Swettenham (Elkayes) and one at Telok Anson (Perak Match Factory). The latter was, at the time of my inspection, suffering from the effects of a boycott by Chinese traders. This boycott in addition to reducing the output of the factory to 25 per cent. of its previous production (equivalent to 12 ½ per cent. of possible production) extended to the staff of the factory which now employs about a dozen Chinese girls instead of 100. Tamil girls are being introduced to undertake the work but the factory was so disorganised that a detailed description would be of no use in a survey of typical methods of employment.

Elkayes Match Factory employs a staff of some 160 persons. Of these some 40-50 are Tamils – mostly men, and about 100 are Chinese women. The machines for peeling the logs and making the boxes are tended by women. [...] All these labourers are paid at daily rates.

The filling of boxes and the wrapping of boxes into packets of ten is done by women – usually Chinese, though a few Tamils are employed. This work is calculated at piece-rates.

Some quarters are provided, and about 80 persons – mostly Tamils with their families – live there. The majority of the workers live in attap huts of their own or of their families in the vicinity. The factory is spacious and well ventilated.

Wages are calculated weekly and are paid weekly – one week in arrear. Each worker has a card on which is entered daily the value of the work done. No wages are payable when sick, but free hospital treatment at the Government hospital is provided. Work continues for seven days a week. In 1986 production was reduced and no work was done on Saturdays, Sundays and holidays. Full time work has been resumed in 1987. The factory hours are 7 a.m.-12 a.m.; 12.30 p.m.-4 p.m., i.e., 8 ½ hours daily. No overtime is worked. There is no method of ascertaining how long the piece-workers work, but it is said to be less than the factory hours. The work is not physically heavy, but the work of the machine attendants is monotonous and that of the fillers requires intense concentration at the speed at which it is done. /

The piece-rate for filling boxes is 9 ½ cents per tray of 345 boxes. An expert is said to be able to do 6 or 7 trays daily, but 3, 4 or 5 seem to be the usual figures of actual production. Wrappers are paid at 3 ¾ cents per 100 boxes.

Average daily wages for each of the four weeks preceding my visit were:

Wrappers	52 cents, 53 cents, 53 cents, 47 cents
Fillers	31 cents, 25 cents, 29 cents, 29 cents

The manager explained that the fillers do not necessarily work full days. When the stock is finished they go home.

Average daily wages for daily-paid labourers (machine attendants) were:

51 cents, 50 cents. 50 cents, 50 cents.

The usual wage appeared to be 40-50 cts. daily.

The following are the wage rates of various additional employees:

Stokers (Tamil)	65 cents daily
Engine drivers (Tamil)	$25 monthly
Machine repairer	80 cents daily
Youths packing sticks	30-40 cents daily
Box makers (women)	35-48 cents daily
Peeling machine (women)	45-50 cents daily
Packing case carpenter	$1.15 daily
Packing case nailer (Tamil)	30 cents daily

SAWMILLS.

There are hand sawmills scattered throughout the Federated Malay States. They are particularly numerous in the Kuala Pilah district of Negri Sembilan. Power sawmills also exist – notably a group at Teluk Anson, Perak, one at Triang, Pahang, and one in the Kuala Pilah district of Negri Sembilan.

HAND SAWMILLS.

These are usually owned by a working proprietor who provides attap kongsi accommodation for the labourers. Payment is at piece rates, varying with the size of the timber sawn. Typical rates are:

6 ½ " x ¾ " x 14'	13 cents per piece
1 ¼ " x 2 ¼ " x 14'	6 ½ „ „
1" x 8" x 14'	20 „ „

Average wage groups gave the following figures for wages at two such places in Negri Sembilan in the seventh and eighth months (Chinese):

A. $38.37;	$23.00
B. $20.00;	$25.50

Advances are made during the month and the proprietor invariably keeps a shop for the supply of provisions. Settlement of wages is effected twice yearly in accordance with the traditional custom of sawyers – during the 6th and 12th months (Chinese). I did not find any instances of the charging of interest on advances. In general hours of work are at the labourer's discretion. /

POWER SAWMILLS.

In the Teluk Anson group, sawyers are usually engaged on daily pay and are provided with free food and lodging. Settlement of wages may be twice monthly (a few days in arrear) monthly or twice yearly. An eight-hour clay is worked. Overtime is reckoned at 3 ½ or 4 hours = one Kung. Typical wage rates were:

Sawyers	$1-$1.50 daily
Improvers	45 cents-$1 daily
General labourers	50 cents-75 cents daily
Engine drivers (Tamils or Malays)	$25-$30 monthly
Stokers (Malay)	$18 monthly

There is, at Teluk Anson, a well-organised Timber Workers' Association which keeps a close watch on conditions of employment and rates of pay. The quarters provided are usually poor and insanitary.

At Triang Sawmill, wages are calculated at piece rates. There is one gang to each saw and the planks cut by each gang are credited to that gang. Rates paid are $1.80; $2 and $2.40 per measured ton, according to the size of the planks.

Each gang keeps its own kung phaai and the earnings are divided among the members of the gang proportionately to the number of days worked. A first division is made at the rate of $1.20 a clay ($1.50 for the ganger). The balance is then divided equally daily as a bonus. Typical cases worked out at the following rates:

	Gangers.	Sawyers.
Fifth Moon	$3.38 daily	$2.18 daily
Sixth Moon	$2.90 „	$2.32 „
Seventh Moon	$2.99 „	$2.39 „

Work restricted to eight hours daily.

There is not, however, work for each day. During these three months the number of days work varied from 1.7 to 26 monthly. Settlement is made twice yearly in accordance with the old Chinese sawyers' custom on 13th of the Sixth Moon and on 24th of Twelfth Moon.

Advances are made to the labourers freely and no interest charged. The proprietor employs a cook and provides meals for the labourers, the cost thereof being debited to their accounts. The amount varies from day to day but appears generally to be between 20 and 22 cents or about $6.50 monthly. No goods other than food are supplied. The sawmill is right at the town of Triang. The labourers appear to be a sturdy independent lot. Newcomers are recruited from Singapore and demand advances of $60 to $90. This and the railway fare is recovered from their wages. I investigated several such cases and had no complaint of overcharge. One man indebted on arrival for $65.85 had reduced this indebtedness in three months to $21.88. Another indebted on arrival for $90 had reduced this after three months to $6.13. There is an excellent new set of lines, but unfortunately the proprietor and his family have moved from the town to occupy part of the lines so that some of the labourers remain in an old dilapidated kongsi.

Along Durian Tipus road in the Kuala Pilah district of Negri Sembilan is a European-owned power sawmill. The labourers here are employed through contractors who provide them with food the cost of which is debited against the labourers. This food charge varied with different contractors from 28 cents to 43 cents daily plus a charge of / 3 cents daily for cook's wages. The low charge of 28 cents occurred in a kongsi of Hailams which had no contractor but worked together with a *kepala* appointed by the men themselves. An eight-hour day is worked and average earnings (before deduction of food charges) varied from $1.20 to $1.60 daily. Felling coolies employed by one contractor at Kung-sz-Kung rate received wages of from 85 cents to $1.20 daily. A few Malays were also employed at 55 cents daily. Monthly settlement of wages by some contractors, six-monthly by others.

PINEAPPLE CANNING FACTORIES.

There are two of these factories, both in the Klang district. The industry is seasonal with two peak harvest periods during November-December and March-April. During these periods the factories are open from 6 a.m. to 12 midnight or 1 a.m. and the cutters may work as long as they please. During the slack seasons there may only be enough pines to keep the cutters employed for a few hours a day or the factories may close altogether. At the time of my visit both factories had been reopened for some ten days only after having been closed for two months.

Cutters are engaged at piece rates, the prices paid varying with the style of cutting (rounds, cubes, etc.), and with the size of the tins filled. The scale of rates is the same as that in operation at the Singapore and Johore factories as agreed between the workers and the employers' association. As a full month had not been worked since reopening I was unable to check the earnings of cutters. Cutters themselves employ boys to help in stacking and removing the tins.

Machine attendants, carrying coolies and miscellaneous workers are paid at monthly rates and receive a full month's pay whether or not there is sufficient work to keep them fully occupied. If necessary they may be required to work from 7 a.m. to 6 p.m. with an hour's break for mid-day meal, without additional payment. Overtime is payable after 6 p.m. at the rate of 10 cents per hour. Typical rates of pay are:

Stamping machines	$15.50 to $33.00 monthly
Sealing machines	20.50 „ 36.00 „
Cooking pines	23.50 „ 36.00 „
Carrying coolies	14.50 „ 34.00 „
Nailing coolies	14.50 „ 36.00 „
Unloading coolies	18.00 „ 19.50 „

One month's notice of resignation or dismissal is required. The company pays for hospital treatment of sick labourers.

There are a few piece-work labourers:

(*a*) Rolling and soldering tins. –
¾ lb. to 3 lbs. – flat rate of 12 ¾ cents per 100 tins.
One 8 lb. tin counts as 8 tins.
One 3 ¼ lb. tin counts as 2 tins.
Turnout of about 800 tins daily.
Earnings say $1 daily.

(*b*) Women fixing rubber bands to tin lids. –
Rates vary with size.
14 ½ cents to 22 cents per 100 lbs. of bands.
Earnings about 35 cents for 6 hours' work. /

(*c*) Women labelling tins. –
Casual labour only, 2 ½ cents a case which may be of two, three or four dozen tins.

Quarters are provided for cutters. The machine attendants frequently live in the town as their employment is more permanent than that of the cutters. All labourers make their own arrangements for food.

Cigar and Tobacco Factories.

There are several cigar and tobacco factories in Perak. One of these employs Burmese women, the others, Chinese women. There is a noticeably large proportion of juvenile labour in the Chinese factories of ages ranging from 12 years upwards. No food or lodging is supplied by the managements. All work is at piece rates, ranging from 8 cents to 12 cents per 100 for cigar making. Women employed on sorting and stripping leaves are paid at 1 to 3 cents a katty. Normal hours of work are 8 to 9 hours, but production is frequently reduced and the day may be reduced to 6 hours. At times work may cease entirely for a few days. Payment of wages is made once or twice monthly. Advances are given with no interest charges at some factories, no advances at others. Earnings are 30 cents to 50 cents daily with some as high as 60 cents. In a full month of full-time earnings are about $15.

BRICK KILNS.

There are brick kilns distributed throughout the Federated Malay States usually owned by small Chinese capitalists or building contractors. Workmen are employed at piece rates. Free quarters – usually attap sheds – are provided.

Typical rates are:

Moulders – Bricks	$24 per 10,000
Tiles	15 ,, ,,
Firers	13 ,, ,,

Work is haphazard according to what supply of bricks is required, and there is no limitation of hours worked. Wage rates for moulders may be between $25 and $32 for a full month. Firers may earn considerably more. Cooked rice may be supplied by the management on payment of a charge to cover rice and cook's wages. Wage-books are made up monthly, but credit balances are frequently left with the proprietor. No interest on advances noticed.

WHARF COOLIES AND UNLOADING COOLIES, PORT SWETTENHAM.

The supply of labour for the unloading of steamers at Port Swettenham is, and has for many years been, in the hands of Mr. Van Tooren, J.P. All labourers are employed and paid direct without the intervention of contractors. A most intricate system of calculation of days worked and of wage rates is in force.

There are some 550 wharf coolies of whom 850 are Tamils, 45 Malays and the remainder Chinese. Thirty days' work constitutes a full month. Hours of work are 7 a.m.-11.30 a.m. and 1 p.m. to 5 p.m., i.e., 8 ½ hours daily. /

There are also some 350 Chinese labourers employed for loading and unloading ships lying off in the stream. For these men 20 days' work constitutes a full month.

7 a.m. to 6 p.m. counts as 1 day.

6 p.m. to 10 p.m. counts as ½ day.

In addition men working through from 7 a.m. to 10 p.m. receive a bonus of 75 cents. Work after 10 p.m. is paid for at 25 cents an hour. All these stream coolies receive free food while actually employed on ships. Advances of 50 cents to $1 are made on alternate days to stream coolies at the company's office.

Newcomers from China are introduced by relatives or friends who have been to China on leave. They start at a wage of $18 monthly plus overtime, and receive annual increments of $1 monthly to $23 monthly. There they await promotion to the more skilled posts as deckhands or winchmen with wages of $27 and $30 monthly, respectively, plus overtime.

Wharf coolies are paid at the rates of $26, $30 or $34 monthly plus overtime which may amount to $8 to $15 monthly. Overtime rates are:

11.30 a.m. to 1 p.m.	20 cents an hour
5 p.m. to 6 p.m.	20 „ „
6 p.m. to 10 p.m.	40 „ „
After 10 p.m.	20 „ „

No food is supplied by the company to wharf coolies.

Free quarters, light and medical attention are provided. Sick labourers receive full pay while in hospital unless suffering from venereal disease. After five years' service a free passage to China is given by the company together with a bonus of a month's pay.

BUILDING LABOURERS.

The employment of building labourers – carpenters, painters and masons – is usually quite straightforward, but interminable trouble is caused by the custom of progressive sub-contracting of almost all building work to such an extent that the ultimate sub-contractor employed is quite unable to meet claims for labourers' wages should one of the sub-contractors higher up the scale default or abscond. It has been suggested that the principal contractor should be responsible for all wages in excess of 14 days, but it is doubtful whether any general definition of the term "employer" in the Labour Code could effect this change without inflicting considerable injustice on employers in other industries. It will probably be advisable to introduce a separate Section or Chapter referring to building labourers alone.

Rates of pay are as follows:

Specialist carpenter	$2 a kung
Carpenter} Skilled	
Mason Grade I	$1.40-$1.60 a kung
Painter „ II	$1.00-$1.20
General labourers	60 *cts.* 90 *cts.* a kung /

None of these labourers receive food. Free lodging is usually provided at a kongsi house erected at the site, but some labourers may prefer to provide their own quarters. Apprentices are paid at $4 monthly plus food and lodging. There are now no apprentice agreements. The Kung is eight hours. Artisans may also be employed on piece-work the rates for which are very variable.

There are considerable numbers of women employed in the building trade, mostly in the earthwork connected with the digging of foundations and in the carrying of cement, stone, sand, etc. They may work a 10-hour day for a wage of 55 cents daily plus food and lodging, or, if no food and lodging is supplied the rate may be 75 cents-80 cents daily.

SHOP INDUSTRIES.
SHOEMAKERS.

Usually employed at piece rates. Food and lodging is not usually provided but there are exceptions to this. Typical hours of business at shoemakers' shops are 7 a.m. to 8 p.m. but the hours worked by the shoemakers are very variable. Wages are usually paid weekly and advances are made as required without interest charges. In some districts employers are required to give one week's notice of dismissal while employees may leave without notice. Apprentices may receive $3 monthly plus food and lodging. The employer may provide a special meal on the 2nd and 16th of each month and on festival days.

The following are typical average monthly wage groups from February to September this year:

February	$23.50	May	$25.47	August	$23.60
March	25.20	June	28.24	September	26.30
April	23.40	July	25.20		

TAILORS.

There are two main types of tailors – those making European-style clothes and those making Chinese style. There are also two groups – Cantonese and Hakka. From time to time general agreements as to wage rates are reached through the arbitration of the Chinese Protectorate, but it is quite usual to find that individual employers though publicly supporting such agreements, have made their own terms with their labourers.

Normally, partly-skilled men are on monthly pay of about $13 p.m., while the majority of the workers – skilled men – are on piece rates. It is usual to require one week's notice of resignation or dismissal. Typical hours of work are 8 a.m.-12 a.m. and 1 p.m.-5 p.m. Food is frequently supplied by the proprietor at a charge of about $5 monthly. Special meals are provided on the 2nd and 16th of the month and on festivals. Wages may be paid in full up to date on the 2nd and 16th of the month or credit balances may be left with the proprietor and advances taken without interest. Apprentices may receive $3 monthly plus food and lodging.

Typical monthly wages are:

$29; $35; $35. /

CARPENTERS.

Skilled carpenters are usually employed at daily rates varying from 60 cents to 72 cents daily plus food and lodging. Hours of work in shops are 7 a.m.-11 a.m. and. 1 p.m.-5 p.m. There may be overtime which is paid for at 1 ½ rate. Special meals are provided on the 2nd and 16th of the month and on festivals. Payment of wages in full is frequently made monthly with advances without interest charges. Apprentices may get $20 yearly plus free food and lodging. There are now no written agreements. The employer may be required to give one week's notice of dismissal. This is not usually required of labourers who resign. Workers employed on constructional work outside usually receive higher wages but no food and sometimes no lodging. The extra pay may amount to 20 cents an hour.

Section VI.

THE LABOUR CODE.

I have, throughout this report, made frequent reference to alterations to the Labour Code which seem to me to be desirable. These suggestions are by no means exhaustive but they do, I think, deal with the more important fundamental shortcomings of the present Code. These proposed alterations are:

(1) The introduction of a Factories Enactment.

(2) The placing of the responsibility for the provision of living accommodation, sanitation, water supply, etc., to Chinese estate labourers upon the management of the estate.

(3) The placing of the responsibility for the provision of living accommodation, sanitation, water supply, etc., to Chinese labourers on mines upon the lessee or occupier of the mine with or without exemption in certain cases at the instance of the Controller of Labour.

(4) The code shall apply to all labourers on estates and mines and that neither the employer nor any person in charge of or supervising such labourers may make deductions from wages or may keep a shop for the supply of provisions to labourers other than in accordance with the truck provisions.

(5) The placing of the responsibility for the payment of maternity benefits to Chinese women employed on estates upon the management.

(6) The introduction of a new section referring to building labourers only, and enacting that the principal contractor shall be liable for the wages, in excess of 14 days, due to all labourers employed on the contract.

In addition to these alterations, the following suggestions should be considered:

(7) The deletion of the whole of Chapter IV – "Special provisions relating to Chinese immigrants". It is never used and the present position can be controlled under the Aliens Ordinance. /

(8) The deletion of Chapter XV – "Interpretation and provisions for the observance of mining usage". The only provision worth retaining is the legalization of nai-cheng agreements. This could be done by an amendment to section 53 – which deals with the period of agreements – to make an exception permitting nai-cheng agreements to be entered into for a period not exceeding six months.

(9) The remodelling of sections 53 and 55 dealing with periods of agreement and dates of payment of wages. A difficulty which constantly arises is the determination of the period of notice which must be given to an employee on daily pay who receives his wages monthly. It is most unusual to find in practice that a month's notice of dismissal or resignation is given or is required; a week is more usual and is probably sufficient. Notice to terminate agreement should be 24 hours in the case of labourers employed at daily rates and paid in full daily, and one week in the case of other labourers no matter how their wages are computed.

(10) The amendment of section 63 to reduce the working day from nine hours to eight hours and to reduce the minimum rate of payment for overtime from double to one and a half times the normal rate.

(11) The amendment of sections 71 and 73 to make it clear that the responsibility for the provision of nurseries and schools rests upon the management of an estate and upon the lessee or occupier of a mine.

(12) The amendment of section 74 to ensure that the employer *and any person in charge of or supervising labour* shall be bound to produce books of accounts, etc. This is necessary because of the system now frequently to be met with whereby the *kepala* – not the employer – provides food for the labourers and keeps accounts of charges made to the labourers therefor. It should also be enacted that all books of accounts, etc., must be kept for a period of six months before destruction.

(13) The creation of an "agreement of co-operation".

In addition to these suggestions there are numbers of proposed amendments to be found in departmental files many of which deal with the legal procedure for the hearing of cases and the recovery of wages. All of these deserve careful consideration.

I agree with the suggestion which has already been made, that the first step should be the framing of a Factories Enactment and that thereafter it will more easily be seen how the Labour Code can best be remodelled. A committee should then be appointed to consider the suggestions made in this report and in the departmental files. /

CONCLUSION.

It has been necessary throughout this report to attempt as far as possible to express the results of inspections as generalizations, both as to methods and conditions of employment and as to wage-rates. Although these generalizations are all based on observed facts, it is necessary to insist that so many differences exist that only a detailed knowledge of conditions at individual places of employment can provide the material necessary for a proper understanding of the conditions of labour and of the changes therein which are taking place. It has been my experience during my tour that Protectorate officers are closely in touch with Chinese labour and with the systems of employment in force throughout their States. A partial reservation to this statement must be made in respect of Pahang which, owing to limited staff, has not received as much attention another States. This should be remedied by the appointment of a Protectorate officer to that State in 1938.

I consider that the regular inspection of places of employment by Protectorate officers is of the first importance. The present staff appears to be adequate in Selangor and Negri Sembilan, but if regular inspection of all places of employment in Perak is to be undertaken it seems necessary to provide for the appointment of an additional Assistant Protector of Chinese in that State.

The provisions of the Workmen's Compensation Enactment are now becoming widely known among the labourers, and it is usual to find that employers – European and Chinese – are insured against accidents to labourers. There appears, however, to be some doubt as to the functions of the Protectorate under the Enactment, and it would be well to consider the issue of a circular defining these functions, as has been done in the Colony. If Protectorate officers are to conduct an enquiry into each case of accident reported to the Commissioners for Workmen's Compensation a great amount of extra work will be involved – again particularly in Perak.

I have been informed of the suggestion that a Labour Department should be constituted to deal with all labour matters – Chinese as well as Indian – and throughout my tour I have kept this idea in mind. Attractive though it is in theory I cannot agree that it would be sound in practice. The protection of Chinese labour was the reason for the establishment of the Chinese Protectorate and though various other functions have since been added to it by legislation and by custom, the Protectorate still remains the tribunal for the settlement of Chinese labour disputes and the organisation for investigating Chinese labour conditions. It has an established tradition and has earned the confidence of labourers and of employers – considerations which are not lightly to be cast aside. At present the Secretary for Chinese Affairs has no powers under the Labour Code other than those conferred upon a Protector for the purposes of Part II of the Code (Immigration). Protectors of Chinese are appointed to be Deputy Controllers of Labour and are vested by *Gazette* notification with certain of the Controller's powers. The Controller is in law the Controller of all labour but in matters concerning Chinese labour he consults the Secretary for Chinese Affairs. This would seem to be a very proper arrangement.

It is also to be remembered that the labour work of the Protectorate constitutes one of the main avenues of connection between the Protectorate – and through the Protectorate between Government – and the Chinese community, and to divert that avenue to a separate department / would be to weaken administrative control over the whole field of Chinese affairs, while increasing the personnel of Chinese-trained officers to staff both departments.

It is, however, clear that the closest co-operation and co-ordination must exist between the Chinese Protectorate and the Labour Department, the more so because of the recent and continuing changes in methods of employment and in the organisation of Chinese labour to which reference has been made throughout this report. I suggest that this co-ordination would be considerably strengthened by the appointment of a Chinese Protectorate officer who might be styled the Assistant Secretary for Chinese Affairs (Labour), Federated Malay States (or Malaya), to be stationed in Kuala Lumpur at the office of the Controller of Labour. Such an officer would have no executive powers. He would study the methods of the Labour Department and consider how far they are applicable to the inspection of Chinese labour; he would collect and collate information about Chinese labour from Protectors in each State and consider the incidence of the Labour Code and Factories Enactment on Chinese labour. He would also study the growth of the Trades Union movement among Chinese and developments of Chinese labour generally, and would discuss with the Controller of Labour any matters affecting Chinese labour. On all these points he would report to the Secretary for Chinese Affairs who would have the benefit of this officer's specialised experience and of his close contact with Protectors and with the Controller of Labour before advising on labour matters. Finally this officer would be the Secretary of the newly formed Chinese Labour Advisory Committee.

GOVERNOR TO BRITISH NORTH BORNEO COMPANY, 21 DECEMBER 1923 (1923)

Governor to British North Borneo Company, 21 December 1923. Chinese Immigration Scheme. National Archives, CO 874/904, pp. 153–8.

A letter to the Secretary of the British North Borneo Company from the Governor of the region, Major General Sir William Henry Rycroft. In addition to acting as Governor (1922–5), Rycroft fought in the Indian Frontier Expedition of 1897, the Boer War (1900–1), Somaliland (1903) and the First World War, during which he was mentioned in despatches seven times. After the War, he served in the Black Sea (1918–20) and Ireland (1920–1). In the letter, he comments on a report written by F. J. Hallifax, President of the Municipal Commissioners, Singapore, on the Chinese community of British North Borneo, the findings of which he questions.

Governor to British North Borneo Company, 21 December 1923 (1923), extract

Sir,

Chinese Immigration Scheme.

With reference to my confidential despatch No.588/23 of 12th September, as the effect of Mr. Hallifax's visit and conversations with Officials and Residents and also with the leading Members of the Chinese Community and his visits to some of the settlements can now be visualized, I have the honour to give my views on the Chinese question.

2. Taking Mr. Hallifax's report seriatim: –
<u>Class of Chinese</u>.

I. I do not pretend to understand the Chinaman but quite realize there must be some reason why more Chinese do not settle in our Territory.

Every inducement has been given by Government to the imported Estate Labourer (Chinese or Javanese) to take up land, but the fact remains that the majority of the Chinese relapse into opium sodden gamblers who are content to remain more or less in debt bondage.

Mr. Lease's scheme which, if successful, should, be adopted by other Estates may therefore prove of great value.

The Chinese shop-keeper and small trader doubtless does well. In out-of-the-way places like the Kinabatangan and Labuk the whole trade of the District is in Chinese hands, and everywhere the Native is more or less indebted to the local Towkay. Though objectionable in many ways this forces the native to work.

The wealthier Chinese do not really welcome our endeavours to import settlers and put them on Government land where they will receive titles.

They prefer to bring in settlers, in many cases paying their Fares, and plant them on their own land.

They finance them in the early stages giving them a long lease, on ruinous terms, and keeping them in their debt, make them purchase their needs and often sell the produce of their farms through their Agency.

II. Effect of Gambling and Opium.

As a big step in the abolition of Wah Weh[1] at end of 1924 has been adopted and seeing that the whole question regarding the consumption of Opium throughout the Far East is now under consideration by the League of Nations, I do not propose to make any comments.

III. Settlers Difficulties.

While it is granted that the heavy Jungle in places must terrify anyone accustomed to open country, there are in each Residency certain areas where Settlers can make a start and Residents, who are forming local Settlers' Committees, are in a position to give all information while Government is quite prepared to assist in clearing and fencing areas and if necessary constructing drains and opening communications putting a small covering rate on lands so favoured.

To say that obstacles are put in the way when Chinese wish to purchase lands or start industries any kind is quite untrue.

IV. General feeling of Chinese Community.

A feeling of antagonism to Government by the Chinese is certainly in evidence, especially at Sandakan, where a few have become rich. /

They like so many young communities throughout the World have aspirations towards self Government.

The provision of an Office for Chinese affairs, where they can air and talk over their supposed or genuine grievances will, I am confident, prove of great value.

Regarding their social position, I have reason to believe that they are inclined to consider that, as Chinese, they should be considered as equal to Europeans and that they would not welcome being invited to, say, an "At Home" to which Native Chiefs had also received invitations.

In my opinion the time has not yet come when any of the Chinese Residents in this country can expect to be so treated though I am glad to receive them at Dinner with their Colleagues of the Council and at "At Homes" to which Native Chiefs would also be present.

With regard to complaints against Customs I am glad to hear that Regulations are followed and am satisfied that they have no just grounds for complaint.

That there was and is antagonism towards the Timber Monopoly is undoubted but the fact remains that the Chinese timber output both for local consumption and export has rapidly increased since 1920, and I am most hopeful that the arrangement now put forward by the British Borneo Timber Company by which large areas are definitely thrown open for outside exploitation will show the Chinese that Government wishes them to have their share in the exploitation of the timber resources of the country: though I regret to say they are at present most stubborn in their hostility to the proposals.

With 10 year licences to cut they should be ready to put capital into the venture. /

3. The simplification of the <u>Land Terms</u> approved by your despatch No.733 of 18.10.23 should remove all complaints as to the difficulties of ascertaining terms etc.

4. With regard to the <u>treatment of Chinese by the Police</u> the officer Commanding the Armed Constabulary reports as follows: –

> "This has never been brought to my notice by any of the influential Chinese, all of whom I have known many years both officially and socially, and from my many years of experience of them they have never been backward in coming forward if they want to complain or want assistance. I have heard outside criticism once or twice with regard to the rough and tumbles on the occasions when Police have been called out to stop the faction fights that have occurred. The Police have been successful on each occasion in quelling the fights but have not come out of them unscathed, far from it. There have been a very few individual cases of individual policemen using perhaps more force in the course of their duty than is perhaps necessary, cases of tempers lost or out of control, but in every such case that I can remember the policeman has been punished and probably transferred from the station. I have not received any reports of rough treatment from the Protector in Sandakan, the Resident, or the Chinese Chamber of Commerce, and as far as it is possible for me to be aware, I can emphatically deny that the Chinese receive any different treatment from the Police than any other of the races. It is difficult to have to reply to impressions when no specific charges or cases or reports are made."

5. From personal observation I have been struck by the quiet manner in which the Police maintain order, but am delighted to know that the Indians, the backbone of the Constabulary, heartily despise the Chinaman as a fighting man.

6. The hardship of the <u>Road Ordinance</u>, if it genuinely existed, has now been removed by your decision that it will not be applied to small holdings of 10 acres or under. /

7. With regard to a <u>tax on dogs</u> this is no new Ordinance though it has been amended in some cases in favour of the Chinese small holder who, it is recognised, has need for one or two dogs but certainly not for a pack, unless it is that he breeds dogs to eat as a delicacy!

If so, he should afford to pay for the luxury, while the Town Dweller whether European, Chinese or Native must expect to be charged a moderate tax on dogs whether kept for safety or pleasure.

8. <u>Settlers' Schemes</u>.

Though these may not have come up to the hopes of the promoters they are not in my opinion such derelict institutions as portrayed by Mr. Hallifax, and

I see no reason why the younger generation viz: – Sons and Daughters of the original settlers should not do well in the land of their adoption.

In this connection I am glad to know that Mr. Mershon of the Seventh Day Adventist Mission is making every effort to bring down Southern Chinese under the new Land Terms which he considers most liberal.

9. Charitable Institutions.

The Chinese at Jesselton are opening a hostel and I hope something of the sort will be done at Sandakan though I quite realize that, when the Vagrant Institutes are opened, a better class of Vagrant may be expected so the need for hostels should be less than at present. /

10. Education.

Government, I understand, intends very shortly to open a good Secondary School at Sandakan where at present, apart from local Chinese Schools, Chinese boys and girls can obtain a good education at the various Church Schools to which Government subscribes in form of capitation grants.

11. Generally speaking my views are: –

(a) The establishment of the Office of Chinese Adviser will establish much closer liaison with the Chinese community.

   (I am confident that anyhow at present this can be amalgamated with the Protector's office).

(b) We should establish an Office at Hong Kong – the specially selected Officer to keep touch with the Chinese and be a persona grata with the Governor's staff especially the Secretary for Chinese Affairs.

(c) The lowering of deck passage money from Hong Kong which is now the subject of negotiations is most important.

(d) The establishment of a Printing Office at Sandakan where proclamations, notices, etc., can be struck off in Chinese is necessary.

(e) The abolition of the Office of Chinese Consul-General so soon as the existing Consul's debt is liquidated. Office to remain in abeyance until a United China is again a fait accompli.

I have the honour to be,

Sir,

Your obedient servant,

Governor.

ANON., *PROCEEDINGS AND REPORT OF THE COMMISSION APPOINTED TO INQUIRE INTO THE CAUSE OF THE PRESENT HOUSING DIFFICULTIES IN SINGAPORE, VOLUME I* (1918)

Anon., *Proceedings and Report of the Commission Appointed to Inquire into the Cause of the Present Housing Difficulties in Singapore, Volume 1* (Singapore: Government Publication, 1918), pp. A1–36, A52–55.

The Commission was chaired by W. George Maxwell, variously the Vice-President of Singapore and the British Resident of Perak. It held thirty-four meetings, received twenty-seven written memoranda, took oral evidence from thirty-three witnesses and its members paid a number of visits, both individually and collectively, to the areas discussed. Its findings make depressing reading; the rapid expansion of the city had resulted in extreme overcrowding, poor hygiene and sanitation and high levels of mortality, particularly from tuberculosis and dysentery. The report advances possible reasons for the lack of housing and building land, records previous attempts to rectify these problems and puts forward a number of its own proposals, including the establishment of a city improvement commission to address housing and overcrowding issues, greater public education on hygiene, changes in property taxation and building regulations and the demolition of insanitary buildings and re-housing of the 'poorer classes'. Unfortunately, its recommendations were largely discounted – a Singapore Improvement Trust was only founded in 1927, given the legal authority to build houses in 1932, and, during its existence, built a mere 23,000 housing units.[1]

Notes
1. H. C. Tim, 'The Origins of Social Welfare in Colonial Singapore', *The Asian Graduate Forum on Southeast Asian Studies, Singapore 2012*, pp. 1–17.

Anon., *Proceedings and Report of the Commission Appointed to Inquire into the Cause of the Present Housing Difficulties in Singapore, Volume 1* (1918), extract

CHAPTER I.

PRELIMINARY. – THE DEATH RATE AND THE CONGESTED AREAS.

[...]

General Lay-out of Singapore.

6. Singapore is well laid out so far as the main roads are concerned: the cross streets and side lanes have been made too narrow on subdivision of titles by private owners. For the lay-out of the oldest main roads we have to thank the foresight of Sir STAMFORD RAFFLES. The action taken by him in 1822 to obtain a lay-out that had regard to future development, as well as present needs, is recorded in some detail in Mr. BRADDELL's memorandum "I", and is referred to in Dr. SIMPSON's Report, and in the evidence of several witnesses. And not only is the lay-out good in the "built-on" area, but the main arterial roads extend, fan-wise, from the centre through the suburban area, and out into the country districts. Singapore has therefore much for which to be thankful. The trouble is that no steps were taken until recent years to prevent property from being completely built over. One of the worst parts of the Southern Congested Area was originally alienated as agricultural land. Much of the land in the Northern Congested Area was originally covered by the compounds of the early European residents. As the property changed hands and became subdivided into building lots, no public authority intervened to insist upon intersecting back-lanes or open spaces being reserved in order to prevent the whole area from being – as it now mostly is – entirely covered with buildings. The result is the existing rows upon rows of back-to-back houses, to which the only access is through the front door, and which have been constructed without any regard to light-planes and air-planes.

Present High Standard of New Buildings.

7. In recent years, however, the danger and the difficulty have been clearly realized. When the Teluk Ayer[1] property was sold by the Government in 1902, spaces for back-lanes were reserved. For some time before Dr. SIMPSON's visit, the Municipal Commissioners had insisted upon a high standard of requirements for all plans of new buildings and of reconstructed buildings, with the result that the evil of Insanitary Houses exists only in respect of the old houses which hitherto have not required reconstruction. Anyone who has read. Mr. J. P. ORR's admirable lectures to Bombay audiences upon "Social Reform and Slum Reform" and "Light and Air in Dwellings in Bombay" will realize how much the community owes to the Municipal Commissioners for the action that they have taken to prevent the construction of new Insanitary Houses. Although, as will be seen, we have much to criticize in their action in other respects, in this respect we consider that high praise is due to the Municipality and its officers.

The Two Congested Areas.

8. The "Congested Areas" are two in number. [...] They are occupied solely by the Asiatic community. Rich, middle-class and poor live there. The northern area (often known as the "Malay Quarter") comprises 150 acres; and the southern one (generally known as "Chinatown") comprises 189 acres. As a rule, there are wide roads and two-storeyed houses in the Northern Congested Area, and narrow roads and houses of three and four storeys in the Southern Congested Area. Much of the overcrowding in the Southern Congested Area is due to the house space in this locality-being cramped by the Bukit Pasoh and Kim Cheng estates, which have been tied up by the wills of former proprietors and which still remain undeveloped. [...]

Tendency to Overcrowding.

14. The tendency to overcrowd in houses is due to the insufficiency of accommodation. In consequence of the demand, a man of the poorer classes cannot afford to pay more than a share of the rent of a house. The result is that large houses are subdivided into a number of single-rooms, or cubicles and small houses, which are perhaps only suited for the accommodation of one family, are, houses, subdivided so as to accommodate (i) two families, (ii) a family and lodgers or (iii) a number of bachelors. /

Density of Population.

15. The three "sample censuses" show (as we have said) a density of population of 796, 826 and 1,304 persons to an acre. The evidence of Dr. GLENNIE (Q. 1614–1618) shows that they are fair samples.

16. We do not wish to be understood to state that we consider this density to be, *per se*, necessarily excessive, even in a tropical city. It is remarkable when compared with the density of the poorer parts of London (Mill End 308, Spitalfields 328, Stepney 396); and, even when compared with the density of the congested area of Bombay* (555), it is high. But it is conceivable that these numbers could be housed with every regard for every requirement of sanitation, if the accommodation were, for instance, a many-storeyed edifice like a West End Hotel in London or a Peabody[2] building. But what we assert, and what we think cannot be denied, is that these densities are (to say the least of it) deplorable when they occur – as we know that they occur – in buildings which are not more than two or three storeys high, and which in every way come under any definition of "Insanitary Houses".

17. In respect of Density of Population, we would observe that it is not so much the number of persons to the acre that matters as the manner in which those persons are housed. What matters, most of all, is the number of rooms occupied by each family. At the risk of being wearisome, we would repeat in this connection that it is essential that in future the Census returns should show the number of persons living in cubicles, single-rooms, etc. The vital statistics of the United Kingdom show that the higher degrees of density of population have a marked effect upon mortality.† There appears to be no reason to believe that it would be otherwise in Singapore.

Infant Mortality.

18. It is in respect of the infant death-rate that we have the most striking statistics of the effect of density of population upon mortality. NEWSHOLME gives figures comparing the infantile mortality in the Liverpool district in 1861–1870 with that in 64 selected healthy areas. ‡He shows that whereas the death-rate for all ages was 228 in Liverpool for 100 in the healthy areas, it was in respect of children under five years of age no less than 369 in Liverpool for every 100 in the healthy areas. The ratio of 228 : 100 in respect of the adult death-rate is shocking: but the ratio of 369 : 100 for the children is appalling. In this connection we invite reference to the "Sample" Censuses. In the Pagoda Street block, in a population of 527 males, and 350 females, there were only 48 children between the ages of 1 and 5 years, and only 6 children under one year old. In the Queen Street block, in a population of 918 males and 135 females, there were only 23 children between the ages of 1 and 5 years, and only 7 under one year old. It is true that in the Pagoda Street block doubts have been expressed as to the morality of some of

---

*   See page C 78.
†   Vital Statistics. NEWSHOLME. Third Edition 1892, page 140.
‡   *Ibid.* p. 138.

the women. Conflicting views are recorded in Questions 1215–1216 and 1619-1621. In any event, the figures returned by the Census are sufficiently striking to call for remark.

19. In evidence before the Committee on Physical Deterioration* it was stated that "in no single case has it ever been asserted that ill-nourished or unhealthy babies are more frequent at the time of birth among the poor than among the rich. The poorest and most ill-nourished women bring forth as hale and strong-looking babies as those in the very best conditions. In fact it almost appears that as though the unborn child lights strenuously for its own health at the expense of the mother, and arrives in the world with a full chance of living a normal physical existence. The child's initial gain is thus the mother's loss; and it seems safe to assume that her impaired vitality must suffer from the insanitary surroundings of her life in a cubicle.

20. The extent to which the child suffers from overcrowding during the first year of life is shown in the figures quoted by Dr. MIDDLETON† on the authority of Dr. CHALMERS.‡ /

Males under 1. Deaths per 1,000. in Glasgow.
(The period is not stated.)

	1 apartment.	2 apartment.	3 apartment.	4 apartment.
	–	–	–	–
Diseases of Digestion	25.32	19.72	10.48	12.02
„ Nervous System	14.06	9.76	8.25	11.22
„ Respiratory Organs	39.76	35.51	26.67	20.03
Infectious Disease	23.82	18.83	10.47	5.61

21. In considering these Glasgow returns full allowance must be made for the fact that the four classes indicated in the columns are not only classes of accommodation: they are, to a great extent, classes of the population. The one-apartment class is poorer than the two-apartment class: and lack of food for the children and excess of drink amongst the parents have much to do with the figures. Probably too ignorance and carelessness, both in preventing and curing disease, are important factors which vary with the gradation in the four classes. Nevertheless, when all possible allowance has been made, the figures are sufficiently striking. As might be expected, diseases of the nervous system show the least, and infectious diseases the highest, variation.

---

*   Minutes of Evidence p. 31. Question 556, Quoted by CHALMERS in "The House as a Contributory Factor in the Death-rate," p. 14.
†   Memorandum "R", Page C 79.
‡   CHALMERS. "The House as a Contributory Factor in the Death-rate". Glasgow 1913. /

Loss to Community from Preventable Sickness and Death.

22. The life of every man, woman and child in the community has a value which can be represented in terms of money. Every death is therefore a loss in terms of money. By preventable deaths the Community of Singapore is the poorer every year by the equivalent of a sum, which we dare not even estimate. Quite apart from the loss arising out of those preventable deaths, there is the loss arising out of the antecedent, and preventable, diseases. Not only is there the expenditure on medicine and nursing, but there is the loss in wages. The working man depends solely upon his fitness to work. For such time as the working man ceases to work, he becomes a burden to the community. When he is infectious, he is a danger to it.

Poverty.

23. It has been said that there is no poverty in Singapore. We are of opinion that there is much poverty. Reference is invited to Dr. LIM BOON KENG's evidence on this point (Q. 2382–2383). The poverty is in the thickly populated slums, and is not obtrusive. Sickness, Poverty, Death, are the three last stages of many of the labouring classes. Even the healthy suffer, for they, until their turn too comes, have to support the sick and the dependents of the dead. It has been said that "however much good health may cost", it after all is the cheapest thing that can "be bought." This quotation might be regarded as the text of this part of our Report. We earnestly ask the Government to consider it when any demand is made for expenditure of money, and to strike a balance between the annual monetary loss to the community from preventable sickness, preventable spread of infection and preventable death on the one hand, and the expenditure upon preventive measures on the other hand.

Causes of Tendencies to Overcrowd.

24. The reason for the tendency to crowd into the "Congested Areas" is attributed to several causes. To a certain extent, there is a tendency for trades to collect in specific streets. Thus, the pottery-dealers are in one street, and the coffin-makers nearly fill another street. This is partly due to trade conservatism, of which examples may be seen in Macao Street, where coffin-makers and tombstone-makers still occupy houses in an expensive locality. They do so now presumably because the trade has always been there, and because every individual maker fears that, if he betook himself elsewhere, he would find but little custom. It is obvious that certain parts of the City must be more favourably situated than others as positions in which a livelihood may be made. Men of the shop-keeping class live as a rule with their families and shop-assistants in their shops, for they cannot afford to keep two houses. Men of the artisan and labouring classes live as close as they can to their work, which as a rule is near the river, the harbour or the wharves. The food-hawkers seek the areas where the class of person that pur-

chases their wares is most densely thronged. They are practically compelled to
live in / the area in which they ply their trade. The various places of amusement,
theatres, cinematographs, restaurants, etc., are also attracted there. The pleasure
seekers follow them, and collect there in the evenings. And still more people
are there to earn the money that they spend. It is amongst the poorest class that
the struggle for existence is keenest. This class therefore is impelled towards the
facilities afforded by the Congested Areas. They have to put up with what they
can get in the way of a room, or a share of a room, for the only choice is between
accepting and giving up the struggle. When therefore we were told* that the Asiatic "cares nothing for sanitation, ventilation or even bare comfort," we cannot
but feel that the position rather is that the persons of the classes, which herd in
the Congested Areas, are so situated that they must live there if they are to live
at all, and, that, that being so, they continue to live there and to endure all the
miseries that are entailed thereby.

25. We are of opinion that the only way of relieving the pressure upon these
areas is (i) by a shift elsewhere of the facilities or amenities in which the localities
at present excel other localities and (ii) by improvements in the traffic facilities, whereby people would be able to live further away from their work. If, for
instance, new wharfage or lighterage facilities were afforded in some other part
of the city, it would relieve the pressure on the lightering trade of the Singapore River, because the people, who now live in the Southern Congested area on
account of that trade, would move to the place where the new facilities had been
afforded. And not only would the labourers and artisans move thither, but with
them would go a number of hawkers, shop-keepers, and others. Our recommendations relating to improvements in traffic facilities are contained in paragraphs
168–177 of this Report.

The Filth Conditions in the Interiors of Houses.

26. Dr. SIMPSON's Report dealt so fully upon the condition of the interiors of
the houses in Singapore that we have not considered it necessary to burden this
Report with a repetition of them. What Dr. SIMPSON found in 1907 still exists
in the Congested Areas of Singapore. [...]

The Death-Rate.

27. The evidence which we have taken upon the death-rate, although, by reason of
imperfect registration, not as complete as we could have wished, shows, nevertheless, that the state of affairs in Singapore is one that should no longer be tolerated.

The figures, which we have cited above to exemplify the inadequacy of the
Census, may be quoted again: –

---

*   Memorandum *B*, page C 3. *See* also Q. 151–157. /

Census 1901	206,286
Deaths in decennial period 1901–1911	101,380
Births ,, ,,	47,196

These figures call for action by the Government.

Since the Census of 1911, the figures, upon which the death-rate has been calculated, have been but little more than a surmise; and percentages must be accepted upon that understanding. The death-rate per 1,000, and the actual number of deaths from the principal diseases in each year from 1901 to 1917 are given in Return X to Dr. MIDDLETON's memorandum "R". The death-rate for 1917 was 35.75 per 1,000, which is lower than that of any year from 1901 to 1911. It is higher than that of the years from 1912 to 1916. The total number of deaths in 1917 was 10,900, which is very nearly what it was in 1902, 1907 and 1910. It is considerably less than the returns for 1911, and higher than the returns for the past four years.

Tuberculosis.

28. We invite careful perusal of the evidence on the subject of tuberculosis, especially in connection with the "cubicle" question, and a study of the four photographs with which this Report is provided. These photographs are reproduced from the plates published with Dr. SIMPSON's report in 1907, and we have it on record in Dr. MIDDLETON's evidence (Question 3779) that they represent conditions to be seen to-day in Singapore. /

29. "Tuberculosis is the disease of darkness." Dr. PAUL JUILLERAT, the head of the Health Department of the Paris Municipality, is the authority for the statement. An instance taken from Paris has a direct bearing upon the conditions in Singapore. In Paris, for some years past, the Municipal Health Department has given special attention to the ravages of tuberculosis in six groups of insanitary houses comprising about 60,000 people. The death-rate from tuberculosis alone between 1905 and. 1912 was nearly equal to the total death-rate of London from all causes. Despite all efforts to ameliorate the conditions in the houses, the disease persists. Owing to the narrowness of the streets in front, and the insufficiency, or absence, of open spaces at the back, the houses are irremediably bad; and nothing short of the complete clearance of the areas will provide a remedy.*

30. The case quoted is of course an extreme one, and is not cited with the object of suggesting wholesale demolition. We are of opinion that our evidence shows that there is an imperative need for special attention to be paid to Tuberculosis. We recommend that an expert be brought out at once to study the question. He should be attached to the Municipal Health Department, and, for administra-

---

*   The Case for Town Planning. ALDRIDGE (No date) page 129.

tive purposes, be under the general control and supervision of the Municipal Health Officer. If on his arrival, he finds that he requires an assistant, or assistants, they should be brought out at once. As soon as he arrives, tuberculosis should be declared to be an "Infectious Disease" under Section 2 of the Quarantine and Prevention of Disease Ordinance, 1915. It would then become a notifiable disease under Section 3 of the Ordinance.

31. When the expert has studied the local aspects of the question he will be in a position to submit his recommendations regarding the action to be taken both to prevent and cure the disease. In our opinion, statistical and other necessary local information regarding tuberculosis, as it presents itself in Singapore, has not yet been obtained to a sufficient extent to warrant us in making any further recommendation on the subject. Consideration of such questions as Tuberculosis Hospitals, Sanatoria, Tuberculin Dispensaries, etc., should in our opinion, be deferred until after the expert has submitted his report.

Dysentery.

32. The general consensus of opinion is that it is not necessary to make dysentery a notifiable disease. As the sewerage system extends, replacing the open bucket system, a diminution in the death-rate from dysentery, which is a flyborne disease, may confidently be expected at present, when a kitchen may often be described as part of the latrine, or a latrine as part of the kitchen, the number of cases of dysentery is inevitably high.

[...]

Popular Education in Hygiene.

34. We strongly urge that the Municipal Commissioners give their most careful attention to the desirability – the necessity even – of educating the people in the elementary principles of hygiene. The Hon'ble Dr. LIM BOON KENG* drew our attention to the excellent results of some 10,000 leaflets prepared by Dr. GLENNIE, translated into Chinese by the Chinese Chamber of Commerce, and issued by it, at its own expense, in connection with the recent outbreak of plague. He informed us that the Chinese community read the leaflet with interest, mastered its contents with the result that they probably knew more about plague than the average European in Singapore knows, and were anxious to be inoculated with the vaccine. We understand that the attitude of the coolie-class towards the activities of the Health Department in this outbreak of plague has been far better than it has been in any former epidemic of any kind; and it is not too much to ascribe that fact to the public spirited action of the Chinese Chamber of Commerce. We believe that much can be done by educational methods if used

---

*   Q.2389. /

with intelligence, tact and discretion. As an example of how a thing should not be done, we would / mention the Federated Malay States Government poster of the Magnified Mosquito and the Malarious Mansion. But even that poster, though it excited ridicule, aroused curiosity. We are convinced that the Asiatic community is not only capable of being educated in municipal and domestic hygiene, but is eager to be educated. As soon as the community understands the position, public opinion will urge the introduction of measures which now, because it does not understand, it either opposes or resents. The question of education in these matters is of considerable importance by reason of the fact that thousands of well-to-do and intelligent Asiatics are now living in Singapore in disease-infected houses amidst abominably filthy surroundings. They know full well how much their houses lack sanitary necessities, light and ventilation But they regard these defects as inevitable. If they could be taught what the remedies were, they would not be slow to apply them. Educational methods would be of the greatest value not only in regard to information on tuberculosis, and the care of infants, but also in regard to subjects such as the following, which bear directly upon the health of the community: –

(i) the general carelessness amongst all classes of the community, European and Asiatic, in the proper disposal of house refuse and nightsoil;[3]

(ii) the particular apathy of the members of the European community, who suffer miseries from the mosquitoes that breed in their compounds;

(iii) the concealment of infectious diseases;

(iv) evasion of vaccination and re-vaccination;

(v) use of polluted, wells;

(vi) preparation and storage of food (especially by hawker-house-keepers) under insanitary conditions;

(vii) storage of water in vessels liable to contamination;

(viii) spitting;

(ix) beri-beri.[4]

[Beri-beri is the result of malnutrition, and its connection with "over-milled." or "polished" rice has been established. What is wanted is an arrangement with the rice-millers for a supply of "undermilled" rice, and propaganda and advertisements to induce the Chinese community to eat it instead of the rice that they now buy. The advertising campaign that put "Standard" bread before the British public is an example of what can be done in this way.]

35. This education should in our opinion be entrusted to a Committee. It is not a matter for the officials of the Government or the Municipality. A single Committee for the Colony and the Malay States would be ideal, if there were not the great practical difficulties arising out of the distance between the various Settlements and States. We fear that such a committee could meet but

seldom, and would tend to become a lifeless formal simulacrum[5] instead of a living force. For this reason, we recommend the institution of a Committee on Sanitary Education for Singapore. It might consist of three medical men and one medical lady nominated by the Governor, and three persons nominated by the Chinese Chamber of Commerce, the Chinese Advisory Board and the Muhammadan Advisory Board respectively. The Chairman should be appointed by the Governor from these seven persons, and for preference should not be either a Government or a Municipal Officer. There should be a Secretary, who might be either a Government or a Municipal Officer, and who should be paid a monthly allowance of say $100 per mensem, for his services. The cost of printing, publishing etc., should be borne equally by the Government and the Municipality; and there Should be provision for this service in the Annual Estimates of both. [...]

Action taken by Sir John Anderson to face the Problem of the Congested Areas.

37. The difficulties connected with the Congested Areas, the Insanitary Houses, and the overcrowding evil received the earnest attention of the late Sir JOHN ANDERSON[6] when he assumed duty as Governor of this Colony. [...] The Legislative Council was then determined to deal thoroughly with the insanitary condition of Singapore, and its resultant disease and death-rate. His Excellency Sir JOHN ANDERSON applauded when Mr. JOHN ANDERSON said that the cost of the remedial measures must be a secondary consideration. The first statutory provision for (i) the construction of back-lanes, and (ii) the reconstruction of unhealthy areas, was made in the Municipal Amending Ordinance of 1907. (Cf. Sections 155 and 153, which correspond to Sections 135 and 136 of the present Ordinance, and Part VIIIA which corresponds to the present Part XIV). The financing of the work was faced by providing the Municipality with an Improvement Rate, by giving the Municipality further and larger borrowing powers, and by dividing the financial burden of the cost of the improvement schemes between the Government and the Municipality. The Government* undertook to bear the cost of improving unhealthy areas where all, or the majority of, the buildings were on ground, held under 99-years' leases. In respect of other areas, the cost was to be defrayed from the Improvement Rate.

38. But these brave words and high aims have failed. The Government has not expended a dollar of Government money in improving a single house on the Crown Lands held under 99-years' leases. On the contrary, it deliberately refused to act upon the first scheme put forward by the Municipality for the

---

*   *See* paragraph 2 of the Objects and Reasons of the Bill (re-printed in paragraph 18 of Appendix I), and the Attorney-General's speech on the first reading (paragraph 21 of Appendix I). *See* also Section 270 K of the Municipal Ordinance of 1907, and Section 313 of the Municipal Ordinance of 1913. /

improvement of such a block. This was the Macao Street-Hokien Street block. The "representation" made by the Municipal Health Officer in May, 1908, under the Part of the Ordinance which deals with the "Reconstruction of Unhealthy Areas and Buildings" is reprinted in Memorandum "N" of this Report. The rebuff administered by the Government to the Municipal Commissioners, when they supported the representation, is described in Memorandum "T". We understand (Q. 842) that the reason for the rejection of the representation was that the Government was deterred by the cost of the undertaking. What is beyond our comprehension is that the cost was that under the Acquisition of Land for Public Purposes Ordinance, 1890, and not under Section 270k of the "Municipal Amendment Ordinance", which had been introduced, only in the previous year, to deal with this particular class of case. In respect of the Macao Street-Hokien Street block, the consequence is that (with the exception of a few houses which have been voluntarily reconstructed by the owners) matters remain exactly where they were when Dr. Middleton made his representation in 1908 – otherwise than that the density of population has risen by 30 per cent and the rentals by 40 per cent. [...]. The result of the attitude taken by the Government in regard to this block has been (Q. 831) that the Municipality has deliberately avoided putting forward any other scheme affecting 99-years' lease-hold blocks, and that the Government has escaped all payment in respect of them. /

39. From the period from 1907 to 1913, very little was done to make back-lanes in the Congested Areas. This may be seen from the returns in Memorandum "Y". The reason was that the cost of compensation both under the "back-lane" Sections and under the "Reconstruction" Part was not only extremely high in itself by reason of the value of the properties affected, but was made prohibitive by the extravagant demands of the proprietors under the Sections of the Ordinance dealing with compensation. The Government decided to amend this in 1913; and the Ordinance of 1913 altered the basis of compensation. But it only altered it by introducing Section 137 dealing with back-lanes; and it left the basis of compensation untouched in the "Reconstruction" Part. The result has been that the cheaper acquisition was under Section 137; and, ever since the Ordinance of 1913 was passed, the Government has insisted upon action being taken by the Municipal Commissioners under Section 137, and not under the "Reconstruction" Part. Consequently in the case of the unhealthy areas where all, or the majority of the buildings were leasehold from the Crown, the cost is removed from the Government and thrown upon the rate-payers. This was not the policy voiced in 1907 in Legislative Council when the Bill of that year was passed.

40. Acting on the advice of the unofficial members (*see* §§ 32-35 of Appendix I) the Government refused the only application, of which we have record, for a loan; and did so for fear of creating a precedent.

The Unsatisfactory Form of the Municipal Bill of 1907.

41. The Hon'ble Mr. W. R. COLLYER, as Attorney-General in 1905, prepared a Bill, which was an adaptation from the Housing of the Working Classes Act; 1890 (53 and 54, Vict. C. 70). It was entitled a Bill "to provide for the Abolition of Unhealthy Dwellings and for the Sanitary ' 'Condition of the Town.'" Though in the light of present experience, we do not think the Bill suitable, as it stood, it was, in our opinion, much superior to the legislation actually enacted. When Sir WALTER NAPIER in 1907 drafted a Bill to give effect to Dr. SIMP-SON's recommendations he also adapted the Housing of the Working Classes Act, 1890; but, unlike Mr. COLLYER, made his Bill one to amend the Municipal Ordinance; and furthermore, instead of keeping entirely separate the provisions relating to Unhealthy Areas (Part I of Mr. COLLYER's Bill) from those relating to Unhealthy Dwelling Houses (Part II of Mr. COLLYER's Bill) he brought in a new Part VIIIA for the former, and wove the latter into the old Municipal Ordinance, an arrangement which is followed in the present Municipal Ordinance. By inserting these and other special provisions as a patchwork in an ancient and quite unsuitable piece of legislation like the Municipal Ordinance, Sir WALTER concealed the special nature of the remedy. We mention this in order to bring out the point that what was, in the first instance required and what has now become imperative was, and is, the appointment of a City Improvement Commission with powers to be conferred by a "Singapore City Improvement Ordinance."

The Need for a Singapore City Improvement Commission.

42. In Chapter IX of this Report we elaborate our recommendations regarding a City Improvement Commission. At this stage of our Report we need only say that in our opinion what is wanted in Singapore is what Bombay, Calcutta and Colombo already have – namely, a permanent body of Commissioners wholly distinct from the Municipal Commissioners. The relative position of the two bodies to one another may perhaps be explained by a simile. The engineering department of a railway administration has a "Construction" branch and an "Open Line" branch. "Construction goes ahead, surveys the line, makes the permanent way, puts up all the buildings and one day informs "Open Line" that a section of railway is ready to be handed over to it "Open Line" inspects the section, and takes it over; and from that day "Construction's" task in respect of it is finished. In Singapore, the Improvement Commissioners would perform the task of "Construction", and "the Municipal Commissioners" would represent "Open Line". The Improvement Commissioners would for instance undertake all improvement schemes (of which back-lane schemes are only a particular form), and would hand over the work, when done, to the Municipal Commissioners. / They would acquire land for an open space or park, and then, when the open space or park had been made, hand it over to the Municipal Commis-

sioners to maintain. But the Improvement Commissioners would not hand over everything to the Municipal Commissioners. If they acquired land for estate-development purposes, they might sell that land to intending builders.

43. In one very important respect we would make the Improvement Commissioners a Court of Arbitrament[7] – namely in respect of "Closing Orders." As we show in paragraph 149, the procedure that is still followed in this Colony was abandoned in Great Britain as futile in 1909. If the Imperial Act of 1909 were followed in that respect, it would be the Municipal Commissioners who would make the Closing Orders. But we think that the Municipal Commissioners, and the general public, would prefer that the decision in such cases should rest with the Improvement Commissioners.

CHAPTER II.

THE CAUSES OF THE PRESENT INSUFFICIENCY OF HOUSES.

A very serious Insufficiency of Houses.

44. In the preceding paragraphs we have considered certain prophylactic[8] measures (and also matters arising out of them) in connection with the problem of "Insanitary Houses" and "Congested Areas". We have indicated that the remedial measures come largely under the heading of a City Improvement Commission. But as that commission contains (we hope) the remedies also for the third difficulty, namely, the insufficiency of houses, it will be convenient to consider that difficulty now.

45. We have no hesitation whatever in finding that there is a very serious insufficiency of housing accommodation for all classes of the community. We have referred in our paragraph 9 to the difficulty of having had no census. Dr. MIDDLETON's memorandum (p. C. 76) contains, however, interesting and valuable information. Taking the three census years 1891, 1901 and 1911, we find that in the first decennial period the population increased by 24 per cent but the houses by 15 per cent only, and that in the second period the increases were 34.4 per cent and 27.8 per cent respectively. The following return is, as Dr. MIDDLETON remarks, significant: –

Year	Population.	Occupied Houses.	Vacant Houses.	Persons per Houses.
–	–	–	–	–
1891	155,683	17,732	1,719	8.7
1901	193,089	21,132	1,245	9.1
1911	259,610	26,196	2,406	9.9
1915	289,375	25,806	1,073	12.5
1916	296,951	25,997	860	11.4
1917	304,815	26,811	581	11.3

46. The estimated increase in the population [by excess of immigration over emigration, despite excess of deaths over births, it must be remembered] is about 8,000 a year. If we take Mr. TOMLINSON's figures [Q. 1595–1598] of an average of eight persons to a house, and an average cost of $4,000 a house (including the land) this means that four million dollars a year represents the cost of housing the *additional* population of the year in 1,000 new houses. The actual record of the building operations in 1917 is in striking contrast to this. Memorandum "X" shows that in 1917 only 114 shop-houses and only 27 dwelling-houses were built. Against this, 28 houses were demolished. The position therefore is rapidly getting worse. /

[...]

Timber imported from Netherlands Indies.

57. The trade in the kapor, poonah and seriah wood which is imported from the Netherlands Indies is in the hands of Chinese saw-mills. A body named "United Sawmills, Limited," was registered in July, 1913, and took over four of the mills. In nine months of 1916, it made a profit of $77,993. When we took evidence in April, 1918 it had not – despite the law on the subject – filed any subsequent balance sheet with the Registrar of Companies. For this state of affairs the only explanation given to us was that the Secretary had not time to do the work (Q. 3106). It was denied by the late managing director (Q. 2168) and by the present manager (Q. 3112) that there was any ring. But the latter admitted that, though the prices at the various mills were not the same, there was very little difference in them. If "profiteering" may be defined as taking advantage of an abnormal state of affairs in order to make an abnormal profit, we consider that there has undoubtedly been profiteering in the timber trade in Singapore. In respect of the trade in timber from the Netherlands Indies, we fear that little or nothing can be done in the way of Government control in this Colony.

Seasoning and Preservation of Timber.

58. In Mr. BALL's Memorandum "O", on p. C. 66, will be found mention of the lack of a proper seasoning plant for timber. It is well known that certain preparations will preserve even soft wood timber. If the Public Works Department were to install suitable plant for seasoning and preserving all timber used in the construction of public buildings, (including those erected by the Municipality and Harbour Board) we have no doubt but that the example will be followed by others to the great advantage of the building industry. The matter is of considerable importance in connection with the construction of the temporary buildings which we advocate in paragraph 125 of this Report.

Cement and Iron-work.

59. Cement is unfortunately an imported article, and its rise in price from about $4 a barrel to about $9 is to a great extent due to the cost of freight. Undoubtedly when stocks are low – as they are from time to time – there is profiteering. Haiphong[9] and Hongkong are the principal sources of supply. We are given to understand that the erection of cement works in Singapore is under the consideration of a local Chinese gentleman. In reply to a letter, the Director of Public Works informed us that the Federated Malay States Government was considering the advisability of purchasing the Batu Caves Cement Works, but that this would not assist the private consumers in Singapore, as the output of cement from the works was too small even to meet the needs of the Federated Malay States Government. We would strongly urge that the Governments both of the Colony and the Federated Malay States give every facility to private enterprise in the manufacture of cement, and that, if private enterprise fails, the Government take the matter up with the object of supplying cheap cement not only for the Government works but for private building.

60. The price of all iron-work has increased enormously as the result of the war. For this there appears to be no local remedy at present.

Artisans.

61. Artisans are scarce owing to the recruiting amongst that class by the Military authorities. Wages of skilled labour have risen from $1 a day to $1.30 a day (Q. 521). The Chinese artisan in Singapore is an inferior workman at any time. Apropos of the need of standardisation of doors, window-frames, etc., Mr. BALL (Q. 887) referred to a case where a Chinese carpenter and a Tamil labourer had / gone to execute repairs to a house and had not only wasted a quantity of timber, but had taken six weeks to execute a job that an English carpenter would have done in a day. This of course adds enormously to the cost of building.

Cost of Building.

62. Taking it all round, the Hon'ble the Colonial Engineer estimates that the cost of building a house for European residential occupation has risen from 20 cents a cubic foot before the war to a price of 35 cents at present. This is an increase of 75 per cent (Q. 525).

THE LACK OF LAND SUITABLE FOR BUILDING PURPOSES.

63. [...] It will therein be seen how little land still remains Crown property. We have referred to the radiation of roads fan-wise from the City into the suburbs and the country district. For convenience of illustration this fan may be divided into three sectors of which the dividing lines are the Singapore River and the Bukit Timah Canal.

At the apex of the Northern sector lies the Northern Congested Area (the "Malay Quarter") and towards its base is a wide expanse of low-lying swamp round the Kalang and Rochore Rivers. Further out are the abandoned brick-fields and sand-pits of Kalang, Seranggoon Road and Balestier Plain. A good deal of the high ground out in the country has been appropriated for Chinese burial grounds.

64. The middle sector, lying between Stamford Canal and the Singapore River, has the Government Offices and Fort Canning at its apex, and the Tanglin district at its base. This area is, for the most part, fairly high undulating land. It is the favourite residential quarter, and it is to a very great extent covered by the compounds of European houses. The disused Tiu-Chiu burial ground, containing 70 acres, extends along Orchard Road from Grange Road to Paterson Road.

65. At the apex of the Southern sector lies "Chinatown" (the Southern Congested Area); and when the ground over which Chinatown would naturally expand is examined, it is found to consist of: –
    (i) land recently reclaimed by the Harbour Board from mangrove swamp;
    (ii) extensive areas of mangrove swamp and low-lying land in the valleys of the branches of the Singapore River:
    (iii) ranges of low hills extending between these valleys, and almost entirely occupied by Chinese burial grounds, both public and private.
It will thus be seen that the bases of the Northern and the Southern sectors, to a very large extent, consist either of swamp or of Chinese burial grounds.

The Chinese Burial Grounds.

66. The number and extent of the Chinese burial grounds of Singapore struck Dr. SIMPSON, as they strike every visitor to Singapore, and are commented upon in paragraph 10 of his Report. He wrote: – "the fact of the dead occupying the high" ground, while the living are dwelling on the adjacent low swampy ground strikes "one as being very remarkable."

67. In a matter of life and death, as this housing question is shown in the opening paragraphs of this Report to be, the claims of the living must prevail over those of the dead. We are confident that the good sense of the Chinese community, guided by the Chinese Advisory Committee, on the one side, and by the Improvement Commissioners, on the other, will realize the urgent necessity of putting an end to an intolerable state of affairs. There is power under the "Acquisition of Land for Public Purposes Ordinance 1890" to acquire these burial grounds. Reference to pages B. 105 and B. 223 of the Legislative Council proceedings of 1907 will show what was done when, in connection with the Teluk Ayer Reclamation Scheme, it was necessary to remove a part of Mount

Wallich, on which there was a Chinese burial ground. It will be seen that the Colonial Secretary expressed the thanks of the Government to the Chinese community for the assistance rendered, by them in the matter. We think that the Government need not anticipate objection to any operation in connection with a Housing Scheme. /

68. [...]. From the mouth of the Singapore River, the sea-front, trending southward, extends first along the reclamation in front of the Singapore Club, thence along Teluk Ayer Reclamation, thence the causeway connecting Teluk Ayer with Tanjong Pagar, and thence the East Reclamation up to the Tanjong Pagar wharves. Thence turning westward, the wharves extend as far as the " King's Dock" at Keppel Harbour. The value of this long mileage of sea front can hardly be estimated. Behind it – pressed up close to it – is the southern part of Singapore City. And behind that (north of the Mount Faber ridge) in the area which would naturally supply the wharves and the city, and which one would expect therefore to be covered by a network of roads, we find nothing but a space that is barren and waste, because almost all that is not swamp is given over to the dead.

69. We feel confident that in Bombay the whole of this area would be acquired compulsorily by the Improvement Trust. Compared with the development work carried out by the Trust in the northern part of Bombay Island (see paragraph 196) it is not a large scheme. We strongly urge the preparation of a scheme to deal with this area. Apart altogether from the lamentable waste of valuable land, the Government must consider that upon it lies the responsibility for the annual deaths from malaria. Dr. MIDDLETON'S evidence (Q. 4418) shows that this is the most malarious part of Singapore.

70. This area might conveniently be dealt with in a number of small separate schemes. But each scheme should fit in, and be part of a great comprehensive scheme, thought out on broad lines and carried out with regard to the requirements of the future.

71. Another very big scheme is that of the reclamation of the swamps in the basins of the Kalang and Rochore rivers, and the connection between Beach Road and Tanjong Rhu. This is referred to in the evidence of Messrs, W. DUNMAN and S. TOMLINSON whose maps,* are submitted with this report. The Tanjong Rhu scheme has also been the subject of a report by the Consulting Engineers.

72. We strongly recommend that, without waiting for the constitution of an. Improvement Commission – which will inevitably take some little time – the Government at once detail a capable and experienced engineer (with a staff of

---

* Not printed. /

assistant engineers) to investigate the Teluk Blanga and the Kalang schemes. They are obviously schemes of the very greatest importance to the future of Singapore, and much preliminary investigation has to be done before any decision can be made.

73. There is one little scheme which requires no such preliminary investigation. It is in respect of the mangrove swamp owned by the Crown between Havelock Road and Mount Zion. There is a hill close by, and as soon as arrangements have been made for its acquisition, and the removal of the graves, the earth from it should be used to fill in this very unpleasant swamp, and to make it available for building purposes. We urge that immediate action be taken upon this scheme.

Assessment of Land and Building Property.

Present Rate of Assessment.

74. House property and building land pay an assessment of 18 per cent upon the annual rental if situated within. Water Limits and 15 per cent if situated outside. If any land is suitable for building, but is not the site of, nor occupied as appurtenant to, any building, and if also it is situated (A) within the Water Limits or (B) within such area as is from time to time defined for the purpose by the Municipal Commissioners with the sanction of the Governor in Council, then that land is liable to an assessment upon its Capital Value. This is effected by the definition of Annual Value in section 3 of the Municipal Ordinance.

75. An area has been defined for the purpose of this section. (Q. 1836–1838). A plan of it was shown to us by Mr. CARPMAEL. The area practically extends only to the "Built-over" part of the City, and is almost entirely within the Water Limits. Inside these two areas (*A*) and (*B*) the assessment is 18 per cent and 15 per cent respectively upon 2 ½ per cent of the Capital value. In other words, it is 45 cents or 37 ½ cents per annum for every $100 of Capital value. Outside the areas (*A*) and (*B*), there is complete freedom from assessment. /

Instances of Undeveloped Property.

76. There should be some limit to the area of land that may be regarded as appurtenant to any house. Mr. CARPMAEL, Municipal Assessor, (page B. 128) gave interesting evidence on this point. The "Broadfields" property extends over 38 ½ acres in Tanglin, and contains three houses only. Its value may be put at 8200,000. The total annual assessment is only $780. The "Ardmore" and 'Draycott" property extends over about 78 acres in Tanglin, and contains only wo houses. Its value may be put at 8350,000. it pays an annual assessment of $639. The "Tyersall" property comprises 108 acres in Tanglin, and contains hree houses (one abandoned) and a hut. It may be valued at $220,000, and pays an annual assessment of $497. These three properties extend over an area of 224 acres and contain 7 dwelling-houses. This should not be.

77. We have it in evidence from Mr. Tomlinson (Q. 1529) that the person who builds a residential house should not pay more than $2,000 an acre for his land. And we have it that much of the vacant land in Tanglin is being held up for more than double that price, and there is an instance (Q. 1543) where three and four times that price is demanded. Hence, in the choicest parts of Tanglin, amidst all the facilities of lighting, water, etc., there are wide areas of vacant land, held up by persons who have no intention of building, and, because of these vacant spaces, houses are being put in places which are as yet unprovided with lighting, water and other Municipal amenities. We are of opinion that this is entirely wrong. It is a direct encouragement to speculators to hold up land for a rise.

Difference of opinion. One recommendation: A Capital Land Value Tax.

78. As to the remedy, we are not agreed. The first, fourth and sixth signatories to this Report submit the recommendations herein contained down to the end of paragraph 84. The recommendations of the second, third and fifth signatories are set forth in paragraph 85. From paragraph 85 onwards, we are all agreed. We recommend that the Municipal Ordinance be amended so as to provide that any land, of which the capital value exceeds $1,000 an acre, shall be subject to a tax of 2 per cent per annum on its Capital value, if it is situated within an area to be defined by the Municipal Commissioners with the approval of the Governor in Council, and a tax of 1 per cent per annum, if it is situated outside; unless it already pays in respect of assessment upon the annual rental a sum equal to, or in excess of, the Capital Land Value Tax. Of course, property would not pay assessment as well as the Capital Land Value Tax: it would pay one or the other, whichever were the greater. In our opinion the area, so defined, should include the greater part of the Tanglin district as well as the whole of the "built-over" portion of the City.

79. We consider that it will be advisable to call the payment in respect of the Capital Land Value a "tax", and to call the payment in respect of the Annual Rental an "assessment." It may be objected that this rate of Capital Land Value Tax is not sufficiently high to exert upon the land-proprietor the necessary pressure to induce him to develop it adequately. Possibly it is not. But that is a fault which can be remedied by subsequent legislation. In this connection we invite particular attention to the quotation, which is given on page B 281 of our evidence, from Sir Thomas Whitaker's Book, "Ownership, Tenure and Taxation of Land."

Not a New Tax.

80. We wish to make it clear that we are not suggesting the imposition of a new tax. What is recommended is that the existing Capital Value Tax on land be altered: –

(i) by increasing it to 1 per cent in some cases and 2 per cent in other cases;

(ii) by extending it to all land, of which the capital value exceeds $1,000 an acre inside Municipal limits;

(iii) by providing that any land shall pay Capital Land Value Tax if that tax exceeds the assessment on the annual rental of the building or buildings on the land;

(iv) by limiting the area of land which may be regarded as appurtenant to any house. /

81. This Capital Land Value Tax is really only a modification of the Undeveloped Land Tax which is provided for by the Imperial Finance Act, 1910, (10 Edw. VII C. 8). In the United Kingdom, where it is a tax *in addition* to income-tax (and of course wholly apart from Municipal rates and taxes) it is not very high. It is one-half-penny in the pound. Here it now is, and will continue to be, a Municipal tax, *in lieu of* Municipal Assessment, and is naturally higher. The limit of $1,000 per acre which we recommend is in place of the limit of £50 an acre under the Imperial Act. If the law is altered in the manner that we recommend, it will probably be found convenient to follow the Finance Act, 1910, so far as it applies. We consider that the tax should be collected, as at present, by the Municipal Commissioners. In respect of property that, by reason of its undevelopment, escapes payment of assessment on the annual rental, they would pay over to the Improvement Commissioners the whole of the sum collected. But in respect of property that is partially developed, and is therefore liable to assessment on the annual rental, they would pay over the difference only between the Capital Land Value Tax and the assessment. For instance, if a property in Tanglin were valued at $100,000 the Capital Land Value Tax would be $2,000. If the assessment on the annual rental amounted to $900, the Municipal Commissioners would collect the $2,000, credit themselves with $900, and pay over $1,100 to the Improvement Commissioners.

82. In regard to limiting the area which may be regarded as appurtenant[10] to any house we recommend that an idea be taken from the Finance Act, 1910, and that every dwelling-house be allowed an area of one acre in every case, and an area of five acres if the land value does not exceed twenty times the rental upon which the assessment is paid. In respect of any land in excess, Capital Land Value Tax should be paid.

83. Although we think that cases of genuine hardship will be rare, we think that provision should be made for them. We recommend therefore that the law provide that any case of hardship – such for instance of impossibility of developing property because of its being a trust-estate, or an infants' estate, or because of restrictive covenants – may be considered, and dealt with by the Governor in Council on petition to him.

A City of Mean Houses.

84. There are many cases in the "built-over" part of Singapore where extremely valuable sites are occupied by small mean dwellings, and where a Capital Land Value Tax on the land of 2 per cent would considerably exceed the assessment on the annual rental. In such cases, this Capital Land Value Tax will act as an incentive to the erection of a suitable building. Singapore in many ways deserves the title of a "City of Mean Houses", and it is beyond doubt that the system whereby a mean house pays a small assessment, irrespective of the site value of the land, has much to do with this fact.

The Alternative Recommendation: An Undeveloped Land Tax.

85. The recommendation of the second, third and fifth signatories (*see* paragraph 78) is as follows. We recommend the imposition of an Undeveloped Land Tax on lines akin to those contained in the English Finance (1909-1910) Act, 1910, 10 Edw. 7 c. 8; and we desire to draw particular attention to the evidence of Mr. SAM TOMLINSON; Q. 4126-4153, inclusive.

Undeveloped land duty in England is a duty on the site value of undeveloped land, which is land that has not been developed by the erection on it of dwelling-houses, or of buildings for the purpose of, or not otherwise *bonâ fide* used for, any business, trade or industry other than agriculture. It also includes land which after having been developed has reverted to the condition of undeveloped land and continued in that condition for the space of a year. Section 17 (3) sets out a number of exceptions; section 17 (4) deals with grounds appurtenant to a dwelling-house and we consider that in place of an acre in England five acres should be allowable in Singapore. Section 17 (1) excepts any land where the site value does not exceed fifty pounds per acre.

The Improvement Commissioners should be given the power to impose this tax upon any undeveloped land within the present Municipal limits which in their opinion ought to be developed. /

We think that in addition to the powers under the English Finance Act, the Improvement Commissioners should be given power to declare land to be undeveloped where the house standing on it is manifestly unfit for the site; *e.g.*, where in an important street and on a valuable site there stands an old building out of all keeping with its surroundings and unsuitable to the neighbourhood.

We think that in place of fifty pounds per acre as in the English Section 17 (1) there should be substituted in Singapore $1,000 per acre. This is better in our opinion than confining the tax to "land suitable for building" an expression which needs interpretation and the meaning of which varies with the interpretation given from time to time.

We further think that as the undeveloped land tax is justifiable only upon the ground that it is necessary for the improvement of Singapore and the alteration of the housing situation the whole proceeds thereof should go to the Improvement Commissioners to be expended by them upon the improvement of the Town. These Commissioners should be given the power to arrange with the Municipal Commissioners, who have the necessary machinery, to collect the tax and place it in their books to the credit of the Improvement Commissioners. The Municipality would go on collecting assessment as at present upon all property within the Municipality which did not fall within the Undeveloped Land Tax.

We further think that a period of at least 3 years should be allowed to lapse before bringing into operation this new tax so that owners of property falling within it should have an opportunity to consider whether they will sell, develop or pay.

Capital Value the Basis for Compensation.

86. When a land proprietor is paying assessment on the Capital Value of his land, he should not be permitted to claim more than that capital value in respect of it in the event of his property being acquired for any public purpose.

Vacant Lands with Unknown Ownership.

87. We are of opinion that a more vigorous policy should be adopted by the Municipality in respect of vacant lands of which the owner is unknown to the Municipal authorities and in respect of which no assessment is paid.* If the Municipality would exercise its legal powers and sell the land, it would undoubtedly tend to stimulate building activities.

No Refunds of Assessment on Vacant Houses.

88. We recommend the abolition of refunds of assessment in respect of vacant houses, and the repeal of section 59 of the Municipal Ordinance, which relates thereto. We invite particular attention to the evidence in Questions 1917–1919 as instances of the abuse of the refund system.

Various Suggestions.

89. We have carefully considered various suggestions regarding quinquennial assessment, payment by the tenant instead of by the landlord, rebates on account of repairs and so on, but are of opinion that the present crude system is more suited to local circumstances than the scientific and more elaborate systems of Europe.

IMPERFECTIONS IN THE LAW RELATING TO BUILDING.

Existing Regulations no longer Suitable.

90. The Building Regulations were framed for the use of the last generation and are no longer suitable for present needs. (Q. 2627. 3455). They do not for instance contain any provision relating to ferro-concrete[11] buildings (Q. 3458,

---

*   See Memorandum "K," §10, and Questions 1790 – 1824. /

2736). Although section 134 of the Municipal Ordinance requires that *plans* shall be submitted, written *permits* are frequently given. The Ordinance should be amended to regularize the practice. In certain respects, the regulations operate unfairly. For instance there is no justification for the rule relating to the height of bungalows. (Q. 3622). Revision of the Regulations has been under contemplation for some time past, but has been deferred as the Supervising Architect to the Municipality has not been able to find time to attend to it. (Q. 3451). /

Revision Committee Necessary.

91. It is unnecessary to urge the vital importance to-the building industry of good Building Regulations: and we recommend that the Municipal Commissioners appoint forthwith a Committee of three architects to revise the regulations. The work can only be clone by professional men (Q. 2628, 3452). The members of the Committee should receive an honorarium for their services.

A More Elastic Code.

92. It will be necessary at the same time to amend certain sections of the Municipal Ordinance 1913 so as to do away with their unyielding rigidity and to substitute a more elastic code. For instance Section 135 must be re-cast in order to give greater discretionary powers to the Commissioners in regard to "open space." [*See* paragraph 165 *infra.*] A good example of the cast-iron rigidity of the present law will be found in paragraphs 158 and 159 of this Report.

THE WANT OF A LAW RELATING TO ARCHITECTS.

No Qualification Required.

93. We have taken a mass of evidence regarding the present system under which any person is allowed to practise as an architect in this Colony. It is certainly an extraordinary state of affairs, Mr. JACKSON, Supervising Architect to the Municipality, told, us of a man, who for many years past has been submitting plans to the Municipality, although he cannot draw. A draftsman employed by a European firm of architects prepares the plans, and this man signs them (Q. 3516–19). There are about 30 or 40 men who make a living by preparing plans for persons who desire to build or to repair; and of them only about six are said to be competent. (Q. 3513, 3514). They hang about the Municipal offices. It has been suggested in evidence that there is an opening for an understanding between them and the subordinates in Mr. JACKSON's office (Q. 2531–33), and Mr. JACKSON admits there is such an opening, (Q. 3445–9).

94. The incompetent men are a nuisance to everyone connected with the building trade. When a plan is returned by the Municipality as not complying with the regulations, they are unable to discover what is wrong with it, and suggest

to their employer that the Municipality is willfully making unnecessary difficulties. Another thing is that the calculation of weights and strains is beyond
them, and that their plans are either unsafe (in which case they are rejected
by the Municipality) or wasteful (in which case the employer bears a wholly
unnecessary expense). An instance of this, in regard to waste in piling,[12] is given
by Mr. JACKSON (Q. 3645). We have no hesitation in recommending that the
Government should immediately introduce a Bill to provide for the licensing of
architects. Surveyors have been licensed in the Colony since the date of operation of the "Surveyors Ordinance 1902" (Ordinance No. XXXVII of 1902);
and we consider that the need for the licensing of architects is at least as great as
that for the licensing of surveyors. [...]

THE WANT OF MUNICIPAL ENCOURAGEMENT AND ASSISTANCE TO INTENDING BUILDERS.

An Instance of Unsympathetic Treatment.
98. A case of unsympathetic treatment to a building scheme is recorded in paragraphs 15 and 16 of Mr. ROBINSON's Memorandum *Q* (page C 72), Mr. ELIAS
was prepared in 1913 to put up fiats in Orchard Road. Owing to the attitude
adopted by the Municipality, the scheme was abandoned, and the land is still
vacant. Those rats would have done much to ease the present housing difficulty.

Model Plans.
99. The initial difficulties by which an intending builder is beset would be made
lighter if the Municipality were to drop its attitude of passivity, and adopt a
policy of active assistance. We strongly recommend that it should have plans of
model bungalows, terrace-houses, tenement houses and shop-houses prepared,
and copies sold at a nominal cost to the public. These plans should be framed
and hung in conspicuous places in the Municipal Offices. A competition, with
prizes for the best designs, might have good results and should be held.

Standardisation.
100. Another way in which the Municipality could render most valuable assistance is by arranging for the standardisation of such things as door-frames and
window-frames. The present utter lack of system causes deplorable waste of timber, and of the workman's time. We invite careful attention to our evidence on
this subject, and are confident that if the Municipality will take the matter up
with energy and determination, it can achieve a great deal of good in this respect.
The Municipal Officers should be able, in conference with the architects, contractors and / sawmill-proprietors, to decide upon various standards for various
articles capable of standardisation, and then the Municipality should make it
known to all architects and contractors that, only in exceptional cases, will plans
be passed for doors, windows, etc., which were not of a standard size.

Water and Light in Suburbs.

101. We realize that the Municipal Commissioners feel that, as custodians of the rate-payers' money, they are compelled to consider carefully how they incur any expenditure in schemes which tend to assist in the development of private property. In respect of the supply of water and light to houses lying in the outer fringes of the suburbs the policy of the Commissioners is undoubtedly cautious. It errs we think on the side of over-caution. The "pioneer" properties deserve every consideration; and, as Singapore is expanding rapidly, there need be no fear at present of the new houses not being followed by many more. We do not urge the Municipality at present to lay down gas or water to stimulate development. That is to say, we do not ask it to lead. But we ask it to accompany development. At present it lags behind it.

Private Roads.

The question of "Private roads" is a difficult one. But we recommend that the- Municipality should adopt a more generous policy for the good of the community.

THE (TEMPORARY) DEMAND FOR WAREHOUSES.

102. Owing to the shortage of shipping space, there are huge accumulations of rubber, copra and other produce in Singapore. The normal warehousing accommodation is wholly inadequate to cope with it; and, because of the impossibility of obtaining corrugated iron, suitable temporary warehouses cannot be erected. As a result, dwelling-houses are being used as warehouses, and the former occupants have had to seek accommodation elsewhere. This difficulty will diminish when shipping facilities improve.

CHAPTER III.

A BUILDING PROGRAMME.

[...]

I. – HOUSING OF THE EMPLOYEES OF THE GOVERNMENT, MUNICIPALITY AND HARBOUR BOARD.

105. With one exception,* our witnesses agree, and we entirely concur, that the Government, the Municipality and the Harbour Board should provide housing accomodation for their employees. /

[...]

---

* Question 2837–2841. /

II. – Housing of the Poorer Classes.

Re-housing must precede Dis-housing.

112. When the Legislative Council, responding to the public demand aroused by Dr. Simpson's report, passed the Ordinance of 1907, it fully realized the necessity of providing Housing accommodation for the persons who would be displaced by the / execution of improvement schemes; and section 306 (*h*) of the Ordinance made the necessary provision. It was taken from section 6 (*i*) (*c*) of the Housing of the Working Classes Act, 1890. The principle is not new therefore to Singapore, although the practice is as yet unknown. It is manifest that provision for accommodation of persons dishoused must precede dishousing. Otherwise a dishousing programme only means intensified overcrowding. If neither private enterprise nor philanthropy will re-house, then provision must be made from public funds. Everyone knows that if Closing Orders were carried out against houses in the Congested Areas, there would be no place to which the tenants could go. It would only be a case of making very bad still worse. [...]

Recommendations regarding Re-housing.

116. Any re-housing operations in Singapore in the immediate future must be carried out on land in the vicinity of the Congested Areas. At present transport facilities are not sufficiently good to enable the poorer classes to live at a distance from their work, and the new buildings must therefore be within easy walking distance. Fortunately there is available open space within close vicinity of both Congested Areas. Most of the land near the Southern Congested Area is the property of the Crown or the Harbour Board. This is still more fortunate. /

117. We appointed a Committee to consider how the vacant lands near the Congested Areas could best be laid out for the erection of a one-storeyed type of building suitable for occupation by the poorer classes, including coolies and rickishaw pullers, prepare a plan of the most suitable type of building, and to make an estimate of the cost. The following gentlemen kindly consented to serve – Mr. B. Ball Chairman, Dr. W. R. C. Middleton, Mr. T. Lornie and Mr. H. A. Stallwood. Their report is published as Memorandum "Z". The problem, was to design a type of cheap, light, temporary building. It had to be light, because in some cases, as at Kampong Kapor, or Kampong Bahru, the land has not yet sufficiently consolidated to stand the weight of a heavy building; and it had to be temporary, because the land, being close to the Congested Areas, will later become too valuable to carry one-storeyed houses economically. We recommend the adoption of their building for the type of house to be erected for the poorer classes of the community but also for the peons and coolies employed by the Government. Municipality and Harbour Board. Alternate blocks contain 10 and 12 rooms. The average cost of a block, without allowing for the cost of the

land, is estimated at $1,500. The rooms can be let for $1 a month, and bring in 10 per cent on the outlay. The initial cost of the building is thus $75 per head.

118. The rectangle of land at Kampong Kapor lying between Hindoo Road and Rowell Road will take 28 blocks containing 308 rooms (616 adults) on its area of 99,749 square feet. The total area of vacant land at Kampong Kapor including this area, but excluding roads, back-lanes, etc., is 684,000 square feet. It will therefore accommodate about 4,000 persons.

119. There is a wide expanse of open, levelled land at Mount Wallich, in respect of which the Government's policy is not known to us. It there is to be a railway station there at some future date, we advocate the use of the land in the meantime for occupation by the cheap temporary houses designed by our Committee. We estimate that it might accommodate 1,500 persons at a cost of $112,500. If the land is not reserved for possible use as a railway station site, we urge that the Government put it to its proper use. The lay-out, already approved by the Municipality, provides for a main road (60 feet wide) from the junction of Neil Road, South Bridge Road and Tanjong Pagar Road to the junction of Wallich Street and Teluk Aver Street, Peck Seah Street and Tras Street should be extended to join it. All titles issued by the Crown in respect of this property should be subject to stringent building conditions.

120. The land already reclaimed by the Government between Havelock Road and Mount Zion, and now being planted up with coconuts lies so close to the densely crowded areas of Havelock Road that it should be used for temporary houses; Mr. PIGOTT informed us (Q. 4394) that about twenty acres, out of 48, had been reclaimed. This should accommodate about 2,500 persons at a cost of $187,500.

121. Along the Kampong Bahru Road, the Singapore Harbour Board owns a block of about 60 acres on the southern side, and a small triangular block of about 3 ½ acres on the North. This land was reclaimed from the Lagoon when the Empire Dock was built. It has not yet consolidated. A road, with a level crossing at the railway, should be made at once to connect Kampong Bahru Road with Keppel Road; and temporary buildings should be erected on the property thus developed. As our Committee point out, a public recreation ground is required here; and this fact should be kept in mind. Buildings accommodating 16,000-persons might be put up there at a cost of $1,200,000, Mr. NICHOLSON (Q. 978) informed us that he would have no objection to giving a twenty-years' lease of this property, as the Harbour Board would not want it in the meantime.
122. The Harbour Board has also a very useful area of open, vacant, grazing land known as the tract Reclamation, and situated within a short distance of one of the most thickly populated parts of Singapore. Mr. NICHOLSON informed us (Q. 987) that he would be prepared to give a lease for part of it. We consider that

such part as is not required for building purposes by the Board within the next fifteen years, should be built over by temporary houses. If only ten acres is taken, accommodation can be found for 2,500 persons at a cost of $187,500. /

123. The Teluk Ayer Reclamation is another area of wasted land. Part of it lies within a few hundred yards of land valued at $40 a square foot. It appears to be the policy of the Singapore Harbour Board to retard the progress of this Reclamation Mr. ROBINSON's evidence (page C. 73 and Q. 2669–2672) shows that prohibitive landing charges are deliberately imposed. As the Board has only a five years' lease of the property, we invite the attention of the Government to the action of the Board. Mr. NICHOLSON informed us (Q. 985) that had it not been for the war, that the reclamation would now have been covered by godowns. Some of this land is in solid, and some is as yet unconsolidated reclamation. In view of the fact (see paragraph 169) that much of the overcrowding in Singapore is due to tenement houses having been converted into warehouses, and of the fact that private enterprise is busy in erecting warehouses, we urge that the Board consider whether they should not forthwith erect "godowns" in the solid part of this property. We do not recommend the erection on it of temporary houses for the poor. When this property is laid out, it is very desirable that part or parts of it should be reserved for parking public motor-buses. The cheap traffic, of which we urge the importance in our paragraph 175 can only be achieved if it is given proper facilities.

124. It will be noticed that the recommendations in the preceding paragraphs are confined to the construction of temporary houses. The reason is that it is imperative that the buildings should be (i) cheap, (ii) quickly put up, and (iii) adapted to land which may be required for other purposes after say 15 or 20 years. The erection of a suitable, permanent building for occupation by the poor is a matter in which it is advisable to proceed cautiously. Most fortunately, the Government has at present a vacant area most admirably suited for the purpose of the erection of a block of model permanent buildings. This is the Cross Street block. We strongly urge that the Government put up either a three-storeyed or four-storeyed building here. The ground floor should be let as shop-premises, and the other storeys should be let in tenements. In view of the importance of making a success of the enterprise, we recommend that the Government call publicly for designs and accept the best one. The building should be in ferro-concrete.

125. The available accommodation for temporary houses may be summed up as follows: –

		$
Kampong Kapor will accommodate about 4,000 persons, at a cost of		300,000
Mount Wallich	1,500	112,500
Kampong Bahru	16,000	1,200,000
East Reclamation	2,500	187,500
Havelock Road – Mount Zion	2,500	187,500
	26,500	$1,987,500

In the first instance, it will suffice to put up temporary houses for 10,000 persons at a cost of three-quarters of a million dollars. [...]

CHAPTER V.

THE PROBLEM OF RECONSTRUCTION.

147. The schemes that will require the *total* demolition and reconstruction of a block of Insanitary Houses will be few. Possibly there may not be any. The greatest of all the problems with which the Government is faced is the one of providing an expeditious and equitable scheme for the partial reconstruction of the houses that are now back-to-back or that abut on "obstructive buildings". The present system (if it can be called a system) has undoubtedly failed. The figures supplied by the Municipal Authorities prove it conclusively. From first to last, in the whole of Singapore City – as the result of the general feeling aroused in 1907, by Dr. SIMPSON's report – there have only 22 completed back-lane schemes under Section 137 of the Ordinance. Only 426 houses in all have been affected. Of this number, only 238 have obtained communication with the back-lane, and 188 are still unconnected. Only 156 houses are affected by the ten schemes now in hand; whilst 512 houses will be affected by 14 schemes in which acquisition proceedings are under negotiation. And that is all that "Schemes" have done up to date. Of course back-lanes have been put in in places without "Schemes" when the owner wished to reconstruct. But the complete list (which includes the figures given above) is only 399.

Dr. MIDDLETON's evidence (Q. 3824) appears to us to sum up the case as well as it can be done. In answer to a suggestion that the present system did not appear to have effected much improvement, he said: –

"I think that the present system has not been tried much so far. What we "have been trying to do with back-lanes has not affected the worst parts of the "town."

On another occasion, in answer to a question [Q. 3307] how long it would be, at the present rate of progress, before there were back-lanes through all the Congested Areas, he said that he doubted whether it would be done in a hundred years. It is therefore obviously high time that something else was tried.

The Closing Order prepares the Way.

148. In Glasgow the principle upon which the Municipality-work is that the "Closing Order" prepares the way for the scheme of improvement or reconstruction.* We recommend that the same principle be applied in Singapore. The law on the subject of "Closing Orders" is contained in Section 227 of the Municipal Ordinance 1913. The order is only made when it is proved to the satisfaction of a Police Court that, by reason of a "nuisance", a dwelling-house is unfit for human habitation. This is practically what the law was under Sections 32 and 33 / of the

---

* "Municipal Glasgow". Issued by the Corporation of the City of Glasgow 1915 – page 260. /

Imperial "Housing of the Working Classes Act 1890", under which the proceedings for the purpose of causing a house to be closed had to be brought before a Court of Summary Jurisdiction. It was found in the United Kingdom that this procedure was futile. Out of dwellings inhabited by a population of 11,000,000, there were only 4,220 closing orders, and 748 demolition orders in the seven years ended 1905. At that rate, it would have taken a century to get rid of the existing insanitary buildings.*

On page B 222 of our evidence will be found particulars of the 55 Closing Orders made in Singapore during the period 1908-1917. Of this number 17 were in one block in one street, and 13 in another street During the past three years, owing to war conditions, and to the insufficiency of housing accommodation, no Closing Orders have been obtained by the Municipal Commissioners.

149. The futility of the procedure in Great Britain made it necessary to amend the law in 1909. Under sections 17 and 18 of the "Housing, Town Planning, Etc., Act 1909," (which repealed sections 17 and 18 of the Act of 1890) the Closing Order is made by the Local Authority. We recommend that in Singapore the order be made, on the application of the Municipal Commissioners, by the Improvement Commissioners. This on the one hand will save the Municipal Commissioners from the always awkward position of combining the roles of prosecutor and judge, and on the other hand will ensure that the application will be heard and decided by a competent authority.

Standard of Fitness for Human Habitation.

150. A standard of fitness for occupation must be fixed by law. This has been done in Ceylon by Section 96 of, and Rule 3 of the Schedule to, the "Housing and Town Improvement Ordinance, No. 19 of 1915". It is there provided that any room which does not comply with a certain standard of fitness for occupation is to be deemed, ipso facto, to be unfit for human habitation. Deprived of technicalities and details, (which, however, are very important) the requirements are as follows: –

(*a*) The room must have an average height of at least ten feet.

(*b*) It must have a clear superficial area of not less than 120 square feet

(*c*) At least one side must be an external wall abutting on the open area.

(*d*) It must be connected with the open air by doors and windows of a certain standard.

The operation of this section has immediate effect in respect of rooms comprised in an Improvement Scheme. But in respect of other existing houses its operation is deferred for a minimum period of five years. We recommend that the same principle be applied in Singapore, with the important proviso that, first of all,

---

*   Handbook to the Housing and Town Planning Act 1909. W. THOMPSON 1910. /

housing accommodation must be provided elsewhere to accommodate the persons dishoused. When a human being can be accommodated elsewhere the only test of whether a room should be used for human habitation is whenever it is fit for human habitation. We have no sympathy with the sentimentalists who plead the case of the landlord who is restrained from renting out his insanitary property. We consider that the difference is not great between him and the owner of an unseaworthy ship, or the purveyor of unwholesome food.

Procedure, Closing Order, and Demolition Order.

151. A "Closing Order" should be of two kinds, viz.: –
(i) an order to close the house;
(ii) an order to close a room or rooms in it.

When a Closing Order has been made, there must be ample provision for marking the premises. In this connection we invite reference to Section 77 of the Ceylon Ordinance, which has been followed by Section 25 of the Federated Malay States Ordinance No. 23 of 1917. In our opinion the Law should provide for conspicuous notice-boards in English, Malay, Chinese and Tamil, consisting of the words "Total Closing Order" or "Partial Closing Order", being exhibited on the door of any house in respect of which a closing order against the house or a room has been obtained. If the order is against a room, a copy of the order must be affixed to the door of the room. The next step after the "Closing Order" is / / The scheme is as impracticable as it is simple. It fails because it has not considered how the partially demolished buildings are to be reconstructed. The Commissioners have never dared to enter into a man's house and demolish that part of it which is upon their land, because the bill for compensation would be ruinous. They therefore have to dodge. This is what happens: the Municipal Commissioners propose to deal with a solid block of masonry [...]: –

157. They prepare a plan which provides for a back-lane access to all the buildings. The typical plan is as follows: –
The Governor in Council approves the plan, and the Municipal Commissioners acquire and demolish the four obstructive buildings Nos. 11, 25, 36 and 50 – and make a back-lane along them. And, there the matter stops.

158. It will be seen that the demolition of these four houses has not affected houses Nos. 12–24 and 37–49 in any way. Nothing can affect them except the forcible entrance of a demolishing party; and though the Municipality has (as we have said) the legal power to demolish their back premises, they simply dare not not attempt it. Houses 1–10 and 26–35 are in a different position: their back premises now abut on to the lanes which occupy the site formerly occupied by the obstructive houses. But they take no action to effect any connection between their back premises and the lane which abuts upon them. They obvi-

ously are not in the perfectly helpless condition of houses 12–24 and 37–49; and therefore the Municipal Health Officer sets to work to cajole or bully them into connecting their premises with the back-lane. It is thoroughly in keeping with the whole ridiculous procedure that the bullying is administered by the Municipal Health Officer by means of serving the owners with "Nuisance Notices".* If the landlord, yielding to cajolery or overcome by Nuisance Notices, decides to connect his back premises (kitchen, bathroom and latrine) with the back-lane, and submits a plan accordingly, he learns still more of the subtilty of the Municipal Ordinance. His plan is rejected – (there is no discretion in the matter: the Municipal Commissioners are compelled by Section 135 of the Ordinance to reject it) – unless he also reconstructs his building in such a manner as to give up one-third of it for an open space.

159. Added humour is provided by the combined effect of Sections 139 and 135. Section 139, aiming at an immediate use of the back-lane, provides that when a back-lane is formed, the owner of a house abutting on it shall provide a / means of access to it from his premises, and that, if he fails to do so, the Commissioners may do whatever is necessary. But unfortunately, this otherwise admirable provision is rendered nugatory by the fact that the Commissioners are also bound by Section 135, and cannot touch the house unless they, in their turn, are prepared to reconstruct it in such a manner as to keep one-third of it for open space.

160. It will also be seen that the owners of houses 13–23 and 38–48 might all rebuild and might all have a back-lane at the back of their premises, and that it would all be unavailing so long as the owners of 12 and 49 on the one side, and 24 and 37 on the other side, remained "back to back", and thus cut them off from through communication with the other part of the back-lane.

161. The result, as may be seen, by an inspection of Chinatown, is that generally all that happens is that, after a vast expenditure of time and trouble, four houses are demolished and that, so far as the other houses are concerned, matters might just as well have remained as they were.

A fair Basis for Compensation.

162. Everything turns upon two questions *firstly* the cost of the operation of reconstruction, and *secondly* the incidence of that cost. It has frequently happened that a landlord with an insanitary house, after years of disputation with the Municipal authorities, has found that he has a sanitary building (reconstructed by himself at the rate-payers' expense), that his property is as valuable as ever it was, and that he is the richer by the amount of a handsome cheque

---

*   See Question 3196. In this connection, particular attention is invited to Dr. MIDDLE-
     TON's evidence Q. 3187–3205. /

for "compensation". The schedule to Mr. LORNIE's Memorandum "AA" gives a number of instances in point. In any scheme of compensation, the case of the properties which are diminished in area must be considered separately from the case of the properties that are undiminished. We refer back to the sketches on page A 34; and will take first the cases of houses 12–24 and 37–49, which are diminished in area. In our opinion, the basis for compensation should be that the proprietor shall give up, free of cost, the area required for one-half of the width of the back-lane behind his premises, and shall, in exchange, have his back premises reconstructed for him, free of cost, by the Improvement Commissioners, according to such scale of reconstruction as they may, in their discretion, consider proper. If by reason of the shape of his lot, any landlord is required to contribute more than one-half of the width of the back-lane behind his property, he will receive as compensation from the Improvement Commissioners the value of that excess area. Conversely, if a landlord is required-to give up less than one-half of the width of the back-lane behind his premises, the value of the difference is payable by him to the Commissioners.

163. The case of houses 1–10 and 26–35 is quite different. They give up no land. The provisions of Section 139 of the Municipal Ordinance 1913 should be transferred to the Singapore City Improvement Ordinance, and strictly enforced against them. Moreover, the owners of these lots have obtained at the back of their premises, an open back-lane in the place of the obstructive buildings that were formerly there. We believe that the cost of the acquisition of lots 11 and 50 – valued as open space – should be divided amongst the owners of houses 1–10, and the cost of the acquisition of houses 25 and 36, also valued as open space, should be divided amongst the owners of lots 26–35. (In passing, we would note that it is only fair that these houses should be allowed to reckon the *whole* width of these back-lanes for open space, instead of one-half only, as at (present.)

164. There will sometimes be cases where, because of the cost of partial reconstruction, it will not be a business proposition to attempt a back-lane scheme. In such a case, the application of the Closing Order should pave the way to a Rebuilding Scheme, of which we give an outline in paragraphs 230–234.

The Need for discretionary Power.

165. It is essential to the whole scheme of the reconstruction of the unhealthy blocks that the Improvement Commissioners should not only have a wide discretionary power in respect of the open space required to be given up, but should also except a considerably lower standard in cases of partial re-construction (for the purpose of back-lane access) than in cases of *total* re-construction (as where a land, lord puts up a new house because he finds the old house unsuitable). The two / cases are entirely different. It is imperative that every house should connect at the earliest possible moment with a back-lane. A landlord's house may be so

constructed that he can give up an open space of one-quarter without much difficulty, but might have to pull down half his house in order to give up an open space of one-third. It will be the duty of the Improvement Commissioners to discriminate between what is practicable and what is impracticable. It is shown in Memorandum "Y" that, after all these years, only 426 houses have been affected by completed back-lanes. It is bad enough that there should be so little to show: but it is much worse that, of those houses, 188 are still unconnected with the back-lanes, as against 238 which have obtained connection. Mr. A. W. STILL in his Memorandum (p. C. 105) has stated, that "the most dangerous enemies of housing reform are the idealists." We entirely agree; and the impracticable standard set (quite unwittingly perhaps) by the Municipal Ordinance – not by the Municipal Commissioners – has had much to do with the lamentable state of affairs set forth in the preceding sentence.

166. [...]

Obstructive Strips of Land.

167. An amendment to the law is required to enable a landlord to make use of a back-lane, in any case where the back-lane has been laid out in such a manner that his land does not extend up to it. He may be cut off from his access by a narrow strip of perhaps only a few feet in width. The owner of this strip, realizing his neighbour's predicament, demands an extortionate price, or (occasionally) refuses altogether to negotiate. We consider that there should be power of compulsory acquisition by any landlord of any land that cuts him off from access to a back-lane. Whenever the Improvement Commissioners certify that certain premises should be provided with access to a back-lane, the owner of those premises should have the power of acquiring compulsorily any land lying between his property and the back-lane; and the provisions of the Ordinance relating to the acquisition of land should apply, *mutatis mutandis*,[13] to the acquisition.

The provisions of such a law would also be useful in cases where any landed property is cut off from access to a public road; and we believe that, in some cases, an obstructive strip of land lying between a building and a public road has hampered the development of building property. In such a case a certificate by the Colonial Secretary might be substituted for the certificate by the Improvement Commissioners. This power should be given to lessees of Crown Land who propose with the consent of the Government to convert their Leases into Grants. It should not be necessary for a lessee to wait until a grant is issued to him before taking advantage of this power. /[...]

CHAPTER XII.

RECAPITULATION.

271. Our recommendations or expressions of opinion, at the case may be, may be summarized under the two headings of Executive and Legislative.

EXECUTIVE: –

(i) That a Census be held in Singapore Municipal Limits in April, 1919: that the following Census be held in 1921 (on the completion of the decennial period) and quinquennially thereafter. (Paragraphs 11 and 12.)

(ii) That an expert (with assistants if necessary) be brought out at once to study Tuberculosis, and that, upon his arrival, tuberculosis be made a "notifiable" disease. (Paragraphs 50 and 31.)

(iii) That encouragement be given to employment of Lady Doctors. (Paragraph 33.)

(iv) That a Committee on Sanitary Education for Singapore be constituted. (Paragraph 35.)

(v) That the constitution of a Health Department for Malaya be considered. (Paragraph 36.)

(vi) That a Municipal Brickworks Department be starred at once. (Paragraph 56.)

(vii) That the forests be systematically exploited for timber. (Paragraph 56.)

(viii) That the Public Works Department instal at once a suitable plant for seasoning and preserving timber used in construction of public buildings. (Paragraph 58.)

(ix) That every facility be given to private enterprise in manufacture of cement, and that, if private enterprise fail, the Government undertake it. (Paragraph 59.)

(x) That an engineer, with an adequate staff of assistants, be put on at once to examine the Teluk Blanga Development Scheme, and the Tanjong Rhu-Kalang-Rochore Reclamation Scheme. (Paragraph 72.)

(xi) That the Government proceed at once with the reclamation of the mangrove swamp at Havelock Road. (Paragraph 73.)

(xii) That the Municipality adopt a more vigorous policy in respect of vacant lands, where the owner is unknown and no assessment is paid. (Paragraph 87.)

(xiii) That a Committee of three architects revise the Building Regulations forthwith. (Paragraph 91.)

(xiv) That the Municipality prepare model plans of buildings, and sell them at a nominal cost to the public. A competition for best designs. (Paragraph 99.) /

(xv) That the Municipality endeavour to introduce standardisation of door-frames, window-frames, etc. (Paragraph 100.)

(xvi) That the Municipal Commissioners adopt a more generous policy (*A*) in respect of water and light supply in the suburbs, and (*B*) in respect of private roads. (Paragraph 101.)

(xvii) That the Harbour Board at once put up coolie lines to accommodate 4,000 coolies, and also put up quarters to accommodate all the clerks who desire to live near Tanjong Pagan (Paragraph III.)

(xviii) That the Government and the Municipality at once provide accommodation for the whole of their staffs. (Paragraph 111.)

(xix) That the Government take under its consideration the policy of the Harbour Board in deliberately retarding the progress of the development of Teluk Ayer Reclamation. (Paragraph 123.)

(xx) That the Government erect a ferro-concrete block of model houses for the working classes at Cross Street. (Paragraph 124.)

(xxi) That temporary houses to accommodate 10,000 persons of the working classes be erected at once. (Paragraph 125.)

(xxii) That the Government make a public expression of opinion upon the failure of the European firms to house their assistants. (Paragraph 126.)

(xxiii) That the Government dispose of the upper part (53 acres) of the "Economic Gardens" to a suitable Tenant Co-partnership Society; and that the 48-acre block of lowland be dealt with later. (Paragraph 135.)

(xxiv) That the Harbour Board dispose of portion of its property at Keppel Harbour to a suitable Tenant Co-partnership Society. (Paragraphs 136 and 137.)

(xxv) That loans be made by Government to Public Utility Societies and, in special cases, to individuals, for building purposes. (Paragraphs in 141.)

(xxvi) That the Government consider offers for certain favourably situated blocks of land for the erection thereon of Flats, and also consider an application for a loan. (Paragraph 146.)

(xxvii) That the extension of the present tramway system to new roads is not desirable. (Paragraph 170.)

(xxviii) That a Municipal Motor-Bus service be started. (Paragraph 171.1)

(xxix) That the widening of some, if not all of, the arterial roads will be necessary. (Paragraph 175.)

(xxx) That there is an urgent need for Open Spaces. (Paragraph 184.)

(xxxi) That the Improvement Commissioners acquire and lay out lands required for the Open Spaces, and hand them over to the Municipal Commissioners. (Paragraph 184.)

(xxxii) That certain areas of Crown Land be handed over to the Municipal Commissioners for maintenance as Open Spaces. (Paragraph 184.)

(xxxiii) That the Harbour Board's land near the Southern Congested Area be made an Open Space. (Paragraph 184.)

(xxxiv) That an "Open Spaces Sub-Committee" of the Municipal Commissioners deal with the open spaces that are now available. (Paragraph 185.)

(xxxv) That the surplus landed property of the Singapore Harbour Board be handed over to the Improvement Commissioners. (Paragraph 215.)

(xxxvi) That the Crown Land at Havelock Road be vested in the Improvement Commissioners. (Paragraph 216.)

(xxxvii) That all canals in Municipal limits above Harbour limits be handed over to the Municipal Commissioners by the Public Works Department. (Paragraph 268.)

(xxxviii) That the female leper asylum be moved. (Paragraph 269.)

(xxxix) That the Federated Malay States Railway be not allowed to remove earth from the new station site to places outside Municipal limits. (Paragraph 270.) /

LEGISLATIVE: –

(i) Introduce a Bill to provide for the Licensing of Architects. (Paragraphs 95–97.)

(ii) Introduce a Bill to provide for the Registration of Co-operative Societies. (Paragraph 142.)

(iii) Repeal Ordinance VI of 1890 and re-enact it, with it the title of the Land Acquisition Ordinance, (Chapter VIII.)

(iv) Introduce a Singapore City Improvement Ordinance. (Chapters IX and X.)

Summary.

272. In a nut-shell, our findings in regard to the housing difficulties are as follows: –

Houses for the European Community. – There is a very serious shortage, due to many reasons. The Government houses most, but not all, of its employés: the Municipality houses only 5 out of 33: the Harbour Board houses practically the whole of its European staff. Much of the present difficulty is due to the failure of the European firms to house their assistants. The remedy is to build new houses: not to buy some of the existing houses.

As bungalow property is not a remunerative investment, co-operative housing is the only solution of the problem of finding houses for the classes who are not employés of the public bodies or the big European firms. The Societies should come under the definition of "Public Utility" (paragraphs 140–141) and operate on Tenant Co-partnership lines (paragraphs 132–134). The tenant of a house would have to hold shares in the Society to the extent of at least one-third of the value of the house. The Government should lend money to the extent of one-third of the Society's capital. Flats would do much to improve the position, and the Government should render financial assistance.

Houses for Clerks. – Practically nothing has been done by the Government, the Municipality or the Harbour Board to provide accommodation for their clerical staffs. This should be remedied.

Co-operative building on the lines indicated above will provide the only other remedy that we can devise.

Houses for the Working Classes. – The Government, the Municipality and the Harbour Board have between them an enormous number of labourers whom they do not attempt to house. This should be remedied. Temporary houses to accommodate 10,000 persons exclusive of the employés of the public bodies should be put up at once to precede a policy of reconstruction of the insanitary houses in the two Congested Areas. A block of model permanent buildings for the working classes should be put up at Cross Street.

Reconstruction of Insanitary Houses. – The law is deficient, and must be amended.

Municipal Enterprise – in the way of Brick-works and a Motor-bus service is recommended.

General. – In order to carry out the Improvement Schemes and Town-Planning Schemes that are necessary for the proper development of the city, it is necessary to constitute a body of Improvement Commissioners distinct from the Municipal Commissioners.

Preparation of Legislation.

273. We fear that the time of the Attorney-General is so fully taken up with work arising out of the circumstances caused by the war that it will be impossible for him to undertake the task of drafting the Bills recommended by us in the preceding paragraph. We therefore recommend that, if this is the case, the Government ask some local legal firm to prepare the Bills.

ANON., 'MEMORANDUM REGARDING THE PROVISION OF HOUSING AND HOSPITAL ACCOMMODATION FOR LABOUR IN BURMA' (1920)

Anon., 'Memorandum Regarding the Provision of Housing and Hospital Accommodation for Labour in Burma', British Library, IOR/L/PJ/6/1666, file 2288, p. 1 to the end of annexture B.

The letter and memorandum discuss the accommodation and medical facilities provided for migrants recruited through the free labour system (see thematic introduction) and reveal that the government adopted no special measures, relying instead on existing legislation. The writer of the letter, H. Tonkinson, from 1926 represented Burma on the Central Legislative Assembly.

Anon., 'Memorandum Regarding the Provision of Housing and Hospital Accommodation for Labour in Burma' (1920), extract

Copy of a letter from the Hon'ble Mr. H.Tonkinson, I.C.S., Secretary to the Government of Burma, Medical Department, to the Secretary to the Government of India, Department of Commerce, No.27/3Z-3, dated Rangoon, the 2nd March 1920.

In reply to your letter No.4625, dated the 25th June 1919, I am directed to submit a memorandum describing briefly the conditions governing the provision of housing and hospital accommodation for labour in Burma.

2. It will be seen that except in the case of certain coolies passing through Rangoon no special measures have been taken by this Government to provide housing for Indian labour, nor has any special provision of hospital accommodation been made. It should however be noted that the conditions of the employment of Indian labour in Burma are in no way analogous with those in Fiji. Facilities for the journey between India and Burma are freely available in ordinary years, when five or six steamers ply each week between Rangoon and the Indian ports, the cost of the passage being within the means of the poorest classes. The conditions of service in Burma are well known among the classes of Indians concerned and there is an annual influx into Burma of some 250,000 labourers, the majority of whom return to India after a term of employment, the duration of which depends almost entirely upon their inclination. These labourers remain within the sphere of the Government of India which is in a position at any time to take in their behalf any special measures that may be called for. The supply of Indian labour is a necessity in Burma at present and has been so for many years. One consequence of this has been that the existing local legislation in towns has to a considerable extent been framed to meet conditions which are affected by the presence of Indian labourers.

3. With regard to the Government of India's enquiry regarding the labourers in the wolfram mines, I am to note that the specific proposals dealt with in the correspondence referred to were subsequently abandoned. As shown in

the attached / memorandum, however, certain provisions regarding the sanitary housing of labour in the wolfram and tin mines in Tavoy were included in the "Mining Act Rules" and private dispensaries were established at mining centres in Tavoy and Mergui.

Memorandum regarding the provision of housing and hospital accommodation for labour in Burma.

The labour in Burma may be classified as follows:–
  (a) labour employed in factories usually situated in Municipal and Notified Areas;
  (b) labour employed in mines and plantations; and
  (c) agricultural labour.

In class (a) the housing accommodation is governed by the byelaws framed under the Burma Municipal Act, except in the few cases of factories situated outside Municipal and Notified Areas when the provisions of the Burma Village Act and the rules framed thereunder apply. Except in the wolfram and tin mines in Tavoy district the only sanitary provisions applicable to class (b) are the provisions of the Village Act and its rules and the same applies to class(c). The labour under class (c) is very largely seasonal, the number of coolies coming to Burma each year from India being about a quarter of a million. During the war when the steamer services between Burma and India were dislocated by the shortage of shipping, temporary barracks were provided by the Rangoon Municipality with government assistance in which the large number of coolies who arrived in Rangoon en route for India and could not at once obtain passages were housed. The question of making permanent provision for this purpose is under discussion.

2. Before referring to the conditions under the Municipal and Village Acts respectively it may be noted that the operation of the Village Act is not confined to the collections of houses which constitute the villages themselves. The whole of Burma outside the limits of Municipalities and Notified Areas is divided into village tracts with the / exception of absolutely uninhabited tracts, like reserved forests. Each village tract is subject to the authority of a headman appointed by the Deputy Commissioner and his authority extends over the whole area of the village tract. The provisions of the Burma Towns Act are neglected because in practice that Act has been confined in its operation to Municipalities and Notified Areas.

3. So far as labourers residing within the limits of a Municipality or Notified Area under the Municipal Act are concerned, employers of labour provide housing for the majority of their employees and there are usually plenty of lodging houses available for the rest. There is no provision compelling employers to pro-

vide housing. The standard of living and sanitary requirements in every case is that ordinarily in force in the locality. The byelaws in respect of buildings and lodging houses provide against overcrowding, the standard laid down for lodging houses in Rangoon being 36 sq. feet for each person or in special cases 24 sq. feet, and in other municipalities 42 to 50 sq. feet. The sanitary byelaws of the locality apply to these barracks, the santitation etc., of which, it may be noted, are matters to which the Municipal Committees are naturally obliged to pay particular attention. The byelaws in question vary in the different towns and it is presumably unnecessary to quote any specific provisions.

4. In factories outside the limits of a Municipality or Notified Area and on mines and plantations, the employers almost invariably supply housing for their labourers though again there is no obligation upon them to do so. The standard of living and sanitary requirements are governed by the provisions of the Village Act and in mines in Tavoy District by rules under the Mines Act also. The relevant provisions of the village Act are described below: –

The public duties of a headman, are defined in section 8 of the Village Act and these include the following: –

"8(1) Every headman shall be bound to perform the following public duties namely: – /

x   x   x   x

(k) to superintend and control and to take such measures as may be prescribed in any rules made in this behalf for –

Firstly, – the prevention of public nuisances;

Secondly, – the cure or prevention of the spreading of any contagious or infectious disease among human beings or domestic animals of any kind;

x   x   x   x

Fourthly, – the general sanitation of the Village-tract;"

x   x   x   x

Similarly the public duties of each person residing in a village tract are contained in section 11 of the Act.

"11. Every person residing in a village tract shall be bound to perform the following public duties, namely: –

x   x   x   x   x

(c) to take such measures as may be prescribed in any rules made in this behalf for –

x   x   x   x   x

(ii) the prevention of public nuisances;

(iii) the cure of prevention of the spreading of any contagious or infectious disease among human beings or domestic animals of any kind;

x   x   x   x   x

(v) the general sanitation of the village tract;   x

x   x   x   x

(d) on the requisition of the headman or of a rural policeman to assist him in the execution of his public duties."

The sanitary rules which have been framed under the Village Act are of a simple nature to meet conditions in rural areas. A copy of these rules is attached as Annexure A. A copy of the rules under the Mines Act applicable to mines in the Tavoy District so far as they deal with sanitation is also attached as Annexure B.

5. The agricultural labourer is not provided with housing other than that of the temporary nature ordinarily made use of / by cultivators. The provisions of the Village Act apply to such buildings.

6. No special measures have been taken to provide hospital accommodation for labourers in Burma. In all Municipalities and Notified Areas and in certain other terms hospitals are maintained which are open to the labourers. Many employers of labour on a large scale provide medical attendance for their employees and in some cases hospitals also. There is however no obligation upon them to do so. In the Mining areas of the Tavoy and Margui districts at the instance of the Local Government several dispensaries were opened at convenient centres among the mines. These were maintained by private firms with Government assistance. With the cessation of work in many of the mines the dispensaries are also being gradually closed down. /

ANNEXURE A.

Rules prescribing duties of persons residing in a village-tract in respect of public nuisances and sanitation.

1. No person residing in a village-tract shall allow any house or land occupied by him to be kept in a filthy or insanitary condition, or overgrown with weeds or rank vegetation.

2. No person residing in a village-tract shall allow any corpse of a human being, unless embalmed or enclosed in an airtight coffin, to be kept unburied or uncremated for more than 48 hours in any house or land occupoed by him without the special sanction in each case of the Deputy Commissioner, Civil Surgeon, Subdivisional Officer or Township Officer: Provided that between the first day of November and last day of February inclusive, corpses may be kept unburied or uncremated for 72 hours.

3. No person residing in a village-tract shall bury a corpse or cause a corpse to be buried at a depth of less than five feet, or within thirty yards of any well, tank or stream, or of any dwelling house. No person residing in a village tract shall throw a corpse or cause it to be thrown into a river, creek or water of any kind.

4. Except with the permission of the headman no person residing in a village-tract shall burn or bury or deposit the corpse of a human being in or at any place other than a burial ground set apart by the headman.

5. No person residing in a village-tract shall allow any latrine or cess-pit on any house, enclosure or land occupied by him to be kept in a filthy or insanitary condition. Cess-pits shall be closed periodically.

6. No person residing in a village tract shall build any new house in any village within 20 feet of the front or back or six feet of the side of any existing house.

Rules prescribing duties of the Headman of a village-tract, in respect of public nuisances and sanitation.

7. The headman shall require residents of the village-tract to carry out the provisions of the preceding rules.

8. The headman shall set apart one or more places in each village-tract as burial grounds. /

9. The headman shall cause to be removed immediately from any canal, tank or other source of water-supply within the limits of his village-tract, the dead body of any animal found therein and shall cause the same to be buried.

10. The headman shall set apart in each village under his control one or more wells for drinking purposes, and shall cuase to be constructed round each well a parapet two feet high, and shall not allow bathing or washing of clothes within 20 yards of any such well, and shall not allow the ground within 20 yards of any such well to be defiled by flith, rubbish or otherwise. If the water-supply is from tanks, the headman shall reserve one tank for drinking purposes only, shall keep

clean the banks thereof, and shall not allow bathing, washing of clothes or watering of cattle therein.

11. The headman shall cause the villagers to undertake annually such measures for the maintenance of any the removal of silt from all drinking water tanks in his village-tract which are not the property of private individuals as the Deputy Commissioner, may, on the advice, if necessary, of the Executive Engineer, direct.

12. If so directed by the Deputy Commissioner of the Myitkyina, District in respect of the village-tracts of Myitkyina, Myoma, Minyat and Shanzu in the Myitkyina District, the headmen of these village-tracts shall, during the months of November to May inclusive, reserve the Irrawaddy river above the American Baptist Mission compound for the drawing of water for domestic purposes, and in such case the headman shall not allow bathing, washing of clothes or other articles, watering of cattle or mooring of boats alongside the bank above the said Mission compound.

13A. In the case of villages which are situated near the bank of a river or stream, the headman shall, as far as possible, keep the foreshore free from houses up to a distance of forty feet from the bank. He shall require all houses hereafter built or re-built to face the bank of the river or stream, and shall not allow latrines to be erected between the houses and the bank of the river or stream: Provided that this rule shall not apply in / Lower Burma except to the Thayetmyo District and the Pegu Division.

13B. In the case of villages which are situated near the bank of a river or stream, the water of which is ordinarily used for drinking purposes, the headman shall, as far as possible, keep the foreshore free from houses up to a distance of forty feet from the bank. He shall require all houses hereafter built or re-built to face the bank of the river or stream, and shall not allow latrines to be erected between the houses and the bank of the river or stream: Provided that this rule shall be in force in the Arakan, Irrawaddy and Tenasserim Divisions only.

14. The headman shall see that all latrines in each village under his control are screened by a sufficient roof and wall from the view of passers-by or persons residing in the neighbourhood.

15. The headman shall cause the streets and lanes in each village under his control to be kept free from weeds, in good order, and in a sanitary condition.

16. The headman shall mark out a place near, but outside each village under his control where rubbish may be deposited, and shall cause the rubbish to be burnt or worked into the land at ploughing time. /

ANNEXURE – B.

Sanitation.

42. No earth, sludge, dirt, tailings or other refuse matter from any mine, mill washing shed, stamping-house, water-course, or other place, shall be disposed of otherwise than in accordance with such instructions as the Inspector of Mines may issue from time to time.

Disposal of earth, etc.

43. All rubbish or refuse shall be removed at least once every three days from camp sites and deposited or destroyed or otherwise dealt with to the satisfaction of the Health Officer of the district at such place as subject to his approval may be fixed from time to time.

Removal of refuse, etc.

44. No latrines or cess-pits shall be built at a distance of less than 100 feet from any human habitation and their position shall be periodically changed. The Health Officer of the district may order the removal of any latrine or cess-pit which he considers insanitary.

Latrines.

45. The Health Officer of the district may for sanitary reasons give such directions as he thinks fit in respect of the situation, location or removal of camp sites, and no camp sites shall be situated, located or removed otherwise than in accordance with such directions.

Camp sites.

46. No barracks or cooly lines shall be built on any ground within a camp site, if in the opinion of the Health Officer of the district such ground is from a sanitary point of view not suitable, for the purpose, and any barracks or cooly lines built on such ground shall, if the Health Officer so directs, be removed from one position to another within the camp site.

Cooly barracks, etc.

47. (a) In all barracks or cooly lines constructed after the issue of these rules accommodation shall be provided as follows: –

Construction of cooly barracks.

   (i) Not less than 250 cubic feet for each person between the floor and a parallel plane at the wall plate level;
   (ii) Not less than 30 square feet of floor area per person.
   (b) The building shall be constructed in such a manner that the floor itself shall not be less than three feet from / the ground, and the wall plate eight feet above the floor level.
   (c) The walls shall have a space of not less than 12 inches at the top for ventilation.
   (d) A window for every eight feet length of building shall be provided.
   (e) No cook-house shall form part of a barrack or cooly line.

Construction of cook-houses. 48. Cook-houses shall be built not less than 25 feet from the main buildings for which they are intended. The floors shall be constructed of raised earth, one foot high, with the surface finished with gravel and shall be of such dimensions as to allow a plinth area space of not less than ten square feet per man.

Cattle shed etc., 49. No cattle shed, pig sty, stable or other erection used for housing animals shall be constructed within 100 feet of any dwelling house, well, tank or stream used for drinking or bathing purposes.

Provision for appeal. 50. An appeal shall lie to the District Magistrate from any decision or order of the Health Officer of the district under this Chapter within twenty days after the receipt of the decision or order by the owner, agent or manager of the mine affected thereby.

FINANCIAL CAPITAL

Currency

In the early part of the period, a major drag on economic growth was the nature of Malayan currency, which comprised a range of coins including the Spanish or Mexican dollar, the British North Borneo dollar, the rupee, the yen, the US dollar and the Dutch guilder plus private bank notes, primarily used to facilitate trade with Britain and issued by the Asiatic Banking Corp., the Oriental Banking Corp., the Chartered Bank of India, Australia and China, the Hong Kong and Shanghai Bank and the Mercantile Bank of India, London and China. The uncertain value of coinage and occasionally shortages of currency disrupted trade, confidence in private bank notes was damaged by the failure of the Asiatic Banking Corp. in 1866 and the Oriental Banking Corp. in 1884 and all the coins were made of silver, the price of which gradually declined. While the supply of the metal increased with the opening of new American mines, demand fell as countries such as Germany, Scandinavia and the Latin Union (France, Belgium, Italy and Switzerland) abandoned or restricted silver coinage and the exchange banks increasingly used council bills rather than silver to remit funds to India. The value of coinage thus fell against gold, on which the currency of Europe was based, damaging Britain's economic presence in the country. Although exports were cheaper, increasing Malaya's competitiveness, the value of profits plus the salaries of colonial officers repatriated to Britain were greatly diminished. Moreover, British imports were more expensive, reducing demand, though this impact was counterbalanced by the fall in world commodity prices, and the fluctuations in the value of silver made it difficult for businesses to plan ahead.

The British government overcame the shortages of currency and lack of confidence in bank notes by establishing in 1898 the silver Straits dollar as Malaya's currency and founding a Currency Board to oversee its distribution and replace the various banks as the issuer of notes. To ensure that the coins and notes could always be exchanged for gold, the Board kept in London a reserve, equivalent to the currency in circulation, 70 per cent of which was invested in the securities of the UK and 30 per cent in colonial government stock, largely Straits Settlement's securities. In 1906, to resolve the problems created by the depreciation of silver, the value of the Straits dollar, along with that of the British North Borneo and Sarawak dollars, was pegged to sterling at a rate of 2*s* 4*d* per dollar.[1]

The linking of the dollar to sterling and the activities of the Currency Board were the subject of much controversy. Supporters claimed that exchange rate stability facilitated trade and that the Board's control of the issue of coinage and notes spared the administration the problems and risks of currency management and reduced the likelihood of over-issue and inflation. The size of the reserve and its investment in UK government securities, meanwhile, gave the currency credibility and the large Malayan holdings helped to maintain the price of these securities, encouraging investors to subscribe to further government loans. Critics argued that the exchange rate had been fixed at too high a level and greatly damaged the economy, especially after 1920 when the terms of trade turned against the region, and linking the currency to sterling made the region more susceptible to fluctuations in world market prices and tightened its trade relationship with Britain, which did not always offer the best prices for its goods. As regards the Currency Board, it deprived the government of control over its own monetary policy, its withdrawal of coins and notes in slumps accentuated economic contraction by reducing credit and increasing loan risk and its reserves benefitted the Imperial economy, helping to underpin British financial institutions and the world role of sterling, at the expense of Malaya. The reserves were too large, the UK government securities in which they were largely invested paid relatively low interest rates and their investment in the local economy would have assisted economic growth, particularly during downturns.[2]

Burma's currency comprised the silver rupee and bank notes initially issued by the Indian presidency banks and, from 1861, the Indian government. As in Malaya, the fall in the price of silver reduced the value of the rupee, which again damaged Britain's economic returns from the country and also increased the size of India's 'home charges', the funds transferred to London to meet its government's various financial commitments in the UK. To overcome these problems, it was first decided in 1893 that India and Burma should have a gold currency, and, in 1898, that the silver rupee should be retained, but its value fixed to gold at an exchange rate of 1*s* 4*d*, substantially lower than that adopted in Malaya. In 1920, the rate was increased to 2*s*, largely because of a rise in the price of silver caused by shortages. Within India and Burma, the First World War had seen the hoarding of coins and had disrupted shipments of specie, and, in the wider world, there were falls in Mexican output, large purchases at high prices by the US to restore its depleted stocks and greater demand for silver coinage fuelled by the post-war boom. Inevitably, the higher rate led to protests from exporters, who claimed that it threatened their livelihoods, and, a mere few months later, it was abandoned and replaced by one of 1*s* 6*d*, which ruled till the end of the period.[3]

Sources of Finance

The main sources of finance in the region were banks, pawnbrokers and mon-eylenders. Malaya was well served with private sector banks possessing in 1940 sixty-eight (15.64 per million population), as compared to French Indo-China's twenty-three (1.07 per million population) and Siam's twelve (1.04 per million population). To provide banking facilities for lower income groups, the government also established a Post Office Savings Bank and promoted the formation of plantation/mine thrift societies and urban loan societies. By the end of the period, there were 57,000 Post Office Savings Bank accounts holding $14.3m, 338 thrift societies with 61,120 members and paid-up capital of $1.9m, and seventy-six loan societies with 30,626 members and paid-up capital of $6.393m.[4] The banking sector comprised European and Chinese institutions. The first European bank to operate in the country was the Oriental bank, which arrived in 1846. It was followed by the Chartered Mercantile Bank of India, London and China in 1856, the Chartered Bank of India, Australia & China in 1859 and the Hong Kong & Shanghai Banking Corp. in 1877; these three organizations dominating the sector until the end of the period. Their high returns and the increase in foreign trade attracted non-British banks and, by the turn of the century, the Netherlands Indies Commercial Bank, the Netherlands Trading Society, N. I. Handelsbank, the International Banking Corp., the First National City Bank of New York and Banque de L' Indochine had all established offices, generally in Singapore and/or Penang. All were international, having branches across South East Asia and in other commercially important countries.[5]

The banks' principal activity was the short-term finance of the region's trade with the West and the provision of foreign exchange, functions facilitated by their close relationships with the major Agency Houses with which they often shared directors. Other activities included the holding of largely European deposits and, in the case of the three dominant institutions, of government funds; the setting of interest rates through the Bankers' Association; the disposal of demonetized coin; and, until 1906, the issue of private bank notes. Theoretically, to ensure that the notes could be exchanged for coin, the issuing banks maintained a depreciation fund, one third of which was in specie or bullion and the remainder in first class securities. In reality, to maximize the money they lent out at interest, they only covered a small proportion of the notes issued and their reserves contained less than first class securities. Oddly, there was little non-foreign trade lending. Managements were reluctant to lock up money for long periods in ventures such as rubber plantations or tin mines, the profitability of which was largely determined by fluctuating world prices. They also had few contacts with the Chinese business community and there was an expectation in Head Offices that overseas branches would annually remit home large amounts of cash. The loans that were made were negotiated by Chinese Compradors, who, working on a commission basis, acted as an intermediary between the bank and the borrower and generally required significant collateral, usually in the form of property mortgages.[6]

The first Chinese Bank was Kwong Yik Bank, established in 1903 in Singapore. It was followed by the Sze Hai Tong Bank in 1906, the Chinese Commercial Bank in 1912, the Kwong Yik (Selangor) Banking Corp. in 1913, the Ho Hong Bank in 1917 and the Overseas Chinese Bank in 1919. By 1934, thirteen banks were in existence, eleven in the Straits Settlements and two in the FMS. Almost all were limited companies obtaining their capital from shareholders, who were largely Chinese businessmen with interests in *entrepôt* and retail trade, mining and plantation agriculture and members of a specific dialect group. Kwong Yik Bank's founders and shareholders, for example, were Cantonese, the Kwong Yik (Selangor) Banking Corp.'s Teochew and Ho Hong Bank's Hokkien. Although they financed trade and provided foreign exchange, their main activities were the taking of deposits and the provision of loans and advances. Less intimidating than their European counterparts and backed by funds from well-known and trusted local businessmen, they attracted large amounts of deposits, many relatively small. As they had few connections with the European business community, these were largely re-lent to Chinese businessman on collateral of up to 50 per cent of the sum lent.[7]

The banks were notoriously vulnerable to collapse. Depositors were quick to withdraw funds and total deposits were closely related to the prosperity of the rubber industry and prone to large fluctuations; quadrupling during the First World War and doubling in 1924/5, but halving between 1919 and 1922 and falling by a fifth from 1929 to 1932. Unlike their European counterparts, they possessed no access to international capital markets, the Currency Boards refused to act as lenders of last resort and their shareholders' fortunes like those of their depositors were closely linked to the rubber industry. Their banking practices also left much to be desired. Influenced by the Western financial community that preferred a laissez-faire commercial environment, the government failed to introduce banking regulation. Chinese bank reserves were thus small or non-existent, large advances were made to directors, other loans granted on the basis of the borrower's creditworthiness or relationship with the bank and loan repayment dates were often deferred, often indefinitely.[8]

The first bank to collapse was the Kwong Yik Bank, which went bankrupt in 1913 as a result of director mismanagement. More disappeared in the early 1920s and, in 1932, a major financial crisis forced the Ho Hong Bank, the Oversea-Chinese Bank and a smaller competitor to merge, forming the Oversea-Chinese Banking Corp. All three banks had lent large sums to the Chinese entrepreneur Tan Kah Kee, whose business empire fell apart in 1931, and held large amounts of unhedged Hong Kong and Indonesian currency, the exchange rate value of which fell when Britain and Malaya left the Gold Standard in September 1931. By 1940, the Chinese banking sector was thus much changed, comprising the Oversea-Chinese Banking Corp. and six far smaller institutions that catered to specific market niches. To avoid a further crash, money was lent only to low risk clients, reserves of 50 per cent of deposits were maintained and held at European banks and all lending was at call, borrowers having to repay sums when required to do so.[9]

Elsewhere in British South East Asia, banking was far less developed. The banking scene in British North Borneo was dominated by the Chartered Bank of India, Australia & China and the Hong Kong & Shanghai Banking Corp., which was also the largest financial institution in Brunei and Siam. In Burma, which in 1940 possessed thrity-four banks (2.31 per million population), the major players were the Chartered Mercantile Bank of India, London & China; the Chartered Bank of India, Australia & China; Dawson's Bank, with eleven branches that concentrated on the provision of long-term loans to Burmese rice growers; and the Bank of Bengal, which had branches in Rangoon, Moulmein and Akyab. The latter bank in 1921 merged with two Indian competitors to form the Imperial Bank of India. Opening branches in Mandalay (1921), Bassein (1921) and Myingyan (1924), this new institution financed the rice trade, lent sums to rice farmers and acted as a central bank, operating the country's cheque clearing system, holding the reserves of the other European banks and providing them with advances during downturns.[10]

As regards non-banking sources of finance, many entrepreneurs and farmers financed their business activities through credit provided by the purchasers of their goods, as discussed in the Trade thematic introduction in Volume 2, or via their own resources, which were invested in land, property and jewellery that could be sold off when needed, pawned or provided as collateral for loans.[11] Others turned to pawnbrokers and moneylenders. Pawnshops were most commonly found in Malaya and first appeared in Penang and Singapore in the early nineteenth century. From 1823 in Singapore, 1830 in the Straits and 1874 in the FMS, governments sold off the right to issue pawnshop licences to the highest bidder, generally Chinese entrepreneurs with interests in mining, plantation agriculture and trade, who generally issued a number of licences to themselves and sold off the remainder. Low Kim Pong, who obtained the right to issue twenty-six licences in Singapore, for instance, personally owned and operated thirteen pawnshops. The main benefit of the system was that it minimized government administration costs. The drawback was that it tended to raise interest rates – successful bidders charged high fees for the licences they sold, which the purchasers passed onto those who pawned their goods, some of whom were charged rates of up to 90 per cent pa.

Aware that the rates slowed economic growth, the Straits Legislative Council in 1889, followed by its FMS counterpart in 1908, established government departments that sold by tender individual pawnshop licences and set maximum interest rates. The resultant falls in revenue prompted the wealthier Chinese capitalists to leave the sector to be replaced by less ambitious entrepreneurs. In the FMS, these were initially Hakka and Cantonese businessmen, many of whom were based in Singapore, and, after the collapse of a Chinese bank in which the Cantonese pawnbrokers were major shareholders, largely Hakka. Their customers comprised Chinese and Indian immigrant workers and Malays, who used the advances obtained to fund various rites of passage ceremonies. The amount advanced was generally far less than the resale value of the article pawned, loan interest rates ranged from 24 to 60 per cent pa, and, if the loan was not repaid, as was the case in 90 per cent of advances provided in Singapore, the pawned article would be sold. To accumulate operating capital, many pawnshops also acted as quasi-banks, taking deposits on which they paid interest.[12]

Moneylending was dominated by the Chettiars from Tamil Nadu, who largely operated in Burma, and, to a lesser extent, in Malaya, the Dutch East Indies, Siam and French Indo-China. They arrived in Burma in the late 1860s and rapidly become the main providers of credit to the rice sector, each firm obtaining the money lent from the owner's own resources and from non-Chettiar and inter-firm deposits. By 1929/30, their total loans amounted to £50m, approximately two thirds of total lending, though in the Hanthawaddy and Tharrawaddy districts this neared 100 per cent. Two thirds of the finance was lent to agriculture, mainly to rice farmers, and the remainder to merchants and businessmen. As discussed in the General Introduction, they provided borrowers with initial capital finance, followed by 'crop' or 'business' loans – advances that were made and repaid each year and corresponded to the cultivators/business owners' annual expenses. Interest rates were high and collateral comprised land or property, with the result that over time as loans went unpaid most Chettiars became major landowners. Not surprisingly, this trend generated much anger within the local agricultural community, particularly in the 1930s, and, after the Second World War, only a few Chettiars recommenced their former activities.[13]

Note: Information on financial capital can also be found in the following sources/themes:

Topic	Source	Volume/Theme
Burmese money lending	F. Noel-Paton, *Burma Rice* (paragraphs 79–86)	Volume 1/Agriculture
Malayan Post Office Savings Bank	C. S Alexander, *British Malaya: Malayan Statistics*	Volume 3/Human Capital

Notes

1. A. Kaur, "'Hantu' and Highway: Transport in Sabah 1881–1963', *Modern Asian Studies*, 28:1 (1994), pp. 1–49, on pp. 13–14; H. A. Shannon, 'The Modern Colonial Sterling

Exchange Standard', *Staff Papers, International Monetary Fund*, 2:2 (1952), pp. 318–64, on p. 340; W. G. Huff, 'Monetization and Financial Development in Southeast Asia before the Second World War', *Economic History Review*, 56:2 (2003), pp. 300–45, on pp. 308–9; D. Sunderland, *Financing the Raj. The City of London and Colonial India, 1858–1940* (London: Boydell & Brewer, 2013), pp. 138–9; W. L. Ken, 'Singapore: Its Growth as an Entrepot Port, 1819–1941', *Journal of Southeast Asian Studies*, 9:1 (1978), pp. 62–3; H. D. Chiang, 'The Origin of the Malayan Currency System', *Journal of the Malaysian Branch Royal Asiatic Society*, 39 (1976), pp. 1–18; W. Bailey and K. Bhaop-ichitr, 'How Important Was Silver? Some Evidence on Exchange Rate Fluctuations and Stock Returns in Colonial-Era Asia', *Journal of Business*, 77:1 (2004), pp. 137–73, on p. 143; F. H. H. King, 'Sterling Balances and the Colonial Monetary Systems', *Economic Journal*, 65:260 (1955), pp. 719–21, on p. 719; Anon., 'A Survey of Singapore's Mone-tary History, *Monetary Authority of Singapore, Occasional Paper*, 18 (2000), pp. 1–34, on p. 15. See also W. E. Nelson, 'The Gold Standard in Mauritius and the Straits Settlements Between 1850 and 1914', *Journal of Imperial & Commonwealth History*, 16:1 (1987), pp. 48–76. In 1898, the Board introduced 5 and 10 dollar notes, followed in 1901 by notes worth 50 and 100 dollars, in 1906 one dollar, in 1917 and 1920 respectively 10 and 25 cents, and, in 1930, 1,000 dollars.

2. W. G. Huff, 'Boom-or-Bust Commodities and Industrialization in Pre-World War II Malaya', *Journal of Economic History*, 62:4 (2002), pp. 1074–115, on p. 1080; A. Booth 'The Transition in Open Dualistic Economies in Southeast Asia: Another Look at the Evidence', *XIV International Economic History Congress* (2006), pp. 1–39, on p. 8; W. G. Huff, 'Currency Boards and Chinese Banks in Malaya and the Philippines before World War II', *Australian Economic History Review*, 43:2 (2003), pp. 125–39, on pp. 127, 132; King, 'Sterling Balances', p. 719.

3. Sunderland, *Financing*, pp. 14, 140, 149–52.

4. G. Huff, 'Gateway Cities and Urbanisation in Southeast Asia before World War II', *University of Oxford Discussion Papers in Economic and Social History*, 96 (2012), pp. 1–45, on p. 39; R. Winstedt, 'Southeastern Asia and the Philippines', *Annals of the American Academy of Political and Social Science*, 226 (1943),), pp. 97–111, on p. 107; Consulton Research Bureau, *The First Hundred Years of the Post Office Savings Bank of Singapore* (Singapore: Post Office Savings Bank, 1977), pp. 11–12.

5. Huff, 'Monetization', p. 320; W. T. Yuen, 'Chinese Capitalism in Colonial Malaya, 1900–1941' (DPhil. dissertation, University of Hong Kong, 2010),), pp. 1–130, on p. 64; L. Sheng-Yi, *The Monetary and Banking Development of Malaysia and Singapore* (Singapore: Singapore University Press, 1974), pp. 66–70. The American International Banking Corp., for example, had offices in China, Japan, India and the Philippines.

6. G. Jones and J. Wale, 'Merchants as Business Groups: British Trading Companies in Asia before 1945', *Business History Review*, 72:3 (1998),), pp. 367–408, on pp. 391–2; Huff, 'Boom-or-Bust', pp. 1082, 1086; Huff, 'Monetization', pp. 320, 328; Huff, 'Cur-rency', p. 131; Yuen, 'Chinese Capitalism', p. 498; D. Sunderland, *Managing the British Empire: The Crown Agents for the Colonies 1833–1914* (London: Royal Historical Soci-ety/Boydell & Brewer, 2004), pp. 246, 248–9; N. Horesh, 'Between Legal and Illegal Tender: The Chartered Bank and Its Notes in and around China, 1864–1939', *Modern China*, 34:2 (2008), pp. 276–98, on p. 282. The reserves of the Chartered Bank of India, Australia and China covered only a third of the $4m notes it had issued by 1898 and contained $237,500 of 5 per cent Japanese stock that was only marketable in Japan (Sun-derland, *Managing the British Empire*, pp. 248–9).

7.   J. Lim, 'Chinese Merchants in Singapore and the China Trade, 1819–1959', *Chinese Southern Diaspora Studies*, 5 (2011–12),), pp. 79–115, on p. 92; Yuen, 'Chinese Capitalism', pp. 462–5; Huff, 'Currency', pp. 129–30 Huff, 'Monetization', p. 321 Smaller banks included the Lee Wah Bank in Singapore, the Bank of Malaya in Ipoh and the Batu Pahat Bank in Batu Pahat, Johore (T. Ee-Leong, 'The Chinese Banks Incorporated in Singapore and the Federation of Malaya', *JMBRAS*, 31:1 (1953),), pp. on pp. 137–8).

8.   Huff, 'Currency', pp. 130, 132; Huff, 'Monetization', p. 322; Yuen, 'Chinese Capitalism', p. 467.

9.   Lim, 'Chinese Merchants', p. 14; Huff, 'Currency', pp. 132, 135–6; Yuen, 'Chinese Capitalism', p. 497; Huff, 'Monetization', p. 322; W. G. Huff, 'Sharecroppers, Risk, Management, and Chinese Estate Rubber Development in Interwar British Malaya', *Economic Development and Cultural Change*, 40:4 (1992),), pp. 743–73, on p. 745. The niche market bankers were the Sze Hai Tong Bank, the United Chinese Bank and the Lee Wah Bank, all of which were based in Singapore, the Kwong Yik (Selangor) Banking Corp. in Kuala Lumpur, the Ban Hin Lee Bank in Penang and the Batu Pahat Bank in Batu Pahat, Johore (Yuen, 'Chinese Capitalism', p. 497).

10. Shannon, 'The Modern', p. 343; Huff, 'Gateway Cities', p. 24; Anon., 'Central Banking at the Periphery of the British Empire: Colonial Burma, 1886–1937', available online at http://www.econ.mq.edu.au/Econ_docs/research_papers2/2005_research_papers/ Centbanking_Burma.pdf [accessed 4 December 2013], p. 6–7.

11. Huff, 'Monetization', p. 331; Winstedt, 'Southeastern Asia', p. 107.

12. Yuen, 'Chinese Capitalism', pp. 438–9, 441–4, 451–2, 455–7; D. Chua and T. T. W. Tan, 'Hakkas in the Pawnbroking Trade', in T. T. W. Tan (ed.), *Chinese Dialect Groups: Traits and Trades* (Singapore: Opinion Books, 1990), pp. 67–77.

13. C. S. Hwa, 'The Chettyars in British Burma', *Peninjarah*, 2:1 (1967), pp. 12–18; M. Adas, 'Immigrant Asians and the Economic Impact of European Imperialism: The Role of the South Indian Chettiars in British Burma', *Journal of Asian Studies*, 33:3 (1974), pp. 385–401; R. Mahadevan, 'Immigrant Entrepreneurs in Colonial Burma – An Exploratory Study of the Role of Nattukottai Chettiars of Tamil Nadu, 1880–1930', *Indian Economic & Social History Review*, 15:3 (1978), pp. 329–58; S. Turnell and A. Vicary, 'Parching the Land?: The Chettiars in Burma', *Australian Economic History Review*, 48:1 (2008), pp. 1–25, on pp. 1, 5–7, 9–11, 15–22.

STRAITS SETTLEMENTS GOVERNMENT LOAN . ISSUE OF £4 PER CENT. FIVE YEAR CONVERTIBLE BONDS SUFFICIENT TO RAISE £5,000,000. AUTHORISED BY ORDINANCE NO. 4 OF 1907 (1907)

Straits Settlements Government Loan . Issue of £4 per cent. Five Year Convertible Bonds Sufficient to Raise £5,000,000. Authorised by Ordinance No. 4 of 1907, National Archives, CAOG 9/36.

The following source is the prospectus for Malaya's first loan to be issued on the London capital market. Colonial securities were floated by the Crown Agents and were sold for a set price and offered a given annual rate of interest. They were bought largely by stock brokers, retailers of securities, who in the fullness of time sold them onto the public at a profit. After flotation, they were quoted on the Stock Market and their post-issue price, which rose and fell according to demand and supply, was published each day in the Stock Exchange *Daily List*. A full description of the issue process and an explanation of the terms used in prospectuses can be found in D. Sunderland, *Managing the British Empire: The Crown Agents for the Colonies 1833–1914* (London: Royal Historical Society/ Boydell & Brewer, 2004), ch. 6. As discussed in the General Introduction, the 1907 loan attracted public subscriptions of only £753,600, forcing £1.5m of the stock to be purchased by the Crown Agents for Crown colony Investment Funds and the remainder by its underwriters, who gradually offloaded their purchases onto the retail market.

Straits Settlements Government Loan . Issue of £4 per cent. Five Year Convertible Bonds Sufficient to Raise £5,000,000. Authorised by Ordinance No. 4 of 1907 (1907)

Price of Issue £99 per cent.

£5 per cent. on application, and the balance payable as under: –

£19 per cent. on the 30th April.	£15 per cent. on the 19th August.
£15 per cent. on the 6th June.	£15 per cent. on the 23rd September.
£15 per cent. on the 15th July.	£15 per cent. on the 28th October.

Interest payable 15th May and 15th November. A Coupon payable 15th November, 1907, representing interest at the rate of 4 per cent. per annum from the dates of the instalments, will be attached to the Scrip Certificates.[1]

The Bonds are convertible at the option of the holders during their currency into Strait Settlements £3½ per cent. Inscribed Stock 1937 – 1967 on the terms mentioned hereafter.

The Government of the Straits Settlements having complied with the requirements of the Colonial Stock Act, 1900, as announced in the "London Gazette" of the 23rd September, 1902, Trustees are authorised to invest in this Stock, subject to the restrictions set forth in the Trustee Act, 1893.

The Loan is raised for the payment of the Award and Costs – £3,390.000 – in connection with the expropriation by the Colonial Government of the Tanjong Pagar Docks, and for providing the funds required for the improvement and extension of such Docks, and for carrying out various other Public Works in the Colony.

THE CROWN AGENTS FOR THE COLONIES, on behalf of the Government of the Straits Settlements, hereby invite applications for the above Loan.

Shareholders of the Tanjong Pagar Dock Company who may desire to participate in the Loan will be granted preferential allotment in respect of their holdings of Shares, provided that they apply on a special form of application, which can be obtained at Whitehall Gardens or No. 1, Tokenhouse Buildings.

The Loan is secured on the General Revenues and Assets of the Government of the Straits Settlements, and will be raised in the form of Debentures representing £1000, £500, and £100 respectively, bearing interest at the rate of £4 per cent. per annum, payable half yearly on the 15th of May and 15th of November in each year.

Interest and Principal will be payable at the Office of the Crown Agents for the Colonies, Whitehall Gardens, London.

And Bonds which may remain unconverted on the 15th of May 1912 will be paid off at par at that date.

Applications, which must be accompanied by a deposit of £5 per cent., will be received at the Offices of the Crown Agents for the Colonies, Whitehall Gardens, S.W., and No. 1, Tokenhouse Buildings, E.C.

The list will be closed on or before Wednesday, the 24th day of April, but applications from Shareholders of the Tanjong Pagar Dock Company resident in this country will be received up to the first post on Friday, the 26th of April; and a further reasonable extension of time will be granted in the case of Shareholders resident in the Straits Settlements.

In case of partial allotment, the balance of the amount paid on deposit will be applied towards the payment of the first instalment. If there should be a surplus after making that / payment, such surplus will be refunded by cheque. Application may be for the whole or any part of the issue, and no allotment will be made of a less amount than £100 or multiple thereof.

The first payment must accompany the application, and the subsequent payment are to be made at the Crown Agents' Transfer Office, No. 1, Tokenhouse Buildings, E.C., not later than the dates above mentioned.

Payment may be made in full on the 30th day of April, or any subsequent date prior to the 28th of October, under discount of £3½ per cent, per annum, but payments made prior to the 30th April will be subject to discount from that date only.

In the case of default in the payment of any instalment at its due date, the deposit and instalments previously paid will be liable to forfeiture.

After payment by the allottees of the instalment due on allotment, they will receive at the Crown Agents' Transfer Office, No. 1, Tokenhouse Buildings, E.C., in exchange for the Letter of Allotment and Receipt, Scrip Certificates, representing the Debentures to which they will become entitled. These Certificates will be ready for delivery on and after the 4th of June.

CONVERSION INTO STOCK.

The holders of fully paid Letters of Allotment or of Scrip Certificates as soon as they are paid in full, and of the Debentures, will have the option at any time prior to the 15th of February, 1912 on surrender of the Certificates or Debentures, with all undue coupons[2] attached, of converting the some into Straits Settlements Government £3½ per cent. Inscribed Stock 1937 – 1967 on the following terms. At any time between –

			Stock.
The 15th May, 1907	and the	14th May, 1908	£105
The 15th May, 1908	"	14th May, 1909	£104
The 15th May, 1909	"	14th May, 1910	£103
The 15th May, 1910	"	14th May, 1911	£102
The 15th May, 1911	"	15th Feb. 1912	£101

for each £100 of Debentures.

The Stock will be repayable on the 15th of May, 1967, by a Sinking Fund to be formed in this country under the management of the Crown Agents, who are appointed Trustees; but the Government of the Straits Settlements wilt have the option of redemption at par on or after the 15th of May, 1937, on giving six calendar months' notice by advertisement in the *London Gazette* and in the *Times* newspaper, or by post to the then Stockholders at their registered addresses.

The interest, at the rate of £3½ per cent. per annum, will be payable half-yearly, on the 15th of May and 15th of November in each year, by Dividend Warrants, which, if desired, may be transmitted by post, either to the Stockholder, or other person, bank, or firm, within the United Kingdom. Principal and Interest will be payable at the Office of the Grown Agents for the Colonies. London.

The Stock will be transferable at the Crown Agents' Transfer Office, No, 1, Tokenhouse Buildings, E.C. without charge and free of stamp duty.

Stock Certificates to Bearer, of the denominations of £1000, £500 and £100, with coupons for the half-yearly dividends attached, will be obtainable in exchange for Inscribed Stock at the Crown Agents' Transfer Office, No. 1, Tokenhouse Buildings, E.C., on payment of the prescribed fees, and such certificates can, if desired, be re-inscribed.

The revenues of the Colony of the Straits Settlements alone are liable in respect of the above Stock, and the dividends thereon, and the Consolidated Fund of the United Kingdom and the Commissioners of His Majesty's Treasury are not directly or indirectly liable or responsible for the payment of the Stock or of the dividends thereon or for any matter relating thereto (Act 40 and 41, Viet. Cap. 59.)

Forms of Application and a Statistical Statement relative to the Revenue, Expenditure, and Trade of the Colony from 1896 to 1906 inclusive, and a Memorandum as to the financial position of the Colony, which has been prepared by the Government of the Straits Settlements, may be obtained by applying at the Offices of the Crown Agents for the Colonies in Whitehall Gardens, S.W., and at No. 1, Tokenhouse Buildings, E.C.; at that or Messrs, MULLENS, MARSHALL and Co., 13 George Street, Mansion House, E.C.; of Messrs, J. and A. SCRIMGEOUR, South Sea House, Threadneedle Street, E.C.; of the Hong Kong and Shanghai Banking Corporation, 31 Lombard Street, E.C.; and of the Chartered Bank of India, Australia, and China, Hatton Court, Threadneedle Street, E.C.; and copies of the Ordinances under which the Loan is raised may be seen on application at the Office of the Crown Agents in Whitehall Gardens.

OFFICE OF THE CROWN AGENTS FOR THE COLONIES,
    WHITEHALL GARDENS, LONDON,
        22nd April, 1907. /

                        No. _____

STRAITS SETTLEMENTS GOVERNMENT

£4 per cent. Five Year Convertible Bonds.

Issue of £4 per cent. Bonds, sufficent to raise £5,000,000.
AUTHORISED BY ORDINANCE No, 4 OF 1907.

To THE CROWN AGENTS FOR THE COLONIES,
        WHITEHALL GARDENS, SW.

GENTLEMEN,

    hereby apply for £ _____ say _____ pounds of Straits Settlements Government £4 per cent. Five Year Convertible Bonds, subject to the conditions contained in the Prospectus of the 22nd April, 1907, and undertake to pay £99 for every £100 of Bonds, and to accept the same, or any less amount that may be allotted to _____ and to pay for the same in conformity with the terms of the said Prospectus.

    _____ enclose the required deposit of £ _____, being £5 per cent. on the *nominal amount* applied for.

Name _____

(*State whether Mr., Mrs., or Miss, and Title, if any.*)

PLEASE WRITE Address _____
DISTINCTLY. Date _____ April, 1907

NOTE. – No commission will be allowed to Brokers unless their name appears on the Application.

N.B. – Application must be for even hundreds of Bonds, and must be accompanied by the amount of Deposit thereon, and the Application must be enclosed in an envelope, marked outside "Application for Straits Settlements Government Loan."

ANON., *AVERAGE PRICES, DECLARED TRADE VALUES, EXCHANGE AND CURRENCY, VOLUME AND AVERAGE VOLUME OF IMPORTS AND EXPORTS, MARKET PRICES AMD COST OF LIVING* (1930, 1939)

Anon., *Average Prices, Declared Trade Values, Exchange and Currency, Volume and Average Volume of Imports and Exports, Market Prices and Cost of Living* (Singapore: Government Publication, 1930), p. 26.

Anon., *Average Prices, Declared Trade Values, Exchange and Currency, Volume and Average Volume of Imports and Exports, Market Prices and Cost of Living* (Singapore: Government Publication, 1939), p. 39.

The following two sources record currency notes in circulation by month (1914–39) and specie in circulation by year (1925–39) within the Straits Settlements. As discussed in the thematic introduction, the issue of currency was controlled by the Currency Board and was positively related to economic activity.

Anon., *Average Prices, Declared Trade Values, Exchange and Currency, Volume and Average Volume of Imports and Exports, Market Prices and Cost of Living* (1930), extract

Table XIV

CURRENCY NOTES IN CIRCULATION

This table is inserted owing to the recognised relationship between the quantity of currency in circulation and prices.

I.

STRAITS SETTLEMENTS CURRENCY NOTES

VALUE IN CIRCULATION ON 1ST OF MONTH

(Extracted from *Gazette* Returns)

Millions of Dollars

	1914	1916	1917	1918	1919	1920	1921	1922	1923	1924	1925	1926	1927	1928	1929	1930
January	43.7	59.8	68.2	87.0	86.4	183.2	96.4	84.5	72.8	81.1	85.4	161.4	163.3	117.8	115.6	104.2
February	43.8	61.0	75.5	87.1	86.4	183.2	94.7	84.5	75.4	83.6	87.7	163.5	163.2	118.7	113.0	101.0
March	43.9	64.2	77.8	87.1	86.4	165.4	92.1	80.6	77.2	83.6	87.7	163.5	150.9	118.7	113.0	99.9
April	43.9	64.2	80.0	87.1	86.4	147.8	92.1	71.9	78.4	83.6	87.8	163.4	147.3	118.7	113.0	95.8
May	43.9	64.1	83.0	87.1	87.2	133.5	86.1	71.9	78.6	83.7	87.8	163.4	143.0	118.8	109.2	92.9
June	43.8	64.0	83.0	87.0	87.2	135.1	85.0	71.9	78.6	83.7	92.0	163.4	135.6	115.6	108.2	91.0
July	43.8	64.0	83.3	86.8	97.1	131.0	84.1	71.9	78.7	83.7	103.5	163.4	130.9	115.7	108.0	91.0
August	48.1	63.9	85.0	86.5	103.1	124.3	84.1	71.9	78.7	83.7	107.4	163.4	130.8	115.7	107.5	88.9
September	48.1	63.8	87.1	86.5	132.5	124.3	84.2	72.0	80.2	83.7	111.6	163.4	119.1	115.5	105.1	87.0
October	48.1	63.7	87.1	86.5	141.9	119.3	84.2	72.0	80.2	83.7	119.1	163.4	117.4	115.6	105.1	84.1
November	48.1	64.1	87.1	86.5	147.1	111.2	84.2	72.2	80.2	83.7	130.1	163.3	117.4	115.6	105.2	84.2
December	48.4	68.3	87.1	86.4	174.6	–	84.5	72.9	80.2	83.7	153.4	163.3	117.4	115.6	105.2	84.3

II.
Specie in Circulation.

Amount of Straits Settlements Specie including subsidiary silver coins, copper coins, and nickel coins, in circulation on the 30th September of each year.

($000's)	
1925	17,609
1926	18,411
1927	19,528
1928	19,275
1929	20,001
1930	18,450

Anon., *Average Prices, Declared Trade Values, Exchange and Currency, Volume and Average Volume of Imports and Exports, Market Prices and Cost of Living* (1939), extract

TABLE 15

CURRENCY NOTES IN CIRCULATION 1914 – 1939

This table is inserted owing to the recognised relationship between the quantity of currency in circulation and prices.

I

STRAITS SETTLEMENTS CURRENCY NOTES
VALUE IN CIRCULATION ON 1ST OF MONTH
(Extracted from *Gazette* Returns)

Millions of Dollars

	1914	1929	1930	1931	1932	1933	1934	1935	1936	1937	1938	1939
January	43·7	115·6	104·2	82·4	67·4	68·5	67·0	75·8	77·1	84·0	105·0	105·3
February	43·8	113·0	101·0	81·4	67·5	68·5	67·0	75·8	77·6	87·8	105·2	105·3
March	43·9	113·0	99·9	80·6	68·1	68·5	67·2	77·0	77·6	92·2	105·2	105·0
April	43·9	113·0	95·8	77·7	68·2	67·0	67·6	77·0	78·0	92·6	105·2	105·1
May	43·9	109·2	92·9	74·3	68·2	66·8	67·6	77·0	78·0	97·6	105·2	105·2
June	43·8	108·2	91·0	74·4	68·3	66·9	67·8	77·0	78·0	97·6	105·2	105·2
July	43·8	108·0	91·0	74·4	68·4	66·9	68·8	77·0	78·0	97·6	105·3	105·3
August	48·1	107·5	88·9	68·7	68·4	66·9	69·7	77·1	80·0	97·6	105·3	107·2
September	48·1	105·1	87·0	63·6	68·4	66·9	72·5	77·1	80·0	99·0	105·3	107·2
October	48·1	105·1	84·1	61·6	68·4	66·9	73·4	77·1	80·8	103·7	105·3	118·0
November	48·1	105·2	84·2	62·1	68·5	66·9	73·9	77·1	82·9	104·4	105·3	123·9
December	48·4	105·2	84·3	63·1	68·5	67·0	74·5	77·1	82·9	104·8	105·3	125·7
Annual Average	45·6	109·0	92·0	72·0	68·2	67·3	69·7	76·8	79·2	96·6	105·2	109·9

II
Specie in Circulation

Amount of Straits Settlements Specie, including subsidiary silver coins, copper coins and nickel coins, in circulation on the 30th September of each year except 1938 and 1939 as under the new Currency Ordinance the accounts are closed on 31st December.

($000's)		($000's)	
1929	20,001	1935	15,777
1930	18,449	1936	15,862
1931	16,428	1937	16,840
1932	15,209	1938	17,205
1933	14,989	1939	17,978
1934	15,379		

ANTHONISZ, *CURRENCY REFORM IN THE STRAITS SETTLEMENTS* (1915)

J. O. Anthonisz, *Currency Reform in the Straits Settlements* (London: R. W. Simpson & Co, 1915), pp. 1–21, 24–46.

James Oliver Anthonisz (1860–1921) was variously the Treasurer of the Straits Settlements and Acting Resident Councillor of Penang (29 April 1910–18 January 1911). The extract from his 1915 book provides an insider's account of the move to a gold based currency and the fixing of the dollar at 2*s* 4*d*.

J. O. Anthonisz, *Currency Reform in the Straits Settlements* (1915), extract

CHAPTER I

CURRENCY CHANGES AND THE MEASURES TAKEN TO ESTABLISH A GOLD STANDARD

[...] In 1890 all the orders regulating legal tender were repealed by an Order in Council, and the Mexican dollar was made the standard, the American Trade dollar, the Hong-Kong dollar and half dollar being made unlimited legal tender, and the subsidiary silver coins were made legal tender for two dollars and the copper coins legal tender for one dollar.

In 1895 the British trade dollar was introduced, owing to the scarcity of the Mexican dollars, on the recommendation of a Departmental Currency Committee appointed in 1893 by the Secretary of State for the Colonies, and was made legal tender in Hong-Kong, the Straits Settlements, and Labuan. By the orders of the Governor in Council of 1895 and 1898, the Mexican dollar was still maintained as the standard coin, and the British and Hong-Kong dollars were declared to be the equivalent of the standard. The first order demonetised the American Trade dollar and the second the Japanese yen. /

As regards subsidiary coinage, there is no complete record of the silver coins struck prior to 1871. After the closing of the Hong-Kong Mint, arrangements were made with the Royal Mint to carry on the work, and since 1871 until very recently all subsidiary silver coins were struck at the Birmingham Mint.[1] The twenty cent piece was the highest denomination until 1886, when a token fifty cent piece was introduced.

At the time, then, when measures were taken to make a Government issue of paper currency, the metallic currency consisted of unlimited legal tender dollars, mainly Mexican and British; subsidiary silver of the following denominations: fifty, twenty, ten, and five cent pieces; and copper coins, one cent, a large proportion of which were British North Borneo and Sarawak cents, and half cent and quarter cent pieces which were gradually disappearing, owing to the general rise of prices following the depreciation of the dollar. The dollars were imported by the Banks in response to public demand and the requirements of trade, the British dollars from the Bombay Mint and the Mexican dollars viâ San Francisco and London. The Government were only responsible for the subsidiary coin, and the profits from this coinage, which were considerable, were paid into revenue. This seemed such a sure and easy way of getting revenue that the administrations of the Malayan Native States, Perak, Selangor, and Negri Sambilan, which absorbed a considerable portion of this / subsidiary coinage, claimed a portion of the profits, and were allowed the privilege of coining what was necessary for their requirements and of keeping the profits. This privilege was withdrawn after the establishment of the gold standard. In addition, there were bank notes issued by the Chartered Bank of India, Australia, and China, and the Hong Kong and Shanghai Bank. They were not legal tender, but were readily accepted.

The most important measure in the history of the Straits currency, before it was put on a gold basis, was undoubtedly the establishment of a Government Note Issue. The Colony is indebted to Sir Alexander Swettenham,[2] the Colonial Secretary, and Mr. F. G. Penney, the Treasurer, for its successful inauguration. The Ordinance regulating the issue of Paper Currency was Ordinance No. 4 of 1899, and it followed the lines of the Ordinance provided for Ceylon by the Colonial Office. It was based on the principle that the reserve should fully cover the value of the notes issued. The reserve was kept partly in coin and partly in securities, the proportion fixed by law being a two-third minimum coin reserve and a one-third maximum security reserve. Discretionary power was given by the Ordinance to the Secretary of State to alter this proportion by public notification, and the reduction of the coin reserve to a minimum of one-half of the notes in circulation was sanctioned a few years after the passing of the Ordinance.

The income from investments was first applied to / defray the annually recurrent expenses of management, and to the payment of one per cent of the cost price of the securities to a depreciation fund, the balance being paid into revenue. The revenue, however, had to make good every year, forthwith on the order of the Governor, the amount of the depreciation of the securities not covered by the depreciation fund.

The notes authorised by the Ordinance were one dollar notes with a limited legal tender of ten dollars, and the following of unlimited legal tender: five, ten, twenty, fifty, and one hundred dollar notes, and any multiple of one hundred dollar notes. The legal tender of these notes did not cover a tender by the Currency Commissioners at their office or a tender by the note-issuing Banks in redemption of their own notes. Issues of five, ten, twenty, fifty, and one hundred dollars were made at the beginning, but no one dollar notes were issued until 1905.

This summary, it is hoped, will sufficiently explain the position of the currency of the Colony when the arrangements for carrying into effect the most important change of all – for placing the currency on a gold basis – were begun.

It will be fitting to deal here with the causes which originated the movement on the part of the public in favour of putting the Straits currency on a gold basis, and which impelled its growth in face of much opposition from influential quarters, especially of the Banking interest. /

The adoption of the gold standard by Germany in 1872 led to large withdrawals of their silver coins from circulation; and the French Mint, which had for nearly eighty years accepted silver at the rate of fifteen and a-half pounds of silver to one of gold had to be closed to the silver of private holders. From that day the value of silver gradually declined, and with it the value of the dollar, until, from an exchange value in the neighbourhood of five shillings in 1872, it reached the value of 2/7 3/8 in 1893. With the exception of complaints from individuals who had to make sterling remittances home, the grievances of public officials and others drawing fixed salaries, there was no general uneasiness. Merchants were able to find cover by making forward contracts,[3] and to protect themselves from loss. Some took comfort in the hope that silver could not go on falling indefinitely, and that a reaction was bound to take place, and others in the popular belief that a depreciating currency simulated local produce, and that the profits from exports would leave more money for the purchase of imports and more than counterbalance the evil effects of the fall in the exchange value of the dollar. In 1893, however, it was brought home to the Straits community that silver would go considerably lower, and was likely to stay there, by two momentous events in monetary history. In that year, in India, the Government closed their mints to the free coinage of rupees, and, in the United States, the Sherman Purchase Act, under which / large accumulations of silver bullion had been made by periodical purchases, was repealed. It was considered time to take some action, and a committee was appointed by Sir Cecil Clementi-Smith, the then Governor, composed of Government officials, merchants, and representatives of the Chinese community, to receive the views of representative men of all classes and to suggest remedial measures. Half of the members of this committee were in favour of extending the Indian currency to the Straits Settlements, but the other half, including all the Chinese members, were in favour of the maintenance of a silver standard. They however, recommended that a British dollar of the same weight and fineness as the Mexican dollar should be supplied by Government. The opinion expressed by the only Banker on this committee, in a separate minute, is fairly typical of the attitude taken up by the Banks throughout this controversy. He concludes as follows: "I am in favour of a British dollar following silver as being likely to give impetus to planting enterprise and production generally in the Malay Peninsula, but the Government, before introducing such a coin, must clearly decide never to make it a token." The suggestion, apparently was that the Government should control the supply of the dollar by confining the coinage to silver purchased by them. The British dollar introduced on the recommendation of the Departmental Committee appointed by the Secretary of State was, however, obtainable by / everyone who chose to send silver to the Bombay Mint.

No further representations from the public appear to have been made to the Government until 1897. The rate of exchange in 1892 (2/7 3/8) had by then gone down to 1/11 15/16. In the meantime it is significant that large bodies of wage earners had succeeded in impressing the justice of their claims on their employers. Government servants with a European domicile were granted exchange compensation, viz., half their salaries were paid to them at the rate of three shillings to the dollar, and a few years after the whole of their salaries were paid at that rate; the municipalities followed suit, and all the Banks, some of the mercantile firms, and the Dock Company gave increases to their employees much on the same lines. Officers and engineers on local steamers secured by a strike a considerable rise in their salaries. Professional men raised their charges, and approval was given by the authorities to an increase in solicitors' fees. As regards the income of natives, I take the following statement from a report of a Sub-Committee of the Singapore Chamber of Commerce, appointed in 1897, specially to inquire into the local currency with a view to calling the attention of the Government to the question of converting the Straits currency to a gold standard: "It would appear that the wages of Chinese immigrants have not risen, in any appreciable degree, during the past seven years. This coincides / with what has come to be regarded as one of the most important features in our import trade with gold standard countries, viz., that the income of natives generally is not elastic, and has not kept pace with the rise in prices caused by the depreciation of the dollar."

However correct this statement may be in respect of contract coolies–and the statement is based on information collected from the contract registers at the Chinese Protectorate–it cannot be said to apply to the majority of the old resident labourers in the Colony. The fact remains that wages of domestic servants went up enormously long before their employers received any compensation, and it formed one of the reasons for granting compensation. The assertion, so frequently made by men of influence and experience that the depreciation of the exchange value of the dollar had not affected its purchasing power in relation to local articles, had come to be accepted as an uncontrovertible fact, and was the reason why a much smaller compensation in proportion to their salaries was given, and at a much later date, to the local men employed by the Government, Municipalities, firms, and other employers. An instructive and an interesting proof to the contrary is furnished by the gradual disappearance from the markets of the Colony of the quarter and half cent pieces, which financed all the pettier purchases of the neccessaries of Eastern life. But, although compensation was given by all employers who were able to afford it, the question / was as far removed from a satisfactory solution as ever. The Sub-Committee of the Chamber of Commerce, already referred to, found that, for the great majority of employers, no compensation in any shape or form seemed warranted by the present position of business affairs in the Colony, and fixity of exchange on some distinctly higher basis than the present had become with them an urgent necessity. The Sub-Committee recommended the adoption of the English sovereign as the basis of the currency with a Straits dollar, fixed at two shillings, subsidiary to it, the present subsidiary silver coinage to remain as it was. The *modus operandi* suggested was that a law should be passed at one sitting of the Legislative Council, and simultaneously in the Federated Malay States, without letting the intentions of Government becoming known, that a notice be issued that, within a period of time sufficiently brief to prevent importation, all dollars then circulating in the Colony and the Federated Malay States would be exchanged for currency notes, and that Government should raise a loan In London and import a gold reserve in sovereigns. The question, having been submitted in this concrete form to the Straits Government, was then referred to the authorities of the Federated Malay States for their views and the views of the representatives of the different communities there. Two of the Residents declared in favour of a gold standard. European planters and miners appeared to be equally divided on the / subject, but the United Planters' Association passed a resolution objecting to fixity of exchange on the ground that it was undesirable in the interests of the planting community. The Chinese generally were reported as being probably in favour of the silver standard. The Resident-General, Sir Frank Swettenham,[4] afterwards Governor of the Straits Settlements, was in favour of a gold standard with a silver token dollar, as recommended by the Singapore Chamber of Commerce. The question remained in abeyance until 1902, when Sir Frank Swettenham, who had succeeded to the Governorship, requested the Secretary of State to refer the question to an expert, preferably with Indian experience; and, as a result of this application, a committee was appointed in London with Sir David Barbour[5] as President. This committee will be referred to in this work as the Straits Settlements Currency Committee.

When the fact became known that this committee had been appointed, numerous petitions were sent in from all classes of the community declaring in favour of putting the currency on a gold basis. The most important of these was a general petition signed by all the firms and public companies in the Colony, by employees, both European and native, and also, by a very large number of wealthy and influential Chinese, revenue farmers, ship owners, bankers, merchants, and landowners. All the representatives in London and on the Continent of Straits Settlements firms also forwarded petitions to / the Committee in favour of a gold standard. The Singapore and Penang Chambers of Commerce, the Municipality of Singapore, and the Federated Malay States Planters' Association* made representations to the same effect. A petition signed by nearly all the principal Asiatic traders of Penang also asked for a gold standard. On the other hand, a large majority of the miners expressed a preference for a silver standard, and a numerously-signed petition, almost exclusively Chinese, was presented to the Legislative Council by the only European unofficial member who was opposed to the adoption of a gold standard. It was clear, beyond doubt, that the weight of opinion was strongly in favour of a gold standard as the only possible method of bringing about stability of exchange.

The Straits Settlements Currency Committee issued their report in May, 1903. As to the expediency of the change, after setting out the arguments for and against it, they made this very guarded statement: "While we do not think that a gold standard should be pressed on the Straits Settlements against the wishes of the Government and the people, we are equally of opinion that no objection should be raised on the part of His Majesty's Government to the principle of the change, if the Government of the Straits Settlements, after considering all sides of the question, / should decide finally in favour of an alteration from the silver to the gold standard."

It can be seen from the report that the importance of the principle that the Government should only give the people the form of currency for which they ask was the dominating feature of their scheme, and has a material bearing on the recommendations made by them. It was partly on this account, and partly on account of the inconvenience that would be caused in changing the system of accounts to a rupee basis, that the Straits Settlements Currency Committee rejected the proposal for the extension of the currency of India to the Colony, a proposal which was advocated by a section of the Currency Committee appointed by the Governor in 1893. The same reason made them put aside the scheme of the Sub-Committee of the Singapore Chamber of Commerce appointed in 1897. They considered that the risk of its failure, owing to the possible suspicion and opposition on the part of the native population to a wholesale substitution of notes for dollars, was so great that they could not recommend its adoption.

The plan which they recommended was:–

(1) Gradually to introduce a dollar of the same weight and fineness as the British dollar current in the East to be substituted for the Mexican and British dollars circulating in the Colony, the latter dollars being demonetised as soon as the supply of the new dollars was sufficient to permit of this being done with

---

*   The change of opinion on the part of the Association was probably due to the difficulty of getting capital out from England.

safety. They suggested that a portion of / the coin reserve held against the note issue should be melted down and converted into the new Straits dollars.

(2) That, with the arrival of the first supply of the new dollars, they should be made legal tender and their export prohibited, and that the import of British and Mexican dollars should temporarily be prohibited.

(3) When the currency was largely composed of the new dollars, the British and Mexican dollars should finally be demonetised.

(4) After sufficient dollars had been coined to meet the requirements of business in the currency area, the coinage of dollars would cease, until the exchange value of the dollar had reached whatever value in relation to the sovereign might be decided on by the Government as the future value of the Straits' dollar. After this stage was reached, the Government would issue the new dollars in exchange for gold at the fixed rate.

(5) When the gold standard was established, it would not be indispensable that any gold coins should be made legal tender in the Colony and in the Federated Malay States; but the Government should be prepared not only to give dollars in exchange for sovereigns at the declared rate, but also to give sovereigns in exchange for dollars at the same rate, so long as gold was available, or to give bills on the Crown agents in London based on this rate. Measures were immediately taken to carry these recommendations into effect. Arrangements were / made with the Indian Government for the Bombay Mint to undertake the coinage of the new Straits dollar. The design of the new dollar was decided upon, and an Order was made by the King in Council on 25th June, 1903, empowering the Governor, with the consent of the Secretary of State, to make this dollar legal tender, by proclamation, in the Colony, and to declare that Mexican and British dollars shall cease to be legal tender. In July, the Currency Note Ordinance was amended to allow of coin being taken out of the Note Guarantee Fund for the purpose of reminting. By the middle of August, dollars to the amount of two and a-half millions had been shipped to Bombay, and the Banks were also given permission to ship a limited number of British and Mexican dollars under Government supervision to the Bombay Mint, which was specially authorised to receive them. As soon as these operations were undertaken, it became known at large that the Government of the Straits Settlements purposed recoining all the British and Mexican dollars current in the Colony and the Federated Malay States. Sterling exchange was at the time higher in the Straits than in China and Indo-China, and the Mexican and British dollars began to flow in in considerable quantities, being imported by the Banks and by Chinese speculators. The Government were strongly urged to prohibit forthwith the further importation of these dollars, but, as the new dollars were not ready, they properly declined to take any action beyond warning / the public that they would give no pledge that new dollars would, ultimately, be given for all Mexican and British dollars

current in the Straits Settlements and Federated Malay States, and beyond taking steps to introduce an Ordinance to regulate the import and export of coin into and from the Colony.* This Ordinance empowered the Governor, with the approval of the Secretary of State, to prohibit the importation of any coin, whether legal tender or not, and the exportation of any coin which was legal tender in the Colony; and, also, to exempt any particular country or state from the operation of any such order. The latter power made it possible to put the States of the Malay Peninsula on a different footing from that of other foreign countries in the matter of currency.

The first supply of the new dollars arrived at the end of September, 1903, and the following proclamations and orders of the Governor in Council were issued, under the authority of the King's Order in Council of 25th June, 1903:–

(1) Proclamation dated 2nd October, 1903, declaring the Straits Settlements dollar legal tender from 3rd October, 1903.

(2) Order of the Governor in Council prohibiting the importation of the British and Mexican dollars from 3rd October, 1903.

(3) Order of the Governor in Council prohibiting the exportation of the Straits Settlements dollars from 3rd October, 1903. /

(4) Order of the Governor in Council exempting the Federated Malay States and Johore from the operation of the two last preceding orders.

(5) Proclamation dated the 5th October, 1903, constituting the new Straits dollar the standard coin of the Colony.

Notices in Malay, Chinese, and Tamil were posted up throughout the Colony, the Federated Malay States and Johore announcing these currency changes.

In addition to these measures, instructions were given not to make remittances from the coin reserve of the Currency Commissioners for investment in England or India, as this would mean throwing fresh money on the market, and would retard the contraction of the currency in circulation which was necessary for carrying out the proposals of the Straits Settlements Currency Committee.

With the cessation of the coinage of dollars except by Government, and the prohibition of the importation of the other legal tender dollars current in the Colony and the Federated Malay States, the first steps were taken to dissociate the Straits currency from a silver basis. [...]

The course of exchange (telegraphic transfer rates) as compared with Hong-Kong, and the average spot price of silver in London are shown in the following table on pages 22 and 23 [not included].

This table may be summarised as follows:– In the last three months in 1903, whilst silver fell from 27 7/8 to 25 3/4, the dollar in Hong-Kong fell from 22 9/16 / to 20 3/8, and the dollar in the Straits from 23 5/16 to 20 15/16. In

---

*   Ordinance xxiv. of 1903.

1904, silver fell from 26 7/16 to 24 31/32 between January and April, the dollar in Hong-Kong fell from 23 1/4 to 20 5/8, and the dollar in the Straits ranged between 23 9/16 and 21 9/16. The lowest limit reached in the Straits was when silver was at 26 7/16 during this period. During the remainder of the year, silver rose from 25 3/8 in May to 27 7/8 in December, the dollar in Hong-Kong rose from 21 5/16 to 23 9/16, and the dollar in the Straits from 21 1/2 to 23 1/2. It will be seen from the following table that, in December, 1904, when silver was at 27 7/8, the Hong-Kong rate was one-sixteenth higher than the Singapore rate. From December, 1904, to February, 1905, the price of silver rose from 27 7/8 to 28 1/16, Hong-Kong exchange rose from 22 13/16 to 24 1/16 in January, and fell to 23 11/16. Singapore kept pace with silver, and rose uniformly from 23 1/4 to 23 13/16. The price of silver dropped again in March, 1905, reaching 26 1/16 in April, whence it rose again to 27 3/4 in August. Hong-Kong exchange dropped with it, and remained in the neighbourhood of 22 3/4 till July, rising to 23 3/8 in August, whereas Singapore kept at a level of 23 7/8, reaching 24 1/16 in July and 25 7/16 in August. Silver rose steadily from 28 17/32 in September to 29 31/32 in December. Hong-Kong exchange rose from 22 15/16 to 25 1/16 and Singapore from 25 5/16 to 26 5/8.

The course of exchange, as compared with the bullion value of silver, did not give any conclusive or even satisfactory indication that the exchange value of the dollar had been completely separated / from silver. It is true that during the period, March to June, 1905, whereas the price of silver was low, Straits exchange kept at a much higher level than Hong-Kong, and above the bullion value of the dollar. This is the only indication afforded us that the Straits currency was following a course separate from silver.

*The situation was complicated by the large speculations of a foreign banker and certain merchants, some of whom speculated on a half-crown dollar being

---

*   It was generally reported and believed that this Bank succeeded in making a corner in dollars and notes, and that the difference between the value of the dollars when this Bank received them and the fixed value of 2/4, which should have accrued to Government in the form of seignorage,[6] went into the coffers of the Bank. This is very far from the truth. The profits were chiefly book profits, a large part of which the Bank was unable to collect. In fact, the Bank ran short of local currency, and had to beg help from the other Banks to replenish its coffers. On one occasion, when further assistance was refused, except at exorbitant rates, this Bank was compelled to purchase local currency from the Currency Commissioners at the gold import point 2/4 5/16 which was then 2/4 5/16 when the Banks' selling rate was quoted at 2/4. Though no seignorage profits accrued to Government from this scheme, all the Government deposits in the Banks and Treasuries appreciated in gold value, whereas, on the other hand, their sterling and Indian investments depreciated to a like extent in dollar value. Had it not been for the payment of the Tanjong Pagar Dock Award, which was given in dollars, the balance would have been in favour of the Government. The losers were those who had invested their dollar sav-

fixed, and some on a double rupee (2/8) value being given to the dollar, whilst others based their calculations on the advance in the price of silver making it impossible for the Government to provide a sufficient margin of safety between the melting point of the dollar and the nominal value of two shillings which it was generally believed and desired that the dollar would be fixed at.

There are also other factors which should / be taken into consideration. If we study the course of exchange as given in the table [not included], we see that the dollar rose on two occasions out of all proportion to the price of silver; and though it is true that a currency based on silver generally follows the fortunes of silver, abnormal rises take place in the exchange value of a currency if there is an insufficient supply of it to meet the requirements of trade, so that if the Banks delay to import, or find difficulty in getting sufficient currency coined, and thus delay the importation of currency to meet a favourable balance of trade, a sharp rise in exchange will take place. In the same way abnormal falls will occur if there is any undue delay or difficulty in the liquidation of debts due to an unfavourable trade balance.

In the midst of these fluctuations due to such various causes, and a rising market in silver which made it difficult for the Government to arrive at a sure judgment as to whether the value of the dollar had been totally separated from the value of silver, / the Straits Settlements Government were confronted with the problem of either fixing the dollar finally, or of giving temporary relief by exchanging dollars for gold at current Bank rates, and indefinitely postponing fixity of exchange. Special legislation had been introduced in March, 1904 (Ordinance IV. of 1904), to enable the Currency Commissioners to issue notes in Singapore against gold tendered to the Crown Agents for the Colonies in London at a rate of exchange to be notified by an order of the Governor in Council with the previous approval of the Secretary of State. This section was intended to give the Government the means of preventing any inconvenient rise in the current rate of exchange before the time arrived for fixing the value of the dollar. This power was never made use of. In the repeal of this section by Ordinance III. of 1905, passed in March, 1905, and the substitution for it of a section providing that gold shall be received in Singapore as well as in London in exchange for notes, and the manner in which it should be used, the original object of this section was apparently lost sight of, and when the time came when it became necessary to relieve the situation, the community were decidedly opposed to a further indefinite prolongation of the state of suspense and uncertainty which had proved so encouraging to speculation and so inimical to legitimate enterprise. Finality was demanded, and finality was given.

---

ings outside the Colony in gold-using countries, and the gainers those who had invested capital in the Colony and the Federated Malay States. The chief losers were the Currency Commissioners, most of whose sterling investments showed a considerably smaller dollar equivalent.

The policy adopted by India of declaring in advance the value at which the rupee was to be / fixed, was not followed in the Straits Settlements. The Straits Settlements Currency Committee were intentionally silent on the question of the value to be given to the dollar, as they considered that it was a matter for the Government to decide in the light of further experience. It was thought that any premature announcement as to the future gold value of the dollar might promote speculation and have a mischievous effect, and that it would be best not to attempt to fix the value of the new dollar at first, but to leave that important point to be decided in the light of the experience that would be gained when further coinage was stopped. The Singapore Chamber of Commerce asked for a two-shilling dollar, and the majority of the witnesses, connected with the Straits, who gave evidence before the Straits Settlements Currency Committee also declared in favour of a two-shilling dollar, and there is no doubt that the authorities, both in the Colony and in England, inclined to this value being given to the dollar.

With a view to avoiding interference with the status of existing contracts, and to obviating hardship in the relations between debtor and creditor, the Straits Settlements Currency Committee made it one of the essential features of their scheme that the dollar should, when fixed, be approximately the current rate of exchange at the time of fixing. The history of the currency of the Straits Settlements has been, since 1872, one of continual fluctuations as regards its exchange value, and the community had become accustomed/ to adapting their transactions accordingly. There could be no reasonable grounds for complaint if an average rate based on the fluctuations of the preceding ten or fifteen years were selected and the dollar fixed at that figure when the rate of exchange either rose or fell to it. There would have been grave injustice .if the unit of value had been arbitrarily fixed without regard to these considerations, and special legislation would have been found necessary to protect the interests of debtor and creditor. It was not considered that this question was likely to arise out of the scheme propounded by the Straits Settlements Currency committee, and this opinion was justified after fixity became an established fact.

Such being the plan, the price of silver and the course of exchange were carefully watched, and, as early as July, 1904, representations were made to the authorities at home. The opinion of the experts consulted was, that, notwithstanding the continuance of the Russo-Japanese War, silver was likely to fall; and, though the outlook even then appeared to be very much against fixing the value of the dollar so low as two shillings, in view of the rising market in silver it was considered undesirable to take any steps to fix exchange, as, owing to the rise in the price of silver, the appreciation of the dollar would have taken place, even if no currency scheme had been initiated.

The final stage of the measures necessary to contract the currency was reached in August, 1904. / By the first week in August 29,975,000 of the new

dollars had reached the Colony, large enough to meet all the currency requirements of the Colony and the Federated Malay States, and it was considered safe
to demonetise the British, Mexican, and Hong Kong dollar. This was done by
proclamation on the 24th of August, 1904. [...]

In the middle of 1904, there was considerable depression of trade in the
Colony, and, though some observers were inclined to attribute it to the currency
changes introduced by Government, there was nothing in their features to distinguish the failures which then took place from the far more serious failures
of the previous decade. It may be seen from the reports of the Official Assignee
and the Chambers of Commerce that these periods of depression occur with
periodical regularity, and invariably follow periods of prosperity. In prosperous
times it is easy to get credit, speculation sets in, credit is extended where it is
already inflated ; when the collapse comes there is an undue restriction, although
many "failures could be averted by a prudent extension of credit, such as was the
case / when the European Banks and firms stopped advances and sales on credit,
and many Chinese, firms were only saved from bankruptcy by the action of the
Chetties, the Indian moneylenders, who found it profitable to come to their res-
cue. There do not seem to me any grounds for the belief which many people
entertained that the currency changes were responsible for the depression which
took place in 1904, There was no such marked stringency of local currency as to
prevent the Banks giving their usual credit, and in 1905, it was the opinion of
some of the leading business firms that no contraction of currency had yet taken
place at Singapore which could be felt by the business community.

However, in the middle of 1905, there was a marked revival of the produce
business in the Colony and the Federated Malay States. The price of tin began
to rise, and considerable outside capital came into the country for investment in
rubber. With a closed currency, with no means of expansion open to the public
either by the tender of gold or silver, this increase of the export trade formed a
most powerful factor in enhancing the value of the dollar, much more so, in my
opinion, than the rise in the price of silver.

In July, 1905, exchange (demand) rose to 2/0 1/8, and it was generally
expected that, owing to the revival of the produce business, it would rise over 2/1
before the end of the year. The proposal to fix the dollar at 2/- was reluctantly
abandoned. In fixing the dollar under the scheme of the Straits Settlements /
Currency Committee two essential conditions had to be complied with. A sufficient margin had to be left between the token value and the bullion value of
the dollar so as to save it from the melting pot, and the value of the dollar had to
be as near as possible the current rate of exchange. The following proposals were
then submitted for consideration, the main object being to keep the value of the
dollar as low as possible consistent with safety, and to fix it whenever the market
rate of exchange approached approximately the rate decided upon.

The first proposal was based on one of the recommendations of the American Commission that the unit of value to be adopted in the Far Eastern countries, which had decided on going in for a gold standard, should be as uniform as possible, and that the value should be fixed at or near the coinage ratio of 32 (silver) to 1 (gold). This was approximately the ratio adopted in the Philippines for their peso. This was also approximately the ratio on which the Japanese silver half-yen was based. If the silver unit were 480 grains, the gold unit would be 15 grains. Working this out for the Straits dollar (416 grains and 900 fineness) and the sovereign as unit (123.27447 grains), the value of the Straits dollar would have come to 2/1 5/16, approximately. The advantages claimed for adopting this coinage ratio in conjunction with the neighbouring countries which had also gone in for a gold standard, were that there would be less danger of other countries giving a higher value to silver by / continuing to purchase above our limit of value; that the purchase of silver bullion would be automatically suspended at practically the same points; when the countries interested stopped purchasing, the tendency to a rise in the price of silver would be effectually arrested, and that the demand for silver would be so distributed that it would be possible to regulate its price and maintain its stability. One very important factor was overlooked in these calculations, and that was the cheapening of the price of gold by over-production. The subsequent rise in the price of silver, which was to a large extent due to the depreciation of gold, compelled Japan and the Philippines to recoin their silver currency at a very much smaller coinage ratio.

The upward movement in the price of silver soon made it evident that the value recommended of 2/1 1/2for the dollar was too low, and that the margin between this and bullion par was not sufficiently safe. An exchange of nine dollars to the sovereign was then suggested, and was accepted as a more convenient rate providing a sufficient margin of safety. By the middle of November, however, when this rate was agreed to, exchange (telegraphic transfer) had risen to 2/2, and the price of silver had also risen to well over 29d. per ounce.[...] /

It was then proposed to reduce the dollar to 800 fineness, so as to ensure a fixed value of $9 to £1 without running the risk of the exportation of our dollars for sale as bullion. This proposal was not agreed to, as it /meant such a wide departure from the proposals of the Straits Settlements Currency Committee. It was considered that it would certainly be necessary to seek further expert advice, and to arrive at a general concurrence before adopting so wide a departure from the accepted scheme.

In December, 1905, the telegraphic rate of exchange rose to 2/2 5/8, only 1/24th of a penny below the proposed rate of $9 to £1. Here, then, was the opportunity to fix the dollar at this rate according to the scheme of the Straits Settlements Currency

Committee; but, owing to the steady rise of the price of silver, no action was taken. The opinion held was that the time for action would come when a decided fall in the price of silver set in again.

In January, 1906, preparations had to be made for the supply of local currency to meet the customary requirements of the Chinese New Year, which fell on the 25th of the month. This, coming on the top of wide-spread speculation in exchange, which had been going on for some months past and were coming due for settlement, unsettled the market and put a stop to nearly all legitimate business. Exchange fluctuated by leaps and bounds, and widely different rates from the opening rates were quoted by the banks in the course of the same day. There were sometimes five or six quotations a day. [...] On the 12th of the /month the Governor, Sir John Anderson, spoke at a meeting of the Legislative Council, and warned the public against the unauthorised rumours as to the intentions of the Government as regards the exchange value to be given to the dollar, stating that the Government's desire was to fix the dollar as low as possible consistently with safety.

The result was that the dollar dropped from 2/4 11/16 to 2/4 on the following day. It rose again to 2/4 1/2 and dropped to 2/3 in the course of three days. The next day it rose again, and continued to rise until it reached 2/4 3/16 on the 27th of January. Owing to the uncertainty of the outlook, nearly all legitimate business was stopped, and it became impossible for the Government to consider tenders for important and urgent public works. It was felt that any risk of failure to maintain a fixed rate was far preferable to the loss to the community and the Government by a prolongation of this uncertainty. Representations were again made to the Secretary of State urging fixity.

Silver had now reached the price 30 ¼ d. per ounce, and it was evident that the margin of safety for a dollar value based on the ratio of $9 to £1, viz., 2/2 2/3, was much too narrow. Besides, the market rate of exchange had long since gone beyond this value. Permission was, accordingly, granted to the dollar being fixed at 2/4, which was considered the lowest rate possible, consistent with safety. At this time the Bank rate stood at 2/41/8, and showed a tendency to go higher. As it was not possible to / make the necessary arrangements for passing the legislation required before the beginning of the following week - an interval of two working days - it was considered advisable to endeavour to steady the market and to check the tendency towards a rise in exchange rates. With this object, tenders were invited for the sale to Government of a telegraphic transfer on London to the amount of £100,000. A few tentative bids were made, but none was accepted. The hint appeared to have been sufficient, and to have had the desired effect of stopping further' speculative transactions.

This procedure led to some very hostile criticism on the part of the Straits Times, which unjustly accused the Government of endeavouring deliberately to get a better rate from the Banks, knowing in advance that the fixed rate would be lower than the Bank rate then prevailing.

On the 29th January, 1906, Ordinance I. of 1906, which enabled the Currency Commissioners to give out notes in exchange for gold locally and against telegraphic transfers in favour of the Crown Agents for the Colonies in London, was passed at one sitting of the Legislative Council, and on the same day an Order of the Governor in Council was passed authorising the Commissioners to receive gold in exchange for notes at the rate of £7 to $60.

On this day the spot price of standard silver was 2/6 1/4 per ounce, and the corresponding value of the silver content of the dollar was 2/1 1/8. For the price of the silver content of the Straits dollar to reach / the value of 2/4, the spot price of bar silver would have to be 2/9 3/16 per ounce, so that when the dollar was fixed a margin of safety of about ten per cent, was provided below the bullion par of 33/ 3/16 of the Straits dollar.

It must be admitted that the plan of not announcing in advance, as was done in India, the exchange value of the dollar to be fixed, did not achieve the object of preventing speculation ; but the chief reason for adopting the cautious policy of controlling the supply of the dollar, and then being guided by experience as to the determination of the value to be given to it, is to be found in the policy adopted by the Straits Settlements Currency Committee of giving the people the currency they wanted, and of avoiding disturbance of trade and of contracts by making the exchange value to be fixed as close as possible to the market rate of the day. These were considered to be the essential features of the scheme. To make the new dollar readily acceptable, it had to conform in weight, fineness, and shape to the old dollar, and to prevent dislocation of business and hardship, between creditor and debtor, the fixed value had to be approximately the market rate ruling at the time of fixing.

This procedure has been the subject of much criticism. It is commented on as follows in one of these criticisms : -

" The weight and fineness of the dollar, once decided upon, seems to have been assumed to be / unalterable. The silver content of the dollar was the fixed thing, so the Currency Committee appear to have reasoned ; the unit of value was the alterable thing. This was to be adjusted to the coin and to be fixed at such a rate as to allow a safe margin above bullion value. But one would, naturally ask, why not reverse the procedure ? The bullion value of token coins is largely a question of convenience. The unit of value, on the other hand, is of the utmost importance. Alterations in the unit of value by their uneven effects on the prices of various classes of commodities, upon wages, and by the derangements they cause in the relations existing between debtor and creditor, profoundly affect the whole economic structure. Variations in the value of precious metals have frequently compelled countries to alter the weight and fineness of their coins.

Within a short time Japan, Mexico, and the Philippines have taken measures in this direction, consequent on the recent high price of silver. The Straits Settlements, however, afford the only instance in recent monetary history of a material alteration in the unit of value, deliberately made to meet such a contingency."*

This was written before the further rise in the price of silver compelled the Government of the Straits Settlements to reduce the weight of their coins. It may be asked what was the unit of value which existed in the Straits Settlements before fixity, / and what was the material alteration made. The exchange value of the dollar fluctuated with the price of silver, and depended on the silver content of the dollar. The local value of the dollar, so far as the majority of the trading community was concerned, was also measured by the value of the silver contained in the dollar. When these dollars found their way into the interior of China, they were dealt with as sycee, viz., weighed and tested and accepted at the value of their pure silver content. There being no permanent unit of value, it cannot be said that there was any material alteration in the value of the unit when the dollar was fixed at 2/4. If anyone will take the trouble to compare the fluctuations in the exchange of the dollar during the twenty years preceding fixity, he cannot escape the conclusion that 2/4 was a much fairer average than the 2/- value which the community and the Government first desired to fix the dollar at. In the Straits Settlements the value of the dollar was fixed below the rate at which it was then circulating. It is contended that it should have been fixed at the rate at which it circulated when these dollars were first made legal tender in 1903, and to prevent their exportation for sale as bullion the silver content of the dollar should have been immediately reduced. The writer† goes on to say that, whereas in other countries a practically existing unit was assumed which would, henceforth, be a fixed unit for the entire currency system, and all / the coins in circulation were all made subordinate to this unit, and although in British India the existing silver rupee was taken as the unit, and in the Straits dollar the existing dollar (since 1903 the Straits dollar), they were not accepted at the value at which they were then circulating. The procedure indicated as the proper method rests on the assumption that no more violent fluctuations would take place from the date of the selection of the value of the unit and the date when a sufficiency of the new currency would be available to displace the existing currency. According to this plan, the selected value would have been of no use if the market value of the dollar, when the new supply was ready, had diverged considerably from the market value obtaining where the unit was chosen.

The essential feature of the scheme suggested by these critics is that there would have been no delay and no period of uncertainty intervening sufficient to

---

*   "A Gold Standard for the Straits Settlements," by E. W. Kemmerer.
†   Dr. G. Visseringh, *Chinese Currency*.

dislocate trade and derange prices. Let us see how this plan would have worked out in 1903-1904, taking three months as the shortest time required for coining the dollars and putting them into circulation. I will take the Hong-Kong rates of exchange, as there was no artificial contraction of the currency in that Colony. In November, 1903, the lowest Hong-Kong rate was 20 7/8 ; it went still lower in December. Suppose, then, that the unit of value was fixed at 21d. and orders were given for the coinage of dollars adjusted to that value for delivery in February. In February, according to / the foregoing criticisms, the authorities would have been able to put these dollars into circulation at the fixed rate, without any dislocation of prices. But, in February, the dollar had gone up to 23 1/4d., and the plan of bringing in a dollar at a unit of value as close as possible to the existing market rate would have been defeated.

It is asserted, with a good deal of confidence, that the bullion content of the unit of value is a matter of comparative indifference, so long as the coin is convenient to handle, does not unduly encourage counterfeiting and -is not so large as to endanger it being melted down. This may be true when once the value of the unit has been completely dissociated from the value of the silver content of the coin representing it, and when the public have thoroughly recognised the fact that it is only a token ; but the authorities in the Straits Settlements had to deal with a public which , for a very considerable period of years, have looked on the value of their standard coin as the value of the metal contained in it. The value of the standard coin had not only fluctuated in relation to articles produced in gold-using countries, but its value, as measured locally, was reflected in the increased prices of local articles and in the increased wages of native employees.

[...] It was thought, in some quarters, that because the Straits public had readily accepted notes, they would have been as ready to accept a lighter weight dollar even before a definite gold value had been given to that coin. It is true that the great majority of the business men in the Colony had great belief in the general acquiescence of the public in a Government issue of one-dollar notes. The / popularity of the Bank-note issues in the Colony and the Federated Malay States, and the prevalence in all the more important towns of the system of chits, which were accepted by petty traders, hawkers, hackney carriage drivers, and even by rickshaw pullers from known residents, were sufficient grounds for this belief ; but I think that the consensus of opinion on the part of the mercantile community was against the theory that a lighter weight coin would be accepted as a final payment. At any rate, a large majority of the merchants who were called as witnesses before the Straits Settlements Currency Committee held a different view, and their evidence goes to show that they were of the opinion that the most essential feature of the currency scheme was the substitution for the existing trade dollar of a Government dollar of the same size and fineness. Those who believe that a lighter coin would have been readily accepted point to the fact that the new and smaller Straits dollar, made legal tender in 1907, was quietly accepted throughout the country. It must be borne in mind that the conditions were then totally different. The one-dollar note had by then largely displaced the dollar ; it had become known that these notes were accepted in Hong-Kong and at the Treaty Ports at a rate based on the sterling rate of 2/4, and commanded a higher value than the British or Mexican dollar; that the sovereign could be obtained at a slight premium over the fixed rate, and at par from the Currency Commissioners, when gold was / available, and that sterling Bank drafts, rupee Bank drafts and drafts on China and Java were based on this rate. To what extent the note had displaced the dollar may be seen from the fact that the coinage of the first Straits dollar amounted to $35,400,576, whilst the total number of the new and lighter Straits dollars and the fifty cent, pieces minted was only $19,006,872. Over twelve millions of these has been held in the currency note reserve and is still so held, leaving less than seven millions in active circulation, in the Banks and Government Treasuries.

It will be seen, therefore, that the popularity of the one dollar note and its known exchange value made the silver content of the dollar a matter of comparative indifference to the community. Another argument in favour of the opinion, that the lighter dollar would not have been willingly accepted at the beginning, can be seen in the fact that the fifty cent, piece, though made a full legal tender coin, never became a popular coin. When it was made an unlimited legal tender coin at the end of 1906, it was expected that, owing to its convenient size, it would soon get into favour with the general public, and the authorities entertained the hope that it would make it possible to retire altogether the more cumbrous coin. However, there was no greater demand for it than before, and some portion of these coins had afterwards to be sold as bullion.

Another criticism, often heard during the course / of our currency changes, was that we should have waited for silver to decline in value before fixing the dollar, and that the method, followed in India, where the value of the rupee was fixed during a falling market in silver, should have been followed in the Straits Settlements. The only advantage from a falling market in silver in connection with their currency changes was that, with the control over the supply of dollars in Government's hands, a sure indication of the dissociation of the dollar from silver would have been afforded, if the dollar had maintained its exchange value and did not decline in value with every fall in the price of silver. To have fixed the dollar at a low rate when silver was low would have been to lull ourselves into a false sense of security. That India carried out her currency changes during a period of declining silver was largely a matter of circumstances and not of deliberate policy. It could not have been foreseen. In fact, the conditions in India were very unfavourable for the establishment of a gold standard, and it took five years before Indian exchange reached the declared value of 1/4, owing to the low price of silver and the excessive amount of rupees in circulation. Attempts were made by the Indian Government to force exchange up to 1/4 by withholding the sale of Council Bills, but they proved unsuccessful, and were given up. It may be here remarked that the Indian Government, in fixing the rupee at 1/4, provided a very good margin between the bullion / par and the value of the silver content of the rupee as prices then ruled, and it will be seen that India was the only country in the East, which had adopted a gold exchange standard, which was not compelled to recoin its standard coinage by reason of the rise in the price of silver.

GERMAN, *HANDBOOK TO BRITISH MALAYA* (1927)

R. L. German, *Handbook to British Malaya* (London: Malay States Information Service, 1927), pp. 114–16.

The following source provides a list of the banks operating in Malaya in 1927. As discussed in the thematic introduction, the majority of banks were European owned.

R. L. German, *Handbook to British Malaya* (1927), extract

BANKS.

POST OFFICE SAYINGS BANK.

A Post Office Savings Bank was started in the Straits Settlements in 1877, in Perak in 1889, and in Selangor in 1893. In 1906 new Enactments established the Savings Bank throughout the Federated Malay States. Savings Bank business is conducted at all Post Offices in the Federated Malay States and Straits Settlements. The rate of interest on deposits in both Banks has been 3 per cent. per annum for many years. Investments are all in British, Colonial and Indian Government Securities. There are no Government or Post Office Savings Banks in the Unfederated States of Kelantan, Johore, or Trengganu, but a Government Savings Bank was established in Kedah in 1923.

The number of depositors in the Straits Settlements in 1925 was 14,455 with $3,067,801 (£357,910) standing to their credit. In the Federated Malay States in the same year there were 25,620 depositors with $3,128,731 (£365,018) to their credit, and in Kedah 329 depositors with $27,376 (£3,193).

OTHER BANKS.

The following Banks operate in the places named: –

SINGAPORE.

Asia Banking Corporation	Incorporated in New York.
Banque de L'Indo-Chine	" " France. /
Banque Industrielle de Chine	" " France.
Chartered Bank of India, Australia and China	" " England.
Chinese Commercial Bank, Ltd.	
China and Southern Bank, Ltd.	" " Japan.
Oversea China Bank, Ltd.	" " Straits Settlements.
Ho Hong Bank, Ltd.	
Hongkong and Shanghai Banking Corporation	" " Hong Kong.
International Banking Corporation	" " U.S.S.

Lee Wah Bank, Ltd.
Mercantile Bank of India, Ltd.   "   " England.
Nederlandsche Handel Maatschappy   "   " Holland.
Nederlandsche Indische Handelsbank   "   " Holland.
P. and O. Banking Corporation, Ltd.   "   " England.
Sze Hai Tong Banking 8c Insurance Co., Ltd.   "   " Straits Settlements.
Bank of Taiwan, Ltd.   "   " Japan.
Yokohama Specie Bank, Ltd.   "   " Japan.

PENANG.

Chartered Bank of India, Australia and China.
Hongkong and Shanghai Banking Corporation.
Ho Hong Bank, Ltd.
Mercantile Bank of India, Ltd.
Nederlandsche Bank of India, Ltd.

MALACCA.

Hongkong and Shanghai Banking Corporation.
Ho Hong Bank.

FEDERATED MALAY STATES,

PERAK.

Hongkong and Shanghai Banking Corporation.
Chartered Bank of India, Australia and China.
Bank of Malaya (Incorporated in the F.M.S.). /

SELANGOR.

Chartered Bank of India, Australia and China.
Hongkong and Shanghai Banking Corporation.
Kwong Yik Banking Corporation Ltd. (Incorporated in Selangor).
Mercantile Bank of India.

NEGRI SEMBILAN.

Chartered Bank of India, Australia and China.

PAHANG.

Mercantile Bank of India (at Kuantan).

UNFEDERATED MALAY STATES.

KEDAH.

Chartered Bank of India, Australia and China.

JOHORE.

Hongkong and Shanghai Banking Corporation.

CHERRY, *ELEMENTARY BUSINESS PRACTICE IN THE STRAITS SENTTLEMENTS AND FEDERATED MALAY STATES. WITH QUESTIONS AND EXAMPLES* (1915)

W. T. Cherry, *Elementary Business Practice in the Straits Settlements and Federated Malay States. With Questions and Examples* (Singapore: Methodist Publishing House, 1915), pp. 35–40, 42–8.

An American, the Reverend William Thomas Cherry arrived in Malaya in 1899, returning home in 1923. During his time in South East Asia, he undertook missionary work in Malaya, Borneo and the Dutch East Indies, managed the Malaya Publishing House, for which he wrote a number of books, and became Secretary of the Trustees of the Methodist Church in Singapore. The extracts from his 1915 business textbook describes the use of cheques, drafts and Post Office and bank remittances. A more in-depth discussion of the various forms of remittance available to traders can be found in D. Sunderland, *Financing the Raj. The City of London and Colonial India, 1858–1940* (London: Boydell & Brewer, 2013), pp. 101–9.[1]

Notes
1.   *Singapore Free Press and Mercantile Advertiser*, 16 October 1941, p. 5.

W. T. Cherry, *Elementary Business Practice in the Straits Settlements and Federated Malay States. With Questions and Examples* (1915), extract

CHAPTER 6.

BANKING PRACTICE.

EVERY business firm must have a *Bank Account*. [...] The Bank sometimes requires a minimum deposit of $500 to open such an account.

The Bank furnishes the Depositor with *(a)* a Cheque Book, *(b)* a Deposit (or Paying-in) Book, and (c) a Pass Book.

A Cheque is in the following form:–

No	. . . . 192 . . . .

THE COMMERCIAL SCHOOL BANK.
SINGAPORE.

PAY ||||||||||||||||||||||||||||||||||||||||||||||||||||||||||||||||||||||||||||||||||||||||||| *or Bearer*

Dollars |||||||||||||||||||||||||||||||||||||||||||||||||||||||||||||||||||||||||||||||||||||||||||

$||||||||||||||||||||||||||||||||| |||||||||||||||||||||||||||||||||||||||||||||||||||||||||||||

Cheques must be stamped, but as this depends upon the law in each separate State, it is left for the Teacher to explain this to the class. In the S.S., cheques over $20 require a 4.cent stamp. [...]

Endorsement. In order to cash the cheque the Payee must write his name across the back. This is called "endorsing" the cheque. He then presents it to a Bank and receives cash in exchange for it. But should the Bank have any doubt about his being the proper person to receive payment, they may require the Payee or Endorser to bring someone to "identify" him–that is, to satisfy the Bank that he is the person named in the endorsement. If the cheque is presented to a Bank other than the one in which the Drawer has his account, the Bank may also require the Payee to have someone "guarantee" the cheque, as the Bank may have no way of knowing whether the Drawer has any account from which he can make payments by cheque.

If the Payee has himself a Bank account, he has merely to endorse the cheque and deposit it to the credit of his own account instead of cashing it. This, in fact, is the way cheques are usually dealt with. /

Unless a cheque bears the words "For account of Payee only" or "not transferable" the Payee may endorse it in favour of another person, who in his turn may endorse in favour of a third person, and so on. For example: A cheque is drawn in favour of John Smith. Smith finds it inconvenient to take it to the Bank, so he goes to his friend K.K. Brown, of the Steam Tongkang Company, and asks him to kindly cash the cheque for him. This Brown is glad to do, so Smith endorses the cheque thus: "Pay to the order of the Steam Tongkang Company. John Smith." This endorsement makes Brown the Payee instead of Smith. Brown lets Smith have the money at once, and sends the cheque to his Bank after endorsing it: "Steam Tongkang Company, K.K. Brown, Manager.

Most business firms, however, dislike having their paper passed from hand to hand in this fashion, and to prevent this they may write across the face of the cheque as explained in the preceding paragraph, or "Not payable after ... days from date."

A cheque payable to Bearer is really payable to any person who may present it, no matter what name may appear as the Payee; and such a cheque, if lost, could be cashed by the finder even though he had no right whatever to use it. To prevent this, it is common custom to strike out the word "Bearer" and write in the word "Order," in which case the Bank will pay no one but the Payee named in the cheque or in his endorsement, and it would be necessary for the Payee to prove to the Bank that he was such person.

Crossed Cheques. Another alteration that is commonly made in a cheque is to draw two lines across its face, writing between the lines the words "& Co." This is what is called a "crossed cheque," and the effect of crossing a cheque is that the Bank will not cash it, but will accept it only as a deposit.

Precautions. In writing a cheque the amount should be expressed in words as well as figures [...]. Any alteration made in a cheque by the Drawer himself, should be initialled.

It is customary under some circumstances to "limit" a cheque. For instance, the Owner of a Rubber Estate in Johore may wish to send his Estate Manager an "open" cheque– that is, a cheque signed, but without the amount written in–that the Manager may himself write in the amount required say to pay the export duty on his monthly shipment of rubber. If no limit were placed on such a cheque, the

Manager might draw many times the amount of money the Owner intended to place at his disposal. So to make this impossible, the Owner may write across the face of the cheque some such words as: "Not to exceed Fifty Dollars." [...]

Overdrafts. It is easy to see that if the Drawer sent a cheque say to Bombay in payment of a bill, it would be about three or four weeks before that cheque would find its way back to be debited to the Drawer's account. In the meantime, suppose the Drawer has spent most of his money in making other payments, so that when this cheque returns from Bombay there is not enough money to his credit to meet the debit occasioned by the arrival of this cheque. His account would thus be "overdrawn."

But the Bank is under no obligation to permit any depositor to overdraw his account. They would in that event notify the Drawer to deposit sufficient money to meet the cheque, and if he failed to do so his cheque would be "dishonoured" – that is, it would be returned to the person or Bank from which it came with the explanation that there were insufficient funds to meet it; or, perhaps, as a matter of courtesy to the Drawer, with the simple note "Refer to Drawer."

A Draft. From the foregoing it will be seen that while a cheque is a most convenient medium of exchange for near-by or prompt transactions, it is not a satisfactory method of remitting money to great distances or to foreign lands where a different system of currency is in use. For such purposes a much better medium is a *Demand Draft*.

To procure a draft the buyer need not have a Bank account at all, as he may pay cash down for the draft, although if he has an account he may pay for the Draft by a cheque in favour of the Bank.

When a draft is wanted, the applicant fills in a form similar to the following:

THE COMMERCIAL SCHOOL BANK. ....19....						
Wanted the Bank's Drafts on						
No. of Draft.	In favour of	Amount.		Rate.	Dollars	Cents.
Dollars						

> *Applicant* . . . . /

The amount may be stated in either one of two ways:–

(1) If you want a draft on London for the equivalent of $178.43 Straits, write these figures in the last column of the application form, and the Bank will make out the draft for the sterling equivalent of this amount at the current rate of exchange. Should the rate be 2s 4d, your draft would be for £20.16.4.

(2) If you want a draft on Bombay for Rs. 240.3.0, write that sum in the column headed "Amount," and the Bank will tell you the amount in dollars and cents that you must pay.

The form of application of course varies in different banks, but the above form embodies the essentials. The columns headed "No. of Draft," "Rate," etc., are to be filled in by the Bank, not by the applicant.

A Demand Draft is in the following or similar form:–

THE COMMERCIAL SCHOOL BANK OF MALAYA.

£||||||||||||||||||||||||||||||| *Singapore,* . . . . 19 . . . . .

On Demand, Pay this FIRST of Exchange (Second of the same tenor and date not paid) to the order of

(1) . . . .

(2) . . . .*Value received.*

To the   THE COMMERCIAL SCHOOL BANK OF MALAYA.

ROYAL BANK OF BRITAIN,

No. 25, Exchange Place, ...
LONDON.   *Manager.*

---

(1) Insert name of Payee.   (3) Insert amount in words.

The Draft is usually issued in duplicate, the Second of Exchange being exactly like the First, except that it reads:– "On Demand, Pay this Second of Exchange (First of the same tenor and date not paid)."

But sometimes the Bank issues what is call a "Sola Bill," which is not in duplicate, and which reads as follows: – "On Demand, Pay this Sola Bill of Exchange to the order of"

The object in issuing a draft in duplicate is to ensure safety in transmission through the mails. If one of the two forms is lost the other may be used. Sometimes the buyer sends the Original by one mail, and the Duplicate by the following mail; or, he may keep the Duplicate until he receives word that the Original has been safely received.

A Draft differs from a Cheque, then, (a) in that it is paid for by the buyer when issued, whereas a Cheque is not debited to the Drawer until it is cashed by a Bank. (*b*) A Draft states the amount to be paid in the currency of the country in which it is payable, but a Cheque is in the currency of the country in which it is issued. / [...]

Deposits. The Form for depositing cash, notes, or cheques in the Bank is as follows:

THE COMMERCIAL SCHOOL BANK		
at		
CREDIT		
By Cash . . . .$		
„ Bank Notes . . . . „		
„ Cheques . . . . „		
Dollars		
. . . .		
	$	
. . . . 19.		
Please write the Total in Words as well as in Figures.		

These forms are usually contained in a book the stub or counterfoil being a duplicate of the above. The Bank tears off and retains the outer form, and the Depositor retains the counterfoil, which is initialled by the Bank's cashier.

Cheques drawn on the Bank in which the deposit is made are entered on a separate form from that used for cheques on other Banks. The name of the Drawer and payee need not / appear on the Deposit slip, but the name of the Bank on which the cheque or Draft is drawn should appear, together with the amount both in figures and words.

Drafts in foreign currency have to be entered without extending the amount in Straits currency, as the Bank has to quote the rate of exchange at which the foreign currency is to be converted into Straits money.

Money Orders and Postal Orders may be deposited in exactly the same way as cheques or drafts. [...]

Signing Cheques, etc. The handling of money, except for cash sales or in small amounts, is not usually entrusted to office clerks, but is the work of the Accountant or Cashier, and the duty of signing and endorsing cheques and other financial documents is generally reserved for the Manager himself or one of the partners.

In large firms employing a number of European assistants, one or more of these assistants may be authorised to sign the firm "per procuration."[1]

The Manager of a firm would endorse cheques, drafts, bills of lading, etc., thus: –

THE COMMERCIAL EDUCATION COMPANY,

John Smith, Manager.

The name of the firm and the office or position of the person who signs would be printed or impressed with a rubber stamp, and the name signed in ink.

In the case of a partnership, a member of the firm would sign the name of the firm without adding his own name. Thus:

Johnston and Dickson.

In cases where some one signs "per procuration" the signature would be in this form: –

THE COMMERCIAL EDUCATION COMPANY,

per pro J. D. Stonewall.

The custom in the case of limited liability companies is for cheques to be signed by one of the Directors and the Secretaries: –

KLAPA DEVELOPMENT CO., LTD.

R. J. Klumpor, *Director.*

Blotter & Co., *Secretaries.*

Cashing Cheques. Occasionally a person will ask the Clerk in a shop or office either to cash a cheque to save them the trouble of going to the Bank, or to accept a cheque in payment for goods bought, and perhaps to return part of the cheque in cash. Where the person making such a request is favourably known, such a request may always be granted with pleasure. But when it is made by strangers, the request should not be granted without reference to the Manager, as the cheque may be worthless. [...]

CHAPTER 7.

REMITTANCES.

MOST payments for goods bought and sold are made, not by cash, but in some form or other of paper which is equivalent to cash. This method prevails because of its greater safety and convenience. The merchant who buys from London does not send Straits money in payment, as it could not be used there; nor does he send English money, as it would be difficult to procure here. It would also be impossible to recover either if lost in transmission. Instead, therefore, he pays his Straits money into the Bank, and in exchange for it he receives a Draft, which the supplier in London can present to his Bank there and exchange it for English money. Both parties have thus dealt with their own currency only, and no money – only a paper document – has been sent to Europe, and that document, if lost, can be replaced. And to prevent an improper person, should he find the lost draft, from using it, the owner of the draft can request the Bank to "stop payment." [...]

The three principal methods of remitting money are: –

1. By Cash.
2. Through the Post Office.
3. Through the Bank.

I. CASH REMITTANCES.

1. Notes may very conveniently be sent at letter postage rates, but as there is always some risk of loss, it is better to register all letters containing notes, and if the amount is considerable, they should be insured also. This is the usual method of sending money to Rubber Estates for paying the coolies. A large sum of money may be insured against loss by the payment of a small fee, this risk being taken either by the Post Office or by any Insurance Company.

The Registration and Insurance of Letters has already been explained in Chapter 3.

2. Coin may not be sent in a letter. It may be sent by parcel post, which method may be used where a considerable amount of coin is to be sent.

This rule makes it impossible to remit coin in payment of fractions of a dollar, but follow original copy.

(1) The remittance, if small, may be made by money order, or, if large, by cheque or draft.
(2) The sender may enclose notes for the bulk of the bill, and stamps for the odd cents or, he may send notes for the nearest number of dollars in excess of his bill, and ask for the return of the balance in stamps. /

Very few firms will object to the payment of small amounts in stamps, but when stamps are used, they should be of small denominations, and if possible of the country to which they are being sent. (F. M. S. or Netherlands Indies stamps might be sent to the Straits Settlements, or vice versa, but Eastern stamps should not be sent to Europe or America in payment of bills.)

II. POST OFFICE REMITTANCES.

Money may be sent through the Post Office in five ways: –

Stamps,
Money Coupons,
Money Order,
Telegraphic Order,
Postal Order.

1. International Money Coupons are useful for remitting small sums.

2. The Money Order is a very common form of remitting money, especially locally. The purchaser of a Money Order must fill in a form, and present it with the cash at the Post Office, when he will receive either

(*a*) *A Money Order* in the form shown on this page, to be forwarded by post to the payee for presentation at the office of payment, or

(*b*) *A Certificate of Issue,* in the form shown on page 44 [not reproduced], in which case payment will be made by means of an order to be issued by the Postal Administration of the country on which it is drawn.

This form is used in remitting to India.

No. . . . .

STRAITS SETTLEMENTS.

Date Stamp.		$	*c.*

MONEY ORDER.

PAY the Person named in my Letter of Advice the sum of

DOLLARS . . . .

To the Post Office at . . . .

. . . .

Postmaster.

The Person to whom this Order is made payable must sign here his or her Christian and Surname at full length, except in the case of Firms, whose usual Signature will suffice.	*Received the above.* { . . . . Signature of Payee.

N.B. – If the Order be not paid before the end of the twelfth calendar month after that in which it was issued all claims to the Money will be lost. AFTER ONCE PAYING A MONEY ORDER BY WHOMSOEVER PRESENTED, THE OFFICE WILL NOT BE LIABLE TO ANY FURTHER CLAIM.

Stamp of Paying Office. /

The Certificate of Issue referred to on the preceding page is in the following form: –

B.

RECEIPT

TO BE RETAINED BY THE REMITTER, THE PAYEE WILL RECEIVE THE MONEY-ORDER FROM THE POST OFFICE IN INDIA.

Date Stamp

SINGAPORE, No. . . . .

RECEIVED Ruppes [*in words*] . . . .
. . . . Annas [*in words*] . . . .
. . . . as detailed below* for a Money Order
payable at . . . . Post Office
to [*name of Payee*] . . . .

* Value of the Money Order . . . . $
Commission . . . . ,,

Total . . . . $

. . . .

Supdt. Money Order Branch.

The Post Office charges a commission on issuing orders. This charge varies according to the amount of the order and the country in which it is payable, but it is never less than 5 cents.

The Postal Guide contains a list of countries on which Money Orders are issued, and that list shows whether the Order is to be sent to the Payee as per the method *(a)* above, or whether a Certificate of Issue is given as per method *(b)* above. If the latter, you should not send the Certificate of Issue to the Payee as you would send a Money Order, but you should keep the Certificate until you know that the remittance reached its destination safely. The way this is done is, the Post Office advises the Payee's Post Office that a remittance has been received from........ for him which will be paid to him upon furnishing particulars. It is therefore necessary for the remitter not only to pay the money in to the Post Office, but also to write advising the Payee that he has done so; otherwise the latter may have difficulty in securing payment.

The form of Application for a Money Order on India from the Straits Settlements is shown on the opposite page.

Telegraph Money Orders may be sent between Post Offices in the Straits Settlements, Federated Malay States and Kedah, provided, of course, that the Offices concerned are Money Order and Telegraph Offices. /

Application to be Filled up by the Remitter of a Money Order on India.

Nothing to be written by the Remitter on the reverse.

For Rs ....As .... payable at ...... Post Office

On Postal Service

In the District of * . . . .

Name of the Remitter   . . . .

Name of the Payee   . . . .

Full Address of the Payee   . . . .

Address of the Remitter   . . . .

Name of the Remitter   . . . .

. . . . 192.

NAME STAMP TO BE IMPRESSED BY THE POST OFFICE

---

* The name of the District should be written only if the Post Office at which the Money Order is payable is situated in the interior of a District.

☛ The Commission for a Money Order is at the rate of one per cent per Dollar or part of a Dollar with a minimum charge of 10 cents.

The particulars as to names shall include the surname, and, at least, the initial of one christian name both of the Remitter and of the Payee, or, in the case of natives of India, the name, tribe or caste and father's name.

The address of the Payee must be given fully and precisely as on it depends the determination by the receiving office of exchange of the office where the Order shall be made payable.

3. Postal Orders. *British Postal Orders* are issued in sterling, and are payable almost anywhere in the British Empire and its Protectorates. The least sum for which a British Postal Order is issued is *6d.,* but fractions of that amount if the sum is over *6d. (e.g. 2s. 9d.)* may be paid by affixing British, S.S., or F.M.S. stamps to the order.

The purchaser of a British Postal Order must, before parting with it, fill in the name of the person to whom the amount is to be paid, and if possible the Post Office, town, or district where that person resides.

4. Cashing Orders. A Money Order will be cashed upon presentation for payment to the Post Office upon which it is drawn, provided it is properly receipted and the name of the Remitter as furnished by the applicant is in agreement with the letter of advice received by the Post Office from the office issuing the Money Order.

It is not customary, however, for business firms to cash Money Orders. The commoner method is to deposit them in the Bank, the same as cheques or drafts.

5. C.O.D. Post. The Malayan Cash on Delivery service is a most convenient method of remitting for goods purchased. /

III. BANK REMITTANCES.

The Bank is the principal medium for transmitting money. Business firms seldom take either the risk involved in sending notes by mail, or the trouble of remitting payments by Post Office. The use of the Money Order is a convenience to the customer rather than to the business house, as it is a handy method of sending small sums, especially if the sender has no bank account on which he can draw a cheque. But the business house *must* have a bank account, and its bills are usually paid either by draft, cheque, or (if local) cash.

This statement must be qualified by one or two remarks:

(a) Cheques between say Kuala Lumpur and Singapore are subject to a discount of one-eighth per cent, or a minimum of 25 cents, besides the four-cent stamp; so the remitter of a small amount will sometimes use a Money Order to avoid this charge.

(b) Drafts are not usually bought for small sums, so if one wishes to remit, say to India, it is more convenient to send a Money Order than it would be either to buy a Draft for a few Rupees, or to send a Cheque which would be discounted, subject to variation in exchange, and would also be many days in returning to the sender's Bank.

Acceptances. The principal bills that import firms are called upon to pay are those representing purchases of stock from abroad. We have already seen that incoming shipments are accompanied by an Invoice, a Statement, the Bill of Lading, and the Certificate of Insurance. The Consignor sends a *copy* of the Invoice and Statement to the Consignee, sometimes a mail in advance, as a notice to him that the documents will shortly be presented to him for his acceptance. The Consignor then proceeds to "draw" on the Consignee.

This Draft, however, is not the Demand Draft to which we were introduced on page 37, but is a Bill of Exchange payable either at sight, or after a stated number of days – usually either 30, 60, 90 or 180 days, though sometimes for only 3 or 7 days.

To explain this, let us suppose that J. Shoemaker & Co., London, are sending a shipment of boots and shoes to The Oriental Department Stores, Singapore.

The Oriental Department Stores are now able to take delivery of their goods, which they could not do until they had secured the B/L.

At the expiration of the "usance"[2] of the draft, say 60/days, plus three days' grace, the Bank clerk again presents the draft, which has now matured, together with a statement of the amount due in Straits currency at the day's exchange rate, and is given cash or a cheque in payment.

Documents against Acceptance. The foregoing method applies to drafts sent D/A (Documents against Acceptance). The usance may of course vary as already stated.

Documents against Payment. Sometimes the Draft may be sent D/P (Documents against Payment). In such cases the Drawee must *pay* the Draft before he can have the documents. The Draft may read "at sight," or it may have a few days' usance. In the former case he would be expected to pay on demand; in the latter case he would accept the draft and pay when due; but in neither case could the Bank surrender the B/L until the Draft was paid.

Shoemaker & Co. make out their draft. /

Shoemaker & Co. then send this draft (in duplicate) with the original Invoice, Statement, Bill of Lading and Insurance Certificate to their Bankers, with the request that they collect from the Consignee, who, we will suppose, has specified in his order that they are to draw through the Hongkong and Shanghai Bank.

£ 78, 10, 8	*London,* Nov. 18th 1922

Sixty *days after sight of this FIRST of Exchange (Second of the same tenor and date not paid) Pay to the order of*

The Hongkong and Shanghai Banking Corporation

Seventy eight pounds ten shillings and eight pence   *Value received.*

To the

Oriental Department Stores,	**J. SHOEMAKER & CO.,**
No. 10 Stamford, Road,	J.K. Overton
Singapore.	*Manager.*

When these documents arrive in Singapore, the Bank's clerk presents them to the Oriental Department Stores for acceptance. The Manager of the Stores writes across the face of the draft:

Accepted 12th Dec., 1922.

THE ORIENTAL DEPARTMENT STORES,
Stewart Last, Manager.

and returns the draft to the Bank clerk, retaining the other documents.

Interest. Some D/A drafts bear interest, others do not. When they do, it is customary to compute the interest from the date when the draft is drawn in London, until the date of arrival in London of the next mail after the draft is paid.

Open Credit. Some firms enjoy the confidence of home manufacturers to such an extent that they obtain goods on open credit: *i.e.,* the documents are sent direct to the Consignee without drawing. In place of the draft, there is an understanding between the seller and the buyer that the latter will pay within a certain time.

Home Offices. Many firms in the S.S. and F.M.S. have head offices in London or some other home city, and all the buying, shipping and paying is done from such offices. The local establishment in such cases remits to head office all the money it can spare. Such remittances might be made by draft, or, if urgent, by telegraphic transfer.

Telegraphic Transfer. This of course means that the money will be available in London the very day (or following day) it is sent from here. The form used by the Hongkong and Shanghai Bank for this purpose is as follows: – /

Singapore, ...19.

To the Manager of the

Hongkong and Shanghai Banking Corporation.

SINGAPORE.

Dear Sir,

TELEGRAPHIC TRANSFER.

Please instruct your Branch/Agent at . . . . *by cable (using your telegraphic code as required) to make the following payment on the understanding that the message and payment are at my/our risk in every respect.*

. . . .

. . . .

. . . .

Signature of sender . . . .
Address . . . .

Brokers. When a firm has to send a great deal of money abroad, as to Europe or America, it is a matter of importance to obtain the most favourable rate of exchange possible. (Calculate the difference between the cost of $25,000 U.S. currency at 52 1/4 and at 52 1/2, to see how much a man would lose if he bought at the higher rate). To ensure himself against such losses, the Manager accepts the services of a Broker, whose business it is to find out, every day, the rate of exchange at which each Bank is willing to buy or sell in exchange with any desired country. For this service the Broker charges a small percentage fee.

Goods on Consignment. Under special circumstances, some firms will place with retailers, as their agents, a stock of goods "on consignment, for sale or return." This means that the maker, and not the retailer, furnishes the capital, so the latter can afford to sell on a smaller margin of profit than would be the case if his own money were invested in the stock. Consignment stock is paid for as sold, or by periodical remittances (say monthly or quarterly), accompanied by a statement of the stock sold. Before remitting, the retailer would deduct his selling commission from the proceeds of sales.

ALEXANDER, *BRITISH MALAYA: MALAYAN STATISTICS* (1928)

C. S. Alexander, *British Malaya: Malayan Statistics* (London: Malayan Information Agency, 1928), p. 129.

The Planters' Loan Board was founded in 1915 to manage and lend money from the Planters Loan Fund, which was established in 1904 with a capital of $500,000 (increased to $1.5m in 1908) to provide 6 per cent loans to rubber planters whose estates showed potential. By 1915, the Fund's capital had been raised to $4m, loans were additionally available for the construction of buildings and to veterans of the First World War, who had been given land under the War Service Land Grant Scheme, and borrowers could obtain up to $50,000. Board members were nominated by the government and served five year terms. The extract gives details of advances made from 1926 to 1928.[1]

Notes
1. J. H. Drabble 'Investment in the Rubber Industry in Malaya C. 1900–1922', *Journal of Southeast Asian Studies*, 3:2 (1972), pp. 247–61, on pp. 249, 250; *The Straits Times*, 3 August 1947, p. 3.

C. S. Alexander, *British Malaya: Malayan Statistics* (1928), extract

PLANTERS LOANS BOARD – FEDERATED MALAY STATES.

Compiled from the Annual Reports of the Chief Secretary to Government, F.M.S.

Particulars.		1926.	1927.	1928.
Loaus to Planters.				
Lent during the year	$'000	106.0	154.9	126.0
Repaid during the year „	"	319.4	198.8	38.2
Loans Outstanding 31st December –				
Number	No.	15	19	23
Amount	$'000	413.3	369.4	457.2
Building Loans (under extended powers).				
Lent during the year	$'000	–	403.0	665.8
Repaid during the year	"	–	21.6	151.3
Loans Outstanding, 31st December –				
Number	No.	–	19	39
Amount	$'000	–	381.4	895.9
Loans under the War Service Land Grant Scheme.				
Total approved Loans, 31st December –				
Number	No.	103	93	84
Amount	$'000	2,513	2,263	2,027
All Loans				
Interest –				
Total received during the year,	"	136.5	202.4	117.4
Paid to Government Revenue,	"	76.1	125.1	57.7
Credited to the Board,	"	60.4	77.3	59.7
Board's Profit on year's working,	"	27.8	37.6	24.8
General Reserve Fund, 31st Dec.	"	525.0	525.0	525.0
Special Reserves	"	50.0	90.0	90.0

STRICKLAND., *REPORT ON CO-OPERATION IN MALAYA* (1929)

C. F. Strickland., *Report on Co-operation in Malaya* (Kuala Lumpur: Government Publication, 1929), pp. 1–19.

C. F. Strickland was for many years Registrar of Co-operative Societies in India. In 1929, he visited Malaya and collected information on the state and future of co-operation from District Officials and Residents in the west and south of the country, where co-operative societies already existed. His report describes the development of the movement, investigates urban and rural societies and the difficulties in forming a Central Co-operative Bank. Unfortunately, his positive prognosis for the future of Malayan co-operation proved misplaced.

C. F. Strickland., *Report on Co-operation in Malaya* (1929), extract

DEVELOPMENT OF CO-OPERATION.

[...]

The Co-operative Societies Enactment was passed by the Federated Malay States Government in 1922, but no corresponding Act was passed by the Government of the Straits Settlements before the end of 1924. The Unfederated State of Kedah passed a similar Act in 1926; its example was followed by Perlis in the same year, and by Johore in 1927.

The earliest societies were created in 1922 and the annual increase in all types has been steady. The first Assistant Director was added to the staff at the end of 1924 and the second at the end of 1927. The number of societies with membership and capital as on 31st December, 1928, is shown in the following table:

	No. of societies.	Total membership.	Working capital.
FEDERATED MALAY STATES.–			
Urban	28	13,906	$2,112,402
Estate Labourers	18	3,724	39,208
Rural Credit	89	3,100	150,800
Total	135	20,730	$2,302,410
STRAITS SETTLEMENTS.–			
Urban	14	5,136	$322,152
Rural Credit	13	450	7,137
Total	27	5,586	$329,289 /
KEDAH.–			
Urban	7	441	$14,360
Rural Credit	25	1,453	26,767
Total	32	1,894	$41,127
PERLIS.–			
Urban	1	211	$13,551
Rural Credit	5	239	5,272
Total	6	450	$18,823
Grand total	200	28,660	$2,691,649

N.B.–All these figures are subject to audit.

In the following paragraphs, and throughout this report except where specific reference is made to the Unfederated States, my comments on the staff, on the number of societies and on the possibility of expansion refer only to the Federated Malay States and the Straits Settlements.

There are at present no registered secondary institutions. The proposal for a non-co-operative Agricultural Bank, based on the Planters' Loans Board, was rejected by the Secretary of State in 1923; a plan for a Co-operative Bank of Malaya, put forward at that time as an alternative by the Co-operation Board, was not approved by the local Government, but when submitted by the Government in an amended form in 1927 it was partially accepted by the Secretary of State, and a new scheme has now been prepared in accordance with the orders passed by him.

The outstanding feature of this brief account, showing the manner in which Co-operation has been initiated in Malaya, is the omission to equip the co-operative officers with first-hand knowledge of the highly technical subject which they were handling, though it has assumed diverse forms and is widely distributed throughout the world. There is also in Malaya itself a remarkable lack of data on rural economic conditions, and little appears to have been done to collate and utilise these data where they exist, save for the purpose of special crops or to meet exceptional emergencies. I fully realise that a succession of emergencies has rendered it difficult to collect and collate data in the manner of other countries, but the nett result is that the co-operative officers have neither received nor been able to impart to their subordinates an adequate training for their task. It is a matter for astonishment that they have been able to achieve a measure of success under such a handicap.

URBAN SOCIETIES.

3. With the exception of a few stores which failed for lack of experience or lack of loyalty on the part of members, the only type of urban institution is that of the thrift and loan society. The first societies were registered in 1922 and developed with unexpected rapidity. So pressed were the salary-earning classes by the burden of debt to money-lenders of diverse communities, that the earlier and larger societies were "rushed," and members have been admitted in a crowd without really understanding the nature of the society which they were joining. Under the circumstances I do not see that this could have been avoided. It has, however, led to certain grave defects, of which the co-operative staff are well aware and which they are doing their best to remedy. The members are thinking rather of loans than of thrift; proxies are used to an entirely un-co-operative degree, and the managing committees have an imperfect conception of their own duties and of the exact enquiries which should be made before issuing a loan. There has

been in consequence an ill-considered distribution of money, while the administration, which should be democratic, has tended to fall into the hands of a group at head-quarters, though the presence of the honorary Presidents and Vice-Presidents has exercised a steadying influence. Unwelcome as the remedies for those defects may be to the committees and main body of members, I have no doubt that the former within a short time, and the latter more gradually, will consent to adopt them. I have recommended to the Director the entire abolition or strict limitation of proxies, and have reinforced the advice which he was already giving with regard to careful examination of borrowers circumstances, the restriction of loans to a figure not exceeding the needs of the / case, the means of the borrower, and a class of objects for which it is beneficial to borrow. I have also suggested a system of special deposits for stated purposes, and a reduction of the percentage of profits which is carried to the reserve fund in case of those societies which effectually encourage thrift on the part of their members. It should not be supposed, as has sometimes been alleged, that these societies have done more harm than good. The number of borrowers in recent years has not exceeded 45 per cent. of the membership at a given moment (1927, 42 per cent.; 1928, 45 per cent.). The societies have relieved many persons of overwhelming debt, enabling them to repay by regular instalments, and I am convinced that on the lines on which the Director is now guiding them they will prove valuable to their members and highly creditable to Government and to the co-operative staff. The deduction of borrowers' instalments and subscriptions from their pay-sheets is an important safeguard, and should be encouraged in all offices of Government and of private firms.

Neither the Usurious Loans Enactment nor the Public Servants Liabilities Enactment appear to have conferred real benefit on the persons whom they were intended to help. The former, as in India, is practically a dead letter, while the latter is economically unsound. The remedy for usury is not to enhance the rate of interest by rendering recovery of the debt precarious, but to provide the debtor with controlled credit and a means of practising thrift.

Apart from societies for the supply of milk, which may perhaps be developed when the staff have greater leisure, the most promising lines of advance in urban co-operation are (1) housing and (2) better living. The ground open to the thrift and loan societies in Malayan towns is fairly well-covered, and I do not anticipate an increase in their numbers beyond a total of 50 in the near future, except possibly by sub-division of the large institutions. Such a sub-division is advisable, since the members of the larger committees are overwhelmed with work and the difficulty of attendance on the part of the borrower is increased by operation over a wide area.

Housing can be assisted either by the formation of separate societies, the nature of which I have discussed with the Director and with some groups of co-operators, or by the issue of special housing loans from the thrift and loan societies. Suitable by-laws for the latter purpose have been suggested. In either case the help of Government and, in particular, of the Town Planning Officers will be needed in the selection of sites, grant of long leases and the supply of expert advice. While accommodation is being provided by Government for its servants during their tenure of office, many clerks wish to build with a view to their old age, and the demand for non-official houses appears to be rapidly growing in a number of centres. By the encouragement of housing societies Government will relieve the salary-earners and persons of middle status from one of the greatest discomforts which trouble them at present.

While encouraging thrift by a system of special deposits in the thrift and loan societies and reducing one burdensome item of expenditure by the formation of housing societies, the urban co-operators will do well to consider the possibility of limiting their high and growing expenditure on marriages and other ceremonies by means of better living societies. This novel type has been developed with success in the Punjab, and has proved to be more effective than was at one time anticipated. If a large number of persons in a single community will pledge themselves to limit their expenditure on such objects to a standard approved by their own committee, and to submit to the penalties inflicted by that committee in case of infringement, the relief will be general, since undue expenditure on ceremonies is rather due to fear of public opinion than to any desire for extravagance on the part of the individuals concerned. The experiment should at least be tried, and I see no reason why it should not attain its object. A draft set of by-laws has been prepared.

RURAL SOCIETIES.

Rubber Factories.

4. A committee appointed by the Federated Malay States Government in 1925 and a similar committee in Negri Sembilan in the same year recommended the formation of societies which would collect the latex and prepare and market the rubber of associated small-holders. An Agricultural Officer reported to the same effect in 1928 and has recently returned from deputation in Ireland, where he examined the co-operative creameries operating on similar lines. This officer together with two temporary officers, with experience as planters, is now engaged in the organization of one or two such factories. I have consulted them in the matter and heard the views of a group of villagers. There is no reason to doubt that the factories can confer a direct economic benefit on the small producer, can establish themselves on a sound footing and pay off whatever / debt it is necessary to incur for building expenses, if the producers will remain loyal to them for a period of years. The question is whether the economic inducement

will be sufficient to hold the loyalty of a producing class, in whose lives economic values do not play so large a part as in other countries. The factories will offer this advantage over the alternative scheme of selling latex jointly to a big estate, that, while the latter method provides only a safe market, the former encourages the Malays to build up a local institution which they may regard as their own and of which they may feel proud. If this idea appeals to them, I think that the rubber societies may flourish; they may expand with reasonable rapidity, which will depend on, the careful guidance of the first two or three societies. I advise that no undue haste be used in their formation.

It is possible that action on the same lines can hereafter be taken with regard to cocoanuts or other crops, and joint purchase and sale may even be organized on behalf of the feckless Malay fisherman, but the rubber experiment should first be fully tried.

ESTATE LABOURERS' SOCIETIES.

5. The thrift societies, which have been formed since 1926 among the labourers (chiefly Indian) on rubber estates, present no difficulties whatever, provided that they confine themselves to thrift and do not embark on the entirely unnecessary enterprise of granting loans in excess of the amount deposited by each member. They have been cordially welcomed by the Planters' Association of Malaya and by nearly all the individual managers of estates to whom their principles have been explained. I anticipate a rapid increase of these societies, and it may be prudent for the co-operative staff to face a certain unpopularity in refusing registration from time to time, either entirely or within stated areas, until their own numbers and the general co-operative position enable them to give to each new labourers' society the attention which a young society must always receive. After the first year or two the misunderstandings will be overcome, but it is clear that with a crowd of illiterate day-labourers on the one side and a European or Asiatic manager with little or no knowledge of co-operation on the other, fairly frequent visits from a European officer will be needed until each society has found its feet. Thereafter the supervision can ordinarily be carried on by an Asiatic subordinate, though changes among the managers will necessitate a European visit from time to time.

The sums collected moreover will be very large, and a Committee of the Co-operation Board together with a number of estate managers have advised that the money be banked in more than one name. Questions on this point may be of a delicate nature but cannot be shirked, and the status and tactful language of the questioner are all-important.

While, therefore, the number of these societies may eventually reach 1,000 or more, it does not appear to me prudent to go beyond (say) 150 within the next three years; nor within the next five years, unless the general position of the movement has been markedly improved. It will be unwise for the co-operative staff to organize a larger number of societies than they can properly supervise. The movement amongst estate labourers is, however, of great importance both on political and on economic grounds. A labourer who saves his money is the best possible advertiser in India of the conditions under which he served, and though he may return home earlier than he would otherwise have done, he is also likely to come again to Malaya, bringing his relatives with him.

Model by-laws of these societies have been discussed with the Director and amendments suggested.

RURAL CREDIT SOCIETIES.

6. The position as regards the rural credit societies, the first of which were founded in 1922, is not entirely satisfactory. It is true that an intelligent group of Malays, collecting their own common fund by instalments of share payments and ending to one another for productive or necessary purposes, can free themselves from subjection to outside creditors, and can repay without difficulty the moderate sums which they need to borrow from the society. The peculiarity, however, of rural credit in Malaya – a peculiarity which I have never observed in my travels on co-operative study in Europe and elsewhere – is that the comparative permanence and security (despite fluctuations in price) of their income from rubber and cocoanuts relieves them of any real necessity to borrow at all, provided that they practise a moderate degree of thrift. On the other hand, they ordinarily make no attempt whatever to practise thrift, and their attitude in economic adversity is a good-tempered but apathetic acquiescence. If prices are bad they tend to wait until they rise, maintaining in the meantime their previous standard of expenditure. If money comes to a Malay's hands he spends it, regardless of the time when he will need it urgently. Were he an economic-minded person, he would, if he owned a small plot / of rubber or cocoanuts, need no credit at all, and would save in advance to meet such occasions of marriage, house building, etc., as are bound to present themselves. The only areas in which recurrent or seasonal credit may be required, and thrift and wise spending may not in themselves be sufficient, are the rice-growing tracts in the neighbourhood of Krian or in the Kedah and Perlis States.* The cultivators in this northern area, who depend largely if not solely on the rice crop, are exposed to those variations of fortune which are the lot of farmers in India and in Europe, and may be compelled after a disastrous harvest to seek for temporary help. Nevertheless even here the distress is not that with which the Indian or European peasants are familiar. If a drought destroys the grain crop in India there is no harvest

---

*   My remarks are confined to the west of the central range. /

whatever, and the seed and expense of cultivation are lost to the cultivator. A wet summer may produce almost, if not entirely, the same result in Europe and America. In Krian, on the other hand, a disastrous harvest is one in which the crop does not exceed 60 per cent. of the normal. It may, therefore, be hoped that here also in the course of time the Malay cultivator will learn to lay by in times of prosperity the savings which will relieve him in times of distress. At present he is not trained to such forethought and may reasonably be expected to require assistance for his cultivation expenses. The extortionate system of trader's credit, known as padi-ratus in Krian or padi-kuncha in Kedah, has been broken up with the assistance of the credit societies; yet I am inclined to suspect that, for lack of trained leaders, some of the cultivators have recently enmeshed themselves again. The societies deserve support to resist this evil alone. The 17 rice-growing societies of Krian have, therefore, been advised to form a small co-operative banking union or central bank, and, when the staff at the disposal of the Director is adequate expansion in the Krian District can prudently be undertaken. In Kedah and Perlis a similar policy with the same proviso is recommended.

Elsewhere, on the other hand, the rural credit society is not an institution which the Malay cultivator or fisherman feels to be so essential to his existence as it is to the Indian or European peasant. If he would save he would seldom or never need credit, and the value of the present societies lies precisely in the education which they give him in the use of money, and. in the avenue of approach towards him which they open. The cultivators, other than those of Krian, Kedah and Perlis, will only need outside assistance, if they need it at all, once in their lives, i.e., for clearing the heavier indebtedness of the members when they first form a society. As the owned capital increases from year to year, a larger and larger amount of this debt-repayment can be arranged by the primary society itself, but while a society is young and possesses only a small capital, it may be inevitable to incur a single loan from outside. This should only be given when the members have shown, by their careful use and punctual repayment, during at least two years, of the small sums advanced to them for current needs by their own society, that they have grasped the meaning of co-operation and can be trusted with a larger advance for their relief (in rotation, but not all at one time) from old creditors. Such relief, when granted, should, on account of their instability of character and on account of the long term required for its repayment, take the form of a mortgage loan. The more heavily indebted members should be invited to borrow with the approval of their primary society directly from a mortgage institution, whether co-operative or other, while the smaller debts can be cleared by a mortgage loan taken (on the security of all the borrowers' lands) by the society itself. These occasional loans to primary societies for the clearance of old debt will not yield a sufficient profit to support a separate financing institution. No central bank, therefore, of the ordinary co-operative type can be created for this purpose, and the societies must be allowed to have recourse, on exactly the same footing as an individual borrower, to such institutions as may be prepared to assist them on the security of mortgages. This will not be recurrent co-operative credit but a single mortgage operation, which aims at clearing the path of a credit society.

The Muhammadan objection to interest[1] appears to have bulked large in the eyes of Malays in certain areas and of European co-operators in Malaya. I have no specific to offer for the removal of this misconception. The distinction between fair interest and burdensome usury is now so apparent in Muhammadan countries, such as Egypt, the Punjab or Bengal (no less than in other parts of India where Muhammadans are less numerous), that common sense must finally triumph also in Malaya. Several of the Rulers have realised the essential distinction between an evil which existed 1,300 years ago, when fair interest was unknown, and a sound commercial operation which has only come into existence in the last 200 years. I recommend no change in the policy of the department, though it is possible that some amendments relating to the distribution of profits in credit societies on the conclusion of the first ten years, and suggested by me to the Director, may incidentally meet to some extent the objections of the Muhammadans. /

The same policy of special deposits for foreseen needs, which has been recommended to the urban branch, should be adopted by the rural societies. The Malay needs thrift rather than credit, and though it is perhaps impracticable to lead him towards thrift in a single stage, he may be gradually weaned from his old ways and educated in wisdom, if the system of deposits is superimposed on that of loans. The necessary amendments in the by-laws have been drafted in consultation with the Director.

For the same reason better living societies should be formed if possible. The restriction of extravagance is the subject of repeated orders by the Sultans, and the better living societies in the Punjab are found almost without exception in the villages.

When a group of villagers have once been brought together and trained to discuss their own needs in the atmosphere of a credit society, they can be induced gradually to undertake the selection of their seed, and the improvement of their poultry, goats and cattle. The improvement of livestock will also be welcomed by the members of the Estate Labourers' Societies and by many of the managers. The distribution of improved rice seed has been discussed with the Economic Botanist, and a scheme prepared for utilising the Krian Banking Union to this end. The problem of improving the livestock of this country is again complicated by the lack of economic data, not only as to the numbers, age, sex and origin of the stock now present, but also as to the cost of maintenance, the prevalence of disease and the openings for organising co-operative sale of the stock or product. It is scarcely conceivable that fresh milk cannot be produced in Malaya at a lower cost than that at which preserved milk is imported, or that any race of human beings will not after a short experience prefer the pure to the medicated article. It will be the duty of co-operation to keep it pure. When the co-operative staff attack this problem they should enter into alliance with the Veterinary Officers, and should concern themselves with Indians and urban residents no less than with rural Malays. Livestock associations can no doubt be formed in many towns, and will be entitled to the aid of the technical departments. Spectacular results at an early date cannot be expected, but the cattle-breeding societies in Europe and India show what can be done by small-holders who are willing to exercise care with a minimum of expenditure, and the net increment of income and of health throughout Malaya from a sound policy of livestock improvement will not be negligible.

I do not recommend the Krian societies to undertake the purchase or management of rice mills as was at one time suggested. The societies are neither numerous nor intelligent enough for such an undertaking at this stage, and the day is far distant at which they will be in a position to contemplate it. The principal weakness of rural co-operation lies in the supervising staff. Until the efficiency of the Malay officers has been substantially enhanced by the thorough system of training which I advocate below, expansion should be extremely cautious; no new States should be entered. New societies should be organized only with the amended by-laws, and in my opinion the total number of rural credit societies in the Federated Malay States and the Straits Settlements should not, certainly within the next three years, nor within five years unless a marked improvement in the staff has taken place, be allowed to exceed 150.

[...]

CO-OPERATIVE BANK OF MALAYA.

21. A brief reference has been made in paragraph 2 to the scheme for a Co-operative Bank, and I have explained in paragraph 6 that a Central Co-operative Bank of the usual type, financing societies for the purpose of seasonal loans, cannot be constituted in Malaya except in a limited area. It is laid down in the letter of the Secretary of State dated 28th February, 1928, that (1) the co-operative movement and the mortgage credit proposals must be kept separate; (2) that the money of the Thrift Societies must not be used for long term loans and (3) that Government assistance should not exceed $4,500,000, and that this should be withdrawn when possible. The by-laws for a Co-operative Mortgage Bank, which have now been prepared do not contemplate the use of this bank as the central institution of the co-operative societies. Since, however, a co-operative society may under certain circumstances require a mortgage loan for definite purposes, it does not appear to infringe the spirit of the Secretary of State's orders, if the

societies are permitted to become members of this bank in the event of such a contingency arising. I do not anticipate that many loans of this kind will be demanded. In their ordinary business the credit societies will finance themselves except in Krian and Kedah, where they will create their own central institution.

As regards the money of the Thrift Societies the situation was imperfectly understood by the Committee which reported to the Secretary of State. The papers forwarded with the proposal for a Co-operative Bank did not explain in detail the terms on which the Thrift Societies hold the money of their members. The greater part of this money is subscribed as an insurance against old age, and is intended to remain in the society until a member retires from service or withdraws from the society itself. In the latter event a notice of 12 months is necessary. The money is therefore not repayable either on demand or on notice of less than a year, and there will be no danger if a certain portion of it is deposited with a mortgage bank for a period not exceeding five years. Some of the loans at present issued by the Planters' Loans Board are for five years or even a shorter period, and this practice will no doubt be continued by the mortgage bank. It has, however, now been laid down in the by-laws that the mortgage bank shall set apart, for repayment of all / money deposited with it by co-operative societies, a portion of its assets falling due for realisation within the term of such deposits, and that these assets be separately shown in the balance sheet. The danger which was anticipated by the Committee will thus be averted, since for every deposit received from a co-operative society the bank will be obliged to allocate cash or a short-term security, from which it will be repaid on due date. It is reasonable to hope that this arrangement will be approved by the Secretary of State, since it complies with the spirit of his orders. The third instruction that the assistance of Government be limited to $4,500,000 presents no difficulty.

It is now for Government to decide whether a Co-operative Mortgage Bank shall be created or not. As a stranger to this country I am unable to estimate the demand which is to be met. The by-laws, as drafted, provide for the admission of agricultural estates, industrial companies and all classes of individuals as members and borrowers, and loans may be issued for both agricultural and industrial development and for the repayment of prior debts. The issue of housing loans is also intended, and it will be possible to relieve the Residents and District Officers of their present duty of.making advances for this purpose. I am, however, strongly of opinion that the bank, if created, should in the first case consist only of a Head-quarter office without branches, and that no proposal for local or State banks should be entertained in the near future. The first need of a mortgage bank is a capable and business-like manager and an efficient office, and this will only be secured if the turn-over of the bank yields an adequate margin of profit. The overhead cost of branch offices or of State banks cannot in the early stages be met without lowering the quality of the management or the office.

The bank, as now designed, will be a large primary mortgage credit society for the development of Malaya and the assistance of individuals, firms and companies who wish to borrow for any purpose whatever which may be approved by the managing committee. The committee will, of course, approve no loans for purposes of extravagance or speculation, and will, as prescribed in the by-laws, take full mortgage security in every case. All persons who wish to borrow will become shareholders.

[...]

THE FUTURE OF THE MOVEMENT.

23. I have limited my proposals to the action which I consider necessary for the next three or at the most the next five years, and have suggested a degree of expansion which can safely be undertaken in that time. The amendment of the Co-operative Societies Enactment and of the notified rules has been discussed with the Director, who is about to submit proposals to Government. The model by-laws of the existing types of society have been re-drafted, and a number of minor improvements proposed with regard to routine procedure of the field staff. The Director has issued certain circulars in consequence, and has other points under consideration. There is no reason whatever why the co-operative movement in Malaya, though it may differ in some respects from the forms assumed in Europe and elsewhere, should not confer great benefits on the country, and become an invaluable agency for strengthening the character of the Malays and all other communities, and also for conveying to them in a form which they can understand the knowledge of the agricultural and other technical departments. If this is to be done it is indispensable that the co-operative staff, both European and Asiatic, be given an opportunity of really understanding the nature of the task to be performed, the instruments which lie in their hands and the results attained by their use throughout the world. They must constantly be trained, and a special officer must be permanently maintained for their training. Before he is in a position to perform his duties he also must be trained. When this has been done the prospects of co-operation in Malaya will be altogether different from the present, and the co-operative staff will be ready for their real work, the development and the reconstruction of the country.

EDITORIAL NOTES

Anon., *Report on the Working of the Municipalities of British Burma for the Year 1882–83*

1. *capitation-tax*: a Poll tax; a tax levied per head of adult population.
2. *night-conservancy*: work conducted at night.
3. *nightsoil*: human excreta.

Anon., *Fifty Years of Railways in Malaya, 1885–1935*

1. *dog spikes*: A dog spike is large nail that is used to secure rails to a sleeper.
2. *ballasted*: Ballast is rock, broken stone, etc., used for the foundation of a railway track.
3. *lighters*: A lighter is a flat-bottomed barge used for transporting cargo. Generally used in loading or unloading a ship
4. *godown*: warehouse.
5. *attap*: nypa frutican, commonly known as the nipa palm or attap. It is native to the coast-lines and estuaries of the Indian and Pacific Oceans.
6. *sounding*: determining the depth of a body of water.
7. *rolling lift bridge*: a bridge over a river that rises to allow large ships to pass through.
8. *Guillemard Bridge*: In December 1941, British forces retreating south to Kuala Krai, destroyed the last span of the bridge to prevent the Imperial Japanese Army advancing. It remained impassable to traffic until it was reconstructed and reopened to traffic on 7 September 1948. In February 1988 it was replaced by the Tanah Merah Bridge.
9. *Sir Cecil Clementi*: Sir Cecil Clementi (1875–1947). Governor of Hong Kong (1925–30) and Governor and Commander-in-Chief of the Straits Settlements (1930–4).
10. *pontoon wharves*: floating wharves.
11. *screw piles*: A screw pile is a pile that has a wide helical blade at its foot and is twisted into position.
12. *coupled wheels*: wheels coupled together with side rods.
13. *tender*: a vehicle drawn behind a steam locomotive to carry the fuel and water.
14. *driving wheels*: A driving wheel is a powered wheel which is driven by a locomotive's pistons.
15. *firebox*: the furnace of a steam locomotive in which fuel is burned.
16. *bogies*: A bogie is a railway carriage or locomotive undercarriage that has a pair of wheels that swivel to enable curves to be negotiated.
17. *double-heading*: the use of two locomotives to pull carriages.

18. *shunting engine*: a small locomotive that travels very short distances and is used to move carriages/wagons, generally in marshalling yards.
19. *sheerlegs*: A sheerleg is a form of two-legged lifting device used by sailboats and dockyards for tasks such as lifting masts and the heavier parts of rigging.

Alexander, *British Malaya: Malayan Statistics*

1. *Trunk*: long-distance.

Nankivell, *A Report on Highways*

1. *f.o.r.*: Free On Rail.
2. *P.W.D.*: Public Works Department.
3. *scarified*: to break up a surface.
4. *tamping*: to pack down tightly by a succession of blows.
5. *screeding*: the use of a strip of material to level off a horizontal surface.
6. *tensible*: capable of being stretched.

Anon., 'The British India Steam Navigation Company Mail and Indian Immigration Contract, 1923'

1. *tongkangs*: A tongkang is a boat or junk used in the seas of the Malay Archipelago.
2. *barratry*: an unlawful breach of duty on the part of a ship's master or crew.
3. force majeure: an unexpected or uncontrollable event.

Anon., *Report of the Commission on the Eastern Shipping or Straits Homeward Conference as Affecting the Trade of the Colony*

1. *Macassar*: an Indonesian port on the south-west coast of the island of Sulawesi, facing the Makassar Strait.
2. *Light Dues*: cost of transporting cargo from a ship too large to enter a port to the landing docks via a smaller 'lighter' vessel.
3. *tramp steamers*: freight vessels that were not part of the conference and did not run regularly between fixed ports; instead taking cargos wherever shippers desired.
4. *carrying trade*: the business of transporting goods from one place or country to another.
5. *bottoms*: ships.
6. *Suez Canal dues*: charges for using the Suez Canal.
7. *Celebes*: Sulawesi, an island in Indonesia.

Anon., 'Report on the Development and Progress of Civil Aviation in Malaya up to and including the Year 1937'

1. *metalled runways*: runways constructed of broken stone.
2. *De Havilland "Rapide"*: a British short-haul biplane passenger airliner designed in 1933.
3. *Douglas D. C. 2 aircraft*: Douglas Aircraft Company; an American aerospace manufacturer based in Southern California, which produced the 'DC' ('Douglas Commercial') series of commercial aircraft.
4. ab initio: *from the beginning.*

5.   *Miles Magister*: the Miles M.14 Magister was a British two-seat monoplane basic trainer aircraft built by the Miles Aircraft Co. for the Royal Air Force and Fleet Air Arm.
6.   *Tiger Moth*: the de Havilland DH.82 Tiger Moth; a 1930s biplane designed by Geoffrey de Havilland.
7.   *Gipsy Moth*: the de Havilland DH.60 Moth; a 1920s two-seat touring and training aircraft.
8.   *Gipsy Major Moth*: a Gipsy Moth with a four-cylinder, air-cooled, inline engine.
9.   *De Havilland Dragonfly*: the de Havilland DH.90 Dragonfly; a twin-engined luxury touring biplane.

Anon., 'Growth of the Postal Service. Illuminating Facts and Figures'

1.   *Batavia*: now Jakarta.
2.   *Apcar steamers*: steamers operated by the Indian owned Apcar shipping line.
3.   *Messageries Imperiales*: The Messageries Imperiales was a French merchant shipping company. In 1871 it was renamed Compagnie des Messageries Maritimes.
4.   *C.O.D*: An abbreviation of Collect On Delivery; a method of payment by which goods are paid for when they are delivered to the customer's home or place of business.

Gerrard, *On the Hygienic Management of Labour in the Tropics. An Essay*

1.   *Lines*: employee living accommodation.
2.   *out fall*: the place where a sewer or drain discharges.
3.   *Jack roof*: a roof held up by timber posts.
4.   *epitomise*: to embody the essential characteristics of.
5.   *prophylaxis*: prevention of or protective treatment for disease.
6.   *Anophelines*: any of various mosquitoes of the genus *Anopheles*, which can carry the malaria parasite and transmit the disease to humans.
7.   *Salvarsan*: arsphenamine: a yellow hygroscopic powder, $C_{12}H_{12}As_2N_2O_2 \cdot 2HCl \cdot 2H_2O$, formerly used to treat syphilis and other spirochetal infections.
8.   *thymol*: a white, crystalline, aromatic compound, $C_{10}H_{14}O$, derived from thyme oil and other oils and used as an antiseptic, a fungicide and a preservative.
9.   *ankylostomiasis*: a disease caused by hookworm infestation. The main symptom is progressive anemia.
10. *Wasserman's reaction*: The Wassermann test or Wassermann reaction is an antibody test for syphilis, named after the bacteriologist August Paul von Wassermann.
11. *lalang*: a coarse weedy Malaysian grass, *Imperata arundinacea*.
12. *Phthisis*: tubercolosis.
13. *Herring bone*: masonry of brick and mortar.

Marjoribanks and Marakkayar, *Report on Indian Labour Emigrating to Ceylon and Malaya*

1.   *crimped*: employed by.
2.   *porterage*: the carrying of goods by porters.

3. *enlarged spleen*: The spleen is a large, highly vascular lymphoid organ, lying in the human body to the left of the stomach below the diaphragm, serving to store blood, disintegrate old blood cells, filter foreign substances from the blood, and produce lymphocytes. Enlargement (splenomegaly) results in abdominal, chest and back pain.
4. *trainage*: transport by train.
5. *bushel*: one bushel = eight gallons of dried goods.
6. *hundis*: a system for remitting money in which a financial obligation between two parties is settled by transferring it to a third party.
7. inter alia: among other things.
8. *mille*: one thousand.
9. *anchylostomiasis*: a disease caused when hookworms (parasites that live in the small intestine of hosts) are present in large numbers and produce an iron deficiency anemia by sucking blood from the host's intestinal walls.
10. *prophylaxis*: preventive medicine.
11. *anopheline*: a genus of mosquito first described and named by J. W. Meigen in 1818. Approximately 460 species are recognized, 100 of which can transmit human malaria.
12. *larvicides*: A larvicide is an insecticide that is specifically targeted against the larval life stage of an insect.
13. *chennopodium*: Chenopodium is a genus of numerous species of perennial or annual herbaceous flowering plants known as goosefoots.

Anon., 'Indians in Malaya'

1. *B.I.S.N Company*: The British India Steam Navigation Company.
2. *Jaffnese*: Sri Lankan Tamils.
3. *poojas*: religious rituals performed by Hindus as an offering to various deities, distinguished persons or special guests.

Blythe, *Methods and Conditions of Employment of Chinese Labour in the Federated Malay States*

1. *chandu*: opium.
2. kepalas: supervisors/contractors.
3. *Dr. Sun Yat Sen*: Dr Sun Yat-sen (1866–1925) was a Chinese revolutionary and first president and founding father of the Republic of China.
4. *kongsi-house*: benevolent organizations found among overseas Chinese communities, whose memberships comprise individuals with the same surname.
5. *Malayan Communist party*: The Malayan Communist Party (MCP), officially known as the Communist Party of Malaya (CPM), was founded in 1930, replacing the South Sea Communist Party.
6. katty: A catty or katty is equal to 500 grams (approximately 1.1 pounds).
7. *Amang*: the byproduct of tin mining, also known as tin tailings.
8. *congee*: a type of rice porridge or gruel.
9. *Jigmen*: employees who operated the apparatus for cleaning or separating crushed ore by agitation in water.
10. *Sampan coolies*: employees in charge of flatbottom boats, usually propelled by two oars, which transported the ore.

11. *palongs*: a gently sloping wooden structure up which tin ore is pumped.
12. *changkol*: a hoe: a long-handled agricultural tool used to move small amounts of soil and for weeding.
13. *bunding*: an embankment.
14. *fathom*: 1 fathom = 6 feet or 1.8288 metres.
15. *scrap*: latex that drips onto the ground. It is collected periodically and produces a low-grade product.
16. *lump rubber*: Some trees will continue to drip after collection and this leads to a small amount of 'cup lump', which is collected at the next tapping.
17. *gantang*: a measurement of dry content equivalent to three litres.
18. *tahil*: equivalent to 38 grams (1 ⅓ ounces).
19. *Tallymen*: employees who checked the count of goods being loaded or unloaded.
20. *Battery men*: employees who broke up the ore.
21. *stopers*: employees who excavated steps in steeply inclined or vertical veins.
22. *Mullockers*: employees who removed the waste material i.e. broken rock from a mine.
23. *dross*: the scum formed, usually by oxidation, on the surfaces of molten metals.
24. *72 Martyrs Anniversary*: Anniversary of the Yellow Flower Mound revolt also known as the Second Guangzhou uprising, a revolt led by Huang Xing and his fellow revolutionaries against the Qing Dynasty in Guangzhou.
25. *lasts*: A last is a mechanical form that has a shape similar to that of a human foot. It is used by shoemakers in the manufacture and repair of shoes.

Governor to British North Borneo Company, 21 December 1923.

1. *Wah Weh*: a form of gambling.

Anon., *Proceedings and Report of the Commission Appointed to Inquire into the Cause of the Present Housing Difficulties in Singapore, Volume 1*

1. *Teluk Ayer*: Telok Ayer is a historic district located in Singapore's Chinatown within the Central Business District.
2. *Peabody*: Peabody Trust founded in 1862, one of London's oldest and largest housing associations.
3. *nightsoil*: human excreta.
4. *beri-beri*: a disease caused by a deficiency of thiamine and characterized by neurological symptoms, cardiovascular abnormalities and edema.
5. *simulacrum*: an unreal or vague semblance.
6. *Sir JOHN ANDERSON*: Sir John Anderson (1858–1918). Governor of Ceylon (1916–18) and Governor of Straits Settlements (1904–11).
7. *Arbitrament*: arbitration.
8. *prophylactic*: acting to defend against or prevent something.
9. *Haiphong*: the third largest city of Vietnam.
10. *appurtenant*: something added to another, more important thing.
11. *ferro-concrete*: concrete strengthened by a core or foundation skeleton of iron or steel bars, strips etc.
12. *piling*: the act of driving piles.

13. mutatis mutandis: the necessary changes having been made; having substituted new terms; with respective differences taken into consideration.

Straits Settlements 1907. Government Loan Prospectus

1. *Scrip Certificates*: stock certificates.
2. *coupons*: Each bond certificate had coupons attached, each of which on the relevant date could be exchanged for the interest due.

Anthonisz, *Currency Reform in the Straits Settlements*

1. *Birmingham Mint*: The Birmingham Mint, originally known as Heaton's Mint or Ralph Heaton & Sons. Based in Birmingham, it began producing tokens and coins in 1850 as a private enterprise, separate from, but in cooperation with the Royal Mint.
2. *Sir Alexander Swettenham*: Acting Governor of the Straits Settlements from 7 December 1899 to 5 November 1901.
3. *forward contracts*: See D. Sunderland, *Financing the Raj. The City of London and Colonial India, 1858–1940* (London: Boydell & Brewer, 2013), pp. 99–100, 102, 105, 113, 137, 209.
4. *Sir Frank Swettenham*: Sir Frank Athelstane Swettenham (1850–1946). The first Resident General of the Federated Malay States (1896–1901), and, from 1901 to 1904, Governor of the Straits Settlements.
5. *Sir David Barbour*: Sir David Miller Barbour (1841–1928). A senior administrator in India, Finance Member of the Indian Viceroy's Council under Henry Petty-Fitzmaurice, fifth Marquess of Lansdowne, writer on monetary topics and Irish loyalist.
6. *seignorage*: the revenue or profit taken from the minting of coins – the difference between the value of the bullion used and the face value of the coin.

Cherry, *Elementary Business Practice in the Straits Settlements and Federated Malay States. With Questions and Examples*

1. *per procuration*: on behalf of the firm.
2. *usance*: the period of time, set by custom, before a bill of exchange (draft) could be redeemed at its destination.

Strickland, *Report on Co-operation in Malaya*

1. *The Muhammadan objection to interest*: Sharia, Islamic religious law, prohibits the fixed or floating payment or acceptance of specific interest or fees for loans of money.

LIST OF SOURCES

Text	Source
Anon., *Report on the Working of the Municipalities of British Burma for the Year 1882–83* (1883)	LSE, Government Publications, shelfmark 591 (R29)
L. Wray Jr, *Notes on Perak with a Sketch of its Vegetable, Animal and Mineral Products* (1886)	British Library, shelfmark T 29790(i)
Anon., *Fifty years of Railways in Malaya, 1885–1935* (1935)	LSE, Government Publications, shelfmark 595 (12)
C. S. Alexander, *British Malaya: Malayan Statistics* (1928)	LSE, Government Publications, shelfmark 595 (119)
K. Nankivell, *A Report on Highways* (1936)	John Rylands Library, Manchester, shelfmark Eastern 10936.375
Anon., 'A Pioneer Shipping Agency. History of Mansfield & Co.', *The Singapore Free Press Exhibition Supplement*, 2 January 1932 (1932)	National Archives, shelfmark CO 273/582/3
Anon., 'The British India Steam Navigation Company Mail and Indian Immigration Contract, 1923' (1923)	John Rylands Library, Manchester, shelfmark Eastern 10936.157
Anon., *Report of the Commission on the Eastern Shipping or Straits Homeward Conference as Affecting the Trade of the Colony* (1902)	LSE, Government Publications, shelfmark 595 (14)
Anon., 'Report on the Development and Progress of Civil Aviation in Malaya up to and including the Year 1937' (1937)	National Archives, shelfmark CO 323/1552/15
Anon., 'Growth of the Postal Service. Illuminating Facts and Figures', *The Singapore Free Press Exhibition Supplement*, 2 January 1932 (1932)	National Archives, shelfmark CO 273/582/3
C. A. Vlieland, *British Malaya: A Report on the 1931 Census* (1932)	LSE, Historical Statistics, shelfmark 595 (HA161)
C. S Alexander, *British Malaya: Malayan Statistics* (1928)	LSE, Government Publications, shelfmark 595 (119)

P. N. Gerrard, *On the Hygienic Management of Labour in the Tropics. An Essay* (1913) — British Library, General Reference Collection, shelfmark 7688.l.5.

N. E. Marjoribanks and A. K. G. Marakkayar, *Report on Indian Labour Emigrating to Ceylon and Malaya* (1917) — LSE, Government Publications, shelfmark 54 MA (76)

Anon., 'Indians in Malaya' (1926) — National Archives, shelfmark CO 273/534/11

W. L. Blythe, *Methods and Conditions of Employment of Chinese Labour in the Federated Malay States* (1938) — LSE, Government Publications, shelfmark 595 (101)

Governor to British North Borneo Company, 21 December 1923 (1923) — National Archives, shelfmark CO 874/904

Anon., *Proceedings and Report of the Commission Appointed to Inquire into the Cause of the Present Housing Difficulties in Singapore, Volume 1* (1918) — LSE, Government Publications, shelfmark 595 (18)

Anon., 'Memorandum Regarding the Provision of Housing and Hospital Accommodation for Labour in Burma' — British Library, shelfmark IOR/L/PJ/6/1666, File 2288

Straits Settlements Government Loan . Issue of £4 per cent. Five Year Convertible Bonds Sufficient to Raise £5,000,000. Authorised by Ordinance No. 4 of 1907 (1907) — National Archives, shelfmark CAOG 9/36

Anon., *Average Prices, Declared Trade Values, Exchange and Currency, Volume and Average Volume of Imports and Exports, Market Prices and Cost of Living* (1930) — LSE, Government Publications, shelfmark 595 (R41)

Anon., *Average Prices, Declared Trade Values, Exchange and Currency, Volume and Average Volume of Imports and Exports, Market Prices and Cost of Living* (1939) — LSE, Government Publications, shelfmark 595 (R41)

J. O. Anthonisz, *Currency Reform in the Straits Settlements* (1915) — British Library, General Reference Collection, shelfmark 08226.f.75.

R. L. German, *Handbook to British Malaya* (1927) — LSE, Government Publications, shelfmark 595 (3)

W. T. Cherry, *Elementary Business Practice in the Straits Settlements and Federated Malay States. With Questions and Examples* (1915) — British Library, General Reference Collection, shelfmark 08245.f.42.

C. S. Alexander, *British Malaya: Malayan Statistics* (1928) — LSE, Government Publications, shelfmark 595 (119)

C. F. Strickland., *Report on Co-operation in Malaya* (1929) — LSE, Government Publications, shelfmark 595 (7)

INDEX

For Product Safety Concerns and Information please contact our EU
representative GPSR@taylorandfrancis.com Taylor & Francis Verlag GmbH,
Kaufingerstraße 24, 80331 München, Germany

Printed and bound by CPI Group (UK) Ltd, Croydon, CR0 4YY

08/05/2025

01864495-0002